The Presidential Odyssey of John Glenn

The Presidential Odyssey of John Glenn

Richard F. Fenno, Jr.
University of Rochester

PRESS

A Division of Congressional Quarterly Inc.
1414 22nd Street N.W., Washington, D.C. 20037

Cover photos: NASA: Bettmann Newsphotos; Sen. John Glenn's office; Marty LaVor
Back cover photo: JFK Library

Printed in the United States of America

Library of Congress Cataloging-in-Publication Data

Fenno, Richard F., 1926-
    The presidential odyssey of John Glenn/Richard F. Fenno, Jr.
        p. cm.
    Includes bibliographical references.
    ISBN 0-87187-577-2
    ISBN 0-87187-567-5 (pbk.)
    1. Presidents—United States—Election—1984. 2. Glenn, John, 1921- . 3. United States—Politics and government—1981-1989. 4. Presidential candidates—United States—History—20th century. I. Title.
E879.F46   1990
973.927'092—dc20   89-49317
                                                            CIP

To Sharon and Amy

Contents

Preface

Political scientists need stories to help them make sense of the world they seek to explain; *The Presidential Odyssey of John Glenn* should be read as one such story. It is the kind of narrative—in depth, over time, and close-up—I believe is most useful. And it concerns a subject that needs study—of a politician at work, pursuing his ambition, interpreting his world, making decisions, and influencing the political life of the country.

My research for this book took place over six years, covering John Glenn's ongoing senatorial career and his presidential campaign. I accompanied Senator Glenn for the first time during his reelection campaign in Ohio in 1980. I talked with him from time to time in Washington during the year I spent there, from the fall of 1981 to the fall of 1982. I traveled with him off and on in 1981, 1982, and 1983 in seven states. I concluded my firsthand observations during his reelection campaign in Ohio in 1986. The study begins outside the Senate, moves inside the institution, goes out into the country, and returns, finally, to the Senate. Set against the background of Glenn's marine-astronaut experience, the book charts his political development from (Senate) campaigning to (Senate) governing to (presidential) campaigning to (Senate) governing and back to (Senate) campaigning. That sequence gives the study its overall perspective—as the story of a campaign embedded in a career.

Running for president is a fairly common senatorial activity. And, although one senator's campaign is insufficient to underpin generalizations about that activity, a single case can provide exploratory grist for those of us interested in such behavior. It can tell us, for example, how a senator's experiences influence a presidential campaign and, in turn, how an unsuccessful presidential campaign influences the subsequent senatorial career.

The book examines a number of relatively unexplored questions concerning presidential nomination campaigns. For example, it pays more attention to a *losing* nomination campaign than political scientists (or journalists) usually do. Assuming that the seeds of losing nomination campaigns are sown well before the first delegate selection votes are cast, the book also gives more attention than political scientists (or journalists) usually give to the long, preliminary *campaign-without-voters*.

Because of its focus, this case study may strengthen our attachments to some familiar generalizations about nomination politics and, perhaps, suggest corollaries or exceptions to others. Among the staples of political science inquiry to be considered are: the relative weighting of personal/candidate factors and process/campaign factors in explaining the electoral outcome; the interplay of candidate character and candidate image; the difference between nomination campaigns and general election campaigns; the nature of (Democratic) nominating constituencies; problems of campaign organization, resource allocation, and decision making; the evolution of campaign strategy; the influence of campaign consultants; the impact of media reporting and interpretation; and the importance of sequence and momentum in the Iowa-New Hampshire-Super Tuesday series of contests. These inquiries are separable, but clearly interconnected. A detailed study of a single campaign may be particularly helpful in suggesting or exposing such interconnections.

The book should not be read as the definitive account of Senator Glenn's presidential campaign, much less of his political career. In terms of his career, the book focuses on a single six-year slice. While it is a particularly consequential slice, it does not do justice to all that Glenn did beforehand, and it does not purport to cover—except for a brief campaign-related epilogue—anything he has done since. In the fall of 1989, for example, Glenn began to receive a good deal of public attention concerning his relationship with a constituent in the savings and loan business. But that subject lies beyond the reach of a presidential campaign analysis. The campaign story, too, has limitations. Its vantage point comes from outside the campaign, from the perspective of a restricted set of participants, from a few intermittent periods of firsthand observation, and from newspaper accounts between times. The campaign it captures is the personal, talking campaign rather than the campaign as seen on television. And it ignores the perspectives of Glenn's opponents in the race. Despite its profusion of detail, the story has numerous omissions and astigmatisms.

The book began as one of several studies designed to illuminate the operation of the U.S. Senate by observing the behavior of some of its members. The idea was to follow the activity of several senators over one complete electoral cycle and to document general patterns and illustrative examples of senatorial behavior from the resulting case histories. Because of the six-year election-to-election design, it was anticipated that the recurrent activities of campaigning and governing would reveal some behavioral regularities. And they have. But the more interesting result of the research has been the development of some highly detailed examples of selective senatorial activity. While these individual studies share the focus on campaigning and governing, they more persuasively illustrate the diverse paths senatorial careers may take.

By design, then, the senators controlled the research focus, and they pulled the researcher in different, sometimes quite unanticipated, directions. In the case at hand, a senator was chosen for study because he was a Democrat running for reelection in a large northern state; he decided, after the election, to run for president. His presidential odyssey became the dominant activity of his six-year term and, by necessity, the centerpiece of my research.

My greatest debt in all this is, of course, to Senator Glenn. He was unfailingly generous in allowing me to hang around so that I might see the world from over his shoulder. He was approachable, informative, and open in talking with me—often when he was pressed for time. I have tried to repay his personal kindness with a fair and appreciative account of his praiseworthy political career.

I am grateful to his staff—most of all to a special friend, Mary Jane Veno—and to Steve Avakian, Dale Butland, Dan Doherty, Carl Ford, Ed Furtek, Rose Harris, Herb Hedden, Mike McCurry, Marian Murphy, Sandy Specter, Kirk Stone, Len Weiss, and Bill White.

For their willingness to read the manuscript and for their helpful suggestions, I thank Larry Bartels, Chuck Jones, John Kessel, and Tom Mann. At various points along the way I received help from Chris Achen, Henry Brady, Bruce Jacobs, Nelson Polsby, David Shribman, Pevrill Squire, Byron Shafer, Harold Stanley, Ray Wolfinger, and Mike Wolkoff, which I gratefully acknowledge. I also record my debt to the journalists with whom I talked and to the more numerous journalists whose written work I have—as the endnotes make clear—relied upon so heavily.

Once again, I thank Janice Brown for her skill and patience in wrestling with the research notes and the manuscript. I thank Nancy, as always, for proofreading it and for living with it. At CQ Press, I was lucky to have the guidance of Joanne Daniels and the expert editing of Carolyn Goldinger. Finally, I acknowledge my great debt to the Russell Sage Foundation, without whose generous financial support this research could not have been undertaken.

Seasons of Preparation:
From Marine to Senator

INTRODUCTION

There are always members of the United States Senate who want to be president. They think about it. They work at it. It is their goal. Their presence has been a feature of Senate life at least since the Civil War, but their prominence has increased in recent decades, prompting descriptions of the Senate of the 1960s and 1970s as a "presidential nursery" and "presidential incubator."[1] In the first speculations preceding the 1984 election, for example, no fewer than nineteen senators received media mention as presidential possibilities.[2] For most senators, the presidency is not a realistic possibility; only a minuscule number of the aspirants succeed. So the Senate also is described as the "Club of Failed Ambitions."[3] Since 1960 no fewer than twenty-two sitting senators have entered the presidential primaries in pursuit of their party's nomination. Only three have succeeded. Three former senators won the nomination by way of the vice presidency.[4]

Still, every senator has—at some time and however fleetingly—entertained the notion. The thought is thrust upon them as soon as they are elected. Those to whom the question is not put by others will put it to themselves—if not immediately then eventually, if not to pursue it then at least to reject it, if not to contemplate the presidency then at least to consider the vice presidency. The idea of higher office comes with the Senate territory. This book is about one senator's pursuit of the idea.

Sen. John Glenn announced his presidential candidacy in New Concord, Ohio, on April 21, 1983. He announced the end of his candidacy in Washington, D.C., on March 16, 1984. His campaign, like most nomination campaigns, failed. That is the bare-bones story line.

Our central research task is to trace the path leading up to and away from his two announcements. The full story—of a campaign embedded in a career—is intriguing and complicated: Glenn's presidential odyssey was no ordinary case of senatorial ambition, no ordinary campaign, no ordinary failure. It was a campaign that was launched amid extraordinary interest, achieved extraordinary promise, and came to an extraordinarily puzzling end.

The day Glenn dropped out of the race, the *New York Times* reporter who had traveled with him described his campaign as "the most compelling subplot" of the nomination drama. "As recently as mid-February," he wrote,

> Senator John Glenn was regarded as the most serious challenger to former Vice President Walter F. Mondale and the Democrat with the best chance of defeating President Reagan. Today, having failed to be better than a weak second in the first dozen tests of 1984, he withdrew from the race.[5]

The same puzzle of unfulfilled promise had been recorded as Glenn approached each of those dozen tests.

Three days before the caucuses in Iowa, the lieutenant governor, a Glenn supporter said, "The ironic part of it is that in a way, [Iowa] is Senator Glenn's ideal constituency.... If you look at polls of where Iowans are on the issues, those polls will model Senator Glenn more than any other candidate. The campaign should be doing better." [6] The day of the New Hampshire primary, the Democratic leader of the state House of Representatives, a Mondale supporter, said, "The natural inclination of New Hampshire is to be more philosophically attuned to John Glenn ... but he didn't do it right." [7] And the week before Super Tuesday, the executive director of the Alabama Democratic party said, "He had it all—the hero image, the conservatism, the lot. Something happened. Nobody can figure it out." [8] The senator himself, no less than these others, did not anticipate the outcome. At one point in the campaign, he believed he would be president.

Two years later, campaigning for reelection in Ohio, Glenn began every appearance with the same story. In south central Ohio, he spoke from a flatbed truck in front of the Hocking County courthouse in Logan:

> Some of you I have not seen since our days when we were running for the presidency. I am sorry we didn't make that race a successful race; but I want you to know it was not my fault that I lost that race for the presidency. It was Annie's fault. (laughter) Let me tell you why. I grew up with Annie up the

road in New Concord, Ohio. Our parents were good friends, and I've known Annie ever since neither one can remember— we were literally babies together. And so I became accustomed very early in life to doing things exactly the way Annie said to do them. And for several years Annie has been telling me that she wanted me to run for the presidency in the worst possible way. That's exactly what I did! (laughter)

The story was an appealing way to capture the continuity between past and present without dwelling on the past. It was also the senator's admission—however oblique and facetious—that his presidential campaign had been a disappointing flop. His judgment reinforces the judgment of others who focused on the intriguing gap between potential and performance. His judgment tells us, too, that the campaign we shall examine in great detail is deserving of such attention. It was a campaign that mattered—really mattered—to an important electoral outcome and to the unfolding of his political career.

PRE-SENATE CAREER

It is impossible to understand anything about Sen. John Glenn without some knowledge of his pre-senatorial experience. There was nothing normal or average about it. It was a spectacular experience, not comparable to that of any other senator of his time. His presidential ambition grew out of that experience; his quest for the presidency was shaped by it; and his failure can be attributed to it.

The argument here is not the conventional one about the general relevance of background characteristics for legislative behavior. It is more directly relevant than that. Nor is it an argument that pre-senatorial experience is a crucial factor in every case of ambition for higher office. It is more dependent on context than that. It is the argument that the adult, pre-Senate experiences of presidential aspirants from the Senate *may be* a causally connected part of any explanation of a senator's presidential quest, and that each case has to be examined for that possibility. Where the importance of the earlier adult career sequence is indisputable, analysis must begin outside the Senate.

Clues to the relative importance of pre-Senate careers can be found in the length of a pre-Senate career and in the proportion of the pre-Senate career devoted to elective politics. In the extreme case of a person who had a long career before entering the Senate and whose career was spent outside elective politics, we would expect that his or her pre-Senate career would be especially consequential for subsequent behavior. In these terms John Glenn does, indeed, represent the extreme case. Among the one hundred members of the Senate in 1984, he was one of only four who were older than fifty when elected and who had never held elective office.[9] Compared to most of his fellow senators, he came very late to political responsibility, and he came without elective office experience. This combination of circumstances suggests the special importance of his lengthy nonpolitical career to his career as a senator and as a presidential hopeful.

His official one-page handout, "Biography of U.S. Senator Glenn," makes it clear that his Senate position should be viewed as the continuation of a string of successes. It begins: "For John Glenn, the opportunity to represent Ohioans in the U.S. Senate is but the most recent honor in a distinguished career." The unembellished facts are these. John Glenn served in the Marine Corps for twenty-three years and as a Project Mercury astronaut for six of those years. As a marine, he was awarded the Distinguished Flying Cross five times and the Air Medal with eighteen clusters. As the first American to orbit the earth, in 1962, he became the nation's *greatest peacetime hero.* His first political venture came at the age of forty-three, in a 1964 race for the Democratic Senate nomination from which he had to withdraw for health reasons. He tried again six years later in 1970 and was defeated in the Democratic primary. During those post-astronaut, pre-Senate years he was a businessman. In 1974, at the age of fifty-three, he won the Democratic primary and was elected to the U.S. Senate. It was his first elected public office.

John Glenn came to the Senate as an amateur, a person with everything to learn about politics. He had learned—through defeat—how to campaign for the Senate. He still had to learn to be a senator. He had to learn how to campaign for the presidency. Quite simply, in a variety of contexts, he had to learn to be a politician, which is one of the basic sequences of politics. It takes time. It is affected by past experience and validated by subsequent experience. Its lessons get internalized by continuous, repetitive experience. But when contexts change, internalized lessons may be inappropriate, and learning may have to begin anew. Every politician engages in this process of learning from successes and failures. But for John Glenn, the amateur, the process was more problematic than for most of his colleagues. Whether he would learn, and if so what, when, and how much remained central problems at every stage of his career.

Glenn's challenge was not just that he was an amateur. He was also a "mature amateur," starting late in life and carrying with him, therefore, a weighty residue of nonpolitical experience. He had to learn a new profession while still under the influence of his old profession, a condition that further defined his problem. His marine-astronaut experience had been lengthy and intense; it could not be confined, subsumed, or forgotten. He had taken to that career easily and naturally. He was very very good at it. He emerged from it with certain personal traits, certain attitudes and values, certain abilities firmly established.

Some of these characteristics proved to be political strengths, some proved to be weaknesses. But all of them persisted throughout his subsequent career. Taken together they posed problems for him, of how to emphasize the assets from his past while minimizing the liabilities, of how to blend the indelible lessons of his earlier career with the changing requirements of his later career. The problems were magnified because he was so good at his military profession. It might have been easier for a second-rate marine to switch careers. In any case, he did not take to the political career as easily and naturally as he had to the military one. Or so his early political defeat seemed to indicate. And the problems of the mature amateur remained with him from the day he decided to run for the Senate in 1964 to the day he gave up the presidential quest in 1984.

As much as a single nonpolitical event can be said to produce a political career, John Glenn's orbital space flight produced his. Without his three trips around the earth in February 1962, there never would have been a Senator Glenn. That historic "first" made him one of America's greatest heroes. And his heroism made possible his politics. Now, almost three decades later, it takes some effort to recapture the national reaction to the event. But we need to recall it briefly because it is the necessary condition for everything that came after.

The facts are that the president of the United States flew to Florida to greet him, decorate him, and escort him back to the White House. He rode with the vice president in a Pennsylvania Avenue parade to address a cheering joint session of Congress. He was given a ticker tape parade in New York City. In his book *The Right Stuff,* Tom Wolfe characterized these events as "something elemental, like a huge change in the weather, a shift in the templates, The Flood, The Last Day, the True Brother Entering Heaven." [10] And Wolfe tried to recapture the emotionalism of it all by noting that "tears ran like a river all over America." "That was what the sight of John Glenn did to Americans at that time. It primed them for the tears." [11]

That extraordinary degree of public attention and emotion can provide—for a person so inclined—a catapult to fame and a resource of name recognition that are ideal for beginning a public career. When, in 1964, Glenn decided that he was so inclined, observers described the two-year capitalization of his assets. "Roads, bridges, streets, schools and hundreds of babies had been named after him, and wherever he went thousands thronged to see him and hear him speak, heaping upon him an adulation few men have ever known." [12] Traveling with Senator Glenn, one is reminded almost hourly of that great precipitating event—by the continuous stream of people who come speaking words of praise and asking for his autograph. They know him as an astronaut and a hero. And it is in the wake of that overpowering stimulus—for better or worse—that John Glenn has pursued his subsequent career.

Though overshadowed by his five hours in space, Glenn's twenty-three years in the military were an equally important part of his pre-Senate experience. His sixteen years as a marine fighter pilot and test pilot earned him the chance to be an astronaut and underpinned his success in the program. He remained a marine colonel throughout his years in the space program, so the marine and the astronaut experiences cannot be separated from one another.

Watching presidential candidate Glenn, in full-dress uniform, participate in traditional ceremonies celebrating the 208th anniversary of the U.S. Marine Corps—first at the Enlisted Men's Ball in New Orleans and then at the Marine League Ball in Des Moines—one could easily sense his "always faithful" pride in his marine associations. When I asked him, at the end of the four-state, five-day November 1983 campaign swing, to rank its twenty-one events in terms of the "personal comfortableness" he felt during each, he replied, "As far as being comfortable is concerned, the two marine balls would have to come first. I guess you could tell that." And he ranked his other nineteen engagements—all of them political events—equally in second place. A lot of the marine has endured within the politician. It is, therefore, the marine-to-astronaut experience, taken as an unbroken sequence, that is the crucial ingredient of John Glenn's long pre-Senate career.

POLITICS AS PUBLIC SERVICE

We need to understand his marine-to-astronaut experience because it gave John Glenn his basic conception of politics, the one he brought with him to the Senate: *that politics is public service.* Politics, to Glenn, is something a citizen does for his or her country. It is a manifestation of patriotism. Politics is, at bottom, similar to military service. They are career corollaries, one of the other. When asked why he decided to enter politics, Glenn replies, "I look upon my entire life as service to my country." [13] And, "I've looked at most of my life as public service." [14] Politics is a logical extension of military service. It is equally worthwhile to spend one's life making the country a more secure place in which to live or making the country a better place in which to live. Both forms of service are built upon a strong sense of community. And community-minded ideas such as "the common good," "the general welfare," "the greatest good for the greatest number," "what's best for the whole country," "one nation, indivisible" fill Glenn's private conversations and public utterances. A recitation of the Pledge of Allegiance, with phrase by phrase interpretation, is a staple of his political speech-making.

Service to the public requires that individuals express and exemplify dedication and pride, devotion to duty, and preservation of traditional values, ideals fostered by the Marine Corps. It requires that action be guided by principle rather than expediency. Not surprisingly, Glenn's personal hero is that most moral and principled of people, Sir Thomas More.[15] Because public service is the highest calling, it requires the most high-minded of motives and the highest degree of personal integrity among its practitioners. Public service politics place a premium on the good man operating from good motives. Public service politics requires that decisions be made on the merits rather than on the politics of the matter. Voter decisions and legislator decisions should be made only after the issues are carefully set forth, with the pros and cons of each issue laid side by side and debated by the candidates without hype and emotion. In this way, votes will be cast on the merits. If you are right on the merits, he believes, you will win in any political arena, and you do not need salesmanship.

There is nothing passive about this conception. It is an activist view. The attractiveness of public service is the opportunity to do something about the nation's problems. Glenn is a gung ho, "let's-set-goals-and-go-for-it" person. Exposure to scientists and engineers during his test pilot-astronaut days gave him a distinctive, problem-solving view of public service. It also instilled in him a reliance on expertise and a strong faith in the problem-solving capabilities of the education-research-technology enterprise in America. He has faith in institutional engineering—in the capacity of rationally constructed arrangements to produce better political performance. If committee conflict leads to inefficiency, well then let's "overhaul the committee system and jurisdictions."[16] If the president and Congress do not get along, well then, let the president come before Congress regularly to explain his policies.[17] These beliefs, in turn, give him an optimism about the nation's future that is all of a piece with his generally optimistic view of politics itself.

Altogether, Glenn's conception of politics is a kind of civics book view that is commonplace among the citizenry. It is free of cynicism, skepticism, alienation, and distrust. It is activist, high-minded, and optimistic. It is consistent with, and may have been influenced by, the community-oriented, small-town setting in which he was raised.[18] But—

and this is the point—Glenn's idea of politics is clearly consistent with, and was certainly influenced by, his more visible, more proximate marine-to-astronaut career.

A conception of politics as public service, however, leaves out or is prejudicial to other possible views, and what he deemphasizes is as important for understanding Glenn's presidential quest as what he emphasizes. The distinction Glenn draws is between politics as public service and politics as an "ego trip" for the politician. He did not, he says over and over again, go into politics for fame, adulation, or acclaim.

In a 1976 interview the new senator gave voice to some of his career-related views.

> I've looked at my service in the Marine Corps, post-World War II days as being public service. I was proud of service to my country in World War II, and stayed in the Marine Corps, through the Korean War, to test pilot work and the space program. And I guess at the age I was at, when I came out of the space program, or after my orbital flight in '62, I felt if there were other areas I could serve my country in, well, I couldn't think of any other use to which I could put my life, so I've looked at it that way. I don't look at it as an ego trip or anything like that. I've had enough attention to last me several lifetimes. So I get a great satisfaction being able to work on some of the things that not only will help solve some of the problems we have here in this country, but perhaps more importantly, to help outline the opportunities—things toward which we could go in the future.[19]

Unspoken, but implied, in Glenn's contrast between politics as public service and politics as an ego trip is the idea that his expressed motives are better than, or preferable to, the alternative. Implied, too, is the notion that because most politicians require ego trips and he does not, he is different from most politicians. He is sensitive to this implication, frequently punctuating his comments with: "I know this may sound self-serving, but . . ." or "I don't mean this in a self-aggrandizing way, but. . . ." Still the implication will not go away.

Moreover, his view does not emphasize politics as the business of reconciling conflict among diverse interests. It does not emphasize politics as the means of promoting a strongly held belief, ideology, or cause. It is not a view of politics as partisan combat. It does not emphasize the attraction of politics for the sheer enjoyment of it. Nor does it see the attraction as the power to manipulate others. Nor is it a view held in praise of the fellowship of politicians or of their profession.

Because these alternate views are precluded by Glenn's attraction to public service politics, his viewpoint is less sensitive to certain inevitable aspects of political life: the existence of organized interest groups, the passion with which certain groups hold their views, the sharpness of conflicting interests, the bargaining that helps resolve such conflicts, the activities that build working relationships between oneself and others in the political process, the pleasurable aspects of such activities, the exercise of manipulative skills, or the practical political arts in general. It would not be correct to say that Glenn's views neglect the emotional and the symbolic side of politics. Far from it. Appeals to love of country and patriotic devotion suffuse his approach to others. But working-level politics involves a variety of less encompassing, but intensely held emotions and evocative symbols, and they suffer neglect in Glenn's outlook.

There is, in all that he neglects, an implicit distinction between service politics and ego politics—the first emphasizing service, consensus, principle, and problem solving, the second emphasizing ego gratification, conflict, expediency, and manipulation. It has been said by observers that John Glenn does not like politics. That is not true. He likes public service politics, not ego politics. "That's what's so exciting about politics," he said when he entered the Senate. "You can help work out problems and plan for our future and by God that's exciting. *But do I enjoy the business of being a politician? Good Lord no.* I had all the ego trips I could handle in seventeen lifetimes." [20] Those preferences and emotions have not changed. When he was asked, later, how he would feel about running for vice president, he said,

> There are pluses and minuses.... It's the same thing as going into politics. *Nobody enjoys running for the Senate.* You can't look forward to the fund raising and the hurly burley of a campaign month after grinding month, but you weigh that against what you might be able to do when you get there. [21]

Glenn's career-long learning process has been focused on adapting to the necessities of ego politics—within the guidelines fixed by public service politics. He has had to learn to be an everyday, working-level, campaigning, coalition-building politician.

One special aspect of Glenn's experience as a marine fighter pilot, test pilot, and astronaut further explains his view of politics and his political career. In all that he did, he was a solo performer. Although part of a large organization, he operated alone. He depended on his ground crew or on mission control, but he did not need to involve himself in their organizational problems. His contribution to the effort was uniquely individual. The "right stuff" was his, not theirs. As a practical matter, he could remain innocent of the organizational side of the operation. At the same time, he could take organizational support for granted. He did not have to ask for it or take action to secure it. He could remain aloof from the supporters he needed. Support came to him, as Tom Wolfe put it, "in advance" and "up front," as a matter of course, on the assumption that he would exhibit the right stuff alone, in the cockpit or in the capsule.

In this aspect of his training, John Glenn differed from Dwight Eisenhower, and the difference was the fundamental flaw in the early comparisons of the two military heroes. Fred Greenstein's excellent study of Eisenhower makes clear that he was, from the outset of his career, trained to do what Glenn never had to do—to command others, and in so doing, to reach out actively to win their support, obligation, and loyalty. Greenstein found for Eisenhower as we have found for Glenn "an extraordinary continuity in his career and leadership style before and after entering [politics]." One such career continuity was Eisenhower's "extraordinary capacity to win the support of other political leaders . . . and [later] the American public." [22] Eisenhower brought a proven talent for command—an "ability to win support in group settings"—to his quest for the presidency.[23] John Glenn did not.

Glenn's particular kind of military service did not require him to think about how one person leads other people. He entered politics, therefore, without a well-developed sense for managing an organization or for winning support from others. He had instead a clear understanding of the important qualities of the individual performer and a sense of self-reliance. Successful politicians probably need some understanding of all these matters. Ultimately, Glenn would have to make up for his deficiencies. In the short run, however, he could capitalize on those things he did understand.

In that regard, the personal qualities that Glenn developed and/or displayed during his marine-to-astronaut experience strongly reinforced his image as a hero and, hence, have been basic to his entire political career. Among observers, there is general agreement on what those are. He is a very nice person. He is a very courageous person. He is a person of impeccable integrity. He is a very stable person. He is a very careful person. He is fair minded and large minded. He is an intelligent and a diligent person. People who know him trust him implicitly. He has personal strengths that make up what most people mean by "character."

Long before "character" became the dominant, trendy theme of 1987-1988 nominating politics, seasoned students of the office told us that character is the basic and essential qualification for the presidency.[24] For that very reason—his obvious strength of character—Glenn's political career was, from its earliest glimmerings, marked by intense interest in his ultimate prospects. From 1974 to 1984 every feature article about politician John Glenn posed the question about President or Vice President John Glenn.[25] He emerged from his pre-Senate career not only as a hero, but as an exemplary kind of hero— Boy Scout hero, all-American hero, Eisenhower-like hero. He is, his biographer Frank Van Riper says, not just Buck Rogers, but John Wayne and Huckleberry Finn as well.[26] As Tom Wolfe's less friendly portrait of Glenn nonetheless makes clear, his personality made him the best known and the best liked of all the astronauts as far as the public was concerned.[27] It was the combination of *heroism plus character* that made possible his political career. Neither would have done it without the other.

From our listing of Glenn's personal strengths, one element has been missing, and that is because he keeps it hidden. It is his ambition. Again, it is a quality that observers agree upon. Wolfe's informants emphasized Glenn's "soaring ambition," Van Riper's his "never banked ambition." [28] It can be inferred both from his steady climb up the ladder of success in the military and from his upward reachings in elective politics. It can also be inferred from his persistence in the face of deeply disappointing failures—to fly in space despite his failure to be the first to do it, to get to the Senate despite two previous failures, to get to higher office despite being turned down for the vice presidency.

The fact of Glenn's ambition seems obvious enough. His presidential ambition was, after all, the driving force of his second term in the Senate. But it would not be worth special mention were it not that his ambition tends to be hidden by his strongly expressed desire to be of public service. He seems not to want to acknowledge its existence. Perhaps ambition smacks too much of the ego politics he so vigorously denigrates. He downplays his ambition to preserve the notion that he is different from other politicians, that he operates from different, and better, motives than they.

Yet there is no incompatibility between public service politics and ambition. One can have public service motives and a driving ambition to achieve the position and stature that make public service possible. One's ego may not require periodic public massaging, but ego may produce a desire to do the best and be the best in whatever one undertakes. In his reflections on astronaut John Glenn and his upbringing, the author of *The Right Stuff* saw no contradiction between public service and ambition. "He was a Presbyterian," says Wolfe. "In the Presbyterian scheme of things there's no problem being both moral and extremely ambitious—no problem at all." [29]

If Glenn had simply assumed the compatibility of public service and ambition, he would have been more likely to see himself as a politician like everyone else. And he would have been more likely to blur the differences between his motives and those of others, more likely to be comfortable engaging in all forms of political activity—service, ego, or otherwise. To the degree that he denies the intensity of his own ambition, self-perceptions may be distorted, the process of learning may be made more difficult, and the fulfillment of his potential as a politician might, therefore, be slowed. In Glenn's assertions about public service, in his denigration of ego trips, and in the implications that he differs from most politicians, there is at least the possibility of a politically damaging self-deception.

On the other hand, Glenn *is* different in one crucial respect. He is one of America's greatest heroes. And that has given him a set of goals slightly different from that of most other politicians. He wants to advance his career, but he has another strong personal desire—if not a felt obligation to his country—to *maintain his hero's reputation*. He has been constrained to adopt a view of politics and a view of his political career that are compatible with the pursuit of his reputational goal. A view of politics as public service, in which personal political ambition is muted, seems ideally suited to the preservation of his hero's reputation. And therein lies another reason for his strong attachment to this view. Glenn's public service politics must be seen as congenial to his presentation of himself as a politician and as congenial to the protection of himself as a hero.

But winning office and protecting a hero's reputation may in some situations conflict with one another. The protectionist stance may dominate in some of those situations. And when it does, that may be the source of Glenn's inability or unwillingness to develop as a politician. We shall examine such situations later. For now, it will help if we acknowledge that the marine-astronaut-hero does, indeed, have something unique to protect and, therefore, that he brings both expansionist and protectionist goals to the pursuit of his political career.

CAMPAIGNING IN OHIO

John Glenn's political career from 1964 to the present can be viewed as a continuous effort, in a variety of contexts, to develop and define a political persona, a political self to present to others, to which others would react and tender their support. The effort has been guided by his public service view of politics, but it has also been shaped by a series of experiences to which he has responded and from which he has learned. For the most part, the relevant contexts and experiences have been his political campaigns.

LEARNING FROM DEFEAT

Glenn's 1964 campaign was a six-week "false start," cut short by an accidental fall and head injury.[30] It was too brief to teach him anything. Afterward he said, "I didn't change any of my basic attitudes, about trading votes or half truths or twisted truths. I hate to see this side of politics, but it seems to be the accepted method of getting elected." [31] This basic attitude never would change much. But the brief campaign highlighted one aspect of politicking he would eventually need to learn: how to deal with the political party whose nomination he sought. At the time of his orbital feat, Glenn, a military man, was a self-proclaimed independent with no party affiliation. He had voted regularly, but there was some doubt as to how he had voted. He was wooed by both parties in Ohio. When he decided—for family and strategic reasons—to throw in with the Democrats, he came with no identification with the party and no attachment to any of its constituent elements; he was without any close personal relationships within the party and without any expressed devotion to its ideology.[32] He felt comfortable enough as a Democrat, but he had to learn to behave like one and to be perceived as one.

His 1964 debut was not auspicious. "He did all the wrong things and alienated all the wrong people," wrote one Ohio observer. "He challenged the aging Steve Young, then the incumbent Democratic senator, in the primary, with not so much as a discussion with a precinct committeeman." [33] Young counterattacked that Glenn was "not a true Democrat." [34] Glenn was, said one reporter, "the politicians' pariah." [35] His plan, from what little evidence there is, was to rely on his heroism and character, to run a personality-oriented "campaign without party" [36] in the primary. Of his formal announcement, two reporters wrote,

> Seldom in the history of American politics has a serious candidate begun a race for high office with so little organized support. Around him as he addressed the reporters was his entire political camp: Bob Voas, the [NASA] psychologist, whose previous experience in politics had been as a poll watcher; Rep. Wayne Hays, a political figure of limited reknown in Ohio; Donald Gosney, Democratic Chairman in a small and remote county; Clarence Graham, an old friend of Glenn's father; and Robert (Mic) McDaniel, a rotund soft drink bottler from East Liverpool.[37]

The amateurish group contained not a clue as to who, in Ohio, might be willing to give strong support to his candidacy. It gave no hint to where he might go to augment his campaign treasury of $65. But his strategy, support, and his skills were not put to the test in 1964.

In 1970, however, his political talents were tested—and found wanting. "From the outset, the 1970 primary was, like the one six years earlier, a disaster." [38] He conducted the campaign very much according to the 1964 plan. "Glenn didn't do much but say 'I'm John Glenn—here I am, vote for me,'" recalled one Ohio reporter.[39] Another reporter echoed, "John's platform was essentially 'I'm a hero, elect me.'" [40] "Glenn believed that the public automatically would nominate him in the 1970 primary because they had automatically made him a folk hero," wrote a third Ohio reporter. "He couldn't distinguish the two worlds." [41] It was a politics-as-public-service point of view—that the Senate was a logical extension of his previous public service.

Why the Senate? "That's where there's clout. Why should I negotiate at the county commissioner level?" [42] This view of his rightful place seemed to be validated by poll results that placed him far ahead of his opponent, Howard Metzenbaum. In retrospect, it was largely a name recognition advantage, one that was wiped out in the campaign's final days by a media blitz that Glenn neither recognized nor anticipated.[43] "We didn't think we could lose," said his campaign treasurer, "because the poll spread was so great it seemed insurmountable.... On election night ... I was shocked." [44] "When I went looking for campaign funds," Glenn recalled, "people would say 'You'll have no trouble beating Howard Metzenbaum. We'll wait for the general election.'" [45] "I was a shoo-in. That's what they told me in 1970." [46] And he believed it. He believed it because it fit his public service notion—that his marine-to-astronaut service had earned him a Senate nomination. And his campaign reflected that point of view. He was simply signing up for another hitch in the marines.

He demonstrated neither the need nor the desire to embrace the Democratic party or any of its organized supporting groups. He "lunched with Rotarians instead of Democrats"; and he "hardly campaigned" in Cleveland's heavily Democratic black wards.[47] A reporter commented, "He never worked the blacks or the ethnics. He was flying solo without any real pros on his staff, and he had no idea what he was doing." [48] He paid little attention to the party's allies in organized labor. Metzenbaum, on the other hand, courted and corralled these groups. His supporters had a different view of how one "earned" a Senate nomination. "Metzenbaum had performed yeomen service in Ohio's Democratic party," said a prominent party leader. "Glenn really had no relations with the party. He had to build from the bottom. Those of us who had given part of our lives to Democratic party politics felt it was a matter of earning your right to get the nomination." [49] Metzenbaum beat Glenn, by 13,000 votes, by overwhelming him in the urban areas where party influence was greatest. Glenn's reaction to his defeat betrayed the persistence of his public service view. "Two wars, cross-country speed run, orbital flight, and then to be rejected by my home state. It wasn't very pleasant." [50]

The campaign also reflected Glenn's lack of the standard working politician's skills. "He was a terrible candidate," said one of his advisers. "He had never done anything like that before." [51] "Glenn came on appearing uncomfortable," said another. "He didn't know how to work the room." [52] He was not accomplished in the political arts, nor was he predisposed to favor those who were. Organizationally, the campaign reflected Glenn's aversion to professional politicians. "It was just a group of friends of John Glenn who wanted to help," recalled one of his top aides. "For example, Vern Alden had been President of Ohio University and had moved to Boston. He suggested a friend of his and he became campaign manager. He didn't do the things a campaign manager should do. It was a mess." Said Glenn, "We got a late start, we didn't get the right people and we had no money." [53] In sum, he was a poor campaigner and he ran a poor campaign.

In that first campaign, there surfaced a central problem in the development of his political persona. The problem was how to create it in the face of the hero's persona, which he brought with him, strongly and completely developed, from his military career. Reflecting on his 1970 experience, Glenn said,

> The people could only think of me as an astronaut. They weren't ready for me as anything else. I'd read up on everything ... just like I'd done before going into anything—but whenever I'd appear some place and go into great detail about what I wanted to accomplish as a Senator, the first question would always be something like, "Mr. Glenn, do astronauts really drink Tang?" [54]

A top campaign aide wrote in a later memo to Glenn that he had lost,

> because [Metzenbaum] was able to convince the voters that you were a fine astronaut and a great national hero but were not really qualified by background and experience to enter political life at the high level of U.S. Senator. Although you drew crowds wherever you went, and were besieged by autograph seekers, you lacked the resources and the record to effectively turn away the Metzenbaum strategy.

This inability or reluctance of the public to perceive Glenn as a political figure has posed, ever since, a dilemma for him whenever he runs for office.

He cannot expunge the astronaut image even if he wanted to—which, of course, he does not. His heroism plus his character are his most important political resources. How to capitalize on those personal assets without letting them prevent the development of his political persona—that has been the dilemma. And it is not helpful to blame the voters, for it is the candidate who must, in the end, act in ways that make them think of him as a political person. Such action requires a full array of political abilities.

In 1970, it seems, he simply did not possess them. Nor did he seem to be convinced that he needed them.

LEARNING FROM VICTORY

Four years later, his view had changed. He and his associates had devised and internalized what Marjorie Hershey calls a "constructed explanation" for his 1970 defeat.[55] It was precisely that he had failed to develop a political persona. Heroism-plus-character was a necessary but not a sufficient condition for his political success. He was deemed to have been insufficiently attentive to people for whom the Democratic party affiliation is a meaningful one, leaving him without a political base among party loyalists. And he was deemed not to have demonstrated the political skills related to such attentiveness. So, looking ahead to 1974, Glenn spent the intervening years trying to remedy those deficiencies. "After we reassessed things," Glenn said,

> I decided to stay right in the—work with the party and make as many contacts as we could within the state and be as active in the party as I could. So I did during that time period after 1970, and I don't think anyone in the whole state, with the possible exception of the governor, spoke at more Jefferson-Jackson Day dinners or fund-raising dinners for different candidates or worked more closely with county, local, and state Democratic officials than I did. When we came into the 1974 campaign we could organize it on a completely different basis—a much broader area of contact and support.[56]

As it turned out, he needed this enlarged support within the party ranks because he was forced, again, to run in a Democratic primary against the very man who had defeated him in 1970.

In 1974 Howard Metzenbaum was the incumbent U.S. senator; he had lost the 1970 general election but had been appointed to a vacancy by Gov. John Gilligan. The governor, party leaders, and labor leaders retained their preference for Metzenbaum. They offered to support Glenn for lieutenant governor, not for the Senate. If Glenn went along with them in 1974, they said, they would support him for the Senate in 1976 or for governor in 1978. Glenn turned down the package and declared his candidacy. It put him in a familiar posture—running against his party's incumbent senator (as in 1964) and running against his party's organization (as in 1970). This time, however, his prospects were brighter. His politicking had put him in a better position to appeal to the party's rank and file. He had learned something about how to make that appeal. And 1974 was a vintage year in which to do it.

His confrontation with the governor and the party hierarchy was an important learning experience for Glenn. It did as much as any single event in his political career to shape his political persona. It solidified his public service view of politics. It helped him carve out a degree of political independence. It uncovered his marine combativeness that could be effective politically as well as militarily. It established him as a resourceful political counterpuncher. It brought him a new level of respect as a political figure. And it taught him strategic lessons he would employ in new contexts—beginning later in the 1974 campaign and continuing in—and beyond—the presidential campaign.

The governor's proposal angered Glenn.

> I didn't think what they were doing was *right*. I felt I *had earned my opportunity by my life in public service to run for the Senate.* . . . I did not want to be told what to do. I see myself as fulfilling a better role than lieutenant-governor. . . . This was my time. If I didn't run for senator, I was going to do something else in public service—maybe go with a foundation . . . besides, *I don't like deals.*[57]

The comment exemplifies his service politics versus ego politics theme. He had been provided with "an opportunity . . . to publicly stand for principles over political expedience." [58]

From this high ground of public service politics, he went on the offensive against his opponents. He attacked their proposal publicly as "backstabbing, backroom bossism"; he accused the governor of "attempting to stomp me into the political mud" [59] through "blackmail"; and he declared his intention to take his fight to the party's rank and file. "I am alone, and I mean alone," he told the party's executive committee. "I am a target now marked for political extinction . . . because I will not go along in a deception of our Democratic voters." [60] And he drew upon his marine fighter pilot background to let them know he would be a tough combatant. "I never pulled out high over targets," he said. "I was the one who went in low and got them—and as a result I was known as Old Magnet Tail." [61] As a fighter pilot he told a later interviewer, "You're either aggressive or you'd better get into another line of work." The interviewer reflected, "His determination to get the other guy . . . sounds savage." [62] He had no intention of quitting. "Push came to shove," he said, "and I shoved back." [63] And he found it worked. "I've never let people push me around in politics," he later generalized.[64]

By painting himself as a victim of unfair treatment at the hands of the powerbrokers, he prepared the way for his successful appeal over the heads of the party leaders to the party rank and file. "I think a lot of people, a lot of Democrats across the state resented the way I had been treated," he said later.

> My name was known—not just from my astronaut days, I didn't mean that—but my name was known from the Gilligan campaign. They knew I had played a major role in his election. They felt he had . . . dealt unfairly with me . . . had lined up all the state party and labor organizations against me. . . . I just wanted to talk to the rank and file people, give my views, and I'd be accepted or rejected on that basis. The people responded to that. So we came through against considerable odds.[65]

His strategy—appealing to the rank and file over the heads of organized Democratic groups—was effective on several levels. It allowed him to combine his established personal strengths with newly won Democratic party support—by coming across as a hero, a man of integrity, and a politician who had paid his dues. It helped him to establish contact with the Ohio business community, which valued his independence and demonstrated its approval with financial support. Finally, his strategy seemed to be one that would be available and fitting throughout his career.

Once he seized the political high ground and uncovered his instinct for combat, Glenn stayed on the offensive during the 1974 campaign. He was aided by his decision in midcampaign to take on, for the first time, a professional campaign manager from Ohio to complement his nationally experienced media and poll consultants. They pushed him to take full advantage of two events. First, it was disclosed that Metzenbaum had paid no income tax in 1969 and was still contesting a payment of back taxes in the two previous years. Glenn made the issue the centerpiece of his campaign, hammering away at those tax problems, with their suggestions of irregularity and/or impropriety.[66]

Second, Metzenbaum blundered by stating that Glenn had never held a job. That, said Glenn, was "a dirty one." "I don't like it when some dumb yahoo tries to run down the idea that someone risked their fanny for the country." [67] Glenn struck back hard in a debate, citing his military record.

It wasn't my checkbook, it was my life that was on the line. . . . You go with me to a veterans' hospital and tell them they didn't hold a job. Go with me and tell a Gold Star mother her son didn't hold a job. Go to Arlington cemetery, watch those flags and tell me those people didn't hold a job. I tell you, Howard Metzenbaum, you should be on your knees every day of your life thanking God that there were some men, some men who held a job.[68]

The fury of that counterattack kept his opponent on the defensive until Glenn's 100,000-vote victory was secure.

Observers concluded that between 1970 and 1974 Glenn had learned a lot about electoral politics. Said one,

Glenn analyzed his [1970] mistakes, concluding that if he was to become a successful politician, he would have to do all the things politicians are required to do. . . . He won the Democratic nomination to the Senate, certainly on his name and charm, but also because he politicked day and night, accepted the advice of professionals, sought campaign funds on his own, and plotted strategy like any other man running for office.[69]

For example, his new campaign manager told him to campaign exclusively in the fourteen most populous Ohio counties and to concentrate on the white ethnic voters there. And he did. "I'm eastern European," said manager Steve Kovacik, "and I know how my people feel about John Glenn. They like him. We hit every place there was kielbasa—and all the Italian wards. We had John going from six in the morning till two the next morning." [70]

A veteran Ohio reporter recalled later,

Steve Kovacik was an ethnic who took John into Northeast Ohio, into the ethnic communities there and got him their support in 1974. John never had problems in Southern Ohio. His problems were in Northeast Ohio, especially Cuyahoga County. Kovacik taught the farm boy how to politick on the ethnic west side of Cleveland. He got John elected in 1974.

When I asked Glenn, campaigning in 1980, what his 1974 campaign had taught him about his state, he confirmed the reporter's observation.

I knew Ohio pretty well. One group I did not know well were the ethnic groups in the northern part of the state—Polish, Hungarians, Slovenians, Serbians, you name it. They are all organized. They are proud of their heritage. They all have their

festivals, their costumes, their dances, their ethnic food. I knew
of them, but I did not know them first hand. Now they are
among my strongest supporters. They are the most patriotic
people in the country. They are first, second, or at most third
generation Americans and they appreciate this country. I think
they feel especially close to me because of my past. I let it all
hang out in two wars; I was an astronaut—all for my country.
They identify with that.

Glenn's newfound strength on Cleveland's ethnic west side offset his
continuing weaknesses on the predominantly black east side. Kovacik's
campaign generalship has been credited as an essential ingredient in
Glenn's victory.

As his own comment indicates, Glenn's 1974 success still rested on
his marine-astronaut past. But the more aggressively he campaigned and
the more people were exposed to him, the more he added to it a political
profile. Glenn noted the change. In 1970, "within the first two or three
questions, somebody would ask about space and we never would get off
it," but in 1974, "we'd go for maybe a week or ten days at a time without
any question being asked about space." [71] He recalled a more specific
perceptual conversion involving a newspaper publisher. "In 1970 I went
around to pay him a courtesy call," said Glenn.

I was "the astronaut" then. I went in, and he said "I believe in
professionalism. What makes you think an astronaut should be
elected to the United States Senate?" So I told him that
scientists could play a useful role, that there were too many
lawyers, that sort of thing. He didn't say anything. He was a
crusty old bastard. In 1974, I went around again. He asked me
again "What makes you think an astronaut would make a good
Senator?" This time I gave it right back to him. He had not
been trained as a newspaperman. "What makes you think you
are capable of running a large newspaper?" He thought about it
for a minute and then he said, "You've got a point." It was like
turning a switch; from that day to this, he's been as nice as he
can be to me.

His polls still showed, according to a later memo, "some concern on the
part of Ohio voters about political experience and potential as a public
servant." But Glenn was making progress—bit by bit—in the transition
from hero to hero-politician in Ohio. It was a very slow transition. And
it was definitely incomplete. In the context of 1974, however, it was
complete enough.

The Gilligan deal, the income tax issue, and the "never held a job"
accusation were made-to-order campaign issues to be exploited by a hero

of unimpeachable character and a public service politician. In each case, he counterattacked. In each case, his counterattack juxtaposed public service against a private advantage view of politics. In each case, he could speak skillfully, with righteous anger, in defense of his personal integrity. By directing his anger at the low-level politics of the establishment, he could make a high-level politics appeal to the rank and file. He could be highly political while seeming to be less so than his opponents. Glenn would display this pattern in other contexts—including his presidential campaign.

But the context would never again be as favorable as it was in 1974, when the revelations of Watergate left people acutely distrustful of politicians seeking personal advantage. In 1974, wrote one analyst, "the times and the man meshed ... the fact that he [Glenn] never saw a day in public office became a virtue ... there was once again a market for a hero." [72] Better still, there was a market for a fighting, underdog hero running a public service campaign. Strength of character, we have said, is John Glenn's basic political asset. But the events of 1974 demonstrate that the asset can be capitalized on only when the context of a campaign elevates character to the status of an issue. Observers of American politics saw that happen in the 1988 presidential nominating contest.[73] But—to get ahead of our story—it did not happen the year Glenn ran for president.

In 1974 the context converged with the candidate and the campaign to make election victory possible for Glenn in the primary and in the general election. Against his Republican opponent, Glenn experienced no difficulty whatever, carrying every county and winning by more than 1 million votes. His spectacular general election success, viewed against a background of primary election difficulty, might have led him to make a sharp differentiation between the two types of elections. But it appears that he did not. The times and the "market" made it possible to conduct the same kind of campaign in both elections, and the overwhelming victory in the second seemed to vindicate the strategy of the first. After his primary victory, Glenn told Ohio's labor leaders that the issues in the general election would be "the same as in the primary." [74] He intended, in other words, to continue on the same independent course that had won him the primary. And when, after the general election, he looked back on his primary, he said, "Sometimes it got lonesome being right; but I'm beholden to nobody." [75] In his view, public service politics had worked equally well in both the general and the primary elections. In 1974 there may have been no need to make any distinction. But that was not the most useful lesson to carry forward into other campaigns, at other times, and in other markets.

FIRST IMPRESSIONS: OHIO, OCTOBER 1980

My earliest observation of John Glenn during his 1980 campaigning in Ohio produced some tentative, but firsthand, notions about his political persona. The following comments are from my notes, written during and after the October visit.

1. The evidence of his great appeal, as a person, is everywhere. We went to a businessmen's breakfast, a Kiwanis luncheon, a union rally, a Democratic party dinner, a Glenn headquarters opening, and a county fair. In each context, there were smiling autograph seekers. And he moved about in a cocoon of warm feeling and/or respect.

2. The tug of war between the hero and the politician is a recognizable problem. At the opening of his Toledo headquarters, his campaign manager watched Glenn signing autographs and commented, "It adds fifteen minutes to every stop. Still, it's not as bad as it was in 1974. He's a little bit more the senator now and less the astronaut." And a local campaign organizer chimed in minutes later,

> We had to kick his ass [in 1974] every minute to make him campaign the way he should. He doesn't stroke people. He doesn't create excitement. It's hard to keep people working for him. They just fall away. He's a great guy and a great senator, but he's not a politician. He's a hero. Look at him signing autographs. He'll never be beaten.

The older astronaut-hero image seems not to have been integrated yet into the newer U.S. senator image. Instead, they coexist somewhat inharmoniously.

3. Glenn capitalizes most effectively on his personal strengths in small groups and in one-on-one situations. At the opening, a woman asked him to sign a copy of *People* magazine's story featuring his wife's winning battle with stuttering. "I'm so proud of what she did. I'd like to stop the campaign, buy up 3,000 copies of that magazine and hand them out on the street corner." Smiles. When we stopped at a cider mill to get something to eat, he sidled over to the one other family sitting at a table and talked quietly with them about picking out "punkins" for Halloween. Smiles. At the Fairfield County Fair, he bought corn dogs and cokes for the high schoolers who had handed out leaflets, and he greeted people he knew. "There's Mary! Look at the hat she's got on." Smiles. (Six years later he spontaneously recalled our visit to the fair and our conversation with Mary.)

At the 1,000-person Democratic party dinner, however, he arrived late, did not mingle with the crowd, did not leave the dais to circulate, and left as soon as the festivities were over. He fretted about his talk beforehand, delivered it quite mechanically, and fretted about it afterward. As a wholesale campaigner, in a political context, he seems uncomfortable, stiff, and distant.

4. He seems to lack an instinct for the normal, bread-and-butter routines of politics. At a political rally of Boilermakers Lodge 85 in Rossford, he gave a let's-not-be-complacent pep talk. He got little reaction during the talk, received a routine round of applause at the end, got down off the podium, and got halfway out of the union hall. The president went to the microphone, thanked him for coming, and remarked that Glenn was once a plumber, too. When Glenn heard that, he shouted, "That's right, I *was* a plumber." He turned, ran back to the podium, jumped up on it, and ran toward the microphone. The president said, "You don't have to come back." Glenn grabbed the mike and said, "My dad was a plumber in New Concord. I spent my summers digging holes for septic tanks and I hated every minute of it." The audience laughed. "I was the pipe threader and reamer and cutter; and I cut, threaded, and reamed miles of pipe. And that was before you had machines. That was hard going." The audience cheered. Glenn waved, jumped down off the podium, and left in a heightened mood of good feeling. A natural, instinctive politician would have made that obvious connection at the very beginning of his talk and built a sense of identification with his listeners—the more so since Ohio's unions had never been very strong supporters of his. John Glenn, I think, is not a natural politician.

5. He gave no evidence of having any well-differentiated notion about his bases of political support. When I asked him point-blank who his strongest supporters were, he looked back to 1974.

> I suppose I could start with the Democrats. I got more votes in the big cities; but that's because more people live there. You hunt where the ducks are. It's not a case where I'm strong in the cities and not in the agricultural areas—or vice versa. We found something interesting when we went back and checked in 1974. We found that in order to get the vote I did in some counties, I had to have gotten at least 50 percent of the Republican vote. We carried all eighty-eight counties in 1974— the first time that had ever been done. So I'd have to say we have support all across the board.

It was a general election answer and made no reference to a core of strong support within the Democratic party.

Later, as we rode into Toledo, I asked, "Is this area a particularly good one for you politically or about average or what?" "I'd say it's a fairly good area, wouldn't you, Irwin? [friend Irwin Silverman] ... Lucas

County is a good Democratic county. But I wouldn't say it's that much better than other Democratic counties. Maybe it's better organized than some." Again, it was an undifferentiated "across-the-board" view of his constituency. It gave no evidence of a "reelection constituency," "primary constituency" distinction. When I asked a top campaign staffer to describe Glenn's strongest supporters, the answer was simply, "the people." When the staffer inquired what I thought, I answered that I was leaving without any idea whatsoever of just who it was in Ohio who would fight, bleed, and die for John Glenn. And I am not convinced that John Glenn knows either.

In 1980 Glenn did not have to know, because he did not have to fight a primary campaign. His interpretation of the 1974 election was not tested. After six years in the Senate, Glenn had assumed an entirely different relationship with the state Democratic party. Instead of his needing the party, it needed him.[76] He was Ohio's most prominent political figure, a finalist in the 1976 vice-presidential sweepstakes and often mentioned as a future presidential possibility. The party's nomination and party support were his for the asking. That did not mean that he had solved the basic problem with which he had begun—how to live with the Democratic party. The relationship was more one of convenience than one of compatibility. He had proven to be a spectacular vote-getter. As such, he was a person to whom aspiring Ohio politicians wished to attach themselves and against whom the more skeptical of the party's elements—labor, blacks—did not wish to contend. But his status was more that of party icon than party leader. He remained the complete hero and the incomplete politician.

In 1980 he confirmed what he had proved in 1974, that he was an untouchable general election candidate. In the preliminary maneuvering, Ohio Republicans floated trial balloons for other celebrities: Neil Armstrong, first man on the moon; Art Modell, owner of the Cleveland Browns; and Woody Hayes, Ohio State football coach.[77] But Glenn's overwhelming partisan and extrapartisan strength give him preemptive dominance. Prospective opposition disappeared. Against a weak opponent, he carried all but one rural county and amassed the largest plurality—1.6 million votes—of any statewide candidate in Ohio history. The victory put him on the path to a presidential candidacy.

GOVERNING IN THE SENATE

John Glenn spent nine years in the United States Senate between his 1974 election and his 1983 presidential campaign. Those nine years provided him the opportunity to further develop and refine the political persona with which he came to Washington. Minimally, he could earn his credentials as a political figure by virtue of his daily participation in the work of the Senate. Beyond that, he could give substance and structure to his political philosophy through the allocation of his legislative energies, his voting record, and his relationships with external groups. More generally still, he had the opportunity to polish and display political skills analogous to those he had been learning in Ohio—persuasive and coalition-building skills among colleagues in the Senate, presentational and networking skills among people outside the Senate.

Glenn took some advantage of all three opportunities. But he took greatest advantage of the credentialing opportunity, and in so doing he enhanced his potential presidential candidacy. The Senate not only stimulates presidential ambitions; it legitimates them. For Glenn, who had no other political experience, the Senate became his proving ground. By his performance, and by journalistic recognition of it, he did indeed prove himself there. He learned to be a senator. And he gained a reputation as a good senator. His Senate performance and his Senate reputation, in turn, gave him legitimacy as a presidential candidate. John Glenn the hero would never have been taken seriously; John Glenn the senator was. From our career and campaign perspective, that was the major accomplishment of his nine years of governing activity in the Senate.

REPUTATION

Glenn's first priority on entering the Senate was to convince the various observers in and around the institution to take him seriously. He wanted as much internal influence as comes from an initial reputation as a "good" senator. For freshmen this reputation is earned through observance of the Senate's most widely held norms, such as legislative work and specialization.[78] The "workhorse" norm came naturally to the marine-astronaut. He was keenly aware, however, that his adjustment period would be marked by an initial skepticism among colleagues and Senate watchers concerning both the purposefulness of a person who came with an established reputation and the ability of a person who lacked political experience.

Most senators *make* their reputations in the Senate. John Glenn had to *change* his.

> I thought the fact that I had become known in a different field might be a major disadvantage—that Senators might look askance at whether I could carry my own weight in this league.[79]

He determined to keep a low public profile and devote himself to the work of the institution. By midsummer of 1975, Glenn could say,

> As soon as I got here I went to work just as hard as I could to become a day-in and day-out working member of the Senate, and I think I have established myself pretty well in that regard.[80]

His devotion to legislative work was duly noticed by the media scorekeepers—the journalists who cover and comment on political reputation and success—and corroborated by insiders.

In July the *Chicago Tribune* wrote that "some Democrats regard him the star of the [ten-member] freshman class." And they quoted a colleague, "He has shown he is willing to put in the time and do his homework.... He doesn't mind long hours. And he listens, and you don't get senators willing to listen every day."[81] A month later the *Los Angeles Times* headlined, "Glenn's Low Profile Pays Off in Senate: Colleagues Rate Him One of Best in '75 Freshman Group." And it quoted a Senate aide, "Don't be fooled just because he is quiet and does not sound off a lot. He is not awfully articulate, but he has a good mind and he is one of the hardest workers round here."[82] He was being taken seriously and was gaining the favorable internal reputation he sought.

He enhanced his reputation by emphasizing his inside work in the face of the persistent outside suggestion that he had bright prospects for higher office. The Ohio senator drew the attention of the *Chicago Tribune* and the *Los Angeles Times*—along with *People* magazine, the *Washington Post*, the *Milwaukee Journal*, and the *Saturday Evening Post*, among others—during his first Senate year precisely because he was already considered a real, and newsworthy, presidential or vice-presidential possibility.[83] Glenn could parry the inquiries by saying, "I'm just trying to be the best senator Ohio ever had" or "If I'm picked for anything else anytime, I want it to be because I'm doing the best job I know how to do right there."[84] And he gathered further credits when he immediately rebuffed suggestions that he become Ohio's favorite son candidate in 1976.[85] He had more opportunities than most to convince observers that he was serious about his Senate career. And he took them.

The legislative norm of committee-based specialization came just as naturally to Glenn as that of legislative work. His military experience with state of the art technology rendered him as respectful of expertise as a person could be. He had campaigned heavily on the theme that "we didn't have any senators in Washington with any appreciable background in science, research, or technology, yet probably half or more of the things voted on in the U.S. Senate have something to do with the physical sciences." [86] So, following a familiar campaigning-to-governing pattern, he decided "to take whatever research and technology background I had and put it to work in what I see as a very key area, and that is on our energy policy for the future in this country." [87] He applied for and got assigned to the Interior Committee, "which handles probably 75 percent to 80 percent of the energy legislation." His second choice was the Governmental Affairs Committee, which handled "some phases of nuclear energy" plus a broad oversight jurisdiction. His early legislative work was in these committees—particularly Interior. "You have to carve out sort of a specialty area to concentrate your efforts in." [88]

His specialty was energy—and in particular those aspects most closely related to his experience and interest—research and development. "I've been very very active in the subcommittee that handles the Energy Research and Development Administration," he said in 1976.

> I've chaired—been chairman day after day after day of hearings on the whole ERDA budget for the coming fiscal year—$6.2 billion total. We're determining where this money will go and what energy sources will be singled out for specific research and development. I've had a major impact on that.[89]

He had no sense that he was serving an old-fashioned apprenticeship on that committee. "I was able to move in and have an impact on legislation almost from the day we started," he said.

> I had only been there about two months when ... [the chairman] Senator [Henry] Jackson [D-Wash.] asked me to help floor manage some of that legislation on the Senate floor. ... It was a move rapidly enough into some position of importance in getting legislation through that I had not anticipated that early in my freshman year. ... My background has enabled me, particularly in Interior, to really have an impact on things.[90]

It was out of this work that Glenn's early reputation emerged. In 1981, he looked back:

> When I came in, everyone knew who I was. At least they knew my name. I was concerned that I not get a reputation as a lightweight here—as someone who got in on his name and nothing else. So I dug into my committee work as hard as I could. A lot of committee work is drudgery. But 90 percent of the work of the Senate is done in committee. I think I got the reputation as a person who would do the drudgery of the Senate.

A workhorse reputation was the best kind of inside reputation for any newcomer to acquire. It was doubly beneficial for a nationally acclaimed newcomer.

Glenn was fully aware that he was a newcomer. On my first visit to his Washington office, he pointed to an illustration of the biblical story of Daniel in the lion's den on the wall.

> The day I was sworn in, my daughter went down to a gallery and brought this picture back to me. That's exactly the way you feel. I don't care where you come from or what you did before you got here, there is something awesome about the Senate. . . . Whether you are a governor, representative, or lawyer you feel a bit like Daniel in the lion's den. It was so appropriate that I bought copies of this same picture and sent one to each of this year's incoming senators. On my note, I said, "I know you feel a little bit like the picture right now, but this too shall pass."

His self-confidence in the new job developed very gradually. As he described it in 1981:

> When you first come to Congress and you sit in committee, you have ideas that you keep to yourself. You believe that all the experts around know more than you do. So, even if you disagree, you hesitate to speak up. That happened to me many many many times. But I began to notice that although the administration position was very different from mine at the beginning, little by little they would come around to exactly the position I had come to instinctively at the beginning. . . . I'd come home fussing that "I had an idea today, but I kept it to myself; and at the end of the meeting, they came around to exactly what I had thought in the first place." And Annie— she's my biggest booster—would say, "See, I told you to speak up. You kept still and someone else got the credit" and so forth. And I would say, "Well, it's over and it will be good for the country." But gradually, after this happened a lot, I began to get a higher estimate of my own ability. My assessment of myself changed; and I got more confidence in my ideas.

It was a learning process for the marine-astronaut inside the Senate that was comparable to the learning process he had gone through in Ohio— same process, different arena. Although the bottom line—election victory—was clearer in Ohio, the object was the same—to win favorable judgments from observers in and out of his chosen profession and to gain confidence in his ability to perform effectively in that profession.

The idea of slow but steady progress toward these objectives permeates all accounts of Glenn's first term. In the beginning, as on the Interior Committee, he won favorable notice by acting within a narrow range of comfortable, technical matters. He put together, during his first year and a half, an unbroken record of victories on floor amendments. And beneath a headline "Workhorse Label Fits Glenn, Observers Say," a political reporter wrote in the *Akron Beacon Journal*, "His diligence and attention to detail have paid off."

> He has sponsored 25 amendments to various bills and won Senate approval of every one.... It is true that some of these amendments were not particularly controversial ... it is also true that on some of them he had potent allies.... Even so, the string of victories is an astonishing feat considering that Glenn is a freshman senator who is not supposed to have mastered the intrigues and intricacies of getting bills passed.[91]

Eventually, this selective, staff-created record of legislative "wins" would be forgotten, but it prompted the best kind of interim outside judgment on the new senator's progress. Two weeks later, the Washington bureau chief of the *Cincinnati Enquirer* entered a similarly positive judgment beneath the headline "Glenn's Challenge: To Grow in His Job." "He has turned into a doggone good senator, learning more every day.... And there is no reason why he can't continue to grow in that job."[92]

In 1977 Glenn left the Interior Committee to go on the prestigious Foreign Relations Committee—the one he had most wanted all along. That change coincided with an expansion of his legislative range. From his vantage point in 1980, the Glenn-watcher of the *Dayton Daily News* described the change:

> Senator John H. Glenn's background as a marine and an astronaut led him to focus primarily on technical areas during his first few years in the Senate. In those days, reporters covering Glenn joked that the freshman senator's amendments would be sure-fire remedies for an insomniac ... good reading only for first year engineering students.... But in 1977, things started to change. Glenn was named to the Senate Foreign Relations Committee.[93]

And Glenn agreed.

> You come up here and you're playing in the majors. You can't help wondering about your own ability in this league.... When I got here, I started on technically oriented things where I felt my expertise was above most of my compatriots. I have since broadened my base.[94]

He never lost his penchant for focusing—where possible—on the technical aspects of an issue. But the range of issues in which he became engaged widened.

A midterm assessment by the reporter from the *Dayton Journal Herald* described Glenn as "in a sort of holding pattern, waiting to score some major legislative triumph that will vault him toward the front of the Senate pack." Glenn indicated to the reporter that he wanted to achieve greater influence—especially on the Foreign Relations Committee. "Anytime anybody does not hope to move up in leadership," he said, "they shouldn't be here." [95]

Shortly thereafter, President Jimmy Carter signed a piece of legislation of which Glenn was the major author, major sponsor, major strategist—the Nuclear Non-Proliferation Act, designed to restrict the spread of nuclear material from peaceful to military uses. It is the legislative accomplishment of which Glenn is most proud. And while it may not have vaulted him to the front of the pack, it gained him a solid reputation as a capable legislator on a nationally important subject. [96]

He had made a substantial contribution in the area of arms control. As such it propelled him authoritatively into the middle of that huge and burgeoning debate. And it gave his subsequent views on SALT II a credibility that may have dictated the outcome of that proposal. He steadfastly opposed the treaty on the technical and political grounds that its provisions could not be verified. And his expertise on the arcane subject of verification, together with his more general credibility on nuclear arms matters may have—through delay—cost Carter the treaty. The performance stamped Glenn as "a man to be reckoned with" in terms of influence in Washington. "The guy is very hard working and tenacious," summed up a top White House official in 1980. "I'd much prefer to have him on my side than against me. In those areas where he has expertise, it is extremely hard for us to win if he is not with us." [97]

Glenn's own lengthy 1981 account of his career on the Foreign Relations Committee repeats the theme of a gradual process of growth in self-confidence and in recognition by others.

> I had given a lot of thought to foreign relations. It was not a committee assignment that was a passing fancy. I had some definite ideas. So I began to speak out; and I found that oftentimes lots of people agreed with me. That boosted my confidence level still further. By the end of the term, I had a good reputation in the committee. Now, this year, a metamorphosis has taken place. My reputation has begun to spread beyond the committee. In the past, the senior members had been more or less the spokesmen for the committee. Or, at least they were better known. When we would come out of a meeting, the reporters would stick the microphones in their

faces. They would talk and the rest of us down the line would either stand back and listen or go about their business. This year, [committee chairman Charles] Percy speaks for the majority side. But on the minority side . . . I get as much attention from the press as anyone. And I have no hesitation whatever in speaking up and saying what is on my mind.

I'll give you another example. Last week I was asked to go on "Good Morning America" to talk about El Salvador. . . . [F]ive years ago I would have declined, despite that great opportunity for national publicity. I would have thought, "I had better study up on El Salvador." This time, I accepted immediately, went over there, and talked about El Salvador. And got a great reception. Senator ___ told me he was in Florida and was just about to turn off his set when he heard I was going to be on. He listened and he said to me, "You put in words exactly what I was thinking." When you hear that from your colleagues, it boosts your confidence level.

By this time, Glenn was testing himself for a presidential run. And so was the press. But the steady growth of his senatorial capacity—what Lawrence Dodd calls "legislative mastery" [98]—was the central feature of his self-analysis.

By 1980 John Glenn had solid credentials as a good United States senator. That is the way he saw himself. That is the way others saw him. He had proved to everyone that he was not a lightweight—just as he had proved the same thing in Ohio politics. He was interested, hard working, capable, respected, and influential. The *Dayton Daily News* summary by its Washington reporter was headlined "Glenn Flies High in Role of Senator." The summary said, "That Glenn has shed the lightweight image is an indication of how far he has come since arriving in the Senate six years ago with his hero credentials in order but his political ones in question." [99] It was the consensus view of Ohio scorekeepers.[100] And it sustained him in the 1980 campaign. By the end of that campaign, he had begun to think of his credentials as sufficient to legitimate an exploration of presidential possibilities. Whether he could utilize his acquired senatorial capabilities to win support from a presidential-sized electorate was, of course, another matter.

PHILOSOPHY

Alongside the gradual development of his credentials as a political figure, Glenn developed some philosophical definition. Like the credentialing process, the process of ideological definition started from scratch and proceeded gradually.

When he first came into public view as an astronaut, Glenn had no identifiable political views. "All at once, we were being asked questions I never dreamed people would ask," said Glenn in 1976. "You could no longer coast along in anonymity. I determined way back in those days, I would answer them. I would give my opinion for whatever it was worth." When you campaign, he continued, "You go into more and more of telling what your views are. Then when you get here [to the Senate] you refine it even further." [101] The perspective is a developmental one. In his 1974 campaign Glenn presented a set of detailed positions on current issues: a seven-point inflation program and statements on national health care and energy. But they were not central to the campaign and did not constitute a usable ideological profile. His 1980 campaign manager spoke of the 1974 effort in developmental terms. "In 1974 we feared issues—any issue—no matter what side we were on. Now, although we worry about them, we know we can handle them. He's much more self-assured." [102] Six years in the Senate had given Glenn a confidence—and a profile—on the issues.

But the profile had not been as clearly delineated as that of many of his colleagues. He was not easily typecast. His first-term self-definitions showed a predisposition to move toward the middle of the ideological spectrum, to remain self-consciously independent of any group that demanded ideological fealty, and to take each issue as it came, in context, and without reference to a fixed philosophical standard. "I don't like labels," he said in 1975, "because labels indicate that you are expected to vote a particular way on a specific piece of legislation no matter what, and I don't like that. I like to consider each bill on its own and in its own time period." [103] "In the liberal-conservative thing I'm somewhere in the middle," he said in 1977, "I don't try to characterize myself too much." [104] In 1978 he told an Ohio reporter, "I'm a hard fish to hold down. . . . I don't like the idea of being pigeonholed into one ideological mold, then have people think I'm going to have a knee-jerk reaction in response to their pressure. . . . I never give it a thought whether [my vote] is going to be looked at as liberal or conservative." The reporter concluded, "He literally defies labeling." [105] His nine-year record fleshed out these earlier tendencies.

As his views developed during his pre-presidential campaign years in the Senate, he became known for his support of a strong national defense. Yet he did not automatically support all weapons systems. He favored the B-1 bomber and a new nerve gas system, but he opposed the MX missile and the rapid deployment force. In foreign policy he supported arms control in the nuclear proliferation area, but he opposed (then later supported) SALT II. On the matter of arms sales, he voted for the sale of F-15 planes to Saudi Arabia and against the sale of AWACS to that country.

In domestic policy, he voted as a liberal on a range of social issues—pro-choice on abortion, pro-ERA, against formal prayer in the public schools. His voting record on civil rights was consistently liberal, and he took an active role in trying to increase black employment on Capitol Hill. He strongly supported increased spending on education and research, but displayed fiscal conservatism on matters such as health care. On regulatory matters, he tended to come down on the side of free enterprise, favoring the deregulation of natural gas, opposing regulation of used car dealers, opposing stringent environmental controls to reduce acid rain. Yet he supported protectionism via domestic content legislation. On the other hand, his prolabor support on that issue could be put beside his antilabor position on common site picketing. He worked hard to eliminate tax loopholes by subjecting all of them to a sunset provision, but he voted for the Reagan tax program of 1981 with its variety of tax loopholes, and he argued strongly for various tax reductions and tax incentives for business.

The reasoning behind each vote ranged, without a doubt, from the broadest concerns for international security to the narrowest concerns for Ohio's interests. But, taken as a whole, the record had two characteristics. First, it was hard to describe its central tendency in ideological terms. It lacked an easily definable or coherent belief structure. It could be described in numerical terms, in the fashion of the conventional summaries by outsiders. And in that fashion, Glenn's overall voting record stood in the middle-to-liberal range of the spectrum. His first-term ADA/liberalism scores, for example, ranged from a low of 50 percent to a high of 67 percent, with a six-year average of 58 percent. His conservative coalition support scores over the same six-year period ranged from a high of 59 percent to a low of 18 percent, with an average of 32 percent.

The second characteristic of Glenn's voting record was the absence of total agreement with any one outside group. He was, in that sense, a notably independent thinker and actor on the issues. No interest group could see him as a safe and predictable supporter. But he had been a reliable supporter of the Democratic party's position—voting with a majority of the Senate's Democrats from 63 percent to 83 percent of the time, averaging 77 percent in his first term.

When Glenn's political views were given a label, the words were usually "middle of the road" or "centrist" plus "independent" or "unpredictable." The Ohio reporters who knew him best in his first term called him "a classic middle-of-the-road Democrat" or "a fiercely independent legislator who is in no one's political camp." [106] Those depictions jibe closely with Glenn's mature self-description in March 1981.

> Some senators think of themselves as liberals or conservatives. I don't. I'm probably somewhere in the middle. I think you have to decide what's best for the nation given the times we are in. If there were money coming in and a surplus, I'd probably be as wild a liberal on spending as anyone around. But when conditions are what they are now, I'm going to be awfully tough to get along with on the same programs. It depends on the condition of the country. I'm not locked into any ideological camp, liberal or conservative. I never have been and I hope I never am.

In the period after 1975, his self-descriptions remained remarkably consistent. Whatever the strengths and weaknesses of this ideological posture were when he arrived in the Senate, they persisted to the time of his presidential candidacy.

An independent, centrist voting record is reflective of what a senator with a public service view of politics probably wants. Such a record is consistent with a thoughtful, case-by-case, on-the-merits, and in-its-time assessment of what is best for the country. As one observer said, "Every vote is a new vote for Glenn." [107] At the same time, a record of this sort may lack philosophical coherence. Thus, an Ohio scorekeeper summed up in 1978:

> Glenn is something of an enigma in the Senate. His voting record places him slightly to the left of center, more a reflection of his affiliation with the Democratic party than a sign of any deeply held political conviction.[108]

And, during the 1980 campaign, the same reporter wrote, "He lacks a strong philosophical position to guide him, and approaches most issues with the detached air of a clinical pathologist." [109] These comments suggest a lack of coherence. They also suggest a lack of deeply held or strong political views. A centrist, independent record may fail to disclose a certain degree of passion—the kind of commitment outside groups desire. Glenn's record overall displayed both the absence of structure and the absence of passion.

But it is not true that the record lacked any pattern or any strong commitments. A better way to gauge a legislator's depth of interest in various issues is to see what issues he expends time and energy on, what issues he talks about most frequently, and what aspects of an issue he emphasizes. By these criteria, Senator Glenn's major interests tended more toward foreign than domestic matters. Within the domestic field, his greatest passion was reserved for education and research and development. Further, on those matters that occupied his interest, foreign and domestic, he tended to view issues through the lens of technology.

A Glenn watcher wrote in 1978 that Glenn's "interests lie mainly in three areas: controlling the spread of nuclear weapons and technology, foreign affairs, and the advancement of military technology." [110] When asked in 1982 to name his three top Senate achievements, Glenn listed "the Nuclear Non-Proliferation Act," "contributions to the Carter energy program," and "work on the Foreign Relations Committee." [111] The foreign policy emphasis was confirmed when his own staffers began to review his legislative record for purposes of the presidential campaign. Although he had voted on every kind of domestic issue, he had not developed a written or oral record indicative of any special interest in many of them.

Compiled from a review of Glenn's speeches and *Congressional Record* statements, a staff memo in 1982 contained the following observations: "has played a low-key role regarding health issues . . . no comments, not one, about national health insurance, catastrophic coverage, or hospital cost containment"; "does not outline any thoughts on the medicare system"; "did not develop any comprehensive thoughts on the environment"; "said very little about [women's issues]"; "does not voice an opinion on the key housing question"; "did not discuss agricultural issues in any comprehensive way"; "has not made crime a priority"; "no mention of . . . busing . . . prayer in schools . . . tuition tax credits." Glenn's immersion in foreign policy matters was not matched by a similar depth of interest in domestic issues—some of which constitute the core of the traditional Democratic party's program and, hence, its appeal to the electorate.

There is, however, one domestic matter in which Glenn took, from the first days of his term, a deep passionate interest. He believes that the strength and the salvation of the country, as a world leader, lies in its research and technology competence. The United States has out-invented and out-produced every other country and led the world in economic, military, and political strength, he believes, because it has been the leader in the research and development enterprise. And the government must, he feels, give support to this enterprise in every area and by every means it can—directly in support of research and development activities and indirectly in support of education in general. In committee, on the Senate floor, and on the campaign trail, his demeanor becomes more animated and his language more emotional when he comes to the subject of basic research.

The first time I ever heard him speak, to a group of business people in Warren, Ohio, in 1980, I made the following notes: he departs from speech and gets more eloquent about R & D needs and on Jacques Servan-Schreiber's thesis that the success of America comes from plowing back a large proportion of GNP into "inquiry." He wants most of all to find a way to store electrical energy. He tells the group, "If we let the Japanese and Germans beat us to the punch in developing a commercially feasible electric car ... we will really take a drubbing in our automobile industry and in our trade."

Two years later, in Washington, I watched him chair a committee hearing on research and development and noted: Glenn says, "If we are successful today as a nation, it is because we had the foresight and good sense to invest heavily in R & D in the past." He pounds the committee table when he criticizes R & D spending cuts. "Why are we cutting back on all these vital vital areas? They are crucial." He gets so excited that he floods the witnesses with questions. "Maybe I should ask questions in good senatorial style one by one, [but] I get going on this subject." He reddens in the face when he opposes policies that "butcher" or "hack" or "zero out" research as "penny wise and pound stupid" and as "eating America's seed corn." He waxes eloquent about his "one wish" for an energy storage system—"a pet of mine." And he compares as he did in Warren the public investment in research and in scientific education among the United States, Germany, and Japan—always to the present detriment and long-run peril of the United States.[112] He talks passionately about these matters, at home and in Washington. And when he does, Glenn reveals his belief that technological superiority made America a world leader, and that America's future depends largely on whether it enhances or surrenders that special set of abilities and advantages.

His intellectual and visceral commitment to scientific and technological activity flows naturally from his years of commitment to space exploration and from the faith he imbibed there in the ability of scientists and engineers to solve problems. This faith in science and research becomes, in turn, the lens through which he sees other issues. On energy matters, his strongest comments are reserved for the promotion of research on energy storage. "If I could have just one wish," he says over and over, "it would be to solve the problem of energy storage." A staffer noted, "On health there's damn near nothing [in his record]. He's sponsored a council to monitor the amount of radiation Americans get. It's the scientist showing, not the social side." And "while he talks about education, he does not talk about tuition tax credits ... or school prayer. He talks about the need for more, a lot more, scientists and engineers."

A foreign policy adviser to another member of the Senate Foreign

Relations Committee contrasted his senator's approach to foreign affairs with that of Senator Glenn.

> I've noticed, sitting there in committee, that Glenn's politics is tangled up in his view of technology. He doesn't respond to the same people my boss does. He sees the technology of arms control, not the people who attended some rally in Ohio. My boss goes to rallies. When he talks about arms control, he sees some woman who has kids and wants peace. Sign the thing! He's not interested in the technical aspects of SALT. Glenn always focuses on the technical issues—verification, the angle of reentry. That's where he feels comfortable. My boss' attitude is, "Who cares?"

It was the staffer's view that Glenn was right on SALT and for the right reasons. But that was beside the point. The tendency to seize on the practical and the technical, rather than the political and the popular, was one more factor making it hard for Glenn to forge a record of philosophical coherence and of ideological clarity. It has fueled the often-quoted lobbyist's criticism of Glenn: "He doesn't see the forest or even the trees, only branches and twigs," and a colleague's remark: "He can see the pieces of the puzzle, but he has trouble putting the puzzle together." [113]

"I believe," Glenn wrote in the fall of 1980, "that my reputation during the first five years of my term was one of a hard working moderate who made independent judgments." [114] It was a fair assessment as far as it went. He had developed a set of political views that were center to left of center and independent of outside influence. But his ideological profile, although solidly Democratic, was lacking in overall coherence, strongly focused on foreign policy, passionate mostly about research and education on the domestic side and technological in outlook. Just how that more complex and less-than-clearly-structured profile would be sold to, and supported by, the electorate of 1984 remained to be seen.

STYLE

Besides developing and displaying a set of credentials and an ideological profile, John Glenn's Capitol Hill years were spent developing and displaying a governing style—a characteristic way of dealing with institutional routines and dealing with people in and out of the institution. This style dovetailed with the reputational and the ideological results previously described.

A basic stylistic characteristic that emerged in the Washington context was the great care with which he made his legislative decisions. It was a style that went hand in hand with the desire to master technical detail in his committee work and with the desire to make independent, case-by-case judgments on legislative issues. It was yet another product of his marine-astronaut background—both in the habitual reliance on expertise and the habitual reluctance to make hasty judgments.

Nearly every person who has done a feature article on Glenn has been given the chance to fly co-pilot with him in his jet plane. And none failed to be impressed—as I was—with the incredible concentration and attention to detail he exhibits during the flights. There was the checklist to be gone through at every stage, the multiple indicators to be constantly monitored, the constant cross-checking with people on the ground, the anticipatory commentary on atmospheric and airport conditions. It was not a time for conducting interviews. It was time to absorb, as best one could, the education offered by the pilot's running explanation of what he was doing and why. All this was done with a matter-of-fact confidence and a relaxed enthusiasm. He was, clearly, in his element. And it was impossible to imagine this man, or this politician, ever making a calamitous mistake.

I picked up strong evidence for such a conclusion on Friday afternoon, January 13, 1982, in Washington. Glenn was planning to fly his plane to Ohio for an important engagement that evening and for a full schedule of home activity for the weekend. Snow had begun to fall at midday, however, and was falling heavily in Washington by afternoon. I was hanging around in the Glenn office, listening as the senator commented on his periodic weather checks with National Airport. At about 3:30, I asked about the latest forecast. "We've just canceled," he said. "There's icing at 6,000 feet." Two hours later, Air Florida Flight 100 took off in the snowstorm, weighed down with ice on its wings, and plunged into the Potomac River, killing seventy-four people.[115] "Some days are not fit for man nor beast," Glenn recalled later, "and that day was one of them." This dramatic juxtaposition of human judgments spoke volumes about Glenn's potential for life-saving leadership.

By the middle of his first term, careful decision making—like the pilot going through his checklist—had become a hallmark of his legislative style. "I guess I'd say I have an inordinate desire to be certain when I make a decision," he said. His military experience had taught him, "You don't make poppycock decisions off the top of your head. Somebody may die because of your rashness."[116] Again,

> In a military situation, you try to get every single fact you can right down to the time you're going to make your decision. And then you make your decision and go and that's it.[117]

In legislative matters, too, he says, it is best "to try to get every bit of information you can clear up to where you have to make a decision. Then you reach the point where time is out and you make it." [118]

When he finally reaches "have-to" time and makes up his mind, he sticks unswervingly—even stubbornly—to his decision. Observers describe him as too cautious, too indecisive. His own view is that he is not cautious but prudent, not indecisive but judicious.[119] "Most people are willing to say where they stand on something far in advance before I am. But I think mine is the more responsible way of doing things." [120] This decision-making style, comfortable for him, does not make for easy alliances with others. They want early commitments, which he will not give; they want a maneuverable ally, which he will not be.

One consequence of his extremely careful decision-making style is a heavy reliance on his staff. From the beginning, Glenn envisioned extensive delegation to staff as a principle of good organization. Indeed, it was the only aspect of leadership about which I have heard him reflect. "When I was at Quantico Marine Officer's School," he recalled in 1980,

> Douglas Southal Freeman came to lecture on leadership. I will never forget it. He had spent his whole life studying Robert E. Lee, and had written the definitive Pulitzer Prize winning biography of Lee. He said he had become interested in Lee because he thought of him as the perfect leader. After a lifetime of study, he told us, he had concluded that the secret of Lee's leadership lay not in his ability to do everything himself, but in his ability to pick the best people available, delegate to them, and remove them if they didn't do the job. And that is why he ended up writing those great books about Lee's lieutenants.

To understand Glenn the politician, it is important to understand how and what he delegates to his Senate staff—or did at the time of his presidential run.

First, he delegates copious, if not complete, authority to others in the internal management of the fourteen-member (as of 1980-1981) staff. This practice was yet another residue of his marine-to-astronaut experience. "I think you have to go back to the senator's experience as a fighter pilot to understand his attitude toward organization," said a veteran staffer.

> He has no use for organization—no, better still, he has no interest in it. If you'd read his biography, you know that by "sniveling," he always circumvented the organization. A pilot has a ground crew, but he says to them, "You take care of it. Don't bother me with your problems. I've got an important job to do."

As it worked out, Glenn delegated a great deal to his administrative assistant. "In the Senate office," said a staffer, "he lets [the AA] handle all organizational matters. When anyone else brought a problem to him, his attitude was 'you and he straighten it out.'" Glenn's aloofness from internal problems left his administrative assistant free to juggle staff responsibilities as he saw fit and to guard the access route to the senator.

It is, it seems, not easy to work for a national hero. It is a relationship that breeds personal distance. Glenn is invariably referred to as "the senator," never "John"—as is the custom in the office of so many younger and more "ordinary" senators. With distance comes a measure of insecurity—a larger measure, even, than is normal in the highly competitive atmosphere of a Senate office. In the pre-presidential Glenn office, at any rate, that insecurity seemed to have reached to the highest levels. The administrative assistant tended to keep staff responsibilities unclear and tentative, hired people at middle levels who were loyal to him, and restricted direct access to the senator to one or two top loyalists. Staffers could work a year or more in the office without ever having a conversation or a sign of recognition from "the senator." Given free rein to run the staff, the AA ran it very largely in ways designed to protect his own power at the top. It was not an office in which the staff worked demonstrably well together, as a team, or exhibited any of the warm sentiments of a family. As offices go, it was more hierarchical, less cohesive, more secretive, and lower in morale than most. And the senator was not disposed to intervene to change it.

What Glenn wants from his staff is information, and he gets it. That is the second respect in which Glenn relies upon and delegates to his staff—the search for, the collection of, and the transmittal of the information he needs to make decisions. "I always check with my staff before I vote," he said in 1981.

> They know what's up. Or they'd better know. I check with them wherever I am. If I'm in committee and have a chance, I'll call them. If I get here [on the floor] I'll go down to the table, see what the description of the bill says, and then call the staff ... I don't think there have been more than two or three times since I've been here that I've voted without checking first with my staff.

But information is all that Glenn wants. Two of his veteran staffers talked about it. "There's a lot in his Senate operation that comes from his experience as a pilot," said one. "He wants all the information he can get. He loves information. A pilot wants all the information there is before he goes up." "But," added the other, "he wants to make the decisions himself. Every pilot wants to make his own decisions." As a counterweight to the general lack of clear staff relationships, Glenn's issue specialists have a good sense of their responsibilities and are able to communicate with him when his decisions fall in their issue area. This is especially true of the committee-based staffers—whose workplace and work routines fall outside the orbit of the administrative assistant. What Glenn does not want from staffers is political judgment. That distinction became clear in the hiring process.

Not surprisingly Glenn took extraordinary care in selecting a staff. "I took it very seriously when I chose the staff," he said. "I hired [a management consultant] to work full time on it." The consultant was Irwin Silverman, a Toledo businessman, who worked for five months full time, culling 1,200 applications and assembling Glenn's "start-up staff." It was a staff heavily weighted toward substantive expertise and Capitol Hill experience. "We had the pick of Washington," Silverman recalled.

> People who graduated cum laude from Harvard, had a law degree from Yale, and a Ph.D. from somewhere else were just average.... You have to understand that John Glenn's chief aim in everything is excellence. It's the mark of everything he has ever done. There's so much pure intelligence on that staff that it can be a problem.

The "problem" would be that Glenn's heavy emphasis on substantive expertise might shortchange other, more political, qualities.

Glenn's priorities were made clear in his negative attitude toward hiring the people who got him elected. "I hired almost nobody from my campaign staff," he said.

> I thought the job was too important to entrust to people just because they had been on the campaign staff. I wanted the most experienced, the most expert staff I could find. That put a lot of my campaigners' noses out of joint. Some of them still don't speak to me. That's just too bad. Of course, I blame it all on Irwin.

There's a familiar whiff of public service orthodoxy in these views—the desire for a staff of experts, hiring by management consultant, downplaying purely political skills. It was further preparation for studious, nonideological, case-by-case decision making on the merits of the issues placed before him.

Because Glenn does not rely on his staff for the political judgments embedded in his Senate decisions, the staff is markedly nonpolitical, despite the fact that, from the outset, media scorekeepers touted Glenn as a presidential prospect. On the Glenn start-up staff were a couple of

Capitol Hill professionals and his Ohio campaign manager. They wanted to make him president. "They were picking out their offices in the White House," said one observer. But Glenn, wanting only to become a respected senator, did not cooperate. He dampened all presidential talk and efforts. When he failed to receive the 1976 vice-presidential nod, the three would-be kingmakers left. His "follow-up staff" was, therefore, even less political than the first, and one indicator is the staffers' relative lack of partisanship or political activism. They do not, as other senatorial staffs often do, spend their spare time or take time off to work for their party's endangered incumbents or promising challengers. Their minimal partisanship reflects, too, the nonpolitical preference of the man for whom they work.

"One thing you might look into," said a staffer in 1981, "is the amount of politicization in Senate offices. Ours is a very unpolitical office, because the senator is very unpolitical." The senator, he went on, is unpolitical in two senses. First, he does not subject his political calculations to the scrutiny of others. Second, his political calculations are notably free of political calculation. "I'm sure if I went in and said to the senator," the aide continued, " 'if you support this measure, you will be clobbered in five newspapers in Ohio,' he would say 'I don't care what they do. I'm right on this.' We almost never ask what the political consequences of a position will be." "He isn't always comfortable with the way politicians see things," echoes a longtime acquaintance. "If he decides something is 'right,' then he'll do it. If not, he won't." [121] A fellow senator commented, "He's hell on wheels once he's convinced he's right. In fact, he's damned near immovable." [122]

This is basic public service politics. Glenn has tended to feel that he does not need anyone to tell him what is right—for the country, or for Ohio, or for the world. And, once he decides what is right, where the merits of the case lie, it follows—for him—that no political consequences can be sufficiently damaging to affect his decision. One veteran aide commented that all Glenn's important votes are made by him alone, "between him and his conscience." Every vote that subsequently caused him special difficulty in his presidential campaign was his alone—on the 1981 tax cut and on a new nerve gas system, for example. They were made against the political judgment of his staff and to their dismay. Typically, they did not know for sure how he would vote until he voted. He kept his own counsel and cast the vote he thought was right. He was prepared as usual to take whatever political consequences followed. But his view was that when other people understood his vote, they would agree with him that it was, indeed, a vote in the best interests of the country. He probably never allowed himself to imagine how likely or how crippling contrary interpretations of his vote might be.

Glenn's preference for substantive expertise over political abilities also produced a start-up staff that was notably short on home state flavor. Glenn's public announcement described it as "a combination of seasoned Capitol Hill and Ohio governmental professionals." [123] But it was much more the former than the latter—by fifteen to five. And the Ohioans, campaigners all, felt swamped by the noncampaigners from the Hill. Said one,

> Senator Glenn believes in Hill experience. He took only five people from the campaign. For the first couple of years, the atmosphere in the office was very tense. The technicians from the Hill knew nothing about Ohio. They even had contempt for Ohio. I almost quit, the situation was so bad.

A couple of them did quit, most significantly Glenn's campaign manager Steve Kovacik, whose task was to supervise and lubricate all Washington-Ohio connections. His departure rendered Glenn's follow-up staff even less Ohio-oriented than at the beginning. Nor was the diminishment of an Ohio connection in Washington offset by a large or active Glenn presence in Ohio. He was slow to establish his Ohio offices. He budgeted less money for those offices than his Ohio colleagues. He placed a smaller proportion of his staff in Ohio than they. He opened fewer constituency offices than they did. His local operations have been criticized for their inefficiency and lack of responsiveness, in comparison to the vigorous constituency outreach pursuits of colleague Howard Metzenbaum. [124]

It is not that Glenn failed to recognize his responsibilities to Ohio—far from it. Whenever he talked about his job, he propounded his "theory of concentric circles of a senator's responsibility." The three concentric circles were: state, nation, and world. The core of the job was working for one's state. "I try to do all I can for Ohio ... Ohio is my basic concern." "At the center is your home state and your responsibility to it," he explains.

> Then there is a larger circle—the country. You are not just a senator from your state; you are a United States senator. . . . And then the final circle is international. . . . So it's like dropping a rock in a pond that makes circles out from the center. The center is your home base; but that is not all there is.

Clearly, he sought a rationale for tending to his strong supra-Ohio interests. But he worked to reconcile the larger circles of interest with the smallest one.

"I am lucky that Ohio is really a microcosm of the country," he said.

"I think that gives me more freedom to think about the country as a whole." And, "One in seven Ohio jobs depends on international trade. . . . That helps me to take an interest in foreign relations." So the lack of zeal for cementing his Ohio connections did not derive from any lack of recognition of his responsibilities to Ohio or any lack of desire to meet them. Rather, they derived from a lack of interest in and/or sensitivity to the myriad methods for building and maintaining his political support there. It was a familiar pattern of neglect where constituency-building activities are concerned and reminiscent of the 1970 campaign. As in the earlier case, Glenn may have thought that if he did his job well, the support problem would take care of itself.

This suggestion is consistent with another aspect of Glenn's governing style—his neglect of public relations. In contrast to his studious concentration on issue-related detail, he displayed an equally distinctive inattention to self-promotional publicity seeking. A veteran Ohio reporter summarized, "He's very effective. But he's self-effacing. He's much more influential than anybody knows, because he does such a poor job of publicizing himself." He noted that on the day that Glenn's greatest legislative achievement, the Nuclear Non-Proliferation Act, was debated and passed by the Senate, there were only two Ohio reporters present in the Senate press gallery. Yet eight Ohio daily newspapers have reporters in Washington, and twenty others are represented there. Glenn complained to one of them, "I worked two and a half years on the nuclear anti-proliferation legislation. It's something that's important to the whole world. But only at the very end, when the bill finally came to the Senate floor did anyone write anything about it." [125] But Glenn himself was largely to blame.

Throughout his pre-presidential days, he kept his Washington press operation small and understaffed. At first, he kept the press secretary position open and "entertained the thought of hiring a super media type for press secretary, such as those who scramble around here for an inch of type in the *New York Times* or *Washington Post*." [126] But he never did. And while Metzenbaum's press secretary was his highest paid staffer in 1980, Glenn's ranked fourteenth, and the press secretary was not even one of the staffers who had direct access to the senator. [127] Glenn's press work left much to be desired. "He hands out press releases," said one reporter, "but often they don't tell you what you need to know. And the quotes from Glenn are dull." In six years, he had never sent out a newsletter to his constituents. And he had never had any kind of press operation in his Ohio offices. Small wonder that when he ran for reelection, according to his campaign manager, polls showed that Ohioans "have a very positive attitude toward him with few negatives, but when you ask them what he's done, they're stumped." [128] "One person's efforts tend to get lost in a maze unless you make a real big effort," Glenn said, "which I haven't done." [129]

During that 1980 campaign, Glenn explained his inattention to public relations. "Some of my problems with the media are of my own making." He continued:

> What I'm going to say will sound self-serving, but it's the truth. I don't get my kicks in politics from the adoration you get. I've had all of that. I want to accomplish something in the Senate ... within the concentric circles I talked about. I don't think about tooting my own horn. Several times, I've had it happen that I've won a big battle on the Senate floor, come back to the office all excited about it, and yet never even told my press secretary about it. I've been very poor on the PR aspects of the job. My attitude was that the press would pick up whatever I did, that they should pick it up. Then I would be amazed later to find that nobody back home knew what I had done. I was taken aback when I went home and found out how little they knew. I didn't think that was part of my job.

Most senators are instinctive publicity seekers. Those who must learn to do it, learn it on the campaign trail. Indeed, the importance of the media to their success is the distinguishing characteristic of a Senate campaign.[130] But like many other lessons of practical politics, it has not come easily to John Glenn. He has absorbed the lessons of practical politicking as slowly and carefully as he has arrived at all his conclusions. Perhaps the orgy of free publicity he received as an astronaut-hero led him to believe that he need not work for it. Perhaps he believed that good work in public service would—because it should—attract the attention it deserved. To hear him talk in 1980 was to see that it took a full term for the lesson to sink in. "I'm disappointed that the press didn't do these things," he said, "but I guess it will ever be thus." And it took a reelection campaign to produce this sense of resignation and to stimulate thoughts of change.

"I've learned that it's part of your job to keep people informed," he said while campaigning. "So I'm going to change ... I'm going to put more effort into telling people what we are doing. I've been thinking about these changes all year. The campaign—going back and forth from Washington—has stimulated my thinking on the subject." He described some of the adjustments he was planning.

> We put out press releases, but we didn't target them. We never made sure that the farm papers had the farm releases or the papers in the cities had the city-related releases. We are going to set up a bigger operation in the office. When I've done

something I think people ought to know about, I'll call six or seven editors around the state and talk to them about it. I hate to waste their time doing it; but I'm going to have to. Another thing, lots of senators put out newsletters. They send them out several times a year under the frank. Most of the time, they serve to glorify the senator involved. I decided not to join that crowd. I think it's a great waste of the taxpayers' money. I didn't make a big thing out of it, but we just didn't send out any newsletters.... Assuming I'm reelected, we are going to start sending out newsletters.

One can discern, in these ruminations, the worries of a believer in public service politics who finds it necessary to engage in and to justify publicity-seeking activities endemic to ego politics. There is conveyed a sense that he is backsliding and in danger of becoming just another politician.

One can also discern another problem in the creation of a political persona distinct from the hero's persona. As long as he chose to downplay the kind of public relations activity necessary to precede, record, and follow up on his work as a senator, for that long would his political persona remain underdeveloped. As long as he retained only a hero's outlook on publicity, for that long would he be perceived only as a hero. Even as he discussed these things, the feature articles on his 1980 reelection campaign were carrying headlines such as: "On the Campaign Trail with an American Hero: He is Still John Glenn Astronaut" and "Astronaut Glenn Overshadows the Senator." [131] If those perceptions were ever to change, John Glenn would have to change them himself.

A final element of the Glenn governing style was his preference for a peripheral role in the Senate's coalition-building processes. He was not one of those senators who was thought of as having party leadership potential within the institution. He was regarded, rather, as something of a loner, a senator who pursued his own interests in his own way, not in any close relationship with internal or external allies. It was a perfectly acceptable, legitimate, respected style. It earned for him, as we have said, a solid reputation as a good senator and an influential voice on several important issues. But his style kept him relatively aloof from the inside politics of the Senate and from the mutually supportive networks with groups outside the Senate. And it kept him more critical than accepting of established practices, internal and external.

His reluctance to enter wholeheartedly into coalition-building activity comes as no surprise, in the light of all we have said so far. It derives, first, from the marine-to-astronaut background of self-reliant lonerism; second, from the public servant's distaste for practical political maneuvering; third, from the absence of predictable ideological alliances; fourth, from the careful, information-laden approach to decision making; and, finally, from the lack of enthusiasm for public relations activity.

Naturally, he does participate in coalition-building activity—because he must if he is to get certain things done. Consider, for instance, the nuclear proliferation bill:

> I worked with [Sen. Charles] Percy [R-Ill.] on that. We wrote the act right here in the office. The bill was about three-fourths mine and one-fourth his. And the Carter people had some ideas. I had been thinking about it for some time. My original bill was too tough. But the Carter bill was a puff ball. So finally, we all got together and worked out a bill all of us could support. It was a tough battle, but we got through. I was most proud of that.

He does not, however, regale the listener with coalition-building exploits.

The only other such activity to break into print during his first term was his unsuccessful attempt in 1978 to build a majority inside the Senate Finance Committee for "his pet legislative proposal." It called for a regular, sunset-type review of all tax loopholes and tax incentives by the committee. After two years of work, Glenn believed he had a majority lined up, only to find that when the vote was taken Chairman Russell Long had secured the allegiance of several putative Glenn supporters. He interpreted the outcome as an unexplainable betrayal of commitments, and three years later still mused, "I don't think I'll ever understand how that sort of thing can happen." [132]

All of which probably reinforces his preference for service politics over ego politics. The larger point, however, is not that Glenn is incapable of pursuing such legislative endeavors, but that he does not choose to do so. He prefers, instead, to expend his energies developing his own positions and expressing himself on these positions with minimum regard for who else is doing what, when, how, and to whom and with what strategic expectations.

People who watched and worked with him described a person lacking in the inclination to plunge into coalition building. The dominant perception was that of someone who worked—more than most—alone and did not pursue the kind of interpersonal relationships that are preliminary to and concomitant with the business of legislative leadership. In 1978 an Ohio journalist, calling him "something of a loner in the Senate" concluded,

> Glenn operates in a somewhat self-imposed political vacuum in the Senate. Beholden neither to special interest, nor to party—

nor for that matter to the White House—he putters along at his own pace and style, mulling over the issues and coming largely to his own conclusions. He is not oblivious to outside influences. He is simply so confident in his own ability to master the mechanics and nuances of legislation that he relies mostly on his own facilities—and those of his staff—to guide him.[133]

Similarly, a national reporter said in 1983 that the Ohio senator "inhabited the borderland between 'loner' and 'independent.' " And he concluded,

He never joined any of the informal caucuses that coalesce around key issues or individuals in the Senate, and Glenn never bid for leadership of such groups himself. . . . Instead of settling into the fellowship of the Senate, Glenn used it as a theatre where he could act out his independent impulses.[134]

Other scorekeepers described his interpersonal relationships as "cordial and slightly distant" or "pleasant—but distant." "Other senators mill about, shaking hands or patting each other on the arm, squeezing out signals of approval. There are few such we-are-all-pals-here gestures in Glenn's repertory." His colleagues have said that "he is a hard man to get to know" or "he doesn't seem to have many friends." "There are guys here who will buy you a beer, chat you up, try to win you over . . . but Glenn's not like that. He's a loner." [135]

Glenn, when asked about his after-hours socializing, confirmed what was said about him. "That's very important here," he said in 1981,

I don't do as much of it as I should. When I came here, I had been so used to attention that my idea of a big evening was to go home, put on my terry cloth robe and my fuzzy slippers, and read or watch television. That was my idea of a real wild evening. So Annie and I don't do as much socializing as we should. We've been talking about it and have decided to have some get-togethers every so often, invite a few people in.

Ross Baker's splendid analysis of friendship patterns in the Senate makes it clear that close personal relationships are a rarity in that body and, further, that such relationships are unnecessary and irrelevant for effective coalition building. Baker also states that somewhere along the spectrum of interpersonal relationships—at the point where "institutional kinship" merges into "alliances"—coalition building is facilitated.[136] John Glenn's relations with his colleagues did not often reach that point.

In terms of coalition-building skills—as well as inclination—observers noted some areas in which Glenn's governing style posed a handicap. For one thing, a person who makes decisions based on the merits or on what is right finds it difficult to enter wholeheartedly into the bargaining aspects of coalition building. It is silly to say that Glenn would not, but he did so less frequently and less enthusiastically than most. For another thing, his slow, late-in-the-game, stubborn decision-making style made it less likely that he was in a position to do so. He entered the forum too late and too inflexibly. A lobbyist noted that Glenn's preference for going it alone rather than choosing up sides made him "almost a political eunuch" in coalition-building terms.[137] And a veteran Glenn staffer noted, "Once he decides which way to go, he'll try to hang on to it. He could improve his compromising skills."[138] But it is not just a matter of skills. The fact is that legislative maneuvering is a form of ego politics, a manifestation of the professional political arts for which Glenn has had scant enthusiasm.

Participants called him "a bit uppity—you know—starchy about tradin' favors."[139] An aide stated flatly, "He doesn't like horse trading."[140] One scorekeeper said that "Glenn was not a natural legislator" when he came to the Senate and doubts that he has learned to become one. He cited, as an example, Glenn's moralistic outburst, in 1981, against President Reagan's arm-twisting on the AWACS vote. "I deplore that kind of political horse trading. It's political bribery."[141] By reaching his own conclusions and digging in to defend them, Glenn may have proved to be a pivotal and, in that sense, influential vote as the process neared the point of decision. He may even, by force of the argument, carry some other senators with him. But his was not a bargaining, persuading style. "His tendency [is] simply to explain the facts and hope they will prove persuasive."[142] In the Senate, as outside the Senate, he did not give top priority to figuring out how to gain the support of others and then reaching, with his powers of persuasion, to get it.

Coalition building is very much a matter of persuasion. And, quite apart from Glenn's disinclination to bargain and negotiate for support, his powers of persuasion were not enhanced by superior communication skills. His rhetorical abilities were thought to be very ordinary. His national reputation as a poor public speaker was established when his keynote address at the 1976 Democratic convention was ignored by the delegates, was harshly judged—"lackluster," "bomb," "ho hum," "uninspired," and "boring" were used to characterize it by media scorekeepers—and the speech was reported to be a critical factor in eliminating him from the vice-presidential sweepstakes.[143] Inside the Senate, as well, Glenn had not been known as a particularly effective speaker or persuader, but there is no direct relationship between oratorical abilities and coalition-building abilities in the institution. Some of the most effective orators have been the least interested in legislative business, and some of the most effective legislative leaders have been indifferent orators. But coalition building does rely on persuasion, persuasion relies on rhetoric, and some parts of the coalition-building process depend on public persuasion and public rhetoric. Themes must be established and elaborated, arguments must be framed and legitimated, positions must be defended or modified—in numerous public forums and in the give and take of public debate.

It was John Glenn's senatorial pattern to deliver set speeches without much sensitivity to the attentiveness of his colleagues, to repeat over and over the phrasing of his arguments, and to abstain from the give-and-take, cut-and-thrust aspects of Senate debate. The pattern resulted partly from his late-blooming decision making. But it also resulted from the lack of certain rhetorical skills—a commanding use of language, an agility in argumentation, a speaking voice of tonality and range. By choosing not to immerse himself in the business of coalition building, he did not need to display—or to develop—such rhetorical abilities. But to the degree that he neither displayed nor developed them, he helped to give himself another kind of reputation as a "dull," "unimaginative," "unexciting" senator. Away from the public eye, he was and is none of these things. But, like it or not, in a media age, politicians are increasingly judged by their style of communication and their rhetorical skills. Glenn's self-reliant lonerism in the Senate brought him enough success there to overshadow whatever lack of communication talents he may have had. Senators are allowed to appear dull, unexciting, and unimaginative. Whether presidential candidates are granted that latitude remains to be seen.

The scorekeepers who observed John Glenn's governing style wondered, from the outset, whether he would or could become a heavyweight inside the Senate. Such assessments are the daily, monthly, yearly grist for the observers' mill. They rest heavily on the coalition-building activities and reputations of each senator. When Glenn lost his tax oversight proposal in the Finance Committee, a veteran Ohio scorekeeper drew a general conclusion:

> For all his fame, being a space age hero has hardly proved a ticket to power and stardom in the United States Senate. And, although he is widely respected, Glenn's clout is no match for old timers like Russell Long.

"Senate committee staffers, lobbyists, and others on Capitol Hill," he added, "who have closely observed Glenn say he has the potential to achieve prominence. But almost to the person, they say he won't." [144]

The reasons given encompassed all the stylistic elements we have discussed. This 1978 assessment had changed very little by 1980, when another longtime Ohio reporter concluded, "Glenn has shed the light-weight image." But he was unprepared to pronounce him a heavy-weight. "The Ohioan," he wrote,

> is still criticized, as he has been ever since arriving in the Senate, for being too slow to make up his mind on important issues and unwilling to make the legislative deals necessary to pass important bills. In addition Glenn is seen by some as too low-key and unspectacular. Some observers think Glenn is simply too dull ever to become one of the Senate's powers.[145]

At that same time, the first reporter offered a very balanced judgment: "While he is not yet regarded as a heavyweight in the Senate, he is widely respected by both his colleagues and their staffs." [146] Respected but not powerful, no longer a lightweight but not yet a heavyweight—that was the senatorial reputation John Glenn carried into his reelection efforts in 1980.

Thinking in terms of a possible presidential candidacy, Glenn's nine years in the Senate had produced an uneven beginning. He had availed himself of the three opportunities—reputational, philosophical, and political—in direct proportion to their nonpolitical content. He had made the most of his reputational opportunity, made less of his philosophical opportunity, and made the least of his political opportunity. He had won solid credentials as a good senator and, hence, as a legitimate presidential candidate. But he had neither produced an easily recognizable ideological profile nor developed a set of impressive political talents. When he began to contemplate his presidential possibilities, therefore, he did so when his political persona remained notably incomplete and underdeveloped.

The reasons why nine years of experience in the Senate did not produce a more developed political figure lie partly, as we have repeatedly emphasized, in the length and intensity of Glenn's prepolitical career. That career had left an unchangeable core of preferences, calculations, character, and behavior. But it is also worth noting that the smallish nine-year change also resulted from the nature of the Senate itself. The highly individualized body of the 1970s and 1980s did not mold the behavior of any of its members. It permitted, instead, each newcomer to do just about as he or she pleased. Those who were more malleable—the "youthful amateurs," perhaps—might be substantially affected by their membership. So, too, might those who aspired to party leadership positions inside the chamber. But the mature amateurs, without leadership aspirations—like Glenn—were left free to pursue their established ways. And they could do so without adverse effects either in their collegial relationships in Washington or their constituency relationships at home.

A consistency of attitude and behavior is one hallmark of John Glenn's adult career. His nine years in the Senate did nothing to disrupt that. The attitudes and the practices he brought with him to the Senate were marginally, if at all, altered there. It is the combination of Glenn's indelible pre-Senate experience and the laissez-faire individualism of the institutional Senate that accounts for this result.

NOTES

1. Neil MacNeil, "The Presidential Nursery," *Harpers*, February 1972; Robert Peabody, Norman Ornstein, David Rohde, "The United States Senate as a Presidential Incubator: Many Are Called but Few Are Chosen," *Political Science Quarterly*, Summer 1976.
2. Richard Stout, "The Pre- Pre-Campaign," *Public Opinion*, December/January 1983.
3. Helen Dewar, "Senate's Club of Failed Ambitions: Twelve Men Who Ran and Lost," *Washington Post*, March 10, 1980.
4. They are John Kennedy, 1960; Barry Goldwater, 1964; George McGovern, 1972. The other nineteen Senate aspirants were: Lyndon Johnson, Hubert Humphrey, Stuart Symington, 1960; Robert Kennedy, Eugene McCarthy, 1968; Edmund Muskie, Henry Jackson, (Humphrey), 1972; Birch Bayh, Lloyd Bentsen, Frank Church, (Jackson, Humphrey), 1976; Edward Kennedy, Howard Baker, Robert Dole, 1980; John Glenn, Ernest Hollings, Alan Cranston, Gary Hart, 1984; Albert Gore, Paul Simon, (Dole), 1988. Richard Nixon, 1960 and 1968, Hubert Humphrey, 1968, Walter Mondale, 1984, had been senators, but became vice president before they ran for the presidency.
5. David Shribman, "With Few Words, Glenn Withdraws," *New York Times*, March 17, 1984.
6. Paul West, "Glenn Can't Get Off Launch Pad in Iowa," *Dallas Times Herald*, February 17, 1984.
7. Carl Leubsdorf, "Big Day Nears in New Hampshire," *Dallas Morning News*, February 26, 1984.
8. Christopher Thomas, "Southern Comfort for Jackson; Cold Comfort for Glenn," *The Times* (London), March 7, 1984.
9. The others were Jeremiah Denton, R-Ala.; Frank Lautenberg, D-N.J.; and John Warner, R-Va.
10. Tom Wolfe, *The Right Stuff* (New York: Bantam Books, 1980), 289.
11. Ibid., 294.
12. Harold Martin and Don Oberdorfer, "What Made John Glenn Run?" *Saturday Evening Post*, February 2, 1964.
13. Myra MacPherson, "The Hero as Politician: John Glenn's Hard Road," *Washington Post*, January 12, 1975.

14. Taped interview with Senator John Glenn, conducted by Steve Troup, Columbus, Ohio, May 8, 1976.
15. "Senatorial Dossier," *Washington Dossier*, May 1985.
16. John Averill, "Glenn's Low Profile Pays Off in Senate," *Los Angeles Times*, August 24, 1975.
17. David Broder, "Into the Well of the House," *Washington Post*, July 31, 1983.
18. See "The Making of a Brave Man," *Life*, February 2, 1962; Paul Healy, "Mr. America in the Senate," *Saturday Evening Post*, December 1975; David McCullough, "Can John Glenn Be President?" *Parade Magazine*, June 13, 1982.
19. Troup interview. See also "Interview: John Glenn," *Omni*, October 1983.
20. MacPherson, "The Hero As Politician."
21. Brad Tillson, "Glenn Remains Calm: Will Carter Tap Him on Shoulder?" *Columbus Daily News*, July 11, 1976.
22. Fred Greenstein, *The Hidden Hand Presidency* (New York: Basic Books, 1982), 10, 18.
23. Ibid., 34.
24. See the discussion by three ex-presidents, five presidential staffers, and six presidential scholars in Howard K. Smith, "Every Four Years: A Study of the Presidency," Philadelphia, PBS, WAYY-TV 1980. A sampling of the obsession with character in the 1987 nomination campaign would include: R. W. Apple, "America Values Moral Character," *Rochester Democrat and Chronicle*, May 8, 1987; Daniel Golden, "Can Anyone Be Clean Enough to Be President?" *Boston Globe*, September 27, 1987; Paul Taylor, "Our People-Magazined Race for the Presidency," *Washington Post Weekly Edition*, November 2, 1987; Jonathan Alter, "Test Cases for a New Political Generation," *Newsweek*, November 16, 1987; Transcript, MacNeil/Lehrer News Hour, September 23, 1987.
25. The speculation began as soon as he won the Ohio Democratic primary in May 1974. Jules Witcover, "Emerging Ohio Figure," *Washington Post*, May 9, 1974; William Farrell, "Victory By Glenn Linked to Image," *New York Times*, May 9, 1974; "Glenn in Orbit," *Newsweek*, May 20, 1974; Rowland Evans and Robert Novak, "John Glenn's Political Orbit," *Washington Post*, September 15, 1974.
26. Frank Van Riper, *Glenn: The Astronaut Who Would Be President* (New York: Empire, 1983), 25.
27. Wolfe, *The Right Stuff*, chaps. 5 and 6; See also, Julian Scheer, "John Glenn's Liftoff into Politics," *New York Times*, February 20, 1975.
28. Wolfe, *The Right Stuff*, 112; Van Riper, *Glenn*, 49. See also "The Making of a Brave Man"; Michael Barone, "John Glenn: Always Moving Up," *Washington Post*, September 6, 1983.
29. Christian Williams, "The Making of 'The Right Stuff,'" *Washington Post*, October 17, 1983.
30. Troup interview. See articles in *New York Times* for January 17, 21, 23, 1964, and March 10, 31, 1964; *Newsweek*, April 10, 1964.
31. Saul Pett, "The Ironic Fate of Our First Spaceman," *Baltimore Sun*, May 10, 1964.
32. On Glenn's early political affiliations, see E. W. Kenworthy, "Glenn Rules Out Political Bid Now," *New York Times*, July 20, 1963; Julius Duscha, "JFK and Brother Robert Backed Glenn Candidacy," *Washington Post*, January 18, 1964; David Jones, "Glenn Enters Senate Race in Ohio," *New York Times*,

January 18, 1964; David Hess, "Glenn: Washington's Middle-of-the Roader," *Akron Beacon Journal*, April 2, 1978; Howell Raines, "John Glenn: The Hero As Candidate," *New York Times Magazine*, November 13, 1983, 70.

33. Edward P. Whelan, "Look Out Folks, John Glenn Has Landed," *Cleveland Magazine*, Summer 1974.
34. Van Riper, *Glenn*, 189.
35. Whelan, "Look Out Folks."
36. Stephen Salmore and Barbara Salmore, *Candidates, Parties and Campaigns* (Washington, D.C.: CQ Press, 1985).
37. Martin and Oberdorfer, "What Makes John Glenn Run?"
38. Whelan, "Look Out Folks."
39. Tom Watson, "Persistence and Eye for Detail Help Glenn Surmout Defeats and Learn the Ways of Politics," *Congressional Quarterly Weekly Report*, November 5, 1983.
40. Joe Klein, "The Right Stuff," *Rolling Stone*, November 24, 1983.
41. Whelan, "Look Out Folks."
42. "Could This Be the Ike of the Seventies?" *People*, January 1975; see also John Finney, "Capitol Critical of Glenn's Move," *New York Times*, January 18, 1964.
43. Nan Robertson, "TV Helped a Winner in Ohio," *New York Times*, May 9, 1970.
44. Whelan, "Look Out Folks."
45. Ibid.
46. Adrienne Bosworth, "On the Campaign Trail with an American Hero," *Columbus Monthly*, October 1980.
47. Whelan, "Look Out Folks."
48. Klein, "The Right Stuff."
49. Watson, "Persistence and Eye for Detail."
50. Michael Kramer, "John Glenn: The Right Stuff?" *New York Magazine*, November 30, 1983.
51. Watson, "Persistence and Eye for Detail."
52. Ibid.
53. "Glenn in Fresh Start for Senate Seat," *New York Times*, December 18, 1973.
54. Kramer, "John Glenn: The Right Stuff?"
55. Marjorie Hershey, *Running for Office* (New York: Random House, 1984), 93-103.
56. Troup interview.
57. Whelan, "Look Out Folks."
58. Raines, "John Glenn: The Hero As Candidate."
59. Brian Usher, "Ohio Politics in '70s: Irony and Change," *Akron Beacon Journal*, December 23, 1979.
60. Whelan, "Look Our Folks."
61. MacPherson, "The Hero as Politician"; Van Riper, *Glenn*, 250.
62. Barone, "John Glenn Always Moving Up."
63. Raines, "John Glenn: The Hero as Candidate."
64. Jack Germond and Jules Witcover, "An Astronaut in the White House?" *Washingtonian*, February 1982.
65. Troup interview.
66. James M. Perry, "Why Glenn Orbits in Ohio," *National Observer*, April 20, 1974; Christopher Lydon, "Rematch of Glenn and Metzenbaum in Ohio Primary: Controversy on Tax Returns Reflects Watergate Impact," *New York*

Times, April 21, 1974; Jules Witcover, "Metzenbaum-Glenn Race Under Nixon Shadow," *Washington Post*, May 5, 197; *Newsweek*, May 6, 1974.
67. Whelan, "Look Out Folks."
68. Brian Usher, "Eyes Up the Presidency," *Akron Beacon Journal*, August 9, 1981.
69. Whelan, "Look Out Folks."
70. Van Riper, *Glenn*, 258.
71. Warren Wheat, "Available," *Cincinnati Enquirer Magazine*, December 14, 1975.
72. MacPherson, "The Hero as Politician."
73. On the contextual nature of the character issue in 1987-1988, see "Test Cases for a New Political Generation," *Newsweek*, November 16, 1987; R. W. Apple, "America Values Moral Character," *New York Times*, May 8, 1987; Daniel Golden, "Is Anyone Clean Enough to Be President?" *Boston Globe*, September 27, 1987.
74. Whelan, "Look Out Folks."
75. "Could This Be the Ike of the Seventies?"
76. See "Democratic Chairman Says Glenn Key to 'Sweep,'" *Daily Sentinal Tribune* (Bowling Green), November 3, 1976; see also AP, "Glenn Working to Create New Image, Style," *Record Herald* (Washington County, Ohio), December 6, 1978.
77. "Neil Sought in Race Against Sen. Glenn," *Lima News*, July 15, 1979; "Modell to Join Game Against Glenn," *Columbus Citizen Journal*, May 19, 1979; "Could Woody Hayes Be the Power Play for GOP in 1980?" *Columbus Citizen Journal*, April 2, 1979; "GOP Herds Lambs to Slaughter," *Akron Beacon Journal*, November 18, 1979.
78. David Rohde, Norman Ornstein, and Robert Peabody, "Political Change and Legislative Norms in the United States Senate" (Paper presented at the American Political Science Association Meeting, Chicago, 1974); Donald Matthews, *United States Senators and Their World* (Chapel Hill: University of North Carolina Press, 1964), chap. 5.
79. Averill, "Glenn's Low Profile Pays Off in Senate."
80. Ibid.
81. Harry Kelly, "Sky Is Limit for Politician John Glenn," *Chicago Tribune*, July 23, 1975.
82. Averill, "Glenn's Low Profile."
83. For citations see this chapter, supra. See also "Glenn Flying in Political Orbit," *Milwaukee Journal*, July 6, 1975.
84. Kelly, "Sky Is Limit"; MacPherson, "The Hero as Politician."; Wheat, "Available."
85. Abe Zaidan, "Glenn Bars '76 Role as Favorite Son," *Washington Post*, August 12, 1975.
86. Troup interview.
87. Ibid.
88. Ibid.
89. Ibid.
90. Ibid.
91. David Hess, "Workhorse Label Fits Glenn, Observers Say," *Akron Beacon Journal*, July 4, 1976.
92. Warren Wheat, "Glenn's Challenge: To Grow In His Job," *Cincinnati Enquirer*, July 18, 1976.

93. Douglas Lowenstein, "Glenn Flies High in Role of Senator," *Dayton Daily News*, August 24, 1980.
94. Ibid.
95. Andrew Alexander, "Holding Pattern: Glenn Still Waits for a Big Break," *Dayton Journal Herald*, January 23, 1978.
96. *New York Times*, February 3, 1978.
97. Lowenstein, "Glenn Flies High."
98. Lawrence Dodd, "A Theory of Congressional Cycles: Solving the Puzzle of Change," in Gerald Wright, Leroy Rieselbach, Lawrence Dodd, eds., *Congress and Policy Change* (New York: Agathon Press), 1986.
99. Lowenstein, "Glenn Flies High."
100. Ibid.; David Hess, "Senator Glenn Survives the 'Distasteful,' " *Akron Beacon Journal*, March 30, 1980; Andrew Alexander, "Astronaut Glenn Overshadows the Senator," *Dayton Journal Herald*, November 1, 1980.
101. James Herzog, "Glenn Finally Making His Mark in the Senate," *Cleveland Press*, December 27, 1977.
102. Alexander, "Astronaut Glenn Overshadows."
103. Averill, "Glenn's Low Profile."
104. Herzog, "Glenn Finally Making His Mark."
105. Hess, "Glenn: Washington's Middle-of-the-Roader."
106. Lowenstein, "Glenn Flies High."; Hess, "Glenn: Washington's Middle-of-the-Roader"; Alexander, "Astronaut Glenn Overshadows"; Herzog, "Glenn Finally Making His Mark."
107. Morton Kondracke, "John Glenn's Right Stuff," *New Republic*, May 26, 1982.
108. Hess, "Glenn: Washington's Middle-of-the-Roader."
109. Hess, "Senator Glenn Survives."
110. Hess, "Glenn: Washington's Middle-of-the-Roader."
111. David Osborne, "Lost in Space with John Glenn," *Mother Jones*, May 1983.
112. "Research and Development in the United States: The Role of the Public and Private Sectors," Hearings before the Subcommittee on Energy, Nuclear Proliferation and Government Processes, Committee on Governmental Affairs, Senate, 97th Cong., 2d sess., March 9, 1982.
113. Osborne, "Lost in Space with John Glenn"; "Glenn: Flying Solo, His Way," *Time*, June 20, 1983.
114. Letter to publisher of *Toledo Blade*, October 30, 1980.
115. *New York Times*, January 14, 16; February 5; March 2, 6, 1982.
116. Herzog, "Glenn Finally Making the Mark."
117. Hess, "Glenn: Washington's Middle-of-the-Roader."
118. Alexander, "Holding Pattern."
119. Ibid.; Hess, "Glenn: Washington's Middle-of-the-Roader."
120. Alexander, "Holding Pattern."
121. Germond and Witcover, "An Astronaut in the White House? "
122. Martha Angle, "Can John Glenn Lure Democrats Into That Old Space Capsule? " *Washington Star*, July 12, 1976.
123. *Toledo Blade*, January 13, 1975.
124. Robert Tenebaum, "John Glenn and Howard Metzenbaum: The Politics of Incompatibility," *Columbus Monthly*, May 1978; *Columbus Dispatch*, September 1, 1979; Abe Zaidan, "Glenn Backers Angry Over Office Staffing," *Akron Beacon Journal*, circa 1975; Alexander, "Holding Pattern"; *Cleveland Press*, March 15, 1975.
125. Tenebaum, "John Glenn and Howard Metzenbaum."

126. Wheat, "Available."
127. Report of the Secretary of the Senate, April 1, 1980-September 30, 1980, 96th Cong., 2d sess.
128. Hess, "Senator Glenn Survives."
129. Warren Wheat, "Concepts Don't Bring Many Votes," *Port Clinton News Herald*, October 17, 1980.
130. Richard F. Fenno, Jr., *The United States Senate: A Bicameral Perspective* (Washington: American Enterprise Institute, 1982), 9-12.
131. Bosworth, "On the Campaign Trail."; Alexander, "Astronaut Glenn Overshadows."
132. Hess, "Senator Glenn Survives."
133. Hess, "Glenn: Washington's Middle-of-the-Roader."
134. Raines, "John Glenn: The Hero as Candidate."
135. For these characterizations, see Eugene Kennedy, "John Glenn's Presidential Countdown," *New York Times Magazine*, October 11, 1981; Kondracke, "John Glenn's Right Stuff"; Kramer, "John Glenn: The Right Stuff"; Klein, "The Right Stuff."
136. Ross Baker, *Friend and Foe in the U.S. Senate* (New York: Free Press, 1980), chaps. 2 and 3.
137. Hess, "Glenn: Washington's Middle-of-the-Roader."
138. Lowenstein, "Glenn Flies High."
139. Hess, "Glenn: Washington's Middle-of-the-Roader."
140. Angle, "Can Glenn Lure Democrats?"
141. Watson, "Persistence and Eye for Detail."
142. Ibid.
143. See *Baltimore Sun*, "Senator Ho Hum," July 13, 1976; Andrew Alexander, "Pressure Off Glenn," *Dayton Journal Herald*, July 16, 1976; Richard Thomas, "Aides Believe Glenn Got Unfair Treatment," *Mansfield News Journal*, July 17, 1976; *Cleveland Heights Sun Press*, July 29, 1976; *National Journal*, September 24, 1976; Walter Taylor, "Sour Note on Glenn Keynoter," *Washington Star*, July 14, 1976; Angle, "Can John Glenn Lure Democrats?"
144. Alexander, "Holding Pattern."
145. Lowenstein, "Glenn Flies High."
146. Alexander, "Holding Pattern."

Seasons of Exploration and Hope

THE CAMPAIGN-WITHOUT-VOTERS

It is not possible to know when John Glenn first thought about running for president. Like many other senators, he began to be asked about it from the moment he was elected. So the idea must have entered his mind very early. Unlike most senators, however, he never stopped attracting national interest as a presidential possibility. Two years after his election he was one of five finalists in Jimmy Carter's well-publicized search for a vice president. An Ohio reporter covering Glenn's arrival at La Guardia Airport for the 1976 convention wrote that he "was greeted like the superstar he had become in preconvention speculation about the vice presidency" and that his family was "treated like the highly prospective second family of the nation they had become." "When the Glenns stepped out of the closed ramp into the waiting area, lights flashed, cameras hummed and several hundred spectators crowded around."[1] Surely, that brief, heady period of intense national attention kindled, or rekindled, thoughts of the presidency. But he did not act as if he were seriously entertaining the presidential idea until after his overwhelming electoral success in 1980. That victory was both the necessary and the sufficient stimulus.

Two weeks after the victory, I asked him if he would be doing more public speaking. "Yes," he would be, he answered.

> Given the election margin I received, and given the fact that I was one of the few senators—especially from a large state— who went against the landslide, I decided that I ought to get out and speak on the things I think are important and criticize

the administration on things I think need criticizing. And, because I've refused to make a Shermanesque statement about the presidency, the press has chosen to interpret it as a signal that I'm starting a move for the presidency. In any job I've ever had, I have never precluded any advancement or any other job it might lead to. So I have refused to make a Shermanesque statement. And I expect to be making more speeches. Where that will lead, I have no idea. But if you are asking me, does this mean I have a big organization in place, geared up to go, the answer is no.

His electoral interpretation included the legitimating of a serious presidential exploration. And later on he underscored the importance of that electoral interpretation:

As far as public service and the Senate are concerned, I had been interested all my life. But I did not think about the presidency until after the 1980 election. . . . There had been talk before, but I never took it seriously. The first time I thought seriously enough about it so that I wouldn't make a Shermanesque statement was after my 1980 victory in Ohio.

He was about to do things that were preliminary to a presidential campaign, while in no way committing himself to that course.

He had come a long way in six years. He had achieved his first-term goal of becoming a good senator, and now he was in a position to entertain a new goal—higher office. As one veteran staffer put it,

So far we've been refusing 99 percent of all the outside speaking requests he's gotten. And he's gotten hundreds of them. Now that he's been reelected, we have changed that policy. We are going to accept them and see what kind of response he gets.

It was a decision that, by tortuously slow increments, led to the formal announcement of Glenn's candidacy a year and a half later.

In the abstract, a campaign for the presidency is like a campaign for the Senate. As John Kessel has carefully generalized, presidential campaigns take place over time and proceed in sequence through a number of stages.[2] For each recognizable stage, there is a recognizable context—different stages, different contexts. Winning campaigns grow out of favorable contexts and the ability successively to exploit them. Among the ingredients that produce that ability are resources, strategies, and a campaign model. In these general terms, all campaigns are alike.

The differences are mostly contextual. Chief among them is the length of the presidential campaign—especially the segment that is of interest to us, the nomination sequence. Informally, the campaign for the nomination goes on for three years before any actual voting for convention delegates takes place. When the formal process finally begins, it takes another three and a half months to select delegates. In reality, this long campaign is a collection of smaller campaigns conducted state by state, under varying sets of rules, in a complexity of local settings. So, the nomination process is not only especially lengthy, but also especially grueling.

As such, it puts a premium on candidate endurance. Winning is, for the most part, a matter of surviving. It is a characteristic of the process that most candidates do not survive. They drop out before the party convention meets to choose its nominees. We can, therefore, approach the subject of nomination campaigns by asking what it takes to survive, or, conversely, what causes the nonsurvivors to drop out? How and why John Glenn became a nonsurvivor will be our perspective on his campaign for the presidency.

From a citizen's standpoint, the long period between the first stirrings of interest in the next presidential election and the first votes for convention delegates has a distinct air of unreality. It is a phony war. Very few people are involved and nothing decisive happens. Whatever does happen is unpatterned and wildly unpredictable. Whatever is written about it is strictly "inside baseball"—by the few, to the few, and about the few. And the content of such writing focuses less on real events than on perception, conjecture, and speculation. There is, in short, little solid, tangible, meaningful, interpretable evidence of what, if anything, is going on that might be related to the ultimate outcome of the presidential contest. Political scientists have tended to agree with the citizen's position that there is little to study or worth studying during this interim period.

That view is unfortunate. It may be a campaign-without-voters, but it is a campaign nonetheless. From the standpoint of the presidential candidate, a great deal happens during this campaign. And what happens is a matter of life or death. Although the campaign-without-voters cannot produce a winner, it produces losers. It may, that is, determine a candidate's likelihood of survival when the actual voting begins. From the candidate's perspective, too, the campaign-without-voters proceeds through identifiable stages and produces describable patterns. As in the formal nomination sequence, early decisions affect later decisions. Resources, campaign strategies, sequences of campaign activity, and indicators of likely success can be identified. A relationship can be found between campaign activity—speechmaking, organizing, fund raising—and the viability judgments of campaign watchers like professional politicians and media scorekeepers. There is even a crude form of citizen participation through polls. There are, in short, recognizable ways of working to ensure—or impede—survival.

Admittedly, this drawn-out period of preliminaries is a good deal less structured than the period of actual voting, which may explain why studies of nomination politics normally focus on the period when voters actually choose delegates. But that does not mean the preceding period cannot be examined and understood. And if what happens during the campaign-without-voters is vitally important to the candidates—as surely it was to John Glenn—we shall have to do our best to analyze it.

Our plan is to follow Glenn's path and explain why he survived as long as he did and no longer. In the titles of the early magazine profiles and in the headlines of the later running accounts of his campaign, we can trace the broad outlines of his effort.

1. October 1981, *New York Times Magazine*, "John Glenn's Presidential Countdown"
2. February 1982, *Washingtonian*, "An Astronaut in the White House?"
3. March 1982, *Newsweek*, "The Right Stuff for '84"
4. May 1982, *New Republic*, "John Glenn's Right Stuff"
5. June 1982, *Parade Magazine*, "Can John Glenn Be President?"
6. April 1983, *Washington Post*, "Glenn With Hero's Send Off Launches Bid for Presidency"
7. July 1983, *National Journal*, "Democratic State Party Leaders See Race Even as Glenn Gains on Mondale"
8. August 1983, *Washington Post*, "Democratic Governors Show Increasing Interest in Glenn"
9. August 1983, *Los Angeles Times*, "Survey Finds Glenn Strong Against Reagan"
10. October 1983, *Washington Post*, "In Last 3 Months, Glenn's Fund Raising Outpaced Mondale's"
11. October 1983, *Washington Post*, "Mondale-Glenn Draw Battle Lines"
12. October 1983, *Washington Post*, "Glenn Encounters Frost in N.H."
13. November 1983, *Washington Post*, "Glenn's Swing South Shows Gap Between Promise, Performance"
14. November 1983, *New York Times*, "Glenn Steps Up His Attacks on Mondale Policies"
15. December 1983, *Washington Post*, "Glenn, Hoping to Make Up for Lost Time, Reorganizes at Top"
16. December 1983, *U.S. News and World Report*, "Bare Knuckle

Time for Glenn, Mondale"

17. December 1983, *National Journal*, "Democratic State Party Leaders See Mondale Pulling Away from Glenn"
18. January 1984, *Washington Post*, "Fund Raising Problems Force Glenn to Cut Staff"
19. January 1984, *Washington Post*, "Temperatures and Glenn Outlook Falling in Iowa"
20. February 1984, *Wall Street Journal*, "Why is John Glenn, Once So Popular, Running So Poorly?"
21. February 1984, *Dallas Morning News*, "Big News is Depth of Glenn's [Iowa] Defeat"
22. February 1984, *Concord Journal*, "New Hampshire Do or Die for Glenn—[says] Aide"
23. February 1984, *Washington Post*, "Hart Upsets Mondale to Win in N.H.; Glenn Third"
24. March 1984, *Boston Globe*, "Glenn Abandons Quest for Presidency"

This view from the media is highly selective, but it conveys the sense of a campaign sequence, of a campaign that went through four identifiable—albeit overlapping—stages. The first stage (titles 1-5) was a period of *exploration*. It began immediately after Glenn's reelection to the Senate in November 1980 and continued until the announcement by Sen. Edward Kennedy, D-Mass., that he would not run, in December 1982. The second stage (headlines 6-10) was a period of *hope*. It began in January of 1983 and continued until the early days of October when Glenn began a head-to-head battle with former vice president Walter Mondale. The third stage (headlines 11-20) was a period of Glenn-Mondale *confrontation*. It lasted from October until the Iowa caucuses. The fourth stage (headlines 21-24) was a period of *defeat*, which lasted from the Iowa caucuses on February 20 until Glenn abandoned the race three weeks later.

Viewed over the shoulder of the candidate, these four stages stand out clearly. But when viewed from the outside, the designations seem arbitrary. Added confidence comes, however, from the recognition that three contextual variables can be used to frame the stages fairly well. They are *the structure of competition, the focus of media scorekeeping,* and *the set of strategic decisions.*[3] The first variable refers to the number of contestants and their relationship to each other in terms of their changing horse-race prospects. The second variable refers to the dominant substantive focus of media scorekeeping. Each substantial recombination of these two variables into a newly identifiable stage created a changed strategic context for the candidate and a distinctive set of strategic decisions associated with it. We shall write the story of the Glenn campaign in terms of its four stages—or its four seasons—and focus on these three variables as we go.

A SEASON OF EXPLORATION: APRIL 1981-DECEMBER 1982

The season of exploration is the time John Kessel calls "early days" and what another observer calls "the exhibition season." [4] The context is one in which a number of politicians are experimenting with the notion of a presidential campaign, trying it on for size. For each of them, it is a time of private calculation. What goals of mine will be served by running? Do I have a reasonable chance of winning? What will be the costs of a campaign? How will I present myself? What themes will I pursue? Where will my support come from? It is also a time of public testing. Each individual engages in a kind of mating dance or, better, a series of mating dances—with prospective supporters. The individual makes himself or herself available to donors, workers, and voters for their scrutiny and judgment; and they circle one another looking for signs of mutual attraction. It is a tentative kind of courtship. Commitments are sought, but none is required on either side.

During this lengthy period, each potential candidate assesses his own resolve and his own prospects in relative isolation from the others. While there is some interdependence of calculation and an implicit competition, there is no direct confrontation. They do not talk about one another, debate one another, or face one another at the polls. When asked to compare himself with the other likely contenders, Glenn typically responded, "I'd prefer not to comment about those kinds of things. I'll just let them say their piece, and I'll say mine, and we'll let the voters judge." [5] The aspirants go about the business of exploration separately. And, in the process, a fair number of them decide not to go forward with a full-scale presidential campaign.

John Glenn's season of exploration lasted twenty months. On April 3, 1981, he traveled to Jackson, Mississippi, to speak at the Democrats' Jefferson-Jackson Day Dinner. It was his first political trip outside Washington since his reelection and the first public sign of his interest in pursuing what his staffers began to call the "presidential thing." Twenty months later, on December 1, 1982, Ted Kennedy, the leading contender for the party's nomination, suddenly dropped out of the contest, and the structure of competition changed. Walter Mondale quickly became the acknowledged front-runner, and John Glenn emerged from the pack of presidential possibilities to take Mondale's place as the prime contender. This new position in the competitive structure made Glenn "the alternative" to Mondale, thereby placing him within striking distance of the nomination.

From April 1981 to December 1982, Glenn had steadfastly maintained that no decision had been reached about running. He was, he said, "expanding my speaking engagements to see what the response will be," or waiting "to see how well Reagan does as president in leading the country," or assessing "the kind of support I can muster— real financial support, not just 'Best Wishes John.' "[6] He was, he said, "thinking very seriously," "looking very carefully," "keeping the options open." Without any doubt the cumulative effects of his political travels, together with the special impetus of events like the June 1982 Democratic mini-convention, moved him progressively closer to a positive decision. So, too, did the gradual acquiescence of his wife, Annie. Most likely, his decision was made somewhere along the way, well before it turned into a commitment.

But the one event that precipitated what he had come to call "a final and irrevocable decision"[7] was Kennedy's withdrawal. As Glenn explained later,

> When Kennedy dropped out, that changed everything. To that point, the media had played up the head-to-head conflict between Kennedy and Mondale. They have to have conflict. So when Kennedy dropped out, I became their new "conflictee." It became Mondale and Glenn. At that point, I had to decide whether or not I thought the direction Reagan was leading the country was the right direction. I decided it was not. I did not like the turn the economy was taking, the drift of foreign policy, policies in areas like civil rights, the elderly, environmental enforcement. So I decided to run. And that decision brought the first phase to an end.

His season of exploration was over. Our analysis begins with a discussion of that season.

MOTIVATION

During the period of exploration, John Glenn had no difficulty knowing why he would run. He would run to serve his country. That is what he had been doing all his life. As he said in late November 1981, "In whatever I've done, I've always thought not about what it would do for me, but about the country. That's the case now." Publicly his standard comment became, "If I do decide to run, it will be for cause, not just to add another line on my biosheet."[8] Or, "I've had ticker tape parades—I'm not looking for attention." [9] Glenn was applying his fundamental distinction between public service politics and ego politics to the presidential arena.

"I'll tell you how I view this thing," he said to a journalist.

> I think some people think that if the Good Lord himself was in the White House and everything was perfect, it wouldn't make any difference. They'd run for the White House because they think it's their due. I don't look at it that way. If I run it will be for a cause—a need for change when we're going off on the wrong track.[10]

Again, the implication is that he is not like most politicians, that he is motivated by service rather than ego. Without doubt, his public rationale concealed a healthy private ambition, but also without doubt, he was expressing a deeply ingrained, consistently held set of beliefs about civic duty. A presidential run—like each of his Senate runs—would be one more hitch in the marines.

RECOGNITION

In assessing his resources, Glenn began with the most obvious—an extraordinary degree of name recognition. In April 1982, 74 percent of the nation's Democrats had "heard something" about him.[11] As a national hero, he would begin a campaign, as he had in Ohio, with that threshold attribute that every candidate must achieve before he or she can contemplate winning. His identification as an astronaut would later become, as it had in Ohio, a mixed blessing. But during the earliest campaign season, it gave him instant visibility, instant access, and instant appeal to the voters and to media scorekeepers. Voters wanted to see him, and media people wanted to write about him. As the titles of the magazine profiles reveal (titles 1-5), Glenn's legendary past provided an irresistibly attractive theme around which to build media assessments. Even more, a lavishly produced movie, based on Tom Wolfe's book, *The Right Stuff*, and highlighting Glenn's exploits, was in the offing for 1983. John Glenn was a celebrity, and the media began cranking out ample reminders of that fact.

John Glenn was also an attractive personality. His political success in Ohio had been grounded in a combination of heroism and strength of character. The national media, like the media in Ohio, fastened onto the same combination and painted a portrait of Glenn that was immensely flattering and had universal appeal. Not only did he enjoy name recognition, but also it was almost uniformly favorable name recognition. In polls, Glenn's "negatives" were amazingly low. It was not just that Glenn was a hero, he was a particular kind of hero—one whose exploits had not gone to his head. At his exploratory gatherings, he was invariably introduced as a "true" or "genuine" or "authentic" or "all-American" or "truly authentic American" hero.

The earliest media profiles described his special qualities as: "a naturalness and a simplicity rarely found in a public figure," "an aw shucks niceness," "stability, moderation, caution, steadiness, and self-confidence," "goodness . . . and serene self-confidence," "integrity and studious application." "Glenn is solid, reasonable, cautious, collected, steady, sure. He is not flamboyant, dazzling, sparkling, soaring, riveting, nifty, or super." He was, they reported, "a genuinely nice person," "a believable man," "as up-to-date as tomorrow's technology . . . and as comfortable as an old shoe," "almost abnormally normal," "a warm Ike," a man who "knows who he is [and is] comfortable with himself," "an admirable human being," and "almost too good to be true." [12] There were doubts expressed about his political persona, but not about his character.

When scorekeepers take their "first look" at each individual, they seek to convey something about the kind of person he or she is. At later stages in the campaign, when they came back for a second or third look, their focus and their questions become more overtly political, and the tenor of their judgments may change. Whatever might come later, the early media judgments were overwhelmingly favorable to John Glenn. Political skepticism would be offset by optimistic assessments of personal appeal. "Don't forget that win in Ohio," Glenn's advisers would say. "He only spent a quarter of what anyone [else] would. . . . He didn't have any organization, no telephone banks, none of that stuff. His big asset is his personality, which portrays his true strength of character." [13] His character was a major resource, along with his heroism. And, as in Ohio, the two reinforced one another to produce the early, favorable name recognition he enjoyed.

STRATEGY

Glenn's sense of his advantage in name recognition had a major effect on his early strategic thinking. He believed that because of his head start in favorable name recognition, he could afford to wait longer than normal before committing himself to the race. "I don't need to be out there like Jimmy Carter for two years before the first caucuses," he would tell his audience. "You need a fourteen- to sixteen-month lead time for the early caucuses." [14] He would make a decision, he told them, "by the end of the year [1982] or early next year," because "that will give us fourteen to sixteen months before the early caucuses and primaries." [15] This idea, that he needed only fourteen to sixteen months of full-scale effort became a fixed star in his strategic reckoning. Looking back, later in the campaign, Glenn explained,

> We just sat down and tried to figure out how long it would take us to mount a campaign and the number we came up with was fourteen or fifteen months. That was the way it was done. . . . It was part of our thinking that I didn't have the problem of name recognition that some of the other candidates had. If you had gone down the street in some town outside of Colorado and asked who Gary Hart was, they would probably have said he was a football player or something. I didn't have that problem. People knew who I was. My problem was that they didn't know my record. We figured fourteen or fifteen months would be just about right to get that across. [16]

This strategic decision about timing was the one decision over which he had the most control. It was the defining decision of the first stage of his campaign. And it was, perhaps, the one with the most consequences.

The decision indicated that there remained, inside the candidate, a great deal of the senator. It repeated his senatorial decision-making pattern—the careful weighing of alternatives, the final choice made only at "have-to" time. And it had the same effects as the senatorial pattern. It allowed Glenn to maintain personal control over the process and to monopolize political judgments for the longest possible time. During his season of exploration, Glenn exhibited the same self-reliant lonerism that had characterized his activity as a marine, as an astronaut, and as a senator.

While he waited, others who needed to move remained frozen in place. It was not possible to raise money until he agreed to form a political action committee (PAC). It was not possible to assemble a campaign team until he designated a chairman or a directorate. It was not possible to say he was a *bona fide* candidate until he said he was. His timetable delayed all these moves. Until very late in his season of exploration, for example, Glenn financed his activity with funds left over from his 1980 Senate campaign. Throughout the entire season, his campaign-related organization consisted almost entirely of his Senate staff. And he steadfastly refused to declare his candidacy.

Despite a good deal of unsolicited advice to the effect that a nominating campaign required "two years of hard work and four years of detailed planning," [17] the senator adhered to his own timetable. "Once you get the idea that you're going to do something, everybody wants to go, go, go," he said in October. "You go at your own pace. . . . Without doing anything, I've moved up . . . within shouting distance of the others in the polls." [18] Indeed, he had. A March 1982 preference poll taken among Democrats and independents reported: Kennedy 32 percent, Mondale 20 percent, and Glenn 13 percent. A May poll among Democrats reported: Kennedy 30 percent, Mondale 15 percent, Glenn 11 percent.[19] He had been carried to this level on the strength of his favorable name recognition. And, so long as he was exhibiting this degree of support, he was being reinforced in his disinclination to turn exploration—or even decision—into commitment.

RECORD

Another basic resource with which Glenn began his quest was his record in the Senate. As he put it, his fourteen- to sixteen-month campaign was calibrated to "get my record across." And that would be the purpose of the campaign. His record, too, carried strategic implications. It had two elements.

First, he had been a senator for eight years and had the requisite experience there to give him validity as a qualified candidate. He was not a Senate "heavyweight," and he did not have to be. Indeed, Senate heavyweights—Robert Taft, Richard Russell, Lyndon Johnson, Henry Jackson, Howard Baker, Robert Dole—have been notorious nonsurvivors of the nomination process. Glenn had become a respected senator with proven legislative capabilities to blend with his proven electoral prowess. He was especially well regarded for his expertise in foreign and defense policy. He was a well-credentialed United States senator and, as such, he commanded serious attention as a presidential possibility.

The second aspect of his record was its content. His support for a strong national defense and liberal social policies, together with a balancing concern for fiscal responsibility, had produced a voting record that we have described, for convenience, as independent and centrist. Glenn described his record that way when he first talked about his speechmaking plans in late November 1981. "I do see myself somewhere in the center of things," he said. "With Kennedy and Mondale on the left and Hollings and Scoop [Jackson] on the right, I see myself somewhere in the middle." It was another perception that he held to the end and that guided his search for electoral support.

In the exploratory period, his Senate record gave him a helpful issue-related identity. And that, too, got factored into the structure of competition. The media classified him just about as he pictured himself: "the possible moderate alternative to Teddy and Fritz," "middle of the road senator," "thoughtful moderate," "a cautious progressive . . . a centrist, but . . . center left," "in the moderate Democratic opposition [to

Reagan]." [20] More important, his record contributed substantially to the plausibility of his candidacy—at least among influential scorekeepers. James Reston of the *New York Times* described him as "a moderate liberal, standing closer to the middle of American politics than either Kennedy or Mondale." [21] James Gannon, whose *Des Moines Register* was a power in Iowa politics, called him "a moderate Democrat [who] would be of broad appeal to the vast center of the American political spectrum," and "a candidate tailor-made to oppose Ronald Reagan." [22] Jack Germond and Jules Witcover commented,

> Aside from his remarkable political success in Ohio, it is his record on issues that has done the most to stimulate curiosity about Glenn in the political community. On the face of it, he seems exceptionally well positioned for the times.[23]

A *New York Daily News* analysis was headlined "Glenn Asset Is Solid Hold on Political Middle Road." [24] Given that strategic position, scorekeepers could imagine sufficient appeal to sufficient segments of the population to make him president.

Altogether, then, Glenn's resources provided him with the requisite elements of initial candidate credibility—name recognition, qualifications, and a plausible chance of winning. Everything he did as a candidate would be built upon that resource base. In June the *National Journal* presented a thumbnail sketch of the assets and liabilities of several prospective candidates. Glenn's read: "*Assets:* Everybody's hero ... Eisenhower reborn ... a man of the middle ... enjoys name recognition ... bright ... sincere ... solid. *Liabilities:* Lacks luster and ability to generate excitement ... ineffective orator ... uncertainty as to what he stands for ... dislikes some aspects of politics." [25] It was an appropriate mix of credibility and uncertainty for an exploratory season.

OBSERVATIONS AND REFLECTIONS: 1981-1982

Prior to his formal announcement, most of John Glenn's public activity involved speechmaking appearances around the country. Table 2-1 conveys the radical shift in his allocative strategy brought about by the decision to test the presidential waters.

I was present on two of those out-of-town occasions—an address to the annual dinner of the Democratic party of Cook County in Chicago on May 14, 1981, and an address to the Jefferson-Jackson Day Dinner of the Democratic party of Arkansas in Little Rock on March 5, 1982. I was also present at the party's mini-convention in Philadelphia in June 1982.

TABLE 2-1   Allocation of Time Outside Washington, 1975-1982

Year	Trips to Ohio	Days spent in Ohio	Trips elsewhere in U.S.
1975	22	33	11
1976	17	36	3
1977	20	31	3
1978	26	44	4
1979	27	53	3
1980	28	97	5
1981	12	16	27
1982 (through June)	—	—	33

Source: Glenn files.

During and after each of these events, I wrote up my observations and reflections. They provide some running commentary on the exploratory stage of the "campaign."

CHICAGO, MAY 1981

The Chicago speech is Glenn's third out-of-town effort for 1981 and, because of its setting in a Democratic stronghold, the most consequential. The posture of the Glenn group—his wife and four Senate staffers—seems more defensive than aggressive, more concerned with damage control than with winning support. The centerpiece is Glenn's speech. And the staff's goal seems to be to avoid the kind of mediocre performance and harsh judgments that many Democrats remember from his 1976 convention speech. Four reporters from Ohio have flown in for the occasion. "The Ohio press has made a very big thing out of this speech. They want to compare it to his 1976 keynote speech," says a staffer. "Of course, an Ohio president would be very important to them. My fear is that they are making too much out of it."

According to my notes, Glenn's speech was perfectly adequate, but not exciting. When the speech—a tribute to the past accomplishments of the Democratic party and a note of optimism for its future as the guarantor of individual opportunity—was over, the mood of the Glenn group was palpably one of relief. Said one staffer later, "We all think it went pretty well, not very well but better than some of us expected it might. There was a high level of anxiety here about the speech. And he didn't bomb." Another staffer agreed. "If you can give a speech and people listen to some of it and you get some applause, that's all you can ask. The Ohio press will compare it to the 1976 convention speech. And by comparison, this one was much better, a big improvement." The senator's judgment was similar.

If you escape with your hide after talking to that group, you can talk anywhere. When the pope has been shot and when people won't even keep quiet while a priest prays for the pope—that's a pretty tough crowd. When I heard the steady noise all the time the man tried to pray for the pope, and in a Catholic city, I said to myself, "This could be a very black evening." But it wasn't. I thought it went very well.

Matched against his last important speech, against a damage control goal, and against modest expectations, the visit was a success.

There was, however, no sense that he had gained ground. Cook County Democrats do not seem to be among John Glenn's most likely supporters. The Chicago newspapers describe him as "a possible presidential candidate," but they also point out that he was selected to give this speech to avoid alienating the Kennedy or the Mondale factions.[26] Rep. Dan Rostenkowski, D-Ill., gave Glenn a glowing introduction:

In our tidal wave of defeat, he survived and by millions of votes. . . . He did what a freckled face pilot had done, give us the true feeling of our country. . . . It is something to have accomplished his sweet victory as an astronaut. It's another to carry on with dignity and with his contribution as a private citizen. . . . I get the feeling that at the right time, we are going to look to this man to take the leadership of the Democratic party . . . his leadership of the party might become the leadership of the country at 1600 Pennsylvania Avenue.

But afterward he said, "Glenn needs an issue, something to be identified with."[27]

I watched for fifteen minutes while Glenn stood stiffly beside Mayor Jane Byrne in the pre-dinner receiving line. They exchanged neither words nor smiles nor gestures. The mayor, lined up after the senator, had a brief interchange with nearly everyone who came through. But she introduced no one to him. Glenn's handshake was pleasant and perfunctory. The politicians seemed content to meet a celebrity; and he was not reaching out to them to suggest any other connections. He seemed no more comfortable with this group of urban politicians than he had been with a similar group in Toledo in 1980. It was a mating dance conducted without excitement on either side.

ARKANSAS, MARCH 1982

In Arkansas Glenn again displayed a noticeable reserve in routine, working-level dealings with local politicians. Arriving in Little Rock, he was greeted by the state Democratic chairman, the mayor, and the city director. He shook hands with each and then sat down off to one side with a staff aide to await his press conference. For ten minutes or so, the local politicians talked to each other, to other members of the Glenn group, or to Arkansas senator David Pryor, who had flown co-pilot on Glenn's plane. Glenn did not seem uncomfortable, just not interested. He did not plunge in to make conversation or forge links with the greeters.

The more general problem is, of course, the still underdeveloped political persona. At the dinner, Arkansas's two senators introduce him more as the astronaut hero than as the senator. Pryor presents him with a local road sign: "Col. Glenn Road." "When I first went to the Senate," he says,

> I knew I was going to meet John Glenn, one of the greatest American heroes of all time. When I met him on the subway, I stuck out my hand and said, "I'm David Pryor," but I couldn't think of anything else to say. I don't know anything about space or science. So I said, "We have a road named after you in Pulaski County."

"When I first met John Glenn," says Dale Bumpers, "I asked him if he wasn't scared sitting on that booster after his flight had already been scrubbed three times. And he said to me, 'Before I had a chance to get scared they lit the thing and I was off.'" Bumpers calls him "a real American hero, every inch a gentleman, and a great Democrat." At the reception afterward, Democrats gather round while a local 1962 recording, "Mighty John Glenn," is played. To wit: "As he rode higher in the sky, the clouds opened up to let John go by. Johnny Glenn, what a man. Yes, Johnny Glenn is a mighty man. He went through space like nobody can...." The relationship between Glenn and his audience was overwhelmingly centered on the astronaut persona. And the total experience was another reminder of the potency of that image.

The Arkansas speech is similar to the Chicago speech in its broad theme of pride in, and praise for, the Democratic party's past and in its optimism for the future of the country. He seems more relaxed about it than a year ago—opening up with the Arkansas call, "Soooo-ee." He repeats his favorite challenge that "given the proper leadership, I say Americans can still out work, out invent, out produce, and out compete anyone on the face of this planet." And he ends with a thematic emphasis on opportunity—"an opportunity not merely to grind for a bare living but to strive for a better life." He closes, as he had in Chicago, with words from Thomas Wolfe:

> To every person their chance; to every person regardless of birth their shining opportunity; to every person the right to

live, to work, to be themselves; to become whatever their ambitions and decisions combine to make them—that is the promise of America.

"When I talk about the right of people to dream," Glenn says afterward, "You can hear a pin drop. People don't want to be told America is finished." Judging by the hush at the end of the speech, he seems correct on both counts. Glenn will not make the presidency as a mass communicator, but he seems more relaxed than a year ago. "I thought it went well," he said. "People seemed to listen to what I had to say. And more people came to the reception afterward than were expected."

The difference from the Chicago speech was the addition of an explicit, broad-based attack on the Reagan administration. A time of national hope had given way to a recession. He told a news conference, "My people back in Ohio are very concerned. The situation is as bad as I've ever seen it in my time in the Senate." [28] And, following his own criterion—the adequacy of Reagan's performance—Glenn had taken a big step along the path to a decision. As he noted on the way home,

> Last year people's attitude was that they wanted to give Reagan a chance. This year people are scared. Last year whenever you mentioned the economy, people just listened. But this year when you talk about the economy, you can see them nodding their heads. The attitude is completely different. There is that great concern.

And he added, "You can't sense the depths of it by reading the *Washington Post*." So, he is learning something from his travels and is revising the content of his speeches as he goes.

He is gradually shaping a set of point-by-point attacks on the president and his administration. But he has developed applause lines better than his programmatic theme. A leading Arkansas Democrat said to me afterward, "If Glenn is our party's nominee, I will support him. But he's got to show me a lot more by way of a program and a vision before he becomes my candidate." Glenn knows that this task is unfinished. "Democrats have to have an idea of where we want this country to go," he said on the way home. "Then we have to hang our domestic and foreign policies onto that. But so far, no one has been able to set forth that vision." Back in Washington, a top staffer is starting work on a document entitled "A Vision of Politics and the Politics of Vision." But it has not yet reached its intended beneficiary.

John Glenn's vision for the nation, when and if it gets articulated, will be heavily influenced by the kind of America he has experienced. Out of his experience he will mold not only a vision for the country, but also a vision of himself in the country. And insofar as that experience has been limited, he has something to learn. Or, perhaps, he can persuade the part of the nation he does not know to share the values of the part he does know.

Flying "co-pilot" on the way back to Washington, I asked him about the kind of feel he was getting for the country as a result of his travels. He began by talking about two farmers with whom he had just had breakfast. "You get a better feel for what people are thinking if you go there than you get by just reading the *Washington Post*. The farmers are having a terrible time. But they are worried about the same things as the Ohio farmers." Then there was a long silence as he monitored the instruments and flew the plane. Finally, he commented—"off the record for now."

> When you take these trips, you see an America you don't see in Washington. You go up and down the East Coast, and there's a jaded attitude about the country. It's an attitude of cynicism and greed. The newspapers feed on it and foster it. It's almost incestuous. In Washington, you live on that Boston-Washington axis. Then, you go across the Appalachians out to Ohio and into the small towns of the Midwest and you find a very different attitude. People are proud of their country. They love their country. They put the flag out on Flag Day. Then you go further west into Wyoming and Idaho and, boy, if you say anything against America, you'd better watch out. Then you get to the West Coast, and it's like the East Coast. Everybody is for himself. Everyone thinks the country is going to the dogs, and there's nothing you can do about it. You have the two coasts, and in between is America. Of course, you have to have the two coasts. But I hate that East Coast crap.

His admonition that the comment be "off the record for now" was the most overt acknowledgment that he was embarked on a politically sensitive endeavor. The comment was a geographical expression of his sense of "at homeness," and as such a clue as to the likely location of his political support. It was also a clue to the sort of me-in-the-country "vision" he might express in his search for support.

PHILADELPHIA, JUNE 1982

From June 25 to June 27 I accompanied the Glenn team to the Democratic National Party Conference in Philadelphia. The conference was the team's first opportunity to present his case to a broad assemblage of Democrats—and to a large contingent of national scorekeepers. While the official emphasis of this midterm, mini-convention was on the development of issues, it was also the first of the many candidate "cattle shows" or "beauty pageants" of the 1984 nominating process. The conference was not a major determinant of that process. But it provided me with an on-the-spot snapshot of Glenn's "presidential thing" one year into its existence.

Organization. To this point, John Glenn has not put together a campaign organization. What is called the Glenn "operation" here consists of his Washington staff (personal and committee), his Ohio staff, and half a dozen politicians and financial backers from Ohio. There are about fifty in all. Given the distinctly nonpolitical character of his Senate staff, the group is markedly amateurish. One recently hired advance man is the only seasoned campaign professional in the group.

But the "operation," under the leadership of Glenn's administrative assistant, Bill White, has generated a substantial amount of logistical support for their candidate's conference activities. They have assembled elaborate press kits bulging with fourteen favorable early stories on John and Annie Glenn, twenty-seven of his Senate speeches, and op-ed articles on various issues. For each delegate they have a campaign button pinned to a list of Glenn's electoral successes in Ohio. Members of the group have been given a specific assignment for the three-day convention—a state delegation to shadow, to shepherd, and to sell; a set of issue workshops and group meetings to attend; a schedule of ten staff meetings or debriefings; and a packet of materials to provide information about the conference, to sign up supporters, and to generate "a cast of thousands" at Glenn's final evening reception. A hospitality trailer is set up at the convention hall to receive the delegates. Glenn's presence is clearly established. "Everywhere I go," White tells the group the second day, "I hear, 'Your people have been here.' It's been a big job moving the office from Washington to Philadelphia. I'm very pleased with what we've done."

Still, the operation is essentially a Senate staff activity. It is not even a rudimentary campaign organization. My own sense of the difference begins on opening day when I run into Lawrence Kirwan, the Democratic party chairman of my home county, Monroe County, N.Y. Kirwan tells me that he has come to the conference with one specific mission, to sign up John Glenn as the featured speaker at the annual county Democratic dinner. I offer to help.

At an earlier staff meeting of the operation, Bill White had told the group, "If you have found someone you think needs to see the senator, let us know. We have moved the Senate office to Philadelphia, and we'll schedule his time just like we always do." I tell Larry that I'm in touch with the Glenn people and that I will convey his request to them. Larry says, "I came here to get a commitment from Glenn that he wants to do business. I don't need a commitment on the date. If he's serious, he'll do it."

At the next staff meeting, the following discussion takes place:

STAFFER: What do we do if someone asks to have the senator speak in their state or city?

WHITE: Take their names, find out what they want, and we'll be in touch with them after we get back to Washington.

STAFFER: What if they put the pressure on and tell you they need a commitment, something to take home with them?

WHITE: Give their name to Mary Jane [Veno] and she will call them when we get back to Washington.

STAFFER: Wouldn't it have symbolic value if Mary Jane were to give them a call herself now and make a contact.

WHITE: That's a good idea.

After the meeting, I give Mary Jane a sheet of paper with details of Larry Kirwan's request and his phone number. She says she will call him "right now." I go back to my room, call Larry, and tell him he will get a call any minute. "So Bill White is not ready to make a commitment," snaps Larry. And I reply, "He can't focus on that question just yet." "I need to know if he's serious," says Larry, "If he isn't, I'll get someone else. I want to make a deal while I'm here." Larry and I agree that Monroe County is natural Glenn territory—moderate, carried by Jimmy Carter, at the edge of the Midwest, and so on. I assume that Mary Jane will contact him shortly. But I'm beginning to wonder whether the operation can possibly do what Larry wants.

Late the next afternoon, when I return to my room, there is a note under the door from Larry telling me that he never got a call from the Glenn people. When I bump into Mary Jane later, I ask her if someone can give Larry a call, just to put him on hold. She is traveling everywhere with the Glenns and managing their ongoing activities. She has time to deal only with incoming calls. Someone else should have that job. "Tomorrow I may have a couple of hours to do it," she says. The system is woefully overloaded. And too few people have too much responsibility. It is the problem of the senator's staff organization all over again. For better or worse, they have, indeed, "moved the Senate office from Washington to Philadelphia."

The next morning I call Larry and learn from his wife that he is having breakfast with Sen. Ernest "Fritz" Hollings of South Carolina. When I find him at the convention hall, he is upset and baffled. "Glenn is our first choice. We are offering him an opportunity. I can't imagine why he wouldn't want to do it. But we can find someone else. I had breakfast with Fritz Hollings." I gave him my best explanation. "It's not that they don't want to do it. They do," I tell him. "It is just that they are absolutely incapable of focusing on the question while they are here. They can't even consider your question." Larry says he'll wait for a call till Wednesday of next week. Later, back home, I learned that the call did not come.[29]

The operation has succeeded in showcasing John Glenn, but it cannot do the bread-and-butter, follow-up activity that turns presentation into support. Until the Glenn people produce enough of an infrastructure so that someone can do business with the Larry Kirwans of the Democratic party, the operation will not become a campaign organization. And the Larry Kirwans of the party will not think John Glenn is serious.

Support. There is a good deal of interest here in John Glenn's potential candidacy. But a great many party people do not know him; nor does he know them. So the mating dance is much in evidence at this time.

I sat in on a meeting that brought together the senator and the state chairs of four southern and border states (and a few other individuals from those states) convened by Paul Tipps, the Ohio state chairman. Tipps spoke of the interest in a possible Glenn candidacy. Glenn said he was thinking "very seriously" about running and wanted to hear what the others had to say "not only about national concerns like the economy or defense or foreign policy, but about any special problems in your state or region." Parts of the conversation went like this:

> STATE CHAIRMAN A: Several of the state chairs were visiting the other day, and we agreed on what I'm going to say. Two of us are here, but know we speak for three others anyway. . . . We are tired of having national candidates that we have to apologize for when we talk to our own people. We won't have to apologize for you. You are the boy scout. . . . You don't have any black marks against you. We can sell you to our people. I'll name the names—Ted Kennedy, Walter Mondale. It would be very hard for me to sell them to the people of my state. I want you to run. But we need to know pretty soon whether you are going to do it or not. You may not want to make the decision public, but if you could let it be known informally that you are going to run, that would help us. You would find committees starting to form as soon as you did that.
>
> GLENN: Obviously we are thinking very seriously about running or we wouldn't be here going through all these things. We're thinking about it very seriously, but no final decision has been

made. I don't think anyone has made a final decision.

STATE CHAIRMAN B: I think I was the one who suggested the get-together that A mentioned. We have heard Paul Tipps talk about you at state chairs meetings. . . . Democrats in our state look upon most of the people in the national party as kooks. Our local candidates for state office or sheriff will run as Democrats, but they completely separate themselves from the national party. If you were our candidate, I don't think we'd have that problem. I'd be happy to have Ted Kennedy as president. But the candidates in my state will not run with him. I'd like to enlist in your campaign, but I have a limited amount of time in which to decide. What I need to know is whether you are going to be a candidate and whether you are prepared to run a mean and tough campaign. If you decide to run, what kind of plans will you make? You're behind.

GLENN: As I said, we are thinking very, very seriously (two verys!) and we will be making a final decision soon. I think that fourteen or fifteen months out from the election is enough time, that in a year and two or three months everything can come together. If we decide to go, we'll hire a big staff. You can't run a presidential campaign with a Senate staff. That's a mistake Ted Kennedy made. We will run as tough a campaign as is necessary. The big problem will be money. You can't do this without a great deal of money. But we will do everything we have the money to do.

STATE CHAIRMAN C: Our governor has been active in the national party and we aren't kooks. . . . The number one problem is the economy, especially these high interest rates. . . . We ought to regulate the banking industry by putting a cap on interest rates.

GLENN: Nothing is going to happen in this economy until interest rates come down. We are going to see a sawtooth pattern, a little up, a little down in the economy. Reagan's great mistake was sticking with the third year of the tax cut. You cannot take that much money out of the economy and still hope to get the deficit down. We've got to get the government out of the borrowing market where it drives interest rates up.

OTHER POLITICIAN: You have two things going for you as a candidate. First, Ohio. We can't win the presidency without Ohio. Second, one problem our party has is that it's attacked for its lack of patriotism. . . . No one is going to attack the patriotism of a marine colonel. You are protected on your right flank. That's what I came to say.

GLENN: I thank you for that.

STATE CHAIRMAN D: You will recall our conversation when you were in my state?

GLENN: I certainly do. We had a nice talk.

STATE CHAIRMAN D: Well, the situation is the same as it was then. . . . I say to you what I say to [the other possible candidates]. This economy is in terrible shape. We've just got to get somebody in there who can turn it around.

GLENN: Our party's problem, you might say, is that we have worked ourselves out of a job. That may seem a strange thing to say, but if you think of when Franklin Roosevelt took over, something like 51 percent of the people were at or near the poverty line in America. The programs out of the New Deal changed that. Yes, some of the programs were excessive; yes, some of them were wasteful; yes, they weren't all well managed. But they took people out of poverty. They brought about the greatest advancement of a whole people in a shorter period of time than has ever occurred in history—except maybe by revolution. These programs were built on the idea I talked about in my speech—opportunity, giving every person a fair shake. Now we have about 10 percent or 9 percent at or near the poverty line. We will continue to care for these people; but we cannot build a party by catering to the needs of 10 percent of our population. The New Deal programs are good, but we have to go beyond them. We have to worry about investment, capital formation. We have to find a new relationship between management and labor. There is a different attitude now. I can go in to a union hall and talk about the need for business investment. If I had done that a few years ago, either they would have walked out or I would have had to leave. We need to rebuild our economy so people can keep the middle class dream of a little white house in the suburbs. A lot of people voted for Ronald Reagan because they saw themselves losing the dream, slipping out of the middle class. So, we don't want to turn our back on the Roosevelt program, but we have to go beyond it.

STATE CHAIRMAN A: That says it. (Everyone nods. Tipps adjourns the meeting.)

The atmospherics of the meeting were cool—calculating on the part of the politicians, correct on the part of the candidate. The state chairs were in the market for a candidate who could help them in their states and they thought John Glenn might very well be it. They were inspecting the merchandise and offering, tentatively, to make a down payment. The senator gave them a look at the product, but did very little to sell himself to them. He tried to keep them interested and he gave them a bit of his philosophy. No bargains were concluded.

Politics is a calculating business. But it is also a business where intensities count. A striking aspect of the meeting was the total absence of enthusiasm, the absence of an exchange of emotion. The state chairs looked upon the senator as a commodity. He gave nothing of himself to them, no personal warmth, no special confidences. They had no shared experiences to recount, no old loyalties to bind them, no prior exchanges to draw upon. So they came into the room strangers; they seemed to leave the room strangers. They communicated, but they did not touch each other. Or so it seemed to me. This encounter was reminiscent of Glenn's reserved behavior in the presence of Chicago and Arkansas— and Ohio—politicians. In situations that are, because of the presence of politicians, structured as "political," John Glenn does not project those personal qualities that make him so attractive and so trustworthy a human being.

Electability. A major—probably the major—element of Glenn's campaign strategy is emerging here. It builds on his centrist ideological position, and it could be glimpsed in the meeting just described. It is the basic argument that John Glenn is a winner. One scorekeeper sums it up: "Mr. Glenn attracts attention from party professionals who think that Mr. Kennedy ultimately cannot be elected and that Mondale is too flat to be nominated." [30] The thinking reflects that of Bill White, who is—if anyone is—the chief strategist of the "presidential thing." White instructs the staff on their mission by means of an acronym: PARTY PROS WIN. The acronym stresses Glenn's electability. And it also is indicative of Glenn's thinking about his special regional strengths—in the South and Southwest.

White tells his troops that each word and each letter of each word are reminders of what the staffers are expected to do in their face-to-face contact with delegates. The word PARTY pertains to Glenn as a candidate: P = tell delegates of Glenn's Plans; A = get the delegates to Analyze politics in their states; R = Review Glenn's activity so far; T = explain Glenn's decision about Timing; Y = ask each delegate, what do You think about 1984? PROS refers to Glenn's eventual nomination: P = Glenn's Popularity as indicated by polls and by his personality; R = Regional strength in the Midwest, South, and Southwest; O = an Open convention, in which uncommitted party leaders will go to Glenn as the most electable; S = the Shift in delegate strength from the Northeast to the South and Southwest. WIN tells the staffers what they are expected to do on their own to help the process along: W = get the Word out about Glenn; I = Initiate applause during Glenn's speech; N = gather Names of prospective supporters.

The idea of Glenn's neophyte staff venturing into the political arena armed with an acronym is an indicator of the amateurish nature of their effort. But it also provides a useful strategic clue. The task of the operation is to focus on John Glenn's electability, to help plant the idea that if the party is looking for a winner in November, he could be it.

Issues. PARTY PROS WIN indicates nothing, however, about issues. At an issues conference, the omission is conspicuous, and it points to a problem area for John Glenn. "What will you say when they ask you what Glenn stands for?" I ask one staffer. "That we haven't developed that side of it yet," he laughs. A second staffer puts his finger on the current problem. Given John Glenn's fairly restricted subject matter concentration in the Senate, he simply does not have an articulated—as opposed to a voting—record on many issues. His ideological centrism is an artifact of his Senate votes and not the result of any broad-ranging intellectual effort.

The second staffer ticks off some examples: "on health, there's damn near nothing there; he hasn't made a statement about voting rights in a year; on drugs, on the Justice Department, nothing; there's nothing in his record about conservation; on the whole gamut of social welfare issues, like school lunch, he is extremely weak, almost nothing; nothing about Social Security solvency; nothing on the entire complex of what the government can do to stimulate the housing industry." With gaps of this sort, the operation is unprepared to encourage much talk about issues. (In August his unpreparedness cost him dearly in media skepticism when he stumbled into an uninformed, impromptu suggestion to reporters that some elements of the Social Security program could be made voluntary.) [31]

The Glenn people are fully aware of the situation. As a remedy they have just formed a fifty-six-member Advisory Selection Group, which will, in turn, select twenty-six specialized advisory groups in particular issue areas. Each advisory group will have about thirty members, and each group will operate within one of six policy clusters. The executive secretary of each group will be a member of the Senate staff. Bill White says that eventually 700-800 people will be involved in this gargantuan effort to develop issue positions for the campaign. [32] For purposes of the conference, however, this formidable apparatus is not available.

And neither is any substitute. One month earlier, Glenn had received the staff memo, "A Vision of Politics and the Politics of Vision." It proposed a set of issues on which he should concentrate. But it warned that he should discuss these with his Senate staff before activating any external advisory groups. "It would be disastrous for you and your staff," said the memo,

> to meet with the Advisory Selection Group without some clear idea of what your views are, what issues you consider most

important and in what direction the advisory process should proceed ... there is precious little structure to this process at present. If you are unable to provide direction for these advisory groups ... [it] would seriously damage your credibility.

The senator had not yet met with his staff. And if Glenn's top Senate staffers did not yet know these things, the amateur shepherds of the operation could hardly be expected to know them.

What is most conspicuous about the lack of articulation on certain issues is that they are matters of domestic policy. It is the converse side of Glenn's strong interest in foreign policy, arms control, energy technology, and research and development. The memo about vision has come, not surprisingly, from the domestic side of his legislative staff. These staffers do not know what Glenn's positions and priorities on the issues are. A third Glenn staffer explained,

> When a foreign policy issue comes up, Senator Glenn has a gut feeling about what is right. And he will fight bitterly for what he thinks is right. The same with nuclear proliferation or research and development. But there are major areas of domestic policy where he has no gut feeling. He ends up voting right, but doesn't fight for his position. He hasn't internalized his values in that area. He doesn't have a gut feeling for the poor. On nuclear proliferation, the staff knows he's excited; they get excited; they have easy access to him; and the excitement is self-perpetuating. Whether the domestic staff doesn't get excited because they know he's not excited or because they can't get him excited, I don't know. But the lack of excitement there is also self-perpetuating. [An Ohio staffer] told me that he [Glenn] had visited the Battelle Labs in Ohio three times, but had not once been to the central city in Cleveland. Maybe the presidential campaign will force him to give more time to these issues.

Surely it will.

But almost as surely—barring the expenditure of prodigious energies—this Senate record will be strategically constraining for him. For one thing, he has already started down the nomination path without a broad domestic issues component and must, therefore, catch up. For another thing, the relative inattentiveness to domestic issues may cause some difficulty as he reaches for the support of certain traditional Democratic party constituencies. And finally, to the degree that Glenn's candidacy is not dominated by issues, it may cause some difficulty in reaching for primary and caucus voters, who tend to be especially issue-oriented. It is, of course, too early to predict the shape of things to come.

No die is cast. But it is worth noting that John Glenn is not attending the issue workshops at the conference. Sen. Gary Hart, D-Colo., by contrast, is plunging into the middle of some of them and is presiding over his own "issues seminar," displaying a thoughtfulness on the issues and proclaiming a devotion to ideas. It seems likely that he and Glenn are embarked on different strategic paths—at least as far as their issue components are concerned. Hart defines himself in terms of ideas and issues. Glenn does not.[33]

Speechmaking.   Once again Glenn has to face the task of exorcising the memory of his 1976 convention speech—and in a comparable setting. Once again, the worries of the staff indicate the problem his speaking style poses for his candidacy. "Senator Glenn has all the wrong instincts when it comes to reading a speech. . . . He invariably picks out the wrong place to put the emphasis," said a staffer. So his speechwriters rehearsed him in Washington, taped him on the ride to Philadelphia, and rehearsed him right up to the morning of his speech. He and four of his cohorts are scheduled to speak one after the other. Glenn draws last place. Mondale speaks first, to a packed, expectant audience. Glenn speaks to a hall half filled with weary delegates. It is not the fairest test. Nonetheless, the audience is reasonably responsive. His early staccato attacks on Reagan draw considerable applause; the middle of the speech, setting forth his own ideas, does not rise much above the din; but his inspirational conclusion recaptures an applauding audience. It ends, with his Thomas Wolfe quotation, on an upbeat note.

Riding back to the hotel, his speechwriters were subdued. "I feel let down," said one. "I'd feel a lot better if people had been crowding around telling me how good it was." "I wish he'd delivered it like he did in his room beforehand," said another. "The important reaction will be what the op-ed pages say tomorrow," a third added.

It is, of course, the media scorekeepers who helped generate and have kept alive the memory of the 1976 speech. This time, media judgments are better balanced. The *Baltimore Sun* reported, "Like Mr. Mondale, Mr. Glenn seemed to have made an impression with his speech . . . he now appears to be sharpening a strong speech that deals with . . . issues effectively.[34] The hometown *Philadelphia Inquirer* said, "Those who stayed gave his forceful attack on the Reagan administration a warm response." [35] The *Washington Post* scorekeeper noted that Glenn tried for "applause lines . . . in an effort to erase the memory of his [1976] flop." And he said, "Glenn's applause lines received applause, but his soft-voiced delivery permitted a steady rise of conversation on the floor, and the hall was emptying before he finished." [36] *Newsweek* said that Glenn "proved once again that he lacks the right stuff as an orator." [37] *Washington Post* reporters said, "Glenn had trouble exciting the crowd," and they quoted an Iowa delegate as saying, "pretty much of a loud ho hum . . . to me he comes off the same way he did in 1976 . . . he didn't pass the test then and he hasn't come too far since then." [38] This kind of scorekeeping ensures that the knock on Glenn—that his speeches lack inspiration—will remain alive.

For Glenn, the challenge of the speech was, once again, the challenge of survival. He and his staff believe he has survived. One speechwriter summed up:

> The main object of the speech was to lift the 1976 monkey off the back of the senator, to show that he can excite an audience, that he can get applause and that he can, at the same time, distinguish himself from the leftish liberals in the party. I think he accomplished both those things in Philadelphia. . . . People who say his Friday speech was anything approaching his 1976 performance have no idea what they are talking about. . . . It was a tremendous improvement over 1976.

On "Meet the Press" afterward, journalist Jack Germond, recalling 1976, said to Glenn, "You've been sort of living with that for these six years." Then he asked, "Do you think you've wiped that away with the speech you gave on Friday in Philadelphia?" Glenn replied,

> Yes I do. I really do. . . . I thought it was very warmly received. I had many comments about it, not only from people at the convention, but newsmen in Philadelphia . . . they said I had applause twenty-seven times, which I think is pretty good. I don't think I had that in '76 in New York. But I was very happy.[39]

John Glenn is not going to win the presidency as a great communicator. But he has worked on his speechmaking and he has improved it to the point where it will not knock him from the race. He should stop worrying about it and put his effort wherever he thinks his comparative advantage lies.

Glenn's private reflections on the speech reveal more about his attitude toward politics in general than toward the speech. "As far as the speech was concerned, which is 90 percent of what the press focused on," he said afterward,

> We didn't do very well. I thought the speech was well received by the people that were there. But we made one mistake. We didn't pack the hall the way Kennedy and Mondale did. I know what they did and I predicted it. You could look out from the

podium and see the Mondale people there with their signs and
their buttons. I said to someone who was standing beside me
backstage, "You wait and see what happens when he finishes
speaking. They will all leave." Sure enough, they all got up and
left. The others of us had to talk to the ones who were left. I
suppose it was smart politically. I suppose if you want to
impress the media, you have to create a big hoopla with signs
and confetti. But the idea is abhorrent to me. I suppose that's
what we should have done—packed the hall and treated it like
show biz.

There is another indication here that he remains uncomfortable with
many of the accepted routines of politics—especially those that involve
the manipulation of partisan emotions. In the public service view of
politics, hoopla and show biz are neither necessary nor right. That
stiffness of attitude is more likely to hurt him than his stiffness in
speechmaking.

Themes.   The media, typically, showed no interest in the content
of Glenn's speech. But anyone interested in the development of his
campaign themes and his campaign tone could read the speech with
profit. And a comparison between the Glenn speech and the Mondale
speech would be even more helpful. Glenn's speech had two themes—
both evolved from his earlier speeches. One is that the unifying
principle of the Democratic party and the country is *opportunity* "that
offers a chance to all who desire one, a hand to all who need one, and a
job to all who want one." Someone who helped write the speech noted,
"The unifying idea for Senator Glenn is opportunity. What distinguishes
him from many other party liberals is that he stresses equality of
opportunity rather than equality of results. One is a less liberal notion
than the other. I hope somebody picks up on that some day."

The second theme is that the party's and the country's ability to
provide opportunity depends on its ability to expand opportunity and
that its ability to expand opportunity depends on its capacity to welcome,
to live with, and to exploit change. Glenn speaks of "the dynamic nature
of our commitment, our willingness to experiment, to try new methods,
and explore new ideas. This adventurous, questing spirit has sustained
our party." He wants the party to be future-oriented. And the policies he
wishes to stress are future-oriented. (Later in the fall as he campaigned for
fellow Democrats, he would regularly emphasize three building-block
policy areas: "a strong system of public education, government investment in research and development, and free enterprise capitalism.") [40]

There is ample evidence in Glenn's speech, as well as in his voting
record, for his strong belief in the government's role in assuring a

minimum standard for the needy. But the spirit of his thinking is to focus on the challenge of the future and the excitement of dealing with the unknown. He emphasizes the role of government in securing educational opportunity and in promoting efforts to push back the frontiers of knowledge. And the centrist nature of his philosophy is reflected in his emphasis on individual initiative in coping with future challenges. The speech is filled with optimism and the excitement of the search. Altogether, it shows Glenn trying to work out a set of views that blend his astronaut experience with the thematic imperatives of an impending presidential candidacy. (Soon he would begin to use the evocative slogan "Old Values and New Horizons." Later, the campaign theme would become "Believe in the Future Again." Finally it would become "Leadership for the Future.")

In contrast, the theme of Walter Mondale's speech is that the Reagan administration has divided the country into the rich and the rest of us, that its policies have favored the rich and that it is the historic task of the Democratic party to concern itself with the groups that have been disadvantaged. Over and over, Mondale paints a picture of group conflict. The administration, he tells the audience, has created "a government of the wealthy, by the wealthy, and for the wealthy"; "two Americas, one where the well-to-do get more and more and one where the rest of us get less and less"; "a huge jagged fault line across this country . . . that ugly line." The people of "Reagan's America," of "mansions" or "Rolls Royces" or "rich parents" or "wealthy executives" or "the very rich" or "bankers" or "those who raise money" are set against those "good solid decent Americans," the "farmers," "auto workers," "government employees," "teachers," "talented kids," "wait-ers," "laid-off steel workers" or "those who raise strong families" who are "suffering," enduring "heartache," are "flat on their backs," "feeling powerless," "waiting to find a job," "sick," "hungry."

It is a call to renew old tribal loyalties, quite unlike Glenn's call to embrace a changing future. It rests on a view of the world that is markedly more group-oriented and more conflictive than Glenn's. In its deliberate pitting of group against group, it helps to highlight the more consensual, unifying, what's-best-for-the-country nature of John Glenn's message and of his thinking. The Mondale speech was not one Glenn would have given, could have given, or would wish to have given.

But speeches do more than convey themes; they also have an emotional impact on the listeners. In this respect, the contrast between the Mondale speech and the Glenn speech was equally striking. Mondale gave his audience a diet of unremitting partisanship expressed in the hottest of rhetoric. It was unabashedly designed to manipulate emotions, and the audience responded with a degree of warmth and noise that went far beyond any effects of orchestration. Glenn's speech, on the other hand, served up no political red meat. A set of well-crafted one-liners criticizing the Reagan administration is no match for a full-throated battle cry of "them against us." Glenn's speech was thoughtful but bland. It drew genuine, but not sustained or heartfelt, applause. In yet one more arena, therefore, Glenn had demonstrated an inability or an unwillingness to manipulate the narrowly political emotions of his listeners, and they had responded without much feeling.

Viewed somewhat differently, the Mondale speech seemed patently designed to help him win the nomination. However much it portrayed a divided country, its purpose was to unify the party. It was couched in rhetoric that would appeal to the old loyalties and/or the new interests of the party's many constituencies. And Mondale described his own life in ways that projected a closeness and a sense of identification with those constituencies, with the rest of us—"a father who was a minister— in small towns," "a mother who taught music and raised a family," and a family "that didn't have any money." Many of them knew him well anyway, and these words were designed to reassure. The words and rhythms of the speech were reminiscent of Hubert Humphrey, and its purpose was to summon up a Humphrey-like nominating coalition.

In contrast, Glenn's speech gave little sense of the kind of coalition he planned to put together for the nomination. It was not couched in terms of groups and did not make very strong appeals to traditional Democratic constituencies. Nor, typically for Glenn, did he reveal anything of himself, his background, his experience—or the sense of strength, courage, or crisis judgment that could be drawn from that experience. These delegates, most of whom did not know him as well as they knew Mondale, were left without any hints as to his personal side. They would have a hard time picturing him as their leader. They might, in a general way, be willing to think of him as a winner; but his speech, at least, did not tell them much about how he proposed to do it.

Staff.   John Glenn's relationship to the operation in Philadelphia bears all the earmarks of the same aloofness that characterizes his relationship with his office staff in Washington. It makes one wonder anew about how effectively he manages and works with a staff. From the start of their preparation in his office, he remained nearly oblivious to what they were doing. And so the operation resembled a surprise party more than a serious campaign effort. "Bill White had put them through more of a drill than I had realized," he said afterward.

I wasn't aware of what he was doing. I suppose I should have been but I was busy with other things. I had an inkling a day or two before. But I did not know how well organized he was. I got more comments that my staff was the best organized, the nicest, and the most helpful of any group there. I was not only surprised by that, I was delighted.

One of the main organizers agreed.

I think the senator was pleased with the way it came together. He didn't even know what we were doing. He knew we were doing something. But he didn't watch over it. He was too busy. He would come into his office and see the interns putting together folders at 9:00 at night. That's not SOP in this office. He would grin and say, "You've got quite a print shop going there," and leave.

It is something of a puzzle, then, why Glenn neither directed nor guided, nor participated in, nor inquired into the first organized effort to promote his candidacy.

The answer, I think, lies in his normal relationship with the members of his staff—his tendency to delegate copiously to the AA and to remain aloof otherwise. On the evening after his speech, he dropped by the staff's champagne celebration. "I want to thank all of you for doing such a good job," he said. "I won't single out people for praise. But there is one person without whom this would never have come together. And I think it really has come together. That person is Bill White. It wouldn't have worked without you, Bill, so I toast Bill White." Everyone smiled and clapped. The Glenns, White, and their entourage stayed for maybe fifteen minutes and left. The staffers were feeling immensely pleased with themselves. The operation was an officewide effort. The speech was a broad-based effort. The next night's reception seemed certain to be packed. "In an office that's very divisional," said a staffer, "we've done something we all can be proud of."

The staff sat around for an hour in a group laughing, talking, drinking beer, and telling jokes—mostly raunchy jokes. What is striking, to one who has sat in on scores of Senate staff parties, is what the Glenn staff did not talk about. They did not talk about John Glenn. They did not talk about politics. They did not reminisce about anything that any of them have done together. They did not make good-natured fun of one another. They did not talk about their past or their future. What they did is trade raunchy stories. It was almost as if they did not know each other very well. There were no common bonds expressed or evoked, save for the pleasure of their present accomplishment.

The "office" in Philadelphia displayed the same lack of group feeling as the office in Washington. One is led to speculate that the emotional distance they felt from one another was related to the emotional distance they felt from the man for whom they worked.

On their first day back in Washington, a sign appeared in the office: "You did a superb job in Philadelphia." It was signed "John and Annie." It rekindled the warm sense of staff accomplishment. But it was also the extent of the exchange between senator and staff on the matter. A couple of weeks later, one of the main organizers of the operation described the relationship:

> He's not very open with the staff. He's not effusive. He put up a little sign thanking us and that was it. People know he's appreciative of what they did. There's a kind of a good soldier attitude among the staff. They'd be shocked if he hung around and talked to them. They don't expect him to. There's no need for the commander to be down among the troops. They know he works ten hours a day holding up his end.

The relationship between Glenn and his staff was not one that predisposed them to fight, bleed, and die for him. This condition, when considered along with the correctness of the meeting with the state chairs and the tepidness of his convention speech, leads an observer to wonder about Glenn's inclination and/or his ability to secure the emotional attachment of others to him or to his cause. Sooner or later, he will need both the inclination and the ability.

TO YEAR'S END:
THE STATE OF THE EXPLORATION

The Philadelphia mini-convention imparted some momentum to the "presidential thing" internally. Glenn called it "a watershed for me," although not enough of one to push him to make the "irrevocable commitment."

> I've been in twenty-eight states, but here were people who had come from every state to a meeting that is preliminary to 1984. They were all very encouraging. The meetings I had with state chairs ... and with labor leaders were all extremely favorable. ... I don't know that I was moved any by it. But my confidence level, that the thing was possible, went up.

It did move him enough to engage in more strategic speculation than I had heard before. For example, of the meeting I had attended with the southern party leaders, he commented,

Of course, nothing is locked up yet. But I think I would get the strongest—maybe pretty solid—support in the South. They don't like Teddy, and they don't feel too strong about Mondale. The South is a pretty big chunk—especially if you remember the early contests are in Iowa, New Hampshire, and then [the South].

Evidently, he held to this view despite his unwillingness to meet the condition some of them had now set.

He added that he was going ahead with the formation of a money-raising committee. "The thing we need now if we are going to continue to investigate this thing, is money. Our money from the Ohio campaign is almost gone. We are down to the short runs there. So we are going to form a PAC, I'm afraid."

"Afraid?" I asked.

"Yes, nobody likes to form a PAC."

"But won't it be a signal to people who are waiting for one?"

"Oh, it will be received enthusiastically in some quarters, I'm sure."

"Did you feel at Philly that people were pushing you?"

"Yes, but I've had that for a long time."

In September he formed his PAC, the National Council on Public Policy, as a vehicle for fund raising. He lagged behind Kennedy, Mondale, Hart, Hollings, Sen. Alan Cranston of California, and former Florida governor Reubin Askew in making this move.[41] He was not plunging in with any gusto. And he seemed suspended somewhere between decision and commitment.

The day after the convention, he appeared on "Meet the Press," and his treatment there, he believed, constituted another watershed for his presidential ambitions. They had treated him—despite an incentive to do otherwise—like a political figure and not an astronaut.

"I thought 'Meet the Press' went well," he said.

But for me it was special. It was my graduation exercise. As I've told you before, when I first ran for the Senate, in 1970, whenever I would speak and then ask for questions, some kid would invariably yell out and ask me how I liked the Tang. They thought of me as an astronaut. It took four years of steady campaigning in Ohio to change that to where it would come up once in a while but not constantly. My session with "Meet the Press" was scheduled the day the space shuttle was launched, and I thought surely they would start by asking me what I thought about our space program. When we went on the air, the shuttle had been launched only one and a half hours before, and it was whooshing around in space. But the very first question went to foreign policy with Marvin Kalb, and not once did they mention space—some of the nation's most hard-bitten reporters. I have not been trying to dodge the space profession. But I have been trying to win my spurs in another line of endeavor. Nothing could have pleased me more.

His pleasure was an indication of his abiding concern for the development of a political persona. However encouraging this encounter had been, it was a small gain in a long battle. National reporters following the mini-convention continued to identify him almost entirely in terms of his astronaut past.[42]

Nothing that happened in Philadelphia indicated that the operation bore the slightest resemblance to a campaign organization. Wiser heads on the staff saw their Philadelphia activity as irrelevant to the future. "People had fun," said one, "but it wasn't a campaign—no delegates to woo, no votes to count, nothing serious to do." The operation's only important consequence for the future was the strengthening of the position of its organizer, Bill White. A White lieutenant commented,

> The senator's confidence in Bill White was high, but it went even higher. . . . He now knows that Bill White is capable of going on to bigger and better things. . . . You were there at the champagne party when he toasted Bill. To me, that was the signal. From now on Bill can do even more on his own.

Until Glenn moved to recruit a campaign organization, his administrative assistant would be the clearly designated de facto manager of the presidential thing. Philadelphia had settled that.

There remained the question of whether and how long the Senate staff could be a surrogate for a campaign staff. In an interview shortly after Philadelphia, Glenn showed he had given the matter some thought.

> I think the biggest mistake Ted Kennedy made was to try and run his campaign with his Senate staff. It can't be done. You could use your Senate staff to do research on the issues. They would be very involved in that part of it; there's a lot of talent in this office. You might want to take some of them off and put them on the campaign staff. Most of them, though, you would use them for background work. The job of running the campaign, however, can't be done by your staff. You need people who read the polls and do the scheduling. You couldn't schedule in the campaign like you schedule as a senator. A Senate staff, an administrative assistant, can't run a campaign. It's too big.

For the time being, however, Glenn did not believe he was in a campaign and, therefore, did not need a separate campaign organization. That being the case, he did not need to worry yet about the disabilities of his Senate staff. So he could safely leave the presidential thing under White's direction. And that is what he did—for the next six months.

Glenn's decision had behind it the enormous self-confidence of both the astronaut and of the public service politician. On the astronaut side, there was the self-reliant loner's desire to retain control of things as much as possible, the desire, manifested in the Senate, to control the decision-making process until the last possible moment. On the public service side, there was the sense that he did not have to do things quite the same way other politicians did. After Philadelphia, he was asked on "Meet the Press" when he planned to start "building a political organization." He answered, as usual, "sometime later this year or very, very early next year." And he added his rationale.

> I think that I have one luxury, I guess, that my name is known around the country. I don't have to go around shaking hands and building up name recognition, so I do think I have that advantage.[43]

It is surely true that he had greater name recognition than those behind him in the pack—though nowhere near that of Kennedy or Mondale. The notion that he does not "have to go around shaking hands," however, suggests once again that he sees himself as different from other politicians. It is a view that originates in his interpretation of politico as public service. But, as we have said, it is also a view that hides his ambition—perhaps even from himself. And hiding one's ambition may also blind one to the strategic imperatives that are necessary to implement that ambition. It is possible that going around shaking hands was exactly what John Glenn should have been doing. Shaking hands was one of the ordinary routines of politics with which he was not yet totally comfortable.

An incident in November underscored this still incomplete conversion from hero to politician. "On election night," recalled a staffer,

> We got the addresses and telephone numbers of all the Democratic senators so he could call them and congratulate them on their victories. But he wouldn't make the calls. We had John Stennis's phone number—dean of the Senate, just won a great victory—and we told the Stennis people that Senator Glenn was going to call. But he didn't. So we had to call the Stennis people the next day to say that Senator Glenn had been

unable to make the call; and we asked where he could get in touch with Senator Stennis. They said Stennis had gone on vacation with an unlisted number but that they would give it to us since Senator Glenn wanted to call. He never called.

John Stennis had introduced Glenn at his first "toe in the water" visit to Mississippi, but even that did not move the senator from Ohio to "horsetrade" compliments. By itself, no incident such as this would matter. But as an indicator of Glenn's natural inclinations and instincts, it pointed to a certain lack of readiness for what lay ahead.

Some people inside Glenn's staff and many people outside did not share the senator's assumption, in the latter half of 1982, that he was not in a campaign. And they worried about its organizational consequences. The idea of entrusting the whole enterprise to Bill White was not comforting to other top staffers. "I'm convinced we're in a campaign now," said one of them in July, "but we have almost no professional help."

> You cannot run a professional campaign with a Senate staff. We are all a bunch of amateurs and we desperately need to hire some real professionals to run the campaign—people for the rest of us to lean on. Do you know we don't even have a press secretary? We aren't even interviewing for a press secretary. How can you even think of a national campaign without a press secretary who knows the national press?

It would be six months before Glenn would designate a campaign press secretary to deal with the national media..

On the wings of his success in Philadelphia, White turned to the preparation of a lengthy planning document. It had been his tactic all along to pull Glenn toward an "irrevocable commitment" by inching forward on his own and then waiting to see whether his boss would object. White's 191-page "Preliminary Strategy Memorandum," delivered to Glenn November 28, 1982, was designed to pull Glenn over the brink. It was written as if a campaign were in progress; it expressed a sense of urgency about organization and fund raising; and it contained hortatory language about the "challenge" and the "experience" to stimulate the juices of the candidate.

White's memo displayed an intelligent overall grasp of the nominating process—its delegate selection rules, its coalition-building requirements, its organizational demands, its several stages, its swiftly changing rhythms, its dependence on media scorekeeping and media expectations. It covered the gamut from early fund raising to convention organization and beyond. It distinguished "the exhibition season in

1983"—during which the party and the media dominated "the score-keepers"—from the three-month period of the next season "when voters will be making decisions on issues and abilities."

Not surprisingly, the memo also displayed a sensitive understanding of the candidate's personal strengths and weaknesses. And, taking those into account, the pages were filled with wise admonitions about what lay ahead in a campaign where sequential activity, constant scrutiny, and shifting judgments would make something "entirely different from the political campaigns to which we are accustomed." By comparing aspects of a presidential campaign to Glenn's prior experience in Ohio, White insinuated some of his special concerns into the analysis. He stressed, for example, the need for greater organizational decisiveness and flexibility in making the "rapid-fire political and media decisions and adjustments required by swiftly moving events all over the nation"; the continuing need to impose "issues, experience, and record" upon the candidate's heroism and personal qualities; and the wholly new need to think about the attraction and the potential of the presidential office itself.

The memo put into words the two strategic premises that had dominated the operation in Philadelphia. White now dubbed them "super-strategies" and declared them to be the necessary conditions for survival in the nomination contest. One was the electability premise, that Glenn "can win in November." The other was the partisan premise, that Glenn is "a hard-working loyal Democrat who pays his dues." White reasoned that among interested Democrats, there existed a "receptivity to an alternative" to Kennedy and Mondale if—and only if—that alternative has "the perceived ability to win in November" and if his "party credentials are in order." "It is your challenge," he wrote, "to establish yourself as the alternative." Sensing, perhaps, a certain vulnerability, White wrote,

> Even if you are able to convey the impression that you can win in November, you will not receive the nomination if a public perception arises that you feel "entitled" to the nomination because of your general election potential, rather than because you have also supported the principles, platform, and candidates of the Democratic party.... Those who are disadvantaged by a strong showing on your part will be looking for opportunities to chip away at you on this point.

On the plus side, the memo emphasized Glenn's perceived political assets—personal and philosophical. White wrote, "the more the voters get to know you, the more likely they are to vote for you" and "you have the middle of the Democratic party road all to yourself." In all respects, the memo had to be instructive for the candidate.

What it lacked, however, was a hard-edged campaign strategy in which support-gathering priorities were set forth. There was much discussion of "coalitions," of "blocs and organizations," of "coalition building" and of the possible elements of a "Glenn coalition." It was to be "a coalition that will unify the party." But there was little sense of what a realistic, winning Glenn coalition might look like. And there was no sense at all of the composition of Glenn's primary constituency, his hard-core support, the people who would fight, bleed, and die for him. The memo's level of generality is, perhaps, to be expected in a preliminary effort. But at points where concrete problems of support call for specification—with respect to particular states or particular elements within the Democratic party—the memo lapsed into a series of dreamy directives instead of posing a set of hard choices.

The tenor of the advice was overwhelmingly to do "everything." "Every primary and caucus should be entered, and an organization should be built in every state." Every endorsement should be sought; every straw poll should be entered. "Relations with House and Senate colleagues" should be improved; state and local party officials should be cultivated with a grass-roots "bottom-up" campaign. All demographic groups should be wooed. There was mention of momentum, but only cursory concentration on the Iowa-New Hampshire-Super Tuesday sequence. Yet, an "ideal scenario" pictured Glenn "moving to the front sometime by mid-May 1984." The memo was a beginning. But if the candidate was ever to locate and solidify a base of support large enough and enthusiastic enough to carry him "from here to there," a lot more hardheaded analysis would be necessary.

In the immediate aftermath of Philadelphia, the reigning consensus among the national press held that a two-tiered contest had developed, with Kennedy and Mondale as the main contenders, and with all the other hopefuls bunched in a pack well behind. The attention of party professionals and media scorekeepers was focused on Kennedy and Mondale. The July Gallup poll ran them head-to-head among Democratic voters.[44] John Glenn was strictly an afterthought. To the degree that their attention turned to the "pack," however, there gradually developed, in the summer and fall, substantial agreement that John Glenn was positioned in third place.

Commentary on the presidential preliminaries began to play this "third man theme." [45] And it was confirmed by the only hard evidence available in the fall—the polls. In October the Penn-Schoen poll of registered Democrats on their nomination preferences reported: Kennedy at 35 percent, Mondale 24 percent, Glenn 11 percent, Hart 3 percent. A November *Los Angeles Times* poll of the same group found:

Kennedy 31 percent, Mondale 18 percent, Glenn 12 percent, and Cranston 3 percent.[46] Bill White's reading of the polls was that "Kennedy leads Mondale by slightly two to one; that [Glenn] is within easy striking distance of Mondale, and that no other potential candidate even registers significantly." There was plenty of confirmation for Glenn's assumptions about his advantage in name recognition.

Glenn's staffers were delighted with the autumn polls. It put them exactly where they thought they were anyway. And it put them exactly where they wanted to stay for the foreseeable future. As one top aide had put it in July,

> We came out of nowhere in Philadelphia and settled comfortably in third place. I hope we can stay in third place while we work behind the scenes and do what has to be done. We aren't prepared for second place yet. This is not the time for our "program for the '80s."

Bill White wanted Glenn to keep media expectations low by staying in third place all the way to the Iowa caucuses, so that he might do "better than expected" there. "A higher profile," he wrote, "would create greater scrutiny, which will come soon enough anyway without accelerating it." In the May staff memo, another aide had written similarly, "Releasing a vision—either of campaign strategy or blueprints for America—will generate more questions than you can have answers for and will only raise doubts about your abilities to solve serious national problems." In effect, Glenn's basic decision about timing had slowed down his own preparation and effectively limited his total effort to a third-place capability. His name recognition had, indeed, carried him into third place, with only a modest effort on his part. He was content to continue the same modest effort and to ride "comfortably in third place" until he was ready to make his move.

Throughout the fall, he continued with business as usual. He continued to present himself at speaking engagements—on behalf of Democratic House and Senate candidates. He continued to fly his own plane accompanied by his wife and one Senate staffer. His elaborate plan for advisory issue groups languished. He altered neither the timetable nor the style of his exploratory effort.

On December 1, however, his season of exploration abruptly and unexpectedly ended—not according to his plan but according to Ted Kennedy's plan. The time for careful investigation had run out. He was pushed to make his "final and irrevocable" commitment, and he did. His swift reaction to Kennedy's withdrawal was to say, "Anytime someone ahead of you in the polls drops out, that's a plus." [47] But his situation was better captured by the top aide, who said the situation "presents opportunities we are ill-prepared to exploit."[48] The White planning memo, not yet one week old, had been prepared with the assumption that Kennedy was in the race to stay. Glenn was not ready for the second place position into which he had been suddenly thrust; it seemed evident, at the same time, that he had now lost his control over the course of events. For example, he could no longer keep expectations low in the manner recommended in the White memo. The state of his preparation would be amply tested in the seasons ahead.

A SEASON OF HOPE:
JANUARY-SEPTEMBER 1983

When Ted Kennedy withdrew, a leading journalist predicted that because "Glenn is already perceived as the 'comer' in presidential politics, the withdrawal . . . naturally could add to his momentum."[49] A month later, John Glenn had become the acknowledged second-place runner behind Walter Mondale. The first post-Kennedy poll found Mondale at 42 percent, Glenn 18 percent, Rep. Mo Udall of Arizona 8 percent, and Hart 3 percent.[50] It was crucial to all Glenn's strategic thinking that he hold onto this position in the new structure of competition—that he remain the recognized alternative to Mondale and that the contest be circumscribed as a Mondale-Glenn contest. "The whole strategic premise of the Glenn campaign," said an adviser later, "was to be the sole alternative to Fritz Mondale and make it a two-man race."[51] It was a necessary deduction from the fundamental premise of his campaign—his electability. And it reflected the reality of the new structure—a well-established front-runner needing only a designated challenger and media scorekeepers occupationally predisposed to a protagonist-antagonist news story.[52]

According to polls and professional judgments, Glenn remained in second place throughout the year. During the summer, it appeared that he was about to become the front-runner. He never quite achieved that status. But by all outward signs, the spring and summer of 1983 were a season of momentum and hope. He recruited a campaign staff, raised $3 million, formally announced his candidacy, began to plan strategy, and rose steadily in the polls. He enjoyed all the harbingers of a winning campaign. And he believed he could win.

In the fall the outward signs began to change. It is hard to say exactly when that happened. A top adviser said later, "The whole first ten days of October were a walking disaster for us."[53] And October did bring a cluster of major changes—in campaign organization and on the campaign trail. It also brought the first public crisis of the campaign. And it brought a major change in the polls. As these changes deserve separate recognition and treatment, we shall think of September as the end of one season and October as the beginning of another.

Glenn's sudden elevation to second place in the sweepstakes brought intensified scrutiny by the professional politicians and the media scorekeepers. These are the two groups with an occupational interest in what is going on during the campaign-without-voters. They talk to one another a great deal, and they talk about what the politicians know and understand best—organization and electability. Media score-keepers, we have said, make serial assessments of presidential cam-paigns. Their "first look" centers on the personal side of the candidate. Their "second look" focuses more on the political aspects of the candidacy. When John Glenn moved into second place, many journalists were ready to take their second look and to focus on matters such as resources and strategy. They were not about to wait for the Glenn people to announce their readiness.

ORGANIZATION

In taking their second look at Glenn, the media people were not making a fresh start; rather they were highlighting a different theme. In some of their early person-oriented profiles they had recorded profes-sional skepticism about the tardiness of Glenn's organizational efforts. In a May 1982 profile, a party leader was quoted: "Glenn's timing is funny. Through delay, ambivalence or lack of aggressiveness, he's lost an awful lot of ground for using 1982 effectively." [54] In October a journalist traveling with Glenn commented similarly on the professional view.

> He has been painfully slow in putting together a staff and a campaign apparatus to supplant the inexperienced Ohio aides on whom he has relied. The lack of organization has become a subject of open concern ... among leading Democratic party figures who see Glenn as an electable contrast to Kennedy and Mondale.[55]

Time is, of course, as precious a resource as favorable name recognition. Time is needed to acquire nonpersonal campaign resources—organiza-tion and money. An opinion was developing that Glenn had squandered too much of it by his reluctance to commit in 1982.

Shortly after the mini-convention, one of those "leading figures," a top official of the Democratic National Committee, described Glenn's strategic position. "It's a three-candidate race," he said.

It's not a two-candidate race. I'm not sure who the third candidate is. I think it is John Glenn. I don't think Hart can get it all together. He may have a future in another election, not this one. But John Glenn is already there. He is the kind of person people want for president—mature, serious, experienced, solid. I think he is the third force in the party. You want to know what I really think? I think that if you took six of the best professional party operatives—took them off the Kennedy and Mondale campaigns—they could make John Glenn the next president of the United States. But he is so badly staffed, it is astonishing.

The effect of Ted Kennedy's withdrawal was to make this judgment about organization and electability more widely circulated and more widely held. The scorekeepers began to move from a "right stuff" theme to a "right stuff, wrong staff" theme.

In late 1982 and early 1983, Glenn recruited a campaign staff. Bill White, on the combined strength of his long relationship with the senator and his mini-convention success, was made campaign chief of staff. Robert Keefe, "a long time Democratic operative with close ties to labor" [56] and a veteran of the Henry Jackson and Birch Bayh campaigns, became a high-level unpaid adviser. Greg Schneiders, a former Carter assistant, became press secretary. Joe Grandmaison, a McGovern organizer, became political director. Glenn's pollster, William Hamilton, was a Democratic political veteran, as was his media adviser, David Sawyer. Robert Farmer, a fund raiser for John Anderson, became his treasurer. By February, these top aides were supported by a staff of forty, which was scheduled to grow to ninety by April.

Media commentary, however, reflected continuing skepticism about the slow start. "The common perception in Washington," said the first major analysis of the staff, in February, "is that even at this premature stage of the race, Glenn is already at a disadvantage ... because of the slowness with which he is putting together his campaign organization." [57] An analysis one month later was entitled "Mondale Covering Bases in Crucial South: Glenn's Organization Trails His Popularity." [58] In April another "second look" was headlined "Glenn's Campaign Staff Off and Walking." [59]

In March a member of the Senate staff reported on the same slow adaptation to new circumstances in that quarter. "This office has issued only three press releases since the first of the year—one on El Salvador, one on [Disarmament Agency head Kenneth] Adelman, and one on the math-science bill," lamented the staffer.

But those are the three issues he's always been interested in. He's said nothing about the 10 percent withholding on interest—the biggest issue in Congress in terms of volume of mail. During all the publicity on EPA and Anne Burford, not a word from Senator Glenn. No press release on the subject. I know he doesn't like to issue a lot of press releases, and I admire him for that. But these are very hot issues. He has to become identified with more than three issues—foreign policy, defense policy, and research. The only issue he's strongly identified with is nuclear nonproliferation. I know patriotism is a strong part of his appeal. But he'll need more than that. Not too many people are going to vote on the basis of the future of the electric car. I'm not even sure what else he stands for.

At a time when the Senate office should have been cranked up to take advantage of the calm before the storm, there was strong evidence of business-as-usual in that important support group.

His new campaign aides, however, publicly defended the Glenn timetable on the grounds that it was not only correct but was being effectively implemented. In February White described the campaign as "on track with respect to the schedule we set forth." Schneiders said they were "a little ahead of schedule. I don't think we have to do things faster. There is a lot of time. . . . The senator has a clear idea of where we are and where we're going." Keefe echoed the Glenn line: "He came with a lot of built-in assets, especially greater favorable public recognition than the other candidates. That's something you can't buy." [60] In April, White said,

> I will acknowledge that we were not quite prepared for Ted Kennedy's withdrawal from the race. We were elevated into the spotlight and we weren't quite ready for that scrutiny. We were behind the curve. But we've made great strides. . . . The complaints about our organization may have been true before. But they are not true now.[61]

Springtime speculation centered on whether an organization so slow to develop, and thus so slow to work out the inevitable kinks, could ever catch up and perform adequately. "If, in September, Glenn's organization is up to speed," said an April observer, "the widespread complaints of this spring will be forgotten. If not, they are likely to be recalled as harbingers of political doom." [62] The success of his organization would become a pivotal test of Glenn's basic strategic decision about timing.

For anyone who had watched John Glenn over a period of time, the tardiness of his organizational effort was the visible symptom of two more basic candidate characteristics, each of which was rooted in his marine-to-astronaut experience and his public service preferences. For one thing, John Glenn, the self-reliant loner, had never been comfortable putting himself in the hands of others. He had been unseasonably late in declaring his Senate candidacies in 1970 and 1974 and in seeking professional help. For another thing, John Glenn had never been comfortable with other politicians, and his discomfort had been evident since his earliest experiences in Ohio. The net result was that he had not worked closely with other politicians and was not well acquainted within the fraternity of politicians. Now, having finally had to let go of the controls and put himself in the hands of others, these others were, necessarily, professional politicians whom he did not know.

He hedged against these uncertainties by placing the one person he did know and trust in the top spot. But Bill White did not know these professionals either. He was nationally inexperienced, and his inexperience was the object of considerable professional criticism. Moreover, the managerial style Glenn and White had worked out in the Senate office was inappropriate to a national campaign. Glenn had delegated copious authority to White, and White had administered so as to maximize the protection of his authority. Glenn's expressed belief, that it would be a mistake to run a presidential campaign with a Senate staff, was correct. Transferring his top Senate aide to the top of the campaign payroll was inconsistent with that judgment.

A year later, a veteran Senate staffer who had participated in the campaign described the adverse effects of these early organizational decisions.

> The campaign staff suffered from the same problems as the Senate staff. But the problem was compounded by the size of the campaign operation. In the Senate, you could use guerrilla warfare, touch a few bases, and find out what was going on. But the campaign operation was too big. There was no organization, no delegation, no flow of communication up and down the structure. Bill began by hiring weak people. He did not give people clear jobs to do. He ran the whole campaign out of his hip pocket. The senator gave him carte blanche. He delegated almost complete authority over the campaign to Bill. He could do whatever he wanted. Glenn wanted to be in on the major policy decisions. But he knew he would be on the road, far away, and that he had to delegate. He trusted Bill. He knew there was a potential problem, but he told me, "We're in a bind. I have no alternative." He didn't know the national politicians, didn't feel comfortable with them. Bill could have delegated authority the way Glenn had delegated to him. But Bill acted as though he was going to lose his job, when there was no way he was going to lose his job.

These organizational mistakes were made early and never got

straightened out. At the moment of choice, it seems, Glenn's career experiences left him without an acceptable alternative.

Another important characteristic of his new organization was also traceable to the candidate's lack of strong attachments to politicians. With the exception of Bill White, Glenn's campaign decision makers were strangers to their candidate. Not one of them had ever worked with Glenn in his office or in his previous campaigns. Conversely, all of the people who had worked with him in Ohio—his managers Steve Kovacik and Steve Avakian, his media adviser Bill Connell—were absent from the presidential effort. The professionals who did sign on had no past ties to Glenn, no personal loyalty to him, no special affection for him. Nor were they attracted to Glenn because of any distinct issue enthusiasms. They were attracted to Glenn because he looked like he might be a winner. There is nothing unusual about campaign professionals attaching themselves to a potential winner. But the proportion of "hired guns" to dedicated loyalists was lopsidedly high in the Glenn organization. By contrast, when Walter Mondale's campaign manager discussed his organization, he could say, "The biggest strength of our organization is the . . . depth of political pros that goes way beyond our payroll—people around the country Mondale met ten, fifteen, twenty years ago, able people we've worked with for years." [63] That is precisely what John Glenn did not have.

Given Glenn's characteristic aloofness from his staff, it was unlikely that this staff of strangers would turn into a staff of loyalists. On the other hand, not being a natural politician himself, he might be unduly swayed by their advice. It seems inherently risky to have a staff of hired guns exerting a great deal of influence over the campaign of a person they do not really know, especially a person whose unique combination of character and heroism is his major political asset, and for whom the presentation of a political persona is his greatest challenge.

STRATEGY

An organization is not an end in itself. It is a resource to be employed in the implementation of a nomination strategy. And the nomination strategy that began to develop in the Glenn campaign was one that pointed away from a strong organizational emphasis. The underlying premise of the campaign was the idea that John Glenn could defeat Ronald Reagan in the general election. "I'm happy to be there [in the middle of the road]," he said. "That's where most of the American people are, and that's what makes me electable. What elects presidents of the United States is the 71 percent in the middle." [64] The corollary was that, among the Democratic candidates, he was the most likely one—if not the only one—who was electable. Referring to "the activists at the convention," Glenn reflected,

> If that group is seeking someone they personally want, they would not necessarily choose me. If they are seeking someone they can generally support and who can win, they might choose me.[65]

Assuming, then, that Democrats wanted, more than anything else, to defeat Reagan, they would make the pragmatic decision and nominate Glenn.

It was a plausible argument—one around which an implementation strategy had to be constructed. Because the electability argument was essentially a general election argument, the main implementation task was to also make it a nominating election argument. This decision meant, at bottom, maintaining an emphasis on defeating Reagan and maintaining the belief that Glenn was a reasonable bet—if not the best bet—to do it. Mostly, however, it meant interpreting and selling Glenn's presumed general election strengths to Democratic caucus and primary voters. Those strengths were: first, his personal appeal based upon a blend of character and heroism and the traditional values embodied in that blend; second, his philosophical position as a centrist and a moderate; third, his political position as an independent, and one more oriented to the future than to the past. Long before the voters of America would be asked to match those strengths against Ronald Reagan, the voters of the Democratic party would be asked to match the same strengths against Walter Mondale and several other hopefuls. Glenn's strategists had to cope with the first problem—getting Glenn nominated—first.

If political scientists know anything about primary and caucus voters, it is that they are not a random sample of all voters. They are the party's activists—more knowledgeable, more connected to groups, more issue-oriented, better educated, more ideological, and less centrist than the rest of the party or than the general electorate.[66] They are motivated and committed. Candidates are incalculably aided in nomination politics if they can find or already have an identifiable core constituency from among these kinds of voters—a group of supporters with whom they have some common bond and who will, in turn, fight, bleed, and die for them. Within the Democratic party, George McGovern and the antiwar activists, Jimmy Carter and southerners, Hubert Humphrey and organized labor come to mind. To describe these primary constituencies is to call attention to a serious political problem for Glenn. He had never been a cultivator of such constituencies.

Indeed, all of Glenn's strengths had propelled him in the opposite direction. He was aloof in dealing with politicians. His centrism left him ideologically vague. His independence signaled unreliability. Public service politics conflicted with endorsement politics. A longtime Ohio observer said, "He won't go out of his way to kiss anyone's ass for an endorsement." [67] And a veteran staffer said that while he will endorse other politicians, he does not like to do it. "He never went in and put his heaviest support behind his endorsement; and therefore, he doesn't really believe other people will stand behind their endorsement. He sees them as perfunctory." In cases where he absolutely had to have endorsements—from Ohio politicians, for example, he was notoriously slow to acknowledge the need and ask for them.[68] He did not see politics in terms of wooing primary constituencies, and he was neither very enthusiastic nor very skilled at the constituency-building efforts that were needed.

The result was that Glenn's relations remained lukewarm with the activists in basic Democratic constituencies. It was Glenn's familiar Ohio dilemma of learning to live with the Democratic party, but in a new setting. In the case of organized labor, he had not been close to the unions in Ohio and had voted against their highly prized common site picketing bill in Washington. Labor leaders strongly opposed him as vice president in 1976.[69] The AFL-CIO was not only planning to endorse Walter Mondale (a historic first) but also they were planning to rush this endorsement into the fall to give a maximum push to his campaign. "No living American politician has spent more hours in union halls than Walter Mondale," explained David Broder.[70]

In the case of the Jewish community, Glenn had voted to sell F-15 airplanes to Saudi Arabia and Egypt in 1978 and had suggested negotiations with the Palestine Liberation Organization (PLO). Reporters wrote, "Many U.S. supporters of a strong Israel do not consider him to be among their ranks"; he has "a reputation as no friend of Israel"; and "he has a significant Jewish problem." [71] In July *Newsweek* said, "Glenn hasn't done nearly as well as Mondale with one important group of contributors: Jewish supporters of Israel." [72]

In the case of the black community, an Ohio leader noted that it "has no negative opinion of Glenn but no real positive opinion either." [73] In the case of women's groups, when Glenn spoke to the National Organization for Women (NOW) convention, it was reported that he was "the only candidate who damaged himself. The delegates . . . booed and hooted disapproval when he said, 'I think we all loafed on ERA.' " [74] In the case of environmentalists, "He doesn't have a record of sensitivity to environmental issues," said a staffer.

His daughter . . . came in one day and said, "If I'm going to make speeches, I'd better know what his positions are. Can you give me all the things he's said on the environment?" I gave her the material. A couple of days later, she came back and asked, "Is this all there is?" I said "yes." She said, "It isn't much." I said, "Don't talk to me, talk to pop."

In all of these cases Glenn was supportive of the groups' major positions. But in every case, the groups did not feel an emotional attachment on his part. Regarding the AFL-CIO, one journalist commented, "In a world where personal loyalties are highly valued, many labor activists said they have felt only an arm's length relationship with Glenn." [75] In the words of a union leader, "When John Glenn spoke to the AFL-CIO Council . . . we were in the dregs of a depression. But he showed no emotion or real passion." [76] A Jewish leader commented, "We just don't trust him. He votes OK on aid to Israel almost all the time, but we know—we just know—that his heart isn't in the right place." [77] The black leader from Ohio said, "Glenn has voted right on most of the issues, but Metzenbaum is an advocate; he takes leadership on our issues." [78] A feminist leader said of his ERA comment, "Sure the remark hurt him. It showed a certain lack of sensitivity." [79] For the environmentalists, his slowness in coming to grips with the problem of acid rain in New Hampshire was the result of his Ohio attachment to smokestack industries. "It's the new litmus test up here. And so far Glenn hasn't passed it," said one activist in May.[80] And later, when Glenn presented a new, presidentially oriented plan, another leader noted, "Oh, he's come a long way on that. It's not quite the position we'd like, but. . . ." [81]

Glenn often found himself on the defensive, explaining a record that was, in fact, extremely supportive of these various constituencies. He went to New York to discuss his record on Israel. Of his speech there, *Newsweek* recorded, "There was little new in what Glenn said . . . nor were Glenn's restated positions markedly different from those of the other Democratic contenders." [82] It did not help. A Glenn staffer recalled later,

> I'd go out to speak to Jewish groups, and everyone there would have had breakfast or lunch or dinner with Walter Mondale more than once. But they didn't know Glenn. If you put Mondale and Glenn's positions side by side on issues that matter to Jewish groups, they aren't very different. But we had never given them the kind of access Mondale had.

It is less a matter of voting record than a matter of wave length, of feeling, of a symbolic commitment to a group or a cause, of an advocacy style. It is, said Walter Mondale, "a subtle thing, but who, emotionally, is most committed in his heart and in his soul . . . not just being correct on an issue, but bleeding." [83] The creation of such emotional bonds is not naturally a part of John Glenn's repertoire or a part of his public service politics.

In May 1982 I listened to a discussion the senator had with his foreign policy advisers on the upcoming nuclear freeze resolution. The resolution was a matter of intense concern to a very active group of Democrats, so much so that Senator Cranston's presidential candidacy was being floated largely on the appeal of the freeze idea and the effort of freeze supporters. It was a prototypical primary election issue, and it brought forth an instructive John Glenn reaction. He could not give the "freezeniks" the response they wanted. He was generally supportive but he could not commit any emotion to the freeze idea.

"Will you vote for the freeze?" asked an aide. "In committee or on the floor?" inquired the senator. And he continued,

> On the floor, if it came down to it or nothing I would probably vote for it, even if it's just like shooting paper airplanes into the Grand Canyon. It won't accomplish a darn thing. That's what bothers me about the freeze. Every time I get into a discussion—we had one the other night among those of us who have different [arms control] plans—all the talk is about perception, not results. All the others talked about was public opinion—what the people would accept. No one talked about what it would accomplish. It was all perception, nothing else.

"Isn't that pretty depressing?" asked a second staffer. "It's darn depressing," replied Glenn,

> It's just political—pfffft—pop! If I vote for it, it will be because I want to show concern for the problem. But I've been concerned about the problem for six years. What we need are results. . . . I don't know whether I can vote for it in committee or not.

The first staffer said, "Anyone who votes against it will carry a lot of heavy political baggage." The "baggage" comment was the only hint of presidential campaign considerations in a one-hour discussion of this sensitive political issue. Later that week, Glenn voted for the nuclear freeze resolution in committee, but his inability to bring an intense commitment to the vote and his uneasiness about taking symbolic—or "just political"—action exemplified his difficulty with primary constituencies.

When he tried to explain his difficulty, he often missed the mark. "I don't always get the buzz words right for the audience," he said when explaining the adverse reaction he got from saying "man and wife" in a press conference. Or, "The credit business comes back to haunt me," he said in explaining a problem with the NAACP (National Association for the Advancement of Colored People).

> I'll stack my civil rights record up against anyone else's in the Congress. But when I went to talk to the NAACP, they don't know my record. They had no idea what I'd done. These other senators, who had issued forty press releases on what they had done, get all the credit. I didn't.[84]

Considering that his voting record gave him a 1975-1982 NAACP support score of 80 percent, compared to 82 percent for Hart, 84 percent for Cranston, and 88 percent for Mondale, it was an understandable complaint.[85] But the problem was not a matter of buzz words or public relations. It was a matter of advocacy in domestic politics and a matter of responding to intensities in dealing with domestic constituencies. Walter Mondale could go to black audiences and say, "We were together in every single fight. . . . I was involved emotionally. . . . I was perhaps the key person—intensely emotionally involved." [86] Glenn could not do that. In politics, intensity of support for primary constituencies gets returned in proportionate degrees of support at election time. In that kind of exchange, John Glenn started well behind most of his Democratic rivals.

A second manifestation of Glenn's constituency problem lay in his model of what a winning primary campaign would look like. The model he worked from was his Ohio campaigns. He had, after all, won three victories there—one of which was a primary campaign. But Glenn, we have seen, did not distinguish between the two types of campaigns. He worked hard at cultivating rank-and-file Democratic party politicians between the 1970 and 1974 primaries, but he did not pursue top party leaders or activists in various primary constituencies. He was opposed by top party people and by organized labor in 1974, but he found he did not need them. Glenn recalled, "In the places where the organization leaders opposed me, I went into the union halls and talked directly to the rank and file. And that's where I got my best vote." When I asked his 1974 campaign manager to describe Glenn's 1974 primary election supporters, he answered,

> I hate to say this, but it's the truth—the people. He could go around the party organization and the labor unions and establish contact directly with the ordinary voter. He had no base whatsoever, and not anywhere, within the party organization.

His 1980 campaign manager said of his support in that contest, "Remember, he has a rural background and had no early experience with labor and not a lot of involvement with liberal causes. The independent voters identify with him strongly." [87]

In Ohio Glenn's perceived primary election support was never well differentiated from his general election support. Both came from "across the board," "the rank and file," "the people," "independent voters." In both contexts, he ran a campaign that appealed to the broadest, most undifferentiated statewide constituency. He tended to see his political constituency as coterminous with his hero's constituency—that is to say, everybody. It was the kind of constituency perception that was most hospitable to a public service politics campaign—one that emphasized consensual themes and community values rather than conflictual themes and group interests. His November 1982 planning memo called similarly for "a broad-based and all-inclusive coalition of Democratic party elements." Its weakness lay in its lack of definition of any "primary constituency." Unless his new advisers intervened forcefully to convince him otherwise, he would predictably follow the Ohio model in his presidential campaign.

His newly minted advisers did intervene, but in ways that totally reinforced Glenn's Ohio-based notions of constituency politics. A memorandum from his new press secretary conceptualized Glenn's potential base of support as "the constituency of the whole." [88] Glenn could win the nomination, Greg Schneiders argued, by reaching beyond the special-interest primary constituencies to win the support of the broad mass of Democrats, those more attuned to Glenn's concerns for "the greatest good of the greatest number" or "the common good" than for the particular group-oriented issues. The constituency of the whole would be the national equivalent of "the rank and file" or "the people" that brought him victory in Ohio. It would make no distinction between a primary election and a general election. It would allow Glenn to press his personal appeal without coddling politicians and activists. It would allow him to pursue his ideological centrism because that was precisely where the constituency of the whole was located. And he could pursue his independence because that quality would be highly valued by people without narrow interests to protect. Given Glenn's lack of rapport with the party's primary constituencies, the memo made a virtue out of a necessity. Not surprisingly, Glenn approved wholeheartedly of this conceptual underpinning for his nomination campaign. In the words of one dismayed Senate staffer, "He swallowed the argument, hook, line, and sinker. He could be the hero and avoid the dirty political work."

A corollary of the constituency of the whole was the idea of "the expanded electorate." If it is true that the normal caucus and primary voters are ideological, partisan, and activist, then a substantial segment of Glenn's constituency of the whole would have to come from people who did not normally participate—the "floating electorate" or "weak Democrats" or "middle Democrats" or "new blood" or "new voters" or "independents." He would have to do something to alter the normal turnout patterns and bring these people into the arena. He would have to locate and motivate an expanded electorate—two problems that puzzled his campaigners from beginning to end.

The major strategic consequence of the idea of the constituency of the whole and the expanded electorate was to cast the campaign as more of a wholesale operation than a retail operation, and more of a nationwide campaign than a selective state-based campaign. Recent history had emphasized the lesson that, as formulated by one who knew,

> running for president is like running for the city council. It's retail politics, not wholesale politics, not TV politics. Running for president now is the business of getting the delegates to caucuses, to conventions, and getting the votes in wards and precincts and districts. And get that early enough to become the front-runner or near the front-runner.[89]

The conception being developed by the Glenn campaigners, however, turned away from this approach, turned away from retail organization and toward the media. And, insofar as organization remained necessary, they projected a broad, long-range organizational effort rather than one tightly focused on the earliest caucus and primary states. Accordingly, the campaign's political director began setting up field offices in thirty states and talking about "the unique *national* nature" of the campaign.[90] Glenn, too, spoke enthusiastically of his "national campaign."

The idea of a national campaign had been fundamental to planning from the beginning. It was a premise of Bill White's original game plan that "the operation must always be national in scope, and we should establish a campaign presence in every state." A reporter who examined the document in February headlined his story accordingly: "A Campaign Blueprint for 1984: Sen. Glenn to Compete in All 50 States as Middle Roader." [91] The original memo did, however, prescribe certain "regional efforts within a national campaign" by "targeting" twelve states for early special effort. They included Iowa on February 20 and New Hampshire on February 28. They also included the Super Tuesday (March 13) states of Florida, Alabama, Georgia, and Mississippi, as well as Texas on May 5th.

It is a particularly striking feature of the memo that it devotes more discussion and pins more hopes on the southern states in March than on

Iowa and New Hampshire in February. It recognizes that Iowa and New Hampshire go first, and it gives them "high priority for obvious reasons." But it contains no supporting analysis—only a vague assumption that all will be well there; for example, "Your base is in the Midwest." On the other hand, the memo is full of phrases such as, "your strength in the South and West," "your anticipated strength in the South," your "potential to do well in the South and West," "your strategies in the South and West," "your appeal in the South and West," and warnings such as, "If you do not run well in the South and West, you do not have much of a chance." "Anything that adversely affects you in the South or West will deny you the opportunity to make a good early showing." In sum, a necessary level of success in the first two states in February is taken for granted; and the memo clearly points toward take-off victories in the southern states on Super Tuesday.

Later accounts suggest that the early emphasis on March 13 persisted. One reporter wrote that Glenn was focusing on "the second Tuesday in March," as the time when "I tend to think I would do very well." [92] Another said Glenn's pollster concurred that "the Ohioan's chances next year rest with such 'broad participation' events as the Southern primaries." [93] A third reported that Glenn's staffers were playing "war games" on the computer and that "their scenario shows Glenn bursting ahead of Mondale in early May." [94] That had been White's "ideal scenario," too. In none of these accounts was there any evidence of special concern for what might happen before Super Tuesday.

The Glenn people felt confident in pointing toward Super Tuesday because they thought of the campaign more in holistic than segmented terms. And it was the media that would make it so. Schneiders's metaphor was that candidates who built their support out of activist constituencies would be swept away by Glenn. As he put it,

> Mondale's strategy is an organizational, constituency-based strategy. In the Glenn campaign, we place a premium on communication that goes directly to the voters. While not ignoring organization, it is possible that organization structure will turn out to be like sand castles on a beach when a tidal wave comes in.[95]

The wholesale, national tidal wave was to be created by the media. "The success or failure of the campaign," Schneiders said later, "depends on communicating the message on television." [96] The media, it seemed, would put all states on an equal footing. Strategy could be mapped without excessive regard for quick starts or preemptive momentum.

Glenn seemed as willing to accept the media emphasis as he was the constituency of the whole. "People buy almost everything they need through television," he said. "They're not going to break that pattern when it comes to electing their leaders." [97] His organizers planned to take advantage of the premiere of the movie *The Right Stuff*, on October 16, to launch their national media campaign with a five-minute ad the night before. Their grand hope was to prepare an ad that would encourage voters to link "Glenn's past heroism to his future leadership potential. They planned to transform the common emotions of America's finest moment into a common willingness to challenge the future. They planned to suggest that Glenn should lead the effort by associating him with John Kennedy." [98] "Mondale will get all these endorsements," said one Glenn strategist,"—the AFL-CIO, the teacher's union—and then the movie's going to open and everyone's going to forget about the endorsements." [99] It would be symbolic politics of the most abstract sort, as a substitute for the symbolic politics of everyday political routines.

Would the media impulse generate a tidal wave? Both the constituency of the whole and the sand castles concept ran counter to history and wisdom. They bespoke a highly experimental campaign. Whether the experiment would be run for John Glenn's benefit or at John Glenn's expense remained to be seen.

MOMENTUM

The Glenn campaigners had adopted a general election strategy to implement their general election assumption—that John Glenn could defeat Ronald Reagan. That was the central strategic decision of the campaign's second stage. The unanswered question was whether the general election strategy would be a winning strategy in the primary election context. For the final answer, they would have to wait for the campaign-with-voters. And the playing out of their plans for a fifty-state, media-oriented, Super Tuesday-powered campaign would proceed in due time. Meanwhile, in the spring and summer of 1983, the senator from Ohio enjoyed momentum in the campaign-without-voters. From the horse-race polls, one could, indeed, tease out the promise of ultimate success in the general election and primary election contexts.

From December 1982 through September 1983, in twenty-nine separate trial heats, posed by five different national polling organizations, John Glenn ran ahead of Reagan eighteen times. And in their matchups, Glenn did better against Reagan than Mondale did in twenty-two cases.[100] "The candidate we were most fearful of was John Glenn, who ran strongest against the president head-to-head," the Reagan-Bush campaign director said later.[101] Some state polls reported similar summertime results.[102] In July the *Los Angeles Times* said,

The claim made by Glenn's strategists that he would be the most easily elected Democratic contender is one of the underpinnings of his candidacy. For the time being, at least, the *Times* poll, as well as other recent surveys, tends to lend credence to that assertion.[103]

However removed these results might be from nomination reality, they were campaign reality. As such they had consequences.

One apparent consequence was the concomitant rise of Glenn in his head-to-head trial heats with Mondale in polls among Democrats. In May *Newsweek* summarized: "The big news was the series of opinion polls that showed Glenn dramatically closing the gap between himself and Mondale—and actually beating him by two percentage points in the LAT [*Los Angeles Times*] sampling."[104] Between March and May the gap between them in the Gallup poll narrowed from 32 percent to 13 percent to 29 percent to 23 percent.[105] From February to June the gap in the CBS-*New York Times* poll narrowed from 34 percent to 9 percent to 34 percent to 32 percent.[106] "By mid-May," wrote one observer, "the fashionable thought in Washington was that the nomination was Glenn's, that Mondale was finished."[107] The July Harris poll also recorded Mondale and Glenn virtually tied at 48 percent to 46 percent.[108] From the perspective of Mondale's campaign manager, "The whole point of that period was John Glenn.... He seemed to be sailing."[109] In August, at the National Governors' Association meeting, one prominent reporter found "a developing trend toward Glenn, particularly among southern, midwestern and western Democrats."[110]

In the threshold state of Iowa, Mondale's lead over Glenn slipped from 55 percent to 17 percent in March to 45 percent to 30 percent in July.[111] In the pivotal state of New Hampshire one poll showed that Glenn had narrowed a twenty-two-point gap in March to a thirteen-point gap in August among likely primary voters.[112] A July polltaker for Mondale showed Glenn in a virtual tie among that same group.[113] And in a July poll in nine southern states, the area where Glenn needed special strength, he *led* Mondale 39 percent to 33 percent.[114] Glenn's own August view was, "If you look at the polls together, there's been almost a straight line up. There's been a steady movement."[115] Between July and September he raised $1.6 million compared to Mondale's $1.2 million.[116] John Glenn clearly had summertime momentum. None of the other candidates was registering any movement during this period.[117] And there was a distinct softness about the front-runner's support that could be exploited.

A July "state of the race" survey among state Democratic leaders by *National Journal* found plenty of evidence among party professionals for the connection between the electability premise and Glenn's rise within his party. That is to say, the general election argument seemed to be working for the primary context as well. The summary concluded, "Glenn is rapidly gaining . . . and has already stolen a share of the lead." It quoted state leaders: "Glenn is gaining because of the feeling he can beat Reagan"; "the distinct sense around the state is that Glenn can beat Reagan and that Mondale can't"; "John Glenn is the leading candidate at this time because the Democrats are looking for someone who is electable, who can beat Reagan." The analysis concludes with a comment by a party leader who said exactly what the Glenn people wanted to hear.

> If the state chairmen have anything to do with it, John Glenn is going to be the Democratic candidate. He's embraced by people wherever he goes, he's a middle of the roader, he's very credible, he's an American hero and his organization is a lot better than reported. You can see how he's doing by his rise in the polls—as a matter of fact, he's had to hold back. In my judgment, he's the only guy in our party who can beat Reagan. We want to win the war, not just the battles.[118]

The electability argument was especially appealing to party professionals, for whom winning was occupationally paramount.

But it seemed, during the summer, to be reverberating elsewhere in the party as well. At the National Education Association (NEA) convention in July, a reporter wrote, "The teachers' fervent desire to get rid of Reagan has made the question of 'winnability' especially important." The reporter continued, "Glenn's recent advances in the polls got the delegates' attention, and his friendly manner and enthusiastic delivery of his message won their praise."[119] In an August article entitled "Electability Issue Gives Glenn Boost" one scorekeeper traveling with him commented, "At political events from Michigan to Mississippi to Maine where Glenn has appeared this summer, many of his supporters said they were drawn to him because they were anxious to see Reagan beaten and believed Glenn had the best chance in the general election."[120] A mid-September *Newsweek* poll of "top Democratic officials and party leaders" found that 51 percent believed Glenn was "most likely" to defeat Reagan—34 percent for Mondale.[121]

Glenn believed that the polls matching him against Reagan were, in fact, contributing to his rise.[122] But he professed some reluctance to use the argument himself. "Polls are so volatile," he said, "I hate to lean everything on polls. I hate to have the case rely solely on polls. But so long as they run that way, perhaps I should be touting that more."[123] He was correct on both counts. An argument grounded in polls taken ten months before anyone cast a ballot was an immensely vulnerable argument—vulnerable to a shift in the polls. Electability is a self-fulfilling prophecy; without constant reconfirmation, it is a self-destructing prophecy. For the time being, however, electability was a consequential argument for his campaign. His professed reluctance to buttress it with poll data was disingenuous—another sign of his reluctance to admit to routine political tactics. Two weeks earlier he had told the Democratic National Committee, "I'm the Democrat who has consistently run better against Ronald Reagan than anyone else." [124] So long as others used it, he did not have to. But when he felt it necessary to make the argument himself, he was quite prepared to do so.

In a July interview, Glenn was markedly upbeat. He talked about the presidency as if he could picture himself in the job. "He really wants it and he really thinks he is going to win," said a staffer. "He believes now that it is just as likely to come to him as to any of the others in the race." To the inquiry, "How's it going?" the senator replied, "Very well. We're moving up steadily."

> I suppose I would rather have saved what we are doing now for next November, so we could move up and carry the momentum right on into the primaries. Right now, Mondale is here (Glenn waving both hands, on different levels) and we're here just below him. Since we're up here, we've got to make sure we don't drop down. We've got to hold our position till the primaries and then move up. We can do it. But we have to beware of people getting candidate fatigue. They get tired of seeing the same candidates and then they begin to look around and say, "Aren't there some other people around here we could consider?". . . We're gaining just the way we planned, except that we're doing it a little quicker than we had hoped. But I'm pleased. The campaign is going well.

He talked about the ideal qualifications of a vice president and how the circumstances of the convention would probably force him to compromise in making his choice. He joked about the desirability of a presidential yacht as a setting for political persuasion. It was a time of maximum momentum and a time of maximum hope.

Students of polling during campaigns-without-voters know that their findings are highly unstable. "In measuring voter opinion on candidates," said Peter Hart, "a month is equivalent to a lifetime, and six months is an eternity." Surveys taken far in advance of the actual voting produce findings that are "etched in wet sand on the water's edge; they are as firmly fixed as the size of the next wave." [125] In his superb study of momentum during the formal stage of presidential nomination politics,

Larry Bartels developed an explanation of voter behavior that seems applicable to the campaign-without-voters as well.[126] And, as such, it helps us to understand John Glenn's position in the summer of 1983.

Bartels suggests that a bandwagon effect exists during the earliest caucuses and primaries, but that this effect dies out fairly quickly thereafter. This earliest period, he argues, is not very well structured in terms of candidate positions and voter information. With preferences not well developed, therefore, a substantial number of voters support the person they expect to win. And out of those votes based on expectations can come the phenomenon of momentum. Because the media has tremendous influence over expectations, it also influences early momentum. As the nomination process continues, however, voters take in more information, develop their preferences, vote their preferences, and project their preferred candidate as the likely winner. Along with this change comes decreased emphasis on diffuse rationales, such as "leadership" or "good man," and an increase in more concrete rationales, such as political persona or candidate positions. Expectations and momentum decline in their effect.

In Bartels's analysis, the beneficiaries of momentum are little-known candidates with a large up-side potential. Nonetheless, the Glenn case suggests that an analogous sequence of surge and decline took place during his campaign-without-voters. During the summer of 1983, he seems to have been the beneficiary of a considerable "bandwagon" effect, as politicians and Democrats who were polled "voted" for a person they thought would win. In Glenn's case these opinions were grounded primarily in existing name recognition. In the absence of other knowledge, rationales tended to be vague: "he's a hero" and "he's electable." In this unstructured context—with information scarce, with Glenn's political persona undefined, and with voter preferences undeveloped—Glenn achieved his summertime momentum. But to the degree that Bartels's arguments are applicable, Glenn's early voter support was highly unstable—at best fragile and at worst temporary. Name recognition bestows a big initial advantage. But it is a quickly perishable one, and vague rationales like heroism and electability perish with it. Glenn's momentum provided hope, but it was an unreliable base on which to build. It would require much positive reinforcement.

As summer ended, media handicappers of the horse race placed Glenn in a close second-place position and, in tandem with Mondale, in a top tier well removed from the pack. "Mondale and Glenn are far ahead of the others in fund raising, public opinion polls and name recognition. Both sides are girding for a long head-to-head struggle they say might not be settled till the convention."[127] Or, "Right on Mondale's heels, in a seven-way race that already seems to have narrowed to a clear Top Two is a genuine American hero. . . . [And] barring unlikely turnabouts, the Mondale-Glenn contest remains virtually the only game in town." [128] This media judgment won for Glenn his fundamental strategic objective—to be the alternative to Mondale. But that achievement meant that a new level of scrutiny—more intense and more broadly based—lay ahead for both candidates.

For Glenn the new level of scrutiny only added urgency to the task of reinforcing his support. Two prominent scorekeepers posed it this way: that Glenn had "to define himself . . . politically" and that he had "to prove that he can take the heat of a presidential campaign." [129] His advisers agreed. "We see the post-Labor Day period as a time of direct communication, in which John Glenn begins to fill in the blanks for the average voter," said one.[130] And another commented, "We've passed through the phase where the media want to know what kind of guy he is. Now they want to know what's his vision for the future and what kind of president he'll make." These tests were severe because they confronted him anew with the central problem of his political career— the development of a winning political persona. Developing that persona was the essential task that had to be completed before the hope of summer could be converted into success when the campaign-without-voters ended.

NOTES

1. George Embrey "Keynoter Glenn Busily Preparing National Address," *Columbus Dispatch*, July 12, 1976.
2. John Kessel, *Presidential Campaign Politics* (Homewood, Ill.: Dorsey Press, 1980), chaps. 2 and 3.
3. On the structure of competition, see Kessel, *Presidential Campaign Politics*; and John Aldrich, *Before the Convention* (Chicago: University of Chicago, 1980). On media scorekeeping, see James David Barber, ed., *The Race for the Presidency* (New York: Prentice-Hall, 1978); and Nelson Polsby, *Consequences of Party Reform* (New York: Oxford, 1983).
4. Rhodes Cook, "In '88 Context, It's What's Up Front That Counts," *Congressional Quarterly Weekly Report*, August 23, 1986.
5. Jon Weist, "Glenn Hits President on Education," *The Shorthorn*, University of Texas at Arlington, September 21, 1982.
6. Missie Parker-O'Toole, "Sen. Glenn Plans Candidacy Committee," *Morristown (Tennessee) Citizen Tribune*, September 19, 1982; Rick Mann, "Glenn Visits Mesquite to Boost John Bryant," *Mesquite (Texas) Daily News*, October 13, 1982.
7. *Nashville Tennessean*, September 19, 1982.
8. *Houston Chronicle*, October 14, 1982; Mike Flanigan, "Country Deserves

Better, Glenn Says of Reagan," *Tulsa World,* October 9, 1982; Steve Nussbaum, "Glenn Campaigns at UTA," *Arlington Daily News,* September 19, 1982; Ron Poppenhagen, "John Glenn Says Reagan Tarnishes 'America's Promise,'" *Southern Illinoisan,* October 3, 1982.

9. Linda Eardley, "Glenn Aids Young, Mrs. Woods, and Maybe His Own Candidacy," *St. Louis Post Dispatch,* September 11, 1982.

10. James Reston, "John Glenn a Mixture of Old Values and New Technology," *Akron Beacon Journal,* October 7, 1982.

11. Gallup Poll, April 23-26, 1982. For contrast, Jimmy Carter and Ted Kennedy were tied for first at 98 percent, Mondale was next at 90 percent, Alan Cranston 35 percent, Gary Hart 21 percent, *Dallas Morning News,* September 18, 1982; also, notes 3, 4, 6, 7, 8 *supra.*

12. Hugh Sidey, "John Glenn Figures to Be Party's Best Best for '84," *Washington Star,* January 18, 1981; William Safire, "Here's an Early Look at 1984 Presidential Hopefuls," *New York Times,* March 28, 1981; George Will, "John Glenn: The Right Kind of Democrat," *Washington Post,* February 18, 1982; Rowland Evans and Robert Novak, "Looking Over John Glenn," *Washington Post,* May 3, 1982; Morton Kondracke, "John Glenn's Right Stuff," *New Republic,* May 26, 1982; David McCullough, "Can John Glenn Be President?" *Parade Magazine,* June 13, 1982; Mark Shields, "Is John Glenn Too Moderate?" *Washington Post,* June 18, 1982; Tom Wicker, "No Parades Needed," *New York Times,* August 8, 1982; James Gannon, "A Candidate Tailor Made to Oppose Ronald Reagan," *Des Moines Register,* August 8, 1982; Michael Barone, "John Glenn: Always Moving Up," *Washington Post,* September 6, 1983; Carl Leubsdorf, "Political Liftoff," *Dallas Morning News,* October 11, 1982; Norman Miller, "John Glenn: Impressions of a Presidential Aspirant," *Wall Street Journal,* October 14, 1982; Reston, "John Glenn a Mixture."

13. Eugene Kennedy, "John Glenn's Presidential Countdown," *New York Times Magazine,* October 11, 1981.

14. Weist, "Glenn Hits President on Education."

15. Parker-O'Toole, "Senator Glenn Plans."; Harold Lynch, "Glenn Eyes Race for President," *Clarksville (Tennessee) Leaf Chronicle,* September 19, 1982; Bob Dunnavant, "Glenn Speaks at Huntsville Fund-Raiser," *Birmingham Post-Herald,* October 16, 1982; Poppenhagen, "John Glenn Says."

16. A public expression of this view will be found in "Meet the Press" transcript, June 27, 1982, 5-6.

17. "House-Hunting with Howard Baker," *Washington Post Weekly Edition,* March 11, 1985; Nelson Polsby, "The Iowa Caucuses in a Front-Loaded System, A Few Historical Lessons" (Unpublished manuscript, February 2, 1988).

18. Leubsdorf, "Political Liftoff."

19. Kondracke, "John Glenn's Right Stuff."

20. Evans and Novak, "Looking Over John Glenn"; Wicker, "No Parades Needed"; Will, "John Glenn: The Right Kind."; Shields, "Is John Glenn Too Moderate?"; Kondracke, "John Glenn's Right Stuff"; "The Right Stuff for '84," *Newsweek,* March 1, 1982.

21. Reston, "John Glenn a Mixture."

22. Gannon, "A Candidate."

23. Jack Germond and Jules Witcover, "An Astronaut in the White House?" *Washingtonian,* February 1982.

24. Lars Erik Nelson, "Glenn Asset Is Solid Hold on Political Middle Road," as

carried in *Warren (Ohio) Tribune Chronicle,* August 22, 1982.

25. Dom Bonafede, "Only 29 Months to Go and Democrats Already in Line for 1984 Nomination," *National Journal,* June 5, 1982.

26. *Chicago Tribune,* May 14, 1981.

27. Brian Usher, "Eyes Up the Presidency," *Akron Beacon Journal,* August 9, 1981. On October 28, 1983, Rostenkowski and almost all the white party leaders of Illinois endorsed Walter Mondale for president. Larry Green, "Chicago Democratic Leaders Endorse Mondale," *Los Angeles Times,* October 29, 1982; *Washington Post,* October 29, 1982, January 5, 1984.

28. Kay Speed, "Roll Back Tax Cuts to Reduce Deficit, John Glenn Says," *Arkansas Democrat,* March 6, 1982; Jerry Dean, "Glenn Fears Effects of Budget Deficits, Says 'People Scared,' " *Arkansas Gazette,* March 6, 1982.

29. It was not a trivial breakdown. On November 24, Larry Kirwan became director of the Mondale campaign in western New York. A few months later he became state chairman of the New York Democratic party—a position he was to hold for seven years. See Michael Clements, "Monroe County Democratic Leaders Siding With Mondale: Glenn Is Running Second But Some Say He Lacks Momentum," *Rochester Democrat and Chronicle,* November 26, 1982.

30. Adam Clymer, "Democratic Hopefuls to Meet in Philadelphia," *New York Times,* June 18, 1982.

31. Judith Miller, "Breakfast Stir: Glenn on Social Security," *New York Times,* August 13, 1982; Albert Hunt, "John Glenn's Chances for the Nomination," *Wall Street Journal,* December 28, 1982; "Washington Wire," *Wall Street Journal,* December 3, 1982.

32. Associated Press Report, June 16, 1982. The advisory group idea eventually collapsed.

33. See David Maraniss, "Tracing the Roots of Gary Hart's Ideas," *Washington Post Weekly Edition,* April 30, 1984.

34. Fred Barnes, "Crown Prince 'Teddy' Holds the Spotlight," *Baltimore Sun,* June 28, 1982.

35. Larry Eichel, "Democrats Look at the '82 Lineup for an '84 Winner," *Philadelphia Inquirer,* June 26, 1982.

36. David Broder, "Democratic Hopefuls Take Turns Venting Wrath on Reaganomics," *Washington Post,* June 26, 1982.

37. "Happy Days—Here Again? " *Newsweek,* July 5, 1982.

38. Martin Schram and Paul Taylor, "Of First Five Would-Be Presidents, Only Mondale Wows the Convention," *Washington Post,* June 26, 1982.

39. Transcript, "Meet the Press," June 27, 1982, 5.

40. Gregg Ochoa, "Glenn Rips GOP at Ford Rally," *Dexter (Missouri) Daily Statesman,* September 13, 1982; Lee Roop, "Glenn Mixes Politics, Nostalgia at Democratic Fund-Raiser Here," *Huntsville (Alabama) Times,* September 25, 1982; Marilyn Duck, "Glenn Ponders Race," *Tulsa Tribune,* October 8, 1982.

41. David Hess, "Presidential Hopefuls Sowing for '84 Harvest," *Charlotte Observer,* September 7, 1982.

42. For example, "Glenn, with his astronaut past and forthright presence," in Martin Schram, "Democratic 'Candidates' Show Their Stuff," *Washington Post,* June 27, 1982; "The senator sounded like an astronaut again," in Francis Clines, "Rivals Line Up Trailers for 1984 Spot," *New York Times,* June 25, 1982; "Glenn whose fame still comes mainly from the trail in space he once blazed," in Martin Schram, "Conference Gave Democrats Lift, But

Uncertainties Still Dog Them," *Washington Post*, June 30, 1982.

43. Transcript, "Meet the Press," June 27, 1982, 6.
44. Adam Clymer, "Poll Says Kennedy Still Has Big Lead: Survey of Democrats Puts Him Ahead of Mondale," *New York Times*, July 18, 1982.
45. Jack Germond and Jules Witcover, "Glenn Is Moving Up in Democratic Polls," *Cincinnati Enquirer*, November 18, 1982; Robert Healy, "Glenn Has Strong Look for '84," *Boston Globe*, November 17, 1982.
46. "Trial Heats: The Public Rates the 1984 Presidential Hopefuls," *National Journal*, February 12, 1983.
47. David Broder, "Rivals in Party Scramble to Fill 'Kennedy Gap,' " *Washington Post*, December 2, 1982.
48. Ibid.
49. Albert Hunt, "Kennedy Exit From '84 Presidential Race Opens Way for a Democratic Free-for-All," *Wall Street Journal*, December 2, 1982.
50. *Newsweek*, January 3, 1983.
51. Jonathan Moore, ed., *Campaign for President: The Managers Look at '84* (Dover, Mass.: Auburn Press, 1986), 67.
52. On the media, see Henry Brady, "Is Iowa News? " (Unpublished manuscript, February 8, 1988).
53. Jack Germond and Jules Witcover, *Wake Us When It's Over* (New York: Macmillan, 1985), 113.
54. Kondracke, "John Glenn's Right Stuff."
55. Leubsdorf, "Political Liftoff."
56. David Broder, "Labor Saving," *Washington Post Weekly Edition*, September 7, 1987.
57. Dom Bonafede, "Glenn Counts on Slow Pace and Strong Finish to Win Race for Nomination," *National Journal*, February 12, 1983. See also *Newsweek*, December 13, 1982.
58. *Washington Post*, March 15, 1983.
59. Martin Schram, "Glenn's Campaign Staff Off and Walking," *Washington Post*, April 26, 1983.
60. All these comments are in Bonafede, "Glenn Counts on Slow Pace."
61. Schram, "Glenn's Campaign Staff Off and Walking."
62. Ibid.
63. Elizabeth Drew, *Campaign Journal* (New York: Macmillan, 1985), 200-201; "Can Anyone Beat Fritz? " *Newsweek*, January 9, 1984; William Shannon, "The Right Stuff Is Not Enough," *Boston Globe*, November 23, 1983; Dom Bonfede, "Mondale Aides Are Veterans of the Past Races," *National Journal Convention Daily*, July 21, 1984.
64. Tom Watson, "Persistence and Eye for Detail Help Glenn Surmount Defeats and Learn the Ways of Politics," *Congressional Quarterly Weekly Report*, November 5, 1983.
65. David Broder, "Mr. Checklist," *Washington Post*, October 13, 1982.
66. Austin Ranney, "Turnout and Representation in Presidential Primary Elections," *American Political Science Review* (March 1972); James Lengle, *Representation and Presidential Primaries* (Westport, Conn.: Greenwood Press, 1981); Polsby, *Consequences of Party Reform;* Walter Stone, "How Representative Are the Iowa Caucuses? " (Paper presented at Conference, "First in the Nation: Iowa and the Presidential Nomination Process," University of Iowa, February 6-8, 1988).
67. David Osborne, "Lost in Space With John Glenn," *Mother Jones*, May 1983.

68. Rowland Evans and Robert Novak, "Glenn's Shaky Base," *Newsweek*, April 22, 1983; "The First Real Primary," *Newsweek*, January 23, 1984; Schram, "Glenn's Campaign Staff Off and Walking."

69. Matt Winkler, "Labor Told Carter: Forget Glenn," *Mount Vernon (Ohio) News*, July 23, 1976.

70. David Broder, "Kirkland and Mondale," *Boston Globe*, August 15, 1983.

71. William Safire, "John Glenn Not Strong Israel Backer," *Rochester Democrat and Chronicle*, February 7, 1983; Richard Cohen, "Friends," *Washington Post*, September 15, 1983; Michael Kramer, "John Glenn: The Right Stuff? " *New York Times*, January 31, 1983. See also "The Right Stuff for 1984," *Newsweek*, March 1, 1982; "Flak Over Glenn's Vote KO's Fund Raising Event," *Dayton Daily News*, June 4, 1978.

72. Howard Fineman, "Playing the Money Game," *Newsweek*, July 18, 1983.

73. Osborne, "Lost in Space with John Glenn."

74. Bill Peterson, "6 Democratic Hopefuls Vow to Consider Woman as Running Mate," *Washington Post*, October 3, 1983.

75. Kathy Sawyer, "AFL-CIO To Endorse in October," *Washington Post*, August 10, 1983.

76. Albert Hunt, "Ohio Hero in His Presidential Bid, John Glenn Is Helped By All-American Image," *Wall Street Journal*, September 14, 1983.

77. Kramer, "John Glenn: The Right Stuff? "

78. Osborne, "Lost in Space With John Glenn."

79. Peterson, "6 Democratic Hopefuls."

80. *Newsweek*, May 9, 1983.

81. Joe Klein, "The Right Stuff," *Rolling Stone*, November 24, 1983. See also *Newsweek*, "Glenn's Acid Test in New Hampshire," May 9, 1983; Dianne Dumanoski, "Politics, Geography and Acid Rain," *Boston Globe*, May 5, 1983; Bill Peterson, "Glenn Blasts President on Environment Record," *Washington Post*, September 13, 1983.

82. "Glenn: A Mission in Fence Mending," *Newsweek*, September 26, 1983. See also David Broder, "Cancelling Trip, Glenn Attempts to Assure Jews He Backs Israel," *Washington Post*, February 15, 1983.

83. Thomas Oliphant, "Mondale Says He'll Confront Hart in New 'Two-Man' Race," *Boston Globe*, March 2, 1984.

84. For example, Ron Sarro, "Glenn is Spearheading Effort to End Senate's 'Last Plantation' Image," *Washington Star*, February 10, 1978.

85. Milton Coleman, "Hollings Defends Civil Rights Stance, Criticizes NAACP Grading Policies," *Washington Post*, July 14, 1982.

86. Art Harris and Martin Schram, "Six Democratic Hopefuls Strut Their Moderation in New South," *Washington Post*, March 9, 1983.

87. Kennedy, "John Glenn's Presidential Countdown."

88. Raines, "John Glenn: The Hero As Candidate"; Rhodes Cook, "Glenn Looks for High Turnout in 1984 Democratic Contest; Low Vote Might Aid Mondale," *Congressional Quarterly Weekly Report*, October 22, 1983.

89. Baker's view as expressed in interview, "House Hunting with Howard Baker."

90. *Newsweek*, June 13, 1983.

91. Martin Schram, "A Campaign Blueprint for 1984," *Washington Post*, February 6, 1983.

92. David Broder, "Mr. Checklist," *Washington Post*, October 13, 1982.

93. Howell Raines, "Mondale and Glenn Vying for Early Lead Toward 1984,"

New York Times, September 11, 1983.

94. Curtis Wilkie, "Tacticians for Mondale and Glenn Now Talk of a 2-Man Race," *Boston Globe,* August 23, 1983.

95. Martin Schram, "Mondale and Glenn Bet on Divergent Paths to the Presidency," *Washington Post,* October 3, 1983.

96. Sidney Blumenthal, "Statecraft as Spacecraft: John Glenn's Media Campaign Is John Glenn's Campaign," *New Republic,* November 14, 1983.

97. "Liftoff for Campaign 1984," *Newsweek,* October 3, 1983.

98. Blumenthal, "Statecraft as Spacecraft"; "Glenn Meets the Dream Machine," *Newsweek,* October 3, 1983; Howell Raines, "For Glenn, 'The Right Stuff' Seems to be Right," *New York Times,* September 21, 1983.

99. Klein, "The Right Stuff."

100. "Trial Heats," *Public Opinion,* February/March 1984.

101. Jonathan Moore, ed., *Campaign For President: The Managers Look at '84* (Dover, Mass.: Auburn House, 1986), 21.

102. "Mass. Poll: Glenn Gaining," *Boston Globe,* August 20, 1983.

103. Robert Shogan, "Survey Finds Glenn Strong Against Reagan," as carried in *Boston Globe,* July 10, 1983.

104. "A Preview of Campaign '84?" *Newsweek,* May 30, 1983. A similar summary assessment is "Ranks of Democratic Hopefuls May Be Winnowed by Straw Polls" by Martin Schram, *Washington Post,* May 31, 1983.

105. "The Democrats and the Polls," *Washington Post,* May 24, 1983.

106. *Washington Post,* February 5, 1983; *National Journal,* July 16, 1983.

107. Drew, *Campaign Journal,* 174.

108. *Washington Post,* July 14, 1983.

109. Moore, *Campaign for President,* 36-37.

110. David Broder, "Democratic Governors Show Increasing Interest in Glenn," *Washington Post,* August 3, 1983. See also Rowland Evans and Robert Novak, "Mondale's Liberalism Criticized," *Boston Globe,* August 4, 1983.

111. David Broder, "Democrats Charge Reagan Has Broken Promises," *Washington Post,* July 14, 1983.

112. Germond and Witcover, *Wake Us When It's Over,* 143.

113. "Opinion Outlook," *National Journal,* October 1, 1983.

114. Rowland Evans and Robert Novak, "Has Glenn Lost the South?" *Washington Post,* December 7, 1983.

115. Curtis Wilkie, "Electability Issue Gives Glenn Boost," *Boston Globe,* August 11, 1983.

116. Thomas Edsall, "In Last Three Months, Glenn Fund-Raising Outpaced Mondale's," *Washington Post,* October 7, 1983.

117. *Washington Post,* May 31, 1983; August 8, 1983.

118. Dom Bonafede, "Democratic State Party Leaders See Race Even as Glenn Gains on Mondale," *National Journal,* July 16, 1983.

119. Kathy Sawyer, "Despite Class Acts, No Democrat Emerges as Teachers' Favorite," *Washington Post,* July 2, 1983.

120. Wilkie, "Electability Issue."

121. David Alpern, "How the Pros See the Race," *Newsweek,* October 3, 1983.

122. Dan Balz, "Democratic Strategists Warn Against Courting Special Groups," *Washington Post,* May 23, 1983.

123. Wilkie, "Electability Issue."

124. David Broder, "Mondale, Glenn Give Democratic Panel Preview of Coming Battle," *Washington Post,* July 15, 1983. See also Wilkie, "Tacticians For

Mondale and Glenn."
125. John Felton, "Public Opinion Polls Play Key, But Also Misunderstood, Role in American Political Arena," *Congressional Quarterly Weekly Report*, March 15, 1980.
126. Larry Bartels, "Expectations and Preferences in Presidential Nominating Campaigns," *American Political Science Review* 79 (1985); Larry Bartels, *Presidential Primaries and the Dynamics of Public Choice* (Princeton, N.J.: Princeton University Press, 1988).
127. Wilkie, "Tacticians for Mondale and Glenn."
128. "Liftoff For Campaign 1984."
129. Martin Schram and Dan Balz, "Democrats Begin the 1988 Campaign in Earnest," *Washington Post*, September 6, 1983.
130. Ibid.

A Season of Confrontation

FROM COMPARISON TO CONFRONTATION: OCTOBER-DECEMBER 1983

In the period between Ted Kennedy's withdrawal in December 1982 and the fall of 1983, Walter Mondale and John Glenn developed and conducted their campaigns separately and at a distance. They seldom came near each other, did not confront each other, and direct comparisons between them were not often attempted.

In May a commentator noted, "The Ohio Senator has not drawn the line on a single issue against the front-runner." [1] Glenn stayed out of all but one summertime straw poll, and it was one that Mondale did not contest. [2] In July their separate appearances before the House Democratic Caucus and the Democratic National Committee (DNC) stimulated some comparison, but a report on the DNC event concluded, "The two men took no direct swipes at each other, emphasizing instead their devotion to party unity." [3] As Glenn's summertime momentum gave him commanding status as one of the "top two" in the "first tier" in the structure of competition, direct comparisons became inevitable. And, as the calendar pushed them steadily toward the start of the formal process, confrontations began to occur—generating still more comparisons. This sequence of Glenn-Mondale comparisons-confrontations-comparisons dominated the last three months of 1983.

It is characteristic of election campaigns that they have no clear beginning. One rule of thumb is that campaigns begin as soon as there are two candidates who recognize one another as serious opponents. By that standard, the Glenn campaign—certainly its testing time—began in the fall of 1983. That view was shared by Walter Mondale. "The real fight begins," he said in September. "We've been wading in the lily pads up to now." [4] Accordingly, it was the time when media scorekeepers started taking their closest look yet at John Glenn. We shall rely heavily on this "third look" to take our bearings on the contest that developed.

These sequential looks, or evaluations, by the journalistic community are not discrete, but cumulative. Each previous set of observations lives within the succeeding set. The national scorekeepers proceed along the path before local scorekeepers do, so there is always considerable overlapping of observations. Still, there is, if Glenn's coverage is any guide, a recognizable pattern to campaign reporting. As we have noted, journalists focus first on personal qualities and second on political resources such as organization and electability. Finally, they focus on the totality of a candidacy by assessing its strengths, weaknesses, and prospects relative to those of rival candidates. This third evaluative look, which concentrates on the "horse race," brings comparisons to the fore and dominates scorekeeping to the end of the nomination process.

During the fall of 1983 media scorekeepers began to make direct comparisons between Mondale and Glenn. At a time when interest in the campaign is low, information scarce, and reality as yet untested, these media comparisons take on added importance. For anyone who cares about the nomination process, journalistic commentary sustains interest, supplies information, and provides the closest available approximation of reality. It also creates the analytic categories that dominate campaign conversations among the interested parties—politicians, activists, and the journalists themselves.

EARLY COMPARISONS

One "third-look" comparison focused on interpersonal political skills. Following the July meeting with House Democrats, for example, Mondale was called the "victor," based on reports that he introduced himself, to applause, as "a politician" and "an unabashed Democrat," that he acted "a lot more confident, a lot more at home," and that he made "a stronger, crisper presentation" than the "stiff and unprepared" Glenn, who reportedly "stumbled on a question regarding his votes in 1981" and "drew a blank on what vote he was being asked to explain." [5] After the DNC appearances, it was said that the two performances "drew a sharp contrast between the polished veteran of political wars and the earnest newcomer to the presidential struggle." [6]

As they began to travel with the two campaigners, reporters came to similar conclusions. One described Mondale as "loose and outgoing from years on the political circuit," while Glenn was "erect and reserved from years in the military." [7] Another found that "in gatherings of his party's elite, Mr. Mondale demonstrated the easy wit, detailed knowledge and political acumen that often seemed lacking in the public performance of . . . Senator John Glenn." [8] We have already described, from our observations, Glenn's discomfort in structured political situations—from his 1980 Ohio campaign to the mini-convention. Now journalists, comparing Glenn and Mondale, were beginning to view Glenn's discomfort as a weakness.

A second comparison centered on the contrasting media and organizational emphases of the two campaigns. Comparisons were drawn between Mondale, "the traditional Democrat [with] the best organized and best financed campaign," and Glenn, "fueled mostly by voters' memories of his heroics." [9] In its cover story about the upcoming movie *The Right Stuff*, *Newsweek* stated that the "contrast between the press-the-flesh style of Fritz Mondale and the larger-than-life image of John Glenn embodies what may well be the central theme of campaign '84." [10] Another assessment said, "The Mondale-Glenn fight will be a test of organizational muscle versus media magic." [11] In this view, "one candidate's strong emphasis on organization and his tendency to woo the party one interest group and one voter at a time" is contrasted with the other candidate's "broad media themes and his disdain for the importance of traditional interest groups." [12] "The Glenn campaign," it is said, "begins and ends with the widespread identification of the candidate as a red, white and blue national hero." [13] And, Glenn "will depend almost entirely on popular appeal to help him stay the distance," while "Mondale's great strength is his organization . . . [which is] beyond dispute . . . the strongest and most skilled thing of its kind in recent campaign history." [14]

Because Glenn's media strength was yet to be seen, while evidence of Mondale's organizational strength existed in the present, reporters emphasized organizational comparisons. And these, as we might expect from our "second look" discussions, continued to be unflattering to Glenn. Describing the Glenn campaign as "relying more heavily on media than on organization," one traveling reporter concluded in October, "Glenn's organizations are rated poorly when compared with those of former Vice President Walter Mondale." [15] In view of Glenn's longstanding disinterest in organization, his late start in organizing, and the unsettled relationships within his staff, comparative judgments of this sort were not surprising.

A third point of comparison centered on the candidates' differing appeals for support—both in content and in target, which are tightly linked. "Mondale and Glenn provide the party with a distinct choice," wrote an observer. "One bases his appeal on traditional Democratic liberalism. The other offers a more centrist appeal that reaches out to independents and even to Republicans." [16] Another said, "A campaign swing with Mondale is a trip through the Democratic party; a similar swing with Glenn is a journey through Middle America." [17] "Mondale's target," wrote a third traveling scorekeeper, "is the traditional organized, active, generally liberal, collection of people—that support the Democratic party—unions, teachers' organizations, feminist societies, environmental clubs, peace groups."

On the other hand, "Glenn is sending his signal to Democratic voters who are less likely to be loyal to constituency organization[s] even though many of them are ... members." [18] Glenn's target, the unorganized Democrats or "the constituency of the whole," could not be easily specified by observers. And, as his Senate record showed, the content of the independent, centrist message he planned to communicate was not easily characterized either. Centrism, as we have said, is more the artifact of a voting record than a philosophical position. Altogether, therefore, Glenn's appeals for support were vague, while Mondale's were specific and aimed at well-defined groups.

Later in the campaign, national surveys consistently confirmed early judgments that Glenn's views matched more closely to those of the general public than did the views of Walter Mondale. Table 3-1 reports the mean scores assigned by registered voters to themselves, to Glenn, to Mondale, and to Ronald Reagan on liberalism-conservatism scales.

In each of three polls, Glenn's philosophy was thought to be closer to the public's than Mondale's. Furthermore, in every case, Glenn's views were closer to the public's than were Reagan's. On ideological grounds, therefore, Glenn always seemed well positioned for a contest—with Mondale and with Reagan—for the support of the general public, but with one proviso. The mean scores do not reflect the percentage of "don't know" answers. As Table 3-1 indicates, these answers occurred much more frequently for John Glenn than for the others. A separate study of the national electorate found that the voters' image of John Glenn remained extremely unstable and indistinct right through the period of the Iowa caucuses and began to crystallize only afterward. [19] Taken together, these surveys point to Glenn's continuing campaign task of fleshing out his political persona and the lengthy time span required to do it.

STRATEGY AND INSTINCT

In combination, the several media comparisons pointed to John Glenn's comparative advantage in a general election setting, and to Walter Mondale's comparative advantage in a primary election setting. Glenn's electoral strength, which had so impressed the politicians and

TABLE 3-1   Ideological Placements: 1983-1984

	December 1983 [1] (10 pt. scale)		January 1984 [2] (7 pt. scale)		February 1984 [3] (5 pt. scale)	
		Don't know		Don't know		Don't know
Mean self-placements	5.71	—	4.32	—	3.19	—
Mean Glenn placements	5.24	24%	4.18	28%	3.28	34%
Mean Mondale placements	5.00	14%	3.89	17%	2.66	15%
Mean Reagan placements	6.45	7%	4.32	10%	3.51	9%

[1] ABC-*Washington Post* Poll: liberal=1; conservative=10.
[2] ABC-*Washington Post* Poll: liberal=1; conservative=7.
[3] *New York Times*-CBS poll: very liberal=1; very conservative=5.

which had triggered his presidential run, was general election strength. His heroism and his character, the value system underlying his public service politics, and his independent centrist record all contributed to his general election prowess. Primaries had been much more difficult for him. His lack of ease around politicians, his detachment from organization, his weak ties to core Democratic constituencies all contributed to this difficulty.

Glenn's confrontations with Mondale in the fall of 1983 were, at bottom, a struggle to win, from participants and observers, a strategically favorable interpretation of the electoral context. Glenn wanted the contest to be seen as one between the Democrats and Reagan—as a general election context in which the essential question is which Democrat has the best chance of beating Ronald Reagan? As he stated his case in late August, "It doesn't do [us] . . . any good to win the nomination. That's not the objective. . . . The objective is going to be who can replace Ronald Reagan in the White House. That's what we have to keep in mind. In that regard, the polls have very consistently shown me to be ahead in that department." [20] Mondale, on the other hand, wanted the basic contest to be interpreted as one between himself and Glenn—a primary election context in which the essential question is which candidate is most representative of the Democratic party? Or, as his campaign manager put it, which is "the most effective spokesman for the Democratic party?" [21] Each man was attempting to exploit his comparative advantage.

Sequence, strategy, and circumstance conspired to give Walter Mondale the initial advantage in the definitional struggle. Because the primaries came before the general election, the intra-Democratic contest also came first. As a strategic matter, Mondale wanted to force the intra-Democratic contest as soon as possible so that he could display his political support. When a Democratic party leader asked him in a public forum in late September to state his differences with Glenn, he seized the opportunity to criticize a series of Glenn's Senate votes. It was the first direct attack of the campaign. A week later, Mondale won the endorsement—plus the money and the workers—of two huge, traditionally Democratic constituencies—organized labor via the AFL-CIO and teachers via the National Education Association (NEA). In that same week, he won a straw poll at the party's Maine state convention, before which he challenged Glenn, saying, "I am a real Democrat." [22] This cluster of intraparty successes gave Mondale a sudden burst of momentum and support for his interpretation of the electoral context. Mondale's actions precipitated a reaction by Glenn, and Glenn's reaction put the two front-runners in direct confrontation.

"When we were expanding our speechmaking and exploring the idea of running," Glenn had said in a mid-July interview, "it was much easier to control events. Once we had decided to run and get into the campaign, we lost a great deal of control. In a campaign, so many things can upset your plans." Glenn was exactly right; he did not anticipate the events of late September and early October, and he could not control them. They disrupted his timetable. "We knew the clash would come," said his campaign manager, "but it came sooner than we had expected. . . . It didn't happen the way we planned it."

As summer ended, the Glenn people had defined their major task as "filling in the blanks" of the candidate's political persona. With their theme of "Leadership for the Future" or "Believe in the Future Again," they planned gradually to portray Glenn as a man of such preparation and character as to be a recognized leader. They would do this by having him speak knowledgeably and moderately about the issues and by launching a fall media campaign that would use his astronaut adventure to gain public attention for his consensual, future-oriented policies and for his leadership potential. Left to their own devices, they believed they could fill out Glenn's political persona by the time of the early primaries, when they would be prepared to take on Mondale at the polls. Glenn preferred this approach, too. He believed, as noted earlier, that his fourteen-to sixteen-month task was to "get my record across." And he wanted to proceed with characteristic care, step by step, along this course.

Neither the candidate nor his advisers wanted an early confrontation with Mondale, but they got one and were forced to sidetrack their positive work on Glenn's record and react. They had to improvise, and, in their improvisation, they had to rely heavily on their political instincts. This situation is endemic to political campaigns, and it posed the first stringent test for the candidate and his organization. Their reaction engaged two of Glenn's basic political instincts. These instincts were not entirely consistent with one another, so choices had to be made in the face of conflicting pressures. The choices altered the course of the Glenn campaign.

One instinct was to avoid negative campaigning. Glenn's belief that campaigns should be positive and upbeat was a deeply held ingredient of his public service politics. It was all of a piece with his near reverence for the country's basic public institutions and his belief in the importance of high-quality public officials. Negative personal campaigning, he believed, damages the public office being sought and the person seeking it. He applied this value system with special force to the presidency.

When we first met, during his Senate campaign of 1980, he voiced these views strongly—in the context of President Jimmy Carter's Ohio campaign.

> When the president came to Ohio, I implored him and the members of his staff to come in with a positive campaign. He didn't. He came in with a completely negative, cut and shoot attack on Ronnie Reagan, Ronnie Reagan, Ronnie Reagan. I almost crawled under the platform. You can't come in preaching morality with your Bible under your arm and proceed to cut someone's balls off. That's not what people want to hear. . . . People hold the president to a higher standard than they do congressional candidates. They may lie to people in their own lives, and cheat people—and even cheat on their wives—but when they vote for president, they want someone up there (points upward), someone who represents what they want to be, not who they are. . . . They want to hear something positive. You can't just cut and shoot.

In July 1983 I asked him whether the pressures of his own campaign had tempted him into negative campaigning. "We have avoided that so far," he answered, "and I will continue to avoid it. To me public office is a calling. You represent someone else. . . . It's easy to score points with personal attacks on your opponent. But that demeans the office you are entrusted with."

Later in the interview, he returned with vigor to the same point. "Some people have a funny attitude about politics," he said.

> George Reedy had an article the other day. . . . He said politics is war, that the object is to win, that how you get there doesn't matter because you can act differently when you get there and so forth. He's completely wrong. If you're a lying, cheating, no good son of a bitch in the campaign, you'll be a lying, cheating, no good son of a bitch when you're in office. You don't put on

a moral cloak when you stand over there on the east front of the Capitol and take the oath of office. You are the same person you always were. You can't campaign one way and govern in a different way.... Reedy was all wet.

This emphasis on the good man, the good campaigner, and the good public official is pure public service politics. It is also vintage marine-astronaut-hero.

Just as deeply embedded within the marine-astronaut, however, was a second, quite different instinct—competitiveness. Throughout his career Glenn had accepted and thrived on challenges. The greater the challenge the more it triggered his competitive instincts—as a fighter pilot in combat or as an astronaut striving to be the first to fly in space. His favorite nickname was Old Magnet Tail, earned because as a fighter pilot he stayed so close to North Korean planes for so long to bring down the enemy that his plane got shot up, too.

Political challenges had brought forth the same instinctive combativeness under fire. And this combativeness, too, had been crowned with success. In 1974 his fierce rhetorical counterattacks—first against the proposed Gilligan "deal" and, second, against the Metzenbaum "never-held-a-job" comment—carried him to victory in that most difficult of all his elections. He had proved to be an adept political counterpuncher when he believed that some aspect of his character was being challenged. Despite his strong disinclination to engage in negative personal campaigning, Glenn was more than willing to counterattack in kind against any opponent who initiated what he considered a personal attack.

Glenn's guide to action in the presence of such conflict goes something like this: his campaigns, he believes, are positive campaigns. He will never, therefore, initiate personal or negative attacks on his opponent. But if his opponent initiates a personal attack on him, he is fully justified in counterattacking in kind. And a counterattack under such provocation does not violate his public service credo. Indeed, his counterattack can be cradled in righteous indignation. He can, therefore, follow his public service and his combative predispositions at the same time. He needs only to wait for an attack on him that he can define as personal and he can, without violating any of his precepts, retaliate. In that act of retaliation, he can give vent to all his competitive instincts. While he strikes at his opponent, however, he will be at great pains to point out that he did not start the conflict and that his response is proportionate to the initial insult. As he put it during his discussion of Carter's Ohio visit in 1980,

I have always believed that if an opponent says something you think is unfair, hit him back. Hit him just as hard as you possibly can. But then, go on to talk positively about your vision for the future, for the kind of world you would want for our children to live in.

That is the rationale he followed in 1974. It was the rationale he was about to follow in 1983.

This reconciliation of his political creed and his personal competitiveness reflected his desire to win elections and his desire to protect his reputation in so doing. He knew that his political strength rested ultimately on his perceived strength of character. He reacted viscerally and relentlessly when he believed it was under attack. But his extreme sensitivity to personal attack was not only a reaction to the immediate electoral context. It was also a much deeper reaction to an attack on his reputation as a national hero, a public reputation that predated and existed independently of his political reputation. Glenn has acted, always, to maintain this independence. He brought an exemplary public reputation to politics, and he does not intend to lose it through politics. The two goals may not always be compatible, for the protectionist goal may constrain the electoral goal. But both help account for his supersensitivity to perceived attacks on his character, for his supercombativeness in reaction to them, and for the electoral rationale designed to explain his actions. In seeking the presidency of the United States, he sought to gain more than most politicians ever gain; but he had more to lose than most politicians ever lose.

CONFRONTATION

On September 26 in a public forum in Syracuse, Gov. Mario Cuomo of New York asked John Glenn to discuss the differences between himself and Walter Mondale. Glenn, following his instinctive distaste for personalized, negative campaigning, demurred. He said that he had thus far avoided the characterization of other candidates or their views, and he proceeded to present only some views of his own. "We have been careful," an adviser said afterward, "not to take the initiative to make the debate personal."[23] Three days later, when Mondale spoke in Rochester, Cuomo asked him the same question, and Mondale answered at length. He picked out Glenn's Senate record on Reagan's 1981 tax cut, SALT II, nerve gas, defense spending, and the B-1 bomber and explained his disagreement on each issue. It was an adroit selection of issues of special symbolic importance to core Democratic constituencies, and it put Glenn on the defensive with the party's activists. A media account described Mondale as "bludgeoning Glenn as a born-again Reaganite."[24] "We were looking at some point to define the difference," explained one of Mondale's advisers. "That's what a campaign is all about." [25] Whereas Glenn had avoided a confrontation, Mondale had welcomed it and had constructed it in terms most favorable to him.

At the Maine convention a few days later, Mondale delivered his "I am a real Democrat" speech, structured to have an intraparty appeal. Glenn, seeing the contest in general election terms, answered, "I am told that the political experts in the White House are afraid of my candidacy. Well, I am not afraid of Ronald Reagan." [26] A few days later in Iowa, Glenn continued to impose his thinking on the contest. He argued, "We're not living in the '40s, '50s, or the '60s; we're living in the 1980s." He said that the Democrats would lose in 1984 by "trying to reinstate all the programs of the past," and he decried the notion "that unless you are willing to put a rubber stamp on all these programs of the past, you somehow are less of a Democrat than someone else." [27] The inference was that Mondale was a creature of and a devotee of those past programs. And the further inference was that Mondale was appealing to core Democratic constituencies on that basis.

Glenn argued that this approach was "undersell[ing] the intelligence of Democrats. We think we have to promise them everything under the sun to get their votes . . . [but] they're smart people and . . . they're going to decide what's in the best interests of this country." [28] He was beginning to articulate his broadest anti-Mondale theme—that Mondale catered to special interests to the detriment of the general interest.

> I could go to an environmental group and promise everything they want to hear. I can go before a labor group and promise jobs right to the hilt. But if you're honest about the environment and jobs balance, you have to do what's in the best interests of the country.[29]

It was, for Glenn, a congenial public service politics argument—indeed, the capstone idea of public service politics. It was also an effort to conduct the contest as if it were a general election.

When Cuomo expressed pleasure at Mondale's New York comments, however, Glenn defended himself explicitly. Cuomo said, "Glenn didn't answer the question and this guy [Mondale] did. It shows he puts more emphasis on issues and is willing to take on this aura of celebrity and celluloid images and replace them with questions of character and issues." [30] The "celluloid images" statement was just the kind of attack on his character that activated Glenn's competitiveness. "I was angry about the comment," he said. When an adviser suggested, "You didn't take it personally," he retorted, "I did too take it personally." [31] At a New York City candidates' forum he struck back.

I went through two wars, and I know what it's like to be in combat.... I wasn't doing *Hellcats of the Navy* when I went through 149 missions. That wasn't celluloid; that was the real thing. And when I was on the top of that booster down there ready to go, it was not "Star Trek" ... it was representing the future of this country.[32]

It was a rebuke in the pattern of his 1974 indignant counterattack against Metzenbaum.

He also sharpened his special interest/general interest charge against Mondale by arguing that the Democrats could not defeat Reagan "if we offer a party that can't say no to anyone with a letterhead and a mailing list." [33] Glenn continued, however, to avoid answering Mondale's specific issue criticisms, nor did he challenge Mondale on any specific issues. So long as Mondale desisted, he would do so. "If [Mondale] escalated," said the Glenn people, "we would have no choice but to respond. And in that case we would have to come back hard." [34] Mondale, in the New York forum, simply ignored Glenn. So, pronounced a scorekeeper, "Mondale was the clear loser and ... Glenn the clear winner." [35] The media was promoting the notion of a two-man, head-to-head horse race. And that conflict was about to take shape.

Mondale, it turned out, was carefully picking his spots. He did not share Glenn's reluctance to escalate a confrontation on specifics. His basic campaign strategy had been from the beginning "to make the pace of the campaign at every stage" and "to consolidate broad party support before ... Glenn got his campaign rolling." [36] And he had every intention of escalating his direct attack on Glenn. A reporter traveling with his campaign said, "Mondale's people would love to coax Glenn into an ideological fight, figuring that there is no way Glenn can win such a fight within the Democratic party." [37] At a candidates' forum in Iowa, three days after the one in New York, the coaxing strategy succeeded.

In his speech Glenn once again sounded arguments about general election success. "Will we offer a party that decries the policies of the 1920s and offers as a replacement the policies of the 1960s? If so, we will lose in 1984 just as we did in 1980." [38] But Mondale launched a second frontal attack on three of Glenn's Senate votes, against SALT II, for a new nerve gas system, and for the 1981 tax cut. Rebutting Glenn's argument that the party—and by inference Mondale—could not win if it was perceived as "pandering" to special interests, Mondale charged that these three Glenn votes were special interest votes. He hit particularly hard at Glenn's vote for the tax cut and, therefore, for Reaganomics. He described Reaganomics as "the most radical measure of our time," "the most comprehensive onslaught against social justice in our time," which favored "the very wealthiest Americans." "Of all the measures in modern history in which the forces of special interests clashed with the profound public interest of our nation," said Mondale, "I cannot recall a single instance where the issues were as clear. . . . That would have been a good time for a Democrat to stand up against the special interests and vote no." [39] Mondale "took the paint off the walls," said the state chairman. The speech was reminiscent of his partisan mini-convention line-drawing of "us against them." [40] Only now John Glenn was portrayed as one of "them." It was the very challenge to Glenn's Democratic party credentials that Bill White had predicted in his planning memo. Once again, Mondale had put Glenn on the defensive.

Glenn and his advisers faced some hard choices. Was a direct response called for? If so, what should it be and when should it be delivered? What consequences might be anticipated? It was a portentous set of choices. But they had to be addressed instinctively, in the crush of the campaign. It was candidate Glenn's first public testing time.

The candidate and his advisers chose to "come back hard" and to come back immediately. At a press conference in Melbourne, Florida, the next morning, Glenn defended his tax cut vote as the only institutionally available alternative to a set of existing policies that had "devastated the economy." "What it came down to," said Glenn, "was, were we going to make some changes from those disastrous, failed policies of the past or were we going to have no change?" "The vote in 1981 was not for Reaganomics . . . it . . . was against the economic policies in place." In support of his argument that "change was absolutely necessary," Glenn noted that 80 percent of the Senate Democrats had voted for the tax cut and that large numbers of "working men and women in this country . . . went over and voted for Ronald Reagan because they were so unhappy with the past policies."

His defense turned into a counterattack against Mondale—one far more substantial than anything Glenn had yet developed. He was charging Mondale with being the vice-presidential producer of "the disastrous failed policies of the past administration" as "part of the [Carter] administration that gave us 21 percent interest rates and 17 percent inflation rates [and left the economy] in deep deep trouble," and as a supporter of "the disastrous policies that he apparently now, I gather, would like to go back to." Referring to Mondale's Iowa attack, Glenn said, "It's a little like the first mate on the *Titanic* criticizing someone for going for a lifeboat." [41]

The swiftness and sharpness of this counterattack sprang from Glenn's strong competitive instincts. He interpreted the situation he was in, characteristically, as one in which he had been personally wronged—unsuspectingly and unfairly—and in which he was justified in overriding his aversion to negative campaigning to strike back. "I was very sorry to see that some of our specific votes were ... taken out and were brought up for specific comment or criticism or ridicule," he said. "I did not start that. In fact, the first time it was done, I ignored it, let it go, hoped it would go away, that it did not get all the press attention." [42] Now that he had been attacked twice, he felt he had no choice but to strike back.

He did, however, have a good deal of choice in the content and the timing of his counterattack. And it was the content—plus the timing—that mattered, not the proprieties. How and when he retaliated could turn a tactical maneuver into a strategic change of course. Glenn had leveled a broadside against the previous Democratic administration and had done so in language that sounded very much like Ronald Reagan. By obscuring the differentiation between himself and Reagan, Glenn had left Mondale as the most easily recognized critic of the president. By criticizing the Carter-Mondale administration, Glenn had been sucked into an issue-oriented intra-Democratic party contest, just as the Mondale people had hoped he would be. And he was allowing Mondale to take over his own task of "filling in the blanks" for Democratic voters.

"If we were going to face Glenn as a hero, a nonpolitician, an astronaut, that's dangerous business," said Mondale's campaign manager later. "[But] if we face [him] on who's better prepared, who has better values, who's better on key issues, that's winnable." [43] They wanted to face Glenn as a Democratic party politician, and Glenn was obliging them. Glenn was, in other words, accepting Mondale's intraparty definition of their nomination contest and, at the same time, making it harder for himself to win such a contest by looking less like a representative Democrat. Mondale's people were described as "ecstatic" over their strategic success. "The nomination is locked up—because of Glenn," said one. [44] And Mondale quickly pressed his interpretational advantage. "I think that Mr. Glenn will be deeply shocked," he said, "by the reaction of Democrats across the country to his decision to base his campaign on his support of Reaganomics." [45] Glenn's flash of competitiveness had the potential for altering the tone and direction of his campaign.

The sweeping content of Glenn's counterattack, not to mention its strategic implications, was quite unplanned. When reporters asked Glenn, in Florida, to cite some of the "disastrous policies" of the Carter administration he had opposed in the Senate, he could not name any. And he treated his remarks as a tactical response that had evened the score and should, therefore, bring personalized hostilities to a halt. "I hope," he said after his counterthrust, "that what he has initiated is not to become the norm in this campaign. If I'm attacked, I'm going to respond and I'm going to respond hard." [46] There is nice care taken here to allocate blame and to outline the Marquess of Queensbury rules of public service politics. But there is not much sensitivity displayed to the dynamics of the campaign. Now that he had given his opponent a strategic advantage, it was not likely that his opponent would be either satisfied or cowed. Predictably, a Mondale adviser dismissed the distinction between initiating and responding with the comment, "What is this? Are we running to tell Mommy?" [47]

Glenn's Melbourne counterattack was the kind of improvised reaction to unanticipated events that must be taken often and under pressure during a campaign. It tests the ability of candidate and organization to stay out of trouble. In this case, the Glenn organization was tested and—as observers had long suspected it would be—it was found wanting. A top staffer rehearsed the sequence.

> At the [Iowa] Jefferson-Jackson dinner, Mondale made an attack on Glenn that caught us completely by surprise. We assumed it would not be complimentary, but we had no inkling that it would be as severe as it was. There was not a single leak. So there was Mondale, with every major figure in the campaign in the audience, laying heavy criticism on John Glenn, after Glenn had spoken and had no chance to reply. I had to admire the professionalism of the performance.
>
> By contrast, our response in Florida was a disaster. After the dinner, a group of us sat around kicking around what we might do. Someone came up with the line about . . . the *Titanic,* and Greg Schneiders checked it out with the reporters to see how the national press reacted to it. The next day, before the press conference, Schneiders and Glenn went over what he would say. And out of that came not just the *Titanic* idea but Glenn's comment on "the failed disastrous policies of the Carter administration."
>
> We had three reporters traveling with us . . . when our press conference was over, they ran to the phones. That meant they felt they had a story, and we had set off a bomb. At the next stop, they jumped all over the senator. "What policies are you talking about?" "Didn't you support the Carter policies?" "Which votes did you cast in opposition?" "Give us specific examples." The senator struggled to answer. Do you know, none of us could think of a single one. The reporters knew it, and they knew we had made a big mistake. . . .
>
> Bill White [campaign manager] had no idea what was happening or what was going to be said. So, no research had been done, and we had absolutely no backup available in

Washington. When we did start researching, we couldn't find a single good example. . . . It was a classic case of organizational failure . . . it presented the flaws of the Glenn campaign, laid out for all the world to see.

Despite Mondale's original attack, the Glenn organization had not prepared a response in anticipation of further attacks. As a general matter, Glenn's agility in an extemporaneous issue-based contretemps was not his strength. He wanted to be well briefed before jumping into an issue-based quarrel. His organization had not prepared him for this occasion. Nor had they thought about the most propitious timing for such a response. Nor did they deem it a problem worthy of consultation or coordination between the "roadshow" and the Washington headquarters. When faced with the renewed attack, they struck back hastily and without the careful consideration of possible consequences. Had they appreciated Glenn's strengths and weaknesses, they would have known he was not ready and they would not have prodded him into battle. In retrospect, the *Washington Post* focused on Glenn's Melbourne performance as "the turning point" of his campaign.[48]

It was, of course, John Glenn's decision—the reaction of a competitive individual who felt twice wronged. He may even have believed, in accordance with his public service political orientation, that his tit-for-tat response would conclude hostilities. But his experienced advisers surely knew that his response would become part of the continuing campaign. The journalists would not let the matter rest, for the confrontation had given them the very stimulant they crave—conflict. And they rushed in to record, define, exacerbate, and then evaluate it.

Reaction.   Reaction began with the reporters on the scene and rippled out to a wider circle of observers. One of the regulars on the Glenn campaign beat described his reaction. "When you are with the campaign every day," he said,

You become totally familiar with the pattern. You can recite the stump speech by heart. And that enables you to watch for change. When something happens—bang!—it hits you. Like Melbourne. Melbourne is where the war of words began. And it is where John Glenn stumbled. He made a mistake and it cost him.

One of the reporters on the scene headlined his next day's story "Mondale-Glenn Draw Battle Lines."[49] Another plunged into a research effort to demonstrate Glenn's strong senatorial support for Jimmy Carter. "Glenn Backed Carter Economic Program, Records Show," read his headline.[50] Others picked up the scent. One syndicated column was headlined "Democrats, Hey This is a Pretty Good Fight."[51] A weekly news magazine story with the headline "The Candidates Draw Blood" described a "campaign [that] has grown increasingly nasty" and in which "the candidates [have] taken the gloves off."[52]

From Glenn's perspective, a number of these stories and commentaries were actually egging him on to continue the fight. One raised the question whether Glenn was "ducking the issues" and said that "he is under increasing pressure to define himself in direct confrontation with his opponents."[53] Another recorded "doubts whether Glenn was ready to risk an ideological clash with Mondale."[54] Another suggested that Glenn "was error prone, not up to the give and take of campaigning."[55] In a column disapproving of Glenn's public service aversion to personal, negative campaigning, still another journalist concluded, "Glenn really hates politics." Part of this critique read,

> It is not every politician who feels that his Senate voting record is not a fit subject for campaign discussion. But the former astronaut seems to regard any such reference as "personal attacks." He wants, it seems, to emphasize his differences with President Reagan, not with other Democrats. . . . Any man who objects to having "specific votes held up for specific comments or ridicule" may have proclaimed himself terminally innocent—and touchy. Glenn's attempt to limit the dialogue to blueprints and visions seems more worthy of someone seeking the presidency of the League of Women Voters.[56]

Media scorekeepers are not passive recording instruments. They are active political participants. In this case, they were challenging Glenn to fight.

Such media taunts did not escape the candidate or his advisers. To one of his top media advisers, the situation was exactly analogous to the Pepsi challenge to Coke and called for the same advice he had given to his Coca Cola account. "People were glad we were fighting back. That's the way I feel about Glenn and Mondale," he said. "You demoralize people if you don't fight back. The greater danger for Glenn is that if he doesn't do it himself, Mondale will describe what he is all about. . . . My worry is not Glenn being on the wrong side, but not being strong."[57] "There is conventional wisdom," echoed Glenn's campaign manager, "that Glenn is not tough enough politically. You hear that." The contretemps with Mondale, he admitted, "came sooner than we expected. But it killed once and for all the idea around town that John Glenn wouldn't get in there and mix it up. That helped us." The Glenn camp seemed to be acting to relieve media pressure on their campaign.

With the media fueling the confrontation, and with Glenn and his advisers paying attention to what they said, it seemed likely that the candidate's competitive instincts were reinforced at the point of his Florida decision. Indeed, one month later, he was still smoldering from what he saw—like the Gilligan and Metzenbaum episodes—as Mondale's personal attack on his integrity. "What I've been critical in him is for misrepresenting my votes, and I'm still unhappy about that." [58] Or, "I resent his misrepresentation of Reaganomics." [59] Or, "I felt things were presented unfairly against me earlier." [60] His staff fed this resentment and channeled it into the campaign.

But why anyone—least of all anyone like Bill White who knew him—would think that the marine-astronaut would not, in his own good time, "mix it up" or act "tough enough" or "fight back" or "be strong enough" defies understanding. The more likely danger was exactly the opposite—that, once engaged in combat, Old Magnet Tail would not back off until either he or his opponent was shot down.

The scorekeepers began almost immediately to comment adversely on the wisdom of Glenn's decision, both its content and its timing. Calling it "a wild departure from party protocol," a journalist questioned "whether John Glenn's spectacular response to Walter Mondale's taunts is a case of terminal Romneyism." [61] Another called the decision "the wrong stuff for Glenn—a poorly executed shift away from ozone-level imagery to the ground-level issues that put the emphasis on his past rather than the great look forward his campaign seeks." [62] Another concluded that Glenn had "burned his bridges with the Democratic establishment" and quoted party leader judgments on his decision as "suicidal," "appalling," and "a disaster." [63] With regard to timing, scorekeepers reflected that Glenn had moved "at a surprisingly early point." [64] Party leaders were quoted as saying, "Glenn has no timing. The Carter issue is a silver bullet I thought they'd save for next spring." And, "It's not going to help him at all in the primaries." [65] Even one of Glenn's top advisers was quoted as saying, "It's not a political campaign." [66] In sum, the Florida episode deepened some longstanding reservations in the political community about Glenn's "surefootedness" and his "political instincts" in campaign maneuver.[67]

A few weeks earlier, Meg Greenfield had written about the presidential race that:

We don't "know" our presidents. We imagine them. We watch them intermittently and from afar, inferring from only a relatively few gestures and reactions what kind of people they are and whether they should be in charge. Much depends on our intuition and their ability at a handful of opportune moments to project qualities we admire and respect. . . . Candidates need this gift to be elected and to lead . . . it is the essence of becoming and being President.[68]

Melbourne and the subsequent days provided an "opportune moment" for people to "imagine" Glenn as president. But it was a moment lost.

What happened in Florida also added to existing doubts about the readiness of Glenn's campaign organization. The episode could be interpreted as evidence that neither the headquarters and the field operation nor the Senate staff and the campaign staff had yet been successfully melded. These doubts were further strengthened when a major staff overhaul took place one week later. The Florida incident was not the reason, but, to the degree that it had exposed organizational weaknesses, it was contributory.

The primary reason was dissatisfaction with the state of the field organizations in the early caucus and primary states. The man in charge of those operations, political director Joe Grandmaison, resigned. An informal adviser, Robert Keefe, was formally designated senior adviser for political affairs. Several other political advisers were given formal assignments, and some managerial types, old friends of Bill White, were brought in to help him with central control functions.[69] Grandmaison thought that too many of the campaign's resources were being allocated to the media instead of to the field organization. Other campaigners believed that Grandmaison was spreading his resources too thinly across the nation instead of in the early voting states. Probably both sides were correct.

Glenn's top campaigners continued to place major reliance on the media. And by every measure and observation, Glenn's field organizations lagged far behind those of the front-runner and of some other competitors as well. His opponents had started earlier and had already gone through the shakedown that Glenn was just beginning. They had tested their field staff in straw polls that Glenn had avoided. "We haven't even had a campaign yet," declared one adviser.[70] Keefe began a search for new campaign directors in Iowa, New Hampshire, Florida, Georgia, Alabama, Illinois, and Massachusetts. "I hope the big difference will be," he said, "that from now on we look smart. We haven't looked smart."[71] Now, however, time, as well as a perceived lack of savvy, was a problem for the organization.

Reinforcement.   Events in Florida revealed yet another organizational problem—one that would not be solved by the staff overhaul. What was lacking in the Glenn camp were people who could reinforce the candidate's basic public service instincts to make sure he did not overreact to the twin challenges of Mondale's primary election strategy and the taunts of the media scorekeepers. Someone needed to remind him that the essential appeal of his personal character was the kind of strength that manifests itself in courage, not the kind of toughness that manifests itself in belligerence. Glenn's Florida response was, at the least, risky, in the sense that it took him down an uncharted path. It also showed an uncharacteristic lack of caution. In his planning memo, Bill White had described Glenn as "even-tempered, cautious, and not prone to overreaction, or 'taking-the-bait.'" "Before I make any decision," said Glenn, "I want the EEI, the essential elements of information." [72] But he did not have them in Florida. Moreover, it was not yet "have-to" time.

The question, however, was whether it was the right context and the right time to get locked into an issue-based, Democratic party dog fight. Those who knew him well understood that once he had made a decision, he very likely would get locked in. Certainly that was his habit in the Senate, as it had been his habit in the marines. In the Senate he was stubborn; in the marines he was aggressive. In addition to Old Magnet Tail, Glenn was known to his fellow pilots as the MIG Mad Marine. "You have to understand one thing about the senator," said one of his veteran Senate staffers,

> When he was in combat, he went for the kill. It's like turning an off-on switch. The hired guns didn't understand that about him, that when they sent him into combat, he wouldn't be content to make a point or jab with a joke. He wouldn't stop halfway or show restraint. He would want to go for a kill.

It was Glenn's deepest organizational failure that he had not surrounded himself with people who knew him well enough or cared about him enough to temper his competitive instincts rather than encourage them. Afraid that he would become too passive, his advisers sent him into battle without the thorough briefings and backup he normally required. Unappreciative of his political strength in terms of personal character, they risked the loss of that appeal by allowing him to follow his competitive instincts into a pier six brawl. Totally absorbed by the horse race they were in, they forgot about the well-being of their candidate.

John Glenn's hired guns knew of their candidate only what they read in the papers. And those who knew the candidate as a personality to protect rather than as a horse to ride were unable to help him at that juncture. There was a simple piece of political advice that was often forgotten in the campaign; it was, to plagiarize, "Let Glenn be Glenn." The problem was that those in a position to push it had no idea what it meant and those who knew what it meant were not in a position to push it.

The campaign was at a critical juncture; the Florida decision had set Glenn on a course of personal, negative campaigning from which he did not desist until his fate had been sealed. He could have stopped at any time. But reinforcing events and acceptable rationales kept him on course. Almost immediately, for example, such an event took place. The Mondale campaign sent a letter, with Mondale's signature, to the Florida delegates, stating that Glenn "has cast himself as the Democrat who is anti-Democrat and as the defender of . . . Ronald Reagan." [73] Characteristically, Glenn took it personally, calling it "a vicious and dishonest attack on myself." [74] He demanded an apology and got it. But in accepting it, he attacked Mondale for using "litmus tests" of "ideological purity" "to read others out of our Democratic party" and to conduct a "political inquisition." [75] The net effect was to escalate the conflict.

In early November, an acceptable rationale for escalation presented itself in the form of national poll results. The ABC-*Washington Post* poll showed that a ten-point Mondale lead in September had widened to a twenty-six-point lead in November.[76] Polling in presumably friendly states revealed equally wide gaps.[77] Mondale's October endorsements and straw poll victories were viewed by Glenn advisers as imparting a degree of front-running momentum that had to be stopped lest it produce an insurmountable lead. Their prescription was continued escalation of the head-on conflict with Mondale. Glenn, they decided, should "spend the rest of the year defining himself by defining Mondale." [78] It was a prescription that flew in the face of a cardinal rule of politics—that you had to build up your own political persona before you started tearing down that of your opponent. Old Magnet Tail, feeling justifiably unhappy about being wronged initially—and mindful of his successful counterattacking strategy in similar situations in Ohio—could easily be persuaded that this was a combat situation in which he had to persist. Soon he was saying, "It does feel good." [79]

In mid-November Glenn confirmed his aggressively confrontational course by launching a direct, concentrated issue-based attack on Mondale. In a speech to a group of prodefense Democrats, he portrayed himself as more supportive of national defense than Mondale. He criticized his opponent's Senate record as showing "a fundamental lack of support for an adequate defense." [80] "Today Fritz Mondale likes to say he's for a strong defense, but when his support was needed, his support was weak." [81]

In a speech at Georgetown University the next day, Glenn portrayed himself as more responsible and moderate on economic issues than Mondale. He emphasized his devotion to deficit reduction by urging restraint on spending and by proposing a 10 percent surcharge on income and corporate taxes. He portrayed Mondale as "a candidate who promises everything to everybody" and, therefore, "can't be serious about controlling the federal budget." [82] "Former Vice President Mondale says he hates deficits as much as anyone, but the promises he's already made would be extremely costly." [83] A day later, in Georgia, he added, "Fritz Mondale has made so many big spending commitments to so many interest groups that, if elected, he would be vulnerable to a breach of promise suit by the American people." [84] And, in defending his vote for new, safer stocks of nerve gas, he counterattacked, "If he [Mondale] says he's against it completely, across the board," Glenn charged, "he's for unilateral disarmament. I think we protect our own people by having that as a deterrent to the Soviet Union." [85]

By drawing these contrasts with Mondale, Glenn hoped to portray himself as a fiscal moderate who was strong on defense. He believed that this was the only issue stance that would produce a general election victory. His favorite tag line became, "I don't believe we Democrats should ever again allow ourselves to be charged with being the party of big spending and weak defense." In Glenn's view, that was the bottom-line requirement for party leadership. He and his advisers hoped that by slowing Mondale down, they could speed themselves up, that they could better define the Mondale candidacy.

Naturally, Mondale defended himself and hit back. A media war of charge and countercharge ensued. The net impact of media reports was to depict Glenn as the aggressor. Consider this array of headlines:

November 16, *New York Times*, "Glenn Accuses Mondale of Being Weak on National Defense"

November 16, *Washington Post*, "Glenn Calls Rival Soft on Defense"

November 16, *Baltimore Sun*, "Mondale Soft on National Defense, Glenn Tells Right-Leaning Democrats"

November 16, *Philadelphia Inquirer*, "Mondale Weak on Defense Glenn Says in Policy Attack"

November 16, *New York Daily News*, "Glenn Calls Mondale a Wimp on Defense"

November 16, *Wall Street Journal*, "Glenn Says Mondale Is 'Weak' on Defense as Struggle in Democratic Party Escalates"

November 16, *Los Angeles Times*, "Glenn Accuses Mondale of Failing to Back U.S. Defense"

November 17, *New York Times*, "Glenn Steps Up His Attacks on Mondale Policies"

November 17, *Washington Post*, "Glenn Asserts Rival Mon-

dale Can't Deliver: Senator Scoffs at Vows on Deficit, Programs"
November 17, *New York Times*, "Mondale Fights Back on
Arms Issue"
November 18, *Washington Post*, "Mondale Aides Rebut
Glenn's Economic Attack"
November 19, *Washington Post*, "Glenn, Defending His
Nerve Gas Vote, Attacks Mondale Anew"
November 22, *Washington Post*, "Mondale Takes Aim at
Glenn: Accuses Rival of 'Desperation,' 'Cooking Figures' "
November 28, *Washington Post Weekly Edition*, "Glenn Tac-
tic: Hit Mondale"
December 5, *Washington Post Weekly Edition*, "A Turn for the
Bitter Between Glenn and Mondale"
December 5, *U.S. News and World Report*, "Bare Knuckle
Time for Glenn, Mondale"

Glenn's "fall offensive" served to lock him ever more tightly into head-
to-head combat with Mondale and to further expose him to the risks that
such a course entailed.

There were two risks. One was that under a persistent frontal attack
by Mondale, Glenn would be unable to hold to the moderate, centrist
ideological position that was a crucial underpinning of his candidacy.
When he first contemplated his candidacy, he believed he could stake a
solid claim to the middle of the political spectrum. "However you define
liberal," he had said,

> Teddy is pretty far over on the left. Fritz is a little less so, and is
> trying to push more over into the middle. But that's very
> difficult for him to do. I'm naturally pretty much in the middle
> and people know it.[86]

Recall Bill White's November 1982 assertion to Glenn: "You have the
middle of the Democratic road all to yourself." But the middle is not a
permanently defined space. Candidates rarely concede the middle to an
opponent; thus, the middle gets defined in the course of political combat.
Glenn was far less secure than he thought he was. The danger for him
was that, in combat, Mondale would push him steadily toward the
conservative end of the spectrum by selectively associating him with
Reagan—by "bludgeoning him as a born again Reaganite." He could put
Glenn on the defensive all the more easily in the absence of any widely
accepted delineation of Glenn's belief system. Glenn's defense of the
vaguely defined middle would require a good deal of agility in ideological combat—a skill that did not come naturally to the Ohio senator.

Glenn, on the other hand, would have difficulty portraying Mondale as too liberal for the party, especially with Jesse Jackson, George McGovern, and, to some degree, Gary Hart securely positioned to Mondale's left. In that situation, the risk was that—in the intraparty context—Glenn would be perceived as more conservative than he actually was, and Mondale would, indeed, take away the middle from him. "I never changed my positions one iota," Glenn lamented when it was over. "But if you get 'stuck with a conservative label,' people tend to think you are a way-over conservative like Jesse Helms." [87] In a fight for the support of activist Democrats, the label would be a severe handicap.

The second risk of Glenn's attack mode lay in the presentation of a political persona more negative than positive, a persona that failed, therefore, to take advantage of Glenn's comparative advantage and failed to accord with popular expectations. In late November two observers wrote, "There are valid questions about whether John Glenn is capable of sustaining this offensive without undermining his reputation as a political Mr. Nice Guy." [88] A couple of weeks later, Gary Hart's campaign manager opined that the attacks had, indeed, been damaging. "Glenn came off very poorly," he said. "He engaged in political hyperbole and he couldn't back it up. . . . The candidate's image was tarnished. He didn't look like the nice guy everyone could trust. He got away from what he did best—being himself." [89] The decision to stay on the offensive was Glenn's. But a question arises once again as to whether his hired guns were serving him well. As they had hoped, some blanks were getting filled, but others worried about the negative content that was being placed in them.

A longtime member of the Senate staff was so upset by Glenn's unnaturally and unwisely aggressive anti-Mondale defense speech that he resigned—for one week. Later, he recalled,

> He attacked Mondale as weak on defense, on the basis of votes Mondale cast ten years earlier. Mondale had come around to a position very much like Glenn's. That wasn't what they [the conservative Democrats] were interested in anyway. Mondale told them what they wanted to hear—that they would have an important place in a Democratic administration. Glenn didn't tell them that. And when he attacked Mondale, he sounded mean. I think this speech and the one in Florida on "failed policies" changed the whole course of the campaign. The strategy devised by Schneiders, Sawyer, and Hamilton was exactly right—right for every other politician they had ever advised. But not for Glenn. John Glenn is not a politician and he never will be. He had to run as the good guy. He might not have won, but he had to go with his strengths. When, in the

last couple of weeks, Glenn finally took charge of the campaign and had it run his way, he did better.

This was the "let Glenn be Glenn" view of someone who knew him as well as anyone, but whose only impact on the campaign was a brief and futile resignation. Words such as "bitter," "bare knuckle," "attack," "accuse," "vicious," "hit," and "mean" do not easily fit with the "right stuff" image of a popular national hero or a public servant of sterling character.[90] Nor would they jibe easily with the media campaign designed to emphasize those favorable images. A mismatch of messages had been initiated that would trouble the campaign to its end.

OBSERVATIONS AND REFLECTIONS: FOUR STATES, NOVEMBER 1983

From November 10 to November 14 I traveled with the Glenn campaign in Mississippi, Louisiana, Iowa, and Nevada. The trip took place between the Florida episode and the attack on Mondale's defense policy. During this time the invasion of Grenada and the situation of U.S. Marines in Lebanon occupied the headlines. The presidential campaign had been driven "underground,"[91] and charge and countercharge had yet to resume. It was a chance to gauge the more constant level of the Glenn effort. Again, my notes provide the skeleton for the text.

THE MOOD

The atmosphere surrounding the campaign effort is noticeably less upbeat than it had been in July. It is not downbeat. It is more a feeling of being embattled; and it is a feeling of being caught up in an agenda or a definition of context that they cannot yet control.

At headquarters, the day before the trip, Bill White said, "I'm worried. We've lost ground to Mondale in several polls among the Democrats—even though we are holding up well head-to-head with Reagan. It was the result of the tremendous publicity Mondale got in October." But White was clearly upset with the performance of his own campaign in October. He was still absorbing the lessons of the confrontation with Mondale. There was a defensive lesson to be learned in responding to criticism of Glenn's Senate votes. "We let that one get too far ahead of us before we shut it down," he said.

Next time we will shut it down real quick. We tried to explain each one . . . going into the details of each vote. . . . That was a mistake. We should have said, "Yes, I voted that way because that's what the country wants. You're the one who is wrong on that issue." Don't explain the vote, don't defend the vote, don't tap dance around. We learned that lesson.

There was also an offensive lesson to be learned. "It didn't happen the way we had planned," said White.

We went too far with the Carter emphasis. We wanted to say that the choice on Reaganomics was whether to try something different or just follow the failed policies of past administra-tions—all administrations, Johnson, Nixon, not just Carter. But it came out as an attack on Carter. That hurt us.

And in a veiled reference to his own isolation from that decision, he concluded, "This campaign will not be won by the things we've planned. It will be won by our reaction to the things that come up and are not planned."

In outlining the tasks ahead, White put a positive face on the confrontation. "The events of the fall were important to the process of differentiation," he said.

Glenn got differentiated from Mondale as far as the party is concerned. The exchange with Mondale showed how they differed on what kind of party they wanted the Democrats to be and who they thought ought to run it. The next step is to move beyond the party to the voters and differentiate Glenn from Mondale as to what they want for the country. We haven't done that yet. That's the stage we're in.

"And when we're through with that," he laughed, "we'll talk about what we want for the world, then the solar system, then the universe."

My best understanding of the shift in focus from party to voters is that it means a shift from party elites to party rank and file. White became mildly enthusiastic in describing that strategic task: "We've got to expand the electorate, get the middle Democrats excited about what's happening to them."

We have to say to them, this is your party. Look what happened to it under the leadership of the extremes. Do you want it? Well, take it back! Take back your party from the extremes. Your leadership doesn't represent you, the rank and file. It's a kind of populist appeal, but we can't call it that.

It was an expression of the "constituency of the whole" idea, a reincarnation of the rank and file on which Glenn had based his primary victories in Ohio. And it remains, as always, vaguely defined.

The instrument for implementing this strategy is, of course, John Glenn. But White expressed no positive ideas about how to mount a Glenn-based appeal—only a continuation of the anti-Mondale approach. "I still think people are very interested in valence issues—character, integrity, trust, things like that," he said.

> But I don't think those issues will work by themselves. They have to come up in the context of other issues and then they will work. For example, we are just waiting for Walter Mondale to tag John Glenn as the tool of corporate interests. Mondale has been a lobbyist for corporate interests. . . . We're ready to nail him to the wall on corporate interests. In that context, the character issue would be important. And we may get some help from the media—like Mary McGrory's article "will the real Walter Mondale please stand up," on how he says one thing in private and another in public. If we just went out and said Walter Mondale is a tool of corporate interests, no one would listen. But if we catch him being holier than thou, we can jerk him back real quickly on that one.

His clear intention is to continue in a confrontational mode with Mondale, to lie in the weeds waiting for him to stumble, and, in general, to play negatively off Mondale rather than play positively off John Glenn. If, as White believes, they are in a postdifferentiation stage of the campaign, they seem to have no commensurate strategy—only the counterpunching of the New York-Iowa-Florida sequence. And that strategy has not been notably successful.

On the campaign trail, the mood is similarly tentative—based on the feeling that October had been a good month for Mondale and a bad month for Glenn. On the morning we left Washington, the *Post* headlined its campaign article, "Mondale Makes Impressive Gains Over Glenn, Polls Show." [92] The same day, one of the three campaign regulars filed his story for the Knight-Ridder newspapers saying that Mondale "has substantially increased his lead" and "the latest poll results lend urgency to Glenn's reorganization efforts and strategy changes." [93] After a summertime of steady gains, he reported, "Glenn is slipping among the registered Democrats." In the Harris poll, Mondale's lead among this group had grown from nine points to twenty points between August and October.

Outwardly the Glenn campaigners appear unruffled. "We have said all along there will be fluctuations in the polls," announced a spokes-

man. "We anticipated October would be a good month for Mondale." [94]
But on the campaign plane, the same spokesman conceded the problem
revealed by the polls.

> He has to reach those Democrats who aren't the leaders, give
> them an argument that he is best for the Democratic party,
> and do some party building. He must identify his program
> with the party. His standard stump speech is good. But it has
> no party partisanship in it. He must develop that appeal to
> the party if he is going to win. Maybe it's too late. I don't
> know.

It is a problem as old as Ohio in 1970. Glenn remarked, "Polls go up,
polls go down. We've generally advanced, and so we're just going to
keep on going, doing what we've been doing." But he also began to
speak of his campaign as "a calculated risk."

Like his manager, Glenn seemed preoccupied with the Mondale
confrontation, even when he was joking. Looking forward to the
holidays in Vail and noting that Mondale sometimes skied there too, he
said, "We could have a ski race, and the one who lost would drop out. . . .
I've been wondering whether I would take such a race and I've just
decided. Yes, I would. But I don't think Fritz would." As a matter of fact,
Glenn was preparing to resume the war, with his double-barreled attack
on Mondale's defense and economic policies.

On the trip back from Nevada, he calmly reviewed the events of the
previous month—without mentioning the preparations in progress.

> I had always hoped we could conduct the campaign on the
> issues and not get into personal attacks on one another. But it
> didn't work out that way. I was the aggrieved party—if you
> want to look at it that way. It all began when Mario Cuomo
> asked me to describe the differences between myself and
> Mondale and I refused. Cuomo got mad, and Mondale knew
> he was mad. As soon as he got the chance, he lit out after me
> on a number of things. I had to defend myself and so I hit
> back. But I said I hoped that would be the end of that kind of
> campaigning and that I hoped we would get back to the real
> issues.
>
> At the Iowa Forum, after I had spoken and had no chance
> to reply, he went after me again. So a couple of days later, I
> replied. Then he printed that three-page attack on me that was
> so bad he had to apologize publicly for part of it. Each time I
> said I hoped that was the end of it. And each time they have
> started it again. Now they are going around Iowa talking
> about binary chemicals, telling everybody that I'm in favor of
> nerve gas. "Glenn is for nerve gas; Mondale is against nerve

gas." Now that is just the worst kind of flat-out demagoguery I've ever heard. It makes me mad, and I don't know what to do about it. I may have to take him on head-on and all-out. There are some things I could say that I don't want to say. I'm not sure Fritz would have the stomach for that kind of battle. But I may have to do it. I can't let them get away with that garbage.

There is, in the comment, a continued emphasis on matters of confrontation and differentiation.

The comment also conveys the familiar notion that Glenn is behaving in a manner fundamentally different from Mondale because he is a different kind of politician from Mondale. It is an exaggeration. At the very time that he was preparing a massive counterattack, Glenn was portraying himself as the reluctant combatant and the consistent peacemaker—the adherent of high-level politics. The self-portrait derives, again, from his basic differentiation between public service politics and ego politics, from the corollary that public service politicians have higher motives than ego politicians, from the assumption that he is a public service-type politician and Mondale is an ego-type politician, and from the deduction that he operates out of more worthy motivations than Mondale. This stance, it seems to me, has not served him well. It encourages him to deny his own ambition. That denial, in turn, leads him to see himself as the aggrieved counterattacker. And that defensive posture steers him away from a more positive, more profitable exploitation of his personal strengths.

Glenn believes that if only he can demonstrate that Mondale is, in fact, a different, less idealistic, ego-type politician, the voters will make the leap and conclude that Glenn is the superior candidate. So he is willing to stay locked into a negative campaign against Mondale, attacking him for the ego politician's willingness to promise everything to everybody. Glenn's problem is that while he may, indeed, have found Mondale's weakness, the voters are not likely to shift their allegiance to Glenn until he gives them a positive reason to do so. Glenn and his campaigners believe that Mondale's weakness shows that he lacks character and that, by comparison, Glenn's superior character will become self-evident. It will not. Glenn's character—thought to be his greatest strength—must be presented in a positive way, true to himself, without regard to Walter Mondale. Because Glenn cannot be expected to give up his public service values, any positive definition of his candidacy must be grounded in those values. That may be a difficult task, but the first task is to realize that, up to now, rigid adherence to the public service distinction has kept Glenn in a defensive posture and, as such, has been more harm than help.

THE RECORD

"Nobody outside the state of Ohio knows anything about John Glenn's record," Bill White said before the trip.

> All they know is that he's an astronaut and he's running for president. And those two things, taken together, are a negative. The meat in that sandwich is "what he stands for." And our job is to put the meat in the sandwich. We need to make the connection between astronaut and president. The voters will not do it for us.

"I began the race in March with a solid base of support from people who knew me from the space program and from my work in the Senate," Glenn told a Las Vegas interviewer.

> On the warmth thermometer pollsters use, I have come across as warm—whatever that means—and with very few negatives. But outside of Ohio, very few people knew my whole record or what I stood for. So that has been our main job.

Lou Harris, describing his October poll results on voter information, concurs. "There is a big gap on Glenn's experience and record." [95]

By his own definition, Glenn's "main job" remains unfinished. He and his campaigners have zeroed in on the notion of experience as the key to success. There may be more to it than that. But experience is the central problem they are wrestling with at this point. Along with his attacks on Reagan's budget deficit and the tax surcharge plan to deal with it, discussions of Glenn's experience dominated the Iowa trip. ("I think people have to have a feeling. Hey, this person is really capable of being president of the United States," Glenn will tell journalist Elizabeth Drew during a similar visit in January. "Once you get beyond that point . . . then all those other things I say on specific issues are likely to be accepted—more fully accepted." [96] When asked later what he most wanted to get across to the voters, the candidate said to Drew,

> Experience—I think that's a major one. . . . Most people think of me . . . as an astronaut I guess. Our job is to flesh it out—that there are lots of other experiences and accomplishments that have something to do with the Presidency of the United States. . . . If we could just get this idea of experience across, I think that could make a big difference." [97])

In each of his half-dozen Iowa speeches, Glenn spoke at considerable length and in the same vein about his experience. It is the old problem of his political persona in its newest form.

His remarks in a private home in West Des Moines are typical:

> I was interested back a few weeks ago to see a report in the paper that my leading opponent for the nomination had said that he thought that this nomination should go to the person with the greatest experience. He's going to be surprised to find out that I couldn't agree with him more. I think he's absolutely 100 percent right. Now, let's just let me take a few minutes and talk about experience. He's talking about Washington experience, I know. I've had nine years experience in Washington; I think I have a good feel for how Washington operates. But there's some other things I think that happen outside Washington, D.C., that bear on the future of this country and that a president of the United States should have some experience [with] perhaps. Not only in solving problems but in taking advantage of some of the opportunities that we have as a nation.
>
> And before I was in the Senate and the nine years I've spent there, I was in international business. I headed up an international corporation, traveled all over the world on business, set deals all over the world, and, you know, one out of every six jobs—industrial jobs—in this country depends on export of the product made. And one-third of our agricultural produce gets shipped outside this country. It's a tremendous factor in international commerce and absolutely vital. And I've had experience in that international commerce area.
>
> Before that, with two other people I started four small businesses, know what it's like to meet a payroll, know what it's like to see interest rates go up and have a project canceled out from under us, know those difficulties of financing and refinancing, and 55 percent of our people are employed by small business in this nation.
>
> Before that, I was an astronaut in the NASA program, worked with some of the finest scientists in the world, continued that association with the scientific community, working on energy matters that I took a lead on when I got to the Senate because there wasn't much being done on them. The nuclear nonproliferation act of 1978 was passed; I was the principal author of that act and pushed and worked to get it through. I wish it were being enforced today by this administration instead of bypassed. But that's another story. So I've had experience in the scientific community, and I think that's an excellent background for making some of the research decisions that are going to make or break this nation into the long-term future.
>
> Before that I was in the Marine Corps for twenty-three

years and I can't think of a better background for making some of the defense decisions on what we need—and please underline/circle the last word *need*—and need only. I don't want to see us buying everything that the last salesman was selling that came up the mall entrance steps of the Pentagon. Let's make it what we need. I can tell you something else that that military background brings with it, too. I do not need to sit and watch late-night TV to know what it's like to be in combat. I've been through two wars—hideous, horrible stuff. I've had to write some of those—too many of those—next-of-kin letters after some missions; I don't want to see that ever visited on anyone again and I can just guarantee you that nobody, but nobody, is going to work any harder to keep the peace than I will. And I pledge that to you this evening. (applause)

He was trying to tell his listeners that he should be viewed as more than an astronaut and more than a lifelong politician. He was trying to tell them that his varied background gave him the competence to make important policy judgments. Altogether, it was an impressive refutation of any notion that he lacked relevant experience.

Yet his speeches, taken as wholes, seem not to help much in establishing a political persona. Voters do not judge "experience" as a list of discrete activities, but as part of an overall judgment on an individual's capacity to handle the job. It is not enough simply to list relevant experience; it is necessary to establish the relevance—the political relevance—of the experience. And that larger task requires that he make connections between the elements of his experience, his past record of achievement, and his policy ideas for the future. It requires, too, that he lay out the connections between his experience and the broadest themes of his campaign. Because the recitation of his experience focuses on his past and looks backward, it is especially important that he connect it strongly to his future-oriented campaign theme— "Leadership for the Future" or "Believe in the Future Again." It requires, in sum, the treatment of his experience in a form that his listeners could easily convert into a sense of his "whole record and what I stood for" or, more generally, a sense of his potential political leadership. That is what, in his Iowa speeches at least, he did not seem to accomplish.

He came closest when he related his experience to his expertise on weaponry and to his commitment to peace. But even here, he accomplished less than he might have. Not surprisingly, what the "boys on the bus"—the reporters who travel with a candidate—have come to call the "pledge" was made in every speech and drew applause in every speech. "I've been through two wars . . . and I can just guarantee you that nobody, but nobody, is going to work any harder to keep the peace than I will." It was an effective way to connect his special background to a deeply felt popular concern. It provided a reassuring answer to questions about his leadership—the more so in view of his prodefense reputation and liberal criticism of his vote for a new nerve gas system.

When the applause ended, in West Des Moines, he added another note of reassuring self-description.

> To those who try to make me out to be some sort of superhawk because I had a career in the military, I can say this. I'm sure, with many of you here, I know of no group of people in this whole world that wants peace any more than those who have actually been in combat. And so I just think it is the opposite when they try and paint me into some corner as a big superhawk. It's exactly the opposite.

But he stopped with this rebuttal of the idea that his military background made him a superhawk. He added nothing positive for the group to hang onto. At the very end of the speech he mentioned in passing that he had a "five-point goal for how we keep peace." But he did not provide any leitmotif or circle back to connect it to his earlier comments about his relevant experience. As long as he does not make those kinds of connections, discussions of his relevant experience—even one that draws applause—will be of less than maximum help to his listeners.

Taken as a whole, Glenn's earnest presentation of his experience fails, I think, to communicate a sense of connectedness to political leadership. To begin with, it was cast defensively—more as an answer to Mondale than as his own most positive presentation of himself. He wanted to make the public service argument, "I'm not limited to being just a professional politician." [98] And he did. But that only increases the necessity for him to tie his many nonpolitical experiences in a positive way to the job he is seeking. Instead, the description of his experience comes across more as the recitation of a vita than as the picture of a potential leader.

Furthermore, the description was invariably a self-contained segment within each speech, detached from specific policy discussions and from broader campaign themes. In his speeches, for example, he typically devotes more attention and more passion to education and research than to any other subject; yet just as typically, he does not link those subjects to his experience within the "scientific community," to his past accomplishments, or to his future policy prescriptions. And, therefore, he comes across as something less than a proven leader in that field, too. All in all, despite his intentions, Glenn's rather mechanical discussion of his experience leaves a very incomplete notion of the kind of president he might be.

After listening to five versions of his basic stump speech, it seems to me that this large task of providing the connective tissue, "the meat in the sandwich," between experience and leadership is inherently difficult for John Glenn. It is difficult because the task demands a configurative or an integrative turn of mind, whereas Glenn's thought patterns are more linear or additive. His is a "let's-set-goals-and-go-for-it" style of thinking. It is not a "let's-fit-it-all-together" style of thinking. He tends to think more in terms of a checklist than in terms of an overall sense of proportion. That habit of mind is what leads him to see experience as a "threshold issue," as something to be settled first before one could successfully move on to other matters. That habit of mind is what leads him to set forth his experiences one after the other in an isolated segment of his speech. In a more configurative approach, his experience would have been presented concurrently with its relationship to broader issues. Experience and policy would have been intertwined, not placed in sequence or treated separately. Experience would not have been thought of as the first hurdle, but as a part of every hurdle.

His decision to emphasize experience and his decision to make it one discrete part of his presentation may explain why he produced a fragmented speech that had little or no issue focus. If so, the net result is that his listeners will have great difficulty receiving any basic policy-oriented message. Or so it seems to me. And it also seems that Glenn needs a policy focus if he is to picture himself as a moderate, centrist alternative to Mondale, if he seriously wishes to convey "my record and what I stand for." The task is also inherently difficult because his Senate record on so many issues of domestic politics is a voting record rather than a widely known record of active commitment. It is also difficult because Glenn's centrism, too, is more a vector of Senate votes than a definable philosophical position. So, unless he works hard to delineate his moderate centrist position, the danger is that "what I stand for" (and what he cares for) will remain unknown. His audiences needed a more positive message to hang onto and to talk about. The way he chose to treat experience was no help.

The fragmentation of the candidate's message was worsened by his difficulty in bringing his speeches to any unifying, summary conclusion. He tends, instead, to return at the end of his speech to pick up those checklist items he has failed to mention earlier. In Council Bluffs, for example, when the question period ended and a thank you seemed imminent, he said, "Let me give you some more details on agriculture," and he outlined a multipoint program. Then, he said thank you, but he continued speaking, about the importance of goals, about the Norman

Rockwell pictures, and about a quotation from Ralph Waldo Emerson. He worked from a set of cards, and it seemed as if he could not stop until he had read something from each one. His audience was left with many discrete parts, but with no coherent whole and, hence, no easily encapsulated message.[99] His speaking style is not—as commonly alleged—his most serious problem. The idea that he is "dull" or "boring" is but a surrogate complaint for what *is* a serious problem, the absence of a compelling message.

Not surprisingly, the question and answer period serves him best because it is congenial to his additive style of thinking. It requires no configuration and can be handled one question at a time. In this fashion, he can display the depth of information about a range of subjects that studious senators acquire, and he can show the mastery of detail he commands in areas of special interest to him. Indeed, the question period did more to establish the relevance of his experience than his stump speech, and he achieved better contact with his audience. Afterward, listeners and scorekeepers alike remarked favorably on the extent of his knowledge. The boys on the bus agreed that he would be well-advised to lengthen the question and answer period and shorten the speech. They also agreed that he should shorten his answers, which tend to be long, repetitive, and lacking in capstone conclusions. In Atlantic, Iowa, for example, it took him four and a half minutes to defend his vote on nerve gas and six and a half minutes to describe his position on nuclear weapons control. In twenty minutes, he answered only five questions. Again, he shows an earnest concern that his listeners understand his thinking. But, in November, he has not yet learned—as Bill White suggested he must—to make pointed explanations of his votes or his positions.

The Astronaut

The central impediment to the development of a political persona remains his astronaut-hero background. It is the same impediment that has been with him from the beginning of his career. Here, all his problems with experience are writ large. Here, his linear, additive style of thinking hurts him the most, for he acts as if he thinks that the way to handle his astronaut past is to pile so many other experiences on top of it that it will be subsumed and put in perspective by the sheer weight of the others. So, in discussing his experience, his only direct reference is the bare bones, "I was an astronaut in the NASA program"—which he then describes as a valuable scientific, research experience. To someone who comes to the campaign wondering how he will handle the matter, it seems clear that he has decided to avoid or downplay the astronaut past. (As he will tell Elizabeth Drew later, "I certainly don't try and downplay it, I just try to add on to it." [100]) Adding on to it is not what seems to be needed.

What is needed is a positive effort to come to grips with his marine-astronaut experience in a way that connects it directly and centrally to the kind of president he will be. If the only thing people know about him is that he was an astronaut, his task is to turn that information into an asset by making it an integral part of his campaign. He needs to put it in perspective not by avoiding or downplaying it or by piling other experiences on top of it, but by confronting it, by talking about it. When, for example, his listeners applaud his pledge, they do so because they want peace, not because Glenn has thus far encouraged them to picture him as America's most effective negotiator for peace. Yet the knowledge he gained and the calm courage he displayed as a marine-astronaut—plus his Senate accomplishments in the area of nuclear nonprolifera-tion—give him a very credible basis on which to stake just such a claim. But he says nothing remotely like it; there is no follow up to the pledge.

As with every other element of his experience, he needs to find ways to connect the astronaut part of it to his policy positions and priorities. He needs to integrate it into his definition of political leadership, so as to force people to think of it that way. In Council Bluffs, he hinted at the possibility of linkage. "I was an astronaut in the NASA program," he said, and he added that he was "very proud of that service back in those days. We were setting objectives, goals. We were proud of excellence. We need some of that objective, goal thing today." But that was all. The possible linkages to future political leadership are neither pursued nor elaborated. It is almost as if he does not himself think his astronaut experience can be linked effectively to the require-ments of the presidency. And yet if he does not make the connection positively and aggressively, how can he expect the voters to make it?

In view of Glenn's reluctance to face his past head-on, it seems a bit incongruous that his first nationwide ad campaign features his space flight and that his campaigners are hoping to reap voter attention (if not support) from the newly released movie *The Right Stuff*. Indeed, the five-minute paid media spot on October 15 was timed to coincide with the movie's release. *Newsweek*'s cover story of October 3 featured the movie, with a cover picture of the actor who plays Glenn. Its caption reads " 'The Right Stuff': Can a Movie Help Make a President?" At this point the question cannot be answered. But the high profile being given to his astronaut past in the media stands in sharp contrast to Glenn's consistent downplaying of it on the campaign trail.

When he is asked about the movie, he typically demurs, saying only that he has not seen it and has "no idea what its impact will be." In Las

Vegas, however, he again ventured his cautious connection. The movie, he says, is about "times when we had that pride in excellence that President Kennedy emphasized ... times when we set goals, had objectives, and were moving ahead. That's the kind of leadership I want to provide." It is surely in keeping with Glenn's essential modesty about his heroism that he should not tout the movie. But it is a certainty that the movie's major effect will be to remind people that he was an astronaut, and the former astronaut must devise a way of dealing with that identification head-on. Also, when the media emphasizes his heroic past and the candidate seems unable to relate it to the goal he seeks, it suggests that the Glenn campaign has not yet decided what its essential message really is.

Naturally, this is not the first time Glenn has confronted the astronaut problem. In Ohio he solved it with the passage of time—over the course of several election campaigns and over a ten-year period. Gradually, but very gradually, Ohioans have come to think of him as a senator as well as an astronaut. Now, he must follow the same course in another setting with a new set of scorekeepers. Because he does not have the time to change that persona, there is urgency to his campaign task, all of which casts even further doubt on his initial strategy decision to delay his entry into the race. Given his experience in Ohio, what made him think he could make a blend of his "whole record and what I stand for" and his astronaut past in fourteen to sixteen months? And, once in the presidential race, what made him think he could produce this blend if he did not direct the process openly and aggressively himself?

His media people apparently have decided they could force-feed the public and telescope the lengthy process. But that may well be another manipulative illusion of the hired guns, who have already given too much emphasis to "filling in the blanks" and too little to integrating the astronaut image already so vividly "filled in." Consequently, perhaps, they have downgraded the necessity for the candidate to undertake the task of integration himself. To this observer, however, there is simply no other way to do it.

THE RECEPTION

Before I left on the trip, I had asked campaign manager White to tell me what he would look for if he were going to Iowa. He said,

> See how serious he is when he speaks. Well, I don't mean serious; he's always been serious. But see how hard he is trying to get his message across. Talk to people after he speaks and ask

them what they thought and whether they felt differently after they heard him speak.

He was curious about the content of Glenn's message and about the receptivity of people to it and to him. I have already spoken about the blurred quality of the message despite the candidate's palpably earnest efforts, but not about the kind of reception he received. And it is, perhaps, symbolic of Glenn's struggle to define a winning political persona that on this trip he received his most rousing reception from the least political audience he faced—the U.S. Marines—and the most lukewarm reception from the most political group he faced—the Mississippi NAACP.

He attended Marine Corps Birthday Celebration Balls in New Orleans and Des Moines. In Des Moines, he began, "I cannot think of any group I could be with in the country, the group with which I would feel more at home or more at ease, than with this group of marines." In the dress uniform of a marine colonel, he participated in the ceremonies and delivered an extemporaneous talk that embodied and evoked the set of values that deeply undergird John Glenn's public service career. Seven times, he used the twin phrases "the devotion to duty and the commitment to excellence" to describe "the hallmark of our corps." He spoke several times about the sense of pride in self, unit, and country that are engendered by the marine experience, and about a marine's service to his country as "a call to a higher purpose and higher cause."

"Marine training," he told them, "makes a marine more afraid of letting his country or his fellow marines down than he is of getting hurt." Marines were leaders, he said, because they observed three themes: "learn the tools of your trade; be a person of honesty, decency, integrity, and responsibility; work together and take care of each other." He punctuated the talk with examples of heroism and sacrifice, and he expressed his own "tremendous pride" at his association with people of such "uncommon valor." The talk was begun and concluded with loud applause and with a variety of enthusiastic cheers. After the trip Glenn said he felt "most comfortable" on those two occasions and ranked all his other appearances an equal distance behind. "I guess you could tell that," he said. It was another reminder of how much of the marine remains in the politician.

Although he made no reference to comfortableness in his speech to the Mississippi State NAACP Convention luncheon in Clarksdale, the relationship was noticeably different. He began by referring to the president of the group, Dr. Aaron Henry, and to the man who introduced him, Dr. James Figgs. "It's a pleasure to be here with my friends Aaron Henry and James Figgs. I know I can rely on them for advice and counsel." But his attachment to the group had been more accurately communicated by Henry in an NBC-TV interview prior to the speech. "Glenn is not well known among the constituencies I'm a part of," said Henry. And he described Glenn's civil rights record as "mediocre." Reporter John Dancy inquired, "You said John Glenn has no name recognition?" And Henry, waving his fingers first in the air then pointing to his chest, replied, "Yes, we don't care anything about people riding up there around the moon. We want to know, 'What has he done for black folks down here?' " (It was a symptom of Glenn's problem with his persona that many people thought—to the very end of his campaign—that he had been the first American to walk on the moon, not the first to orbit the earth.)

As he had many times before, Glenn stated, "I am proud of my record on minority issues." He distributed an elaborate brochure entitled "John Glenn Answers the Black Community's Questions," setting forth his position on matters of interest to blacks. He repeated some of them in his speech—praise of Jesse Jackson, criticism of the administration, ideas about job training, employment, hunger, education, business, and civil rights enforcement. None of it was very specific. He drew applause only once, when he stated his opposition to "constructive engagement" as a policy toward apartheid in South Africa.

Afterward, Glenn described the speech as "wholesale politics," whereby "you talk to large numbers of people and hope they will talk with others." "If news of my NAACP speech travels through the black community network, it will be very important," he said. But the next morning on the NBC "Today Show," reporter John Dancy presented his interview with Aaron Henry juxtaposed against Glenn's statement of pride in his civil rights record. It is the TV report that is likely to travel farthest and carry the most impact from his visit.

Thus, the visit becomes another reminder of Glenn's essential weakness with the core constituencies of the Democratic party. His top black staff member, a former NAACP official, feels Glenn's problem with blacks acutely, and believes it can be handled only by a different campaign strategy. "We need threshold credibility," he said in Mississippi.

> And the fact that he was an astronaut doesn't give it to us. The opposition has played up the astronaut thing beautifully; and it's a negative. All the buildup about the movie is a negative. It is so blinding that it shuts out everything else. Individual groups want to know how he affects their concerns. To my way of thinking, the mass appeal is wrong.

In his press conference before the speech, in the speech itself, and in his new brochure, Glenn addressed the question of Jesse Jackson's very recent entry into the race. He praised Jackson, but repeated his determination "to compete for every black vote and every black delegate in the nation." When Walter Mondale spoke to a similar group in Arkansas he told his audience, "You know me. I'm not here to get my civil rights card punched. We've been together in many fights for twenty-five years. You know it and I know it. I haven't just been right. I've been there." [101] There is a dimension of commitment to Mondale's civil rights record that John Glenn cannot match. If Glenn expects any degree of success, it seems he will have to fashion a much warmer, much closer attachment to the black community than he has yet done. It is hard to see when and how he can do so.

In Iowa, where one reporter notes that his audiences are "white, middle class, and middle America," all observers comment that Glenn drew excellent crowds. At dinner one night, the boys on the bus agree they felt an unexpected uptick in the campaign. A front page story from Sioux City on November 12 in the *Des Moines Register* began,

> If sheer numbers count, Senator John Glenn may not be in as much organizational trouble as political experts think. The Democratic presidential candidate drew large enthusiastic crowds here, in Council Bluffs and Atlantic.[102]

On the same day, under a headline, "Glenn Draws Good Crowd at Stop Here," the *Sioux City Journal* began:

> Senator John Glenn may have gained a step on Walter Mondale Friday night in Sioux City. The crowd that Glenn addressed at the Elk's lodge was as large—if not larger—than a gathering Mondale addressed Wednesday night.[103]

Inside the Glenn camp, the feeling was similarly encouraging. On the way back to Washington, the candidate said,

> Campaigning in Iowa is retail politics. You meet people one at a time in small groups. You judge political importance by the size of the group and by the enthusiasm. That is, did more people come out than you expected and did they show any special enthusiasm? We were talking about it afterwards that more people showed up all over Iowa than we had expected—more people than we saw the last time we were here. And there was more enthusiasm.

A staffer who accompanied him on every trip commented, "We were down, but these last two days in Iowa showed we are coming up again. I could feel it when we were down and I can feel it when we're coming up."

It is difficult for a one-shot observer to make comparisons either with previous performances by a candidate or with current performances by other candidates—much less gauge audience response. But it seemed to me that the enthusiasm of the crowds was registered as visibly by their presence as by their response to what they heard. As always, Glenn had difficulty injecting excitement or inspiration or punch into his remarks. The pledge was the only sure-fire applause line in his speeches. It produced the only applause from audiences in Atlantic, Council Bluffs, and West Des Moines. It was one of only two applause-producing comments in Carroll and Sioux City. His audiences listened intently, but they registered almost no enthusiasm. Glenn was, as usual, serious and sincere ("He's the most earnest of all the candidates," remarked one reporter), but he did not deliver emotion. This absence of emotion—plus the fragmentation of the message—results in the same speechmaking problems I had observed in Chicago, Little Rock, and Philadelphia. Glenn's speeches convey more of the dutiful soldier than the enthusiastic missionary.

(At the end of her three-day Iowa trip with Glenn in January, Elizabeth Drew had a similar reaction.

> His audiences may well like him and admire him, but he does not seem to get much out of them, because he doesn't give them much. He is agreeable but remote, automatic. He makes no personal connection with his audiences. Skilled politicians establish a connection with their audiences, joke with them, give them some emotion, get some back. An appearance by a skilled politician turns into a chemical experience. Glenn offers no emotion. There is nothing personal in these appearances. It is as if all the audiences were the same for him. Most skilled politicians take the measure of a crowd and find ways to relate to it specifically. It is as if Glenn were doing a walk-through. Undoubtedly, he comes across as nice and sincere—as John Glenn—and as a man of common sense and plain American values. But little seems to happen.[104])

He does not take maximum advantage of his appearances to build intense attachments to specific groups.

A question that naturally comes to mind is whether the large crowds are more the result of curiosity about the astronaut-hero than about likely support for the candidate. And a related question is whether the Glenn campaigners have been deceived and somewhat lulled by the appearance of large crowds. Journalists traveling with the campaign apply a discount to crowd size, suggesting that an unknown percentage of his Iowa audiences are Republicans. The Iowa state Democratic chairman will venture later that Glenn's handlers mistakenly scheduled him before Rotary Club-type audiences that "aren't going to be around on caucus night." [105] In their profile of John Glenn in Iowa, the state's two top scorekeepers will soon pose the question this way: "Will these people who waited in Mason City to snap his picture, collect his autograph and grasp his hand trudge through the snow in February and spend 3 hours in a school house . . . to help him become President?" [106] It is an old question—about Glenn's performance in manipulating intensities and cultivating constituencies in politics.

If the enthusiasm of Iowa's crowds does reflect—as Glenn's entourage believes—a true enthusiasm for his candidacy, then the question turns back to organization, for that is what it will take to harden initial enthusiasm into ultimate support. To date, existing accounts of Glenn's Iowa organization have been uniformly negative—too little and too late. Three days before this trip a "prominent Iowa Democrat" was quoted as saying,

> Up to now, the Glenn campaign has been the greatest waste of a presidential candidate I've ever seen. They have an ideal candidate who has enormous popular appeal, but in between those two things there has been one of the worst organizational efforts I have ever seen. There are a lot of people here who are ready to march for John Glenn if someone will give them the word.[107]

As our trip began, it was announced that a new Iowa campaign manager had been named, and a major staff shakeup followed. The need to generate more organizational follow-up was given special attention by the new team.[108] A top Iowa reporter, along for our trip, took special note that "while Glenn talked, his aides scurried behind the scenes to collect the names of Iowans who attended the events." And he quoted Glenn's new press secretary to the effect that "those people who sign volunteer lists can expect to be asked to help." [109] At best, this new staff effort means a slow beginning to an eventual turning of a corner. The question in Iowa centered on whether there would be a changed emphasis and whether enough time remained to turn the corner. And the matter was urgent. The day we left the state, a *Des Moines Register* front page story contained this prophetic sentence: "The Ohio Senator says a candidate can't afford a bad showing here because 'he has no chance to recover.' " [110]

POST MORTEM

When I left the campaign November 14, I had gained no clear idea of how successful John Glenn might be. I had been given only the partial perspective of the campaign trail—speechmaking, public display, and preoccupation with the present. I had picked up a pervasive sense of uncertainty, but no sense that the cause was lost. Anything seemed possible. I did, however, recognize a set of familiar problems. The ability of the candidate and his campaigners to cope with these concerns seemed not to have increased substantially since my last look-in, and now there was much less time in which to do so. That juxtaposition was, perhaps, my best first-hand clue to the slow progress of the campaign.

Once again the contrast between the public candidate—stiff and aloof—and the private person—spontaneous and warm—presented itself. It remained as striking to this observer as it had been in Ohio four years earlier. In political situations, the candidate struggles mechanically with his message, his past, his persona. In nonpolitical situations the down-to-earth hero is immensely appealing. When, for example, the flustered president of the National Association of Realtors, Harley Snyder, says to Annie, "Hello, I'm Harley Glenn," the candidate turns immediately to his wife and says, "Hello, I'm John Snyder." (Smiles) On the campaign plane, *Time* photographer P. F. Bentley tells the group he is waiting to present Glenn with a picture of himself with a funny hat on. (Smiles) Bentley, a campaign regular, explains the joke.

> We have this running gag. . . . He will not pose with a hat on, and I keep trying to get a picture of him with a hat on. He'll put a hat on, I'll raise my camera, and he'll take it off. We will go through this routine several times—hat on, camera up, hat off, camera down. He loves it. People say John Glenn is a stiff. They are completely wrong. He has a great comic sense.[111]

In his speechmaking, Glenn always starts with a self-deprecating joke. It sets a nice tone, but the remainder of his presentation is humorless. He remains totally comfortable with himself, but almost as uncomfortable with the conventional routines of politics. How to take advantage of Glenn's appealing personality is still an unsolved problem.

As formal speechmaking is not John Glenn's political strength, one wonders anew why his strategists have not run a truly retail campaign— putting him face to face before small groups in the places where Democrats gathered. Media people who see him in one-on-one situations—in informal settings with voters or with editorial boards—find him appealing and knowledgeable.[112] Certainly their accounts are vastly more flattering than their accounts of his speechmaking. Surely his Ohio campaigners had considered his person-to-person abilities a great as-set.[113] And Iowa is known as a face-to-face, retail state *par excellence.* Perhaps Glenn refused to do it this way. Perhaps his national campaign-ers believed the media would do it for them. Perhaps these hired guns did not think he could do it that way. Perhaps they never thought of it.

Other problems remain visible. He cares passionately about the country and about good government, but he cannot communicate his blend of patriotism and public service to politically oriented audiences. He has not yet articulated any message that will appeal to people apart from their constituency base. He is wedded to a general election strategy, with a national focus and a media emphasis. But he has not figured out how to adapt these strategic choices to the realities of nomination politics. He knows a great deal about many issues, but he cannot package a discussion of them in a way that illuminates personal strength or his leadership potential. His political persona remains undeveloped, as does his organization. In both respects, he is con-strained by a timetable set by his earliest campaign decision. And, in his confrontation with Walter Mondale, he remains unwilling and/or unable to extricate himself from a context not of his making and not to his benefit. All in all, he has not found a public voice that is positive and persuasive or a base of support that is informed and intense. It remains unclear as to where, how, and when he can do so.

Running for the presidency in the whole country is much harder than running for the Senate in one state. A new set of standards applies—standards that involve intimations of leadership ability at the highest and broadest levels. Even if people learn that Glenn has been a good senator for Ohio and spectacularly successful in getting reelected, they will ask for something more. They will ask for signs of the positive, motivating, directing kind of activity that characterizes political leader-ship. They will ask for indications of boldness and a willingness to expend political capital in pursuit of worthy goals. Looking back on John Glenn's presidential quest—from Chicago in 1981 to Iowa in 1983—the observer is struck by the defensive, protective stance he has taken. He campaigns too often as if he has much to lose and does not want to risk losing it. He does not campaign often enough as if he needs to reach out, plunge ahead, and energize others to win.

The fact is that he does have a great deal to lose, perhaps more than the rest of us can begin to fathom. He came to politics as a hero of unimpeachable character, after a model career of service to his country. He brought with him a stellar personal reputation and an unbreakable bond of esteem from his fellow citizens. He has acted in politics as if, above all, he did not want to lose the reputation and the esteem. He has adopted a set of public service ideas that prescribe for him higher standards of political conduct than for most politicians—standards that call for a muted ambition and a remoteness from everyday political machinations. These guiding ideas have been reflected in his political life. He has reacted indignantly and protectively to any perceived attack or denigration of personal character. He has remained uncomfortable in situations structured as "political." He has not relished the workaday activities of coalition building. He has had difficulty weaving the bonds of emotion or obligation or loyalty that nurture primary supporters.

In sum, he has adopted a stance and pattern of activity that are most protective of the flawless personal reputation and public respect he brought with him to the political arena. In Ohio he has succeeded, but only with the spur of defeat and the luxury of time and only as he gave in to the necessities of partisan and interpersonal constituency building. His personal reputation is his greatest political asset. But in protecting it, rather than spending it, he can diminish its usefulness. His contentedness in defining himself by contrast with Mondale and his willingness to counterpunch against Mondale is the present case in point. The constraints of his public service politics seem now to be thwarting, rather than aiding, his ambition to be president. He needs to think positively about the demands of political leadership and present himself in those terms. In Meg Greenfield's terms, he needs to help people "imagine" him as president.

Looking back on this five-day trip, I think Glenn's most memorable effort to come to grips with these various problems came during the question period in Sioux City. It came in answer to the question: "I realize you did not get the AFL-CIO endorsement, but would you give us some of your thoughts on the labor movement and unions?" His answer:

> Sure would. I love the union label, not necessarily the union leader label—a little bit different. The polls across the country have shown a fairly even split of union households between those who will vote for Mr. Mondale and those who will vote for me. Yet labor leaders went about 90 percent, almost 91 percent for him. Well, you know, I had an experience back home in Ohio with opposition many years ago and I determined then to go right straight to the rank and file. And that's the way we've set up this whole campaign this year. I did not set out in this campaign to make it centered around endorsements, be it individual or organization. I'm happy to accept endorsements along the way ... but I didn't make it the centerpiece of my candidacy. I think people over the past twenty or twenty-five years through television, and through newspapers, through magazines, and through radio are well

enough informed that they want to make up their own minds. I think we've lost the day where leadership of any organization, I'm not talking just about labor, but any organization, just says that "here's the way you ought to vote" and all members of the organization fall in line. . . . They can make up their own minds by comparing the records of these people and what we are proposing to do once we get in office. That's where it gets easy to overpromise—promise everything to everybody. "Yeah, I'm with you. I'll give you anything you want. I'm your candidate."

You know, the art of government is not that simple. The art of government is the balance that we have to set, back and forth between conflicting interests. To produce jobs, you have to have investment. To have investment and having people put their hard-earned savings into investment, you need good management. So there's a balance here between investment and management and labor's interest back and forth. You can't go all to labor and you can't go all the other way to business either. We set these balances in our society and that's what we have to take into account. That's what it means to be out in the middle of the political spectrum. It means you're considering these balances that keep our nation going on what is the greatest good for the greatest number of people.

We could tell you right now that we are going to set up environmental laws that are going to be the best, that we are going to make the cleanest environment, and we are not going to have any problems whatsoever for the future. We could put them into effect tomorrow morning, and what would we do? We would probably put 10 million people out of work, too. And so there is that kind of a balance back and forth, too. On the other hand, you can't say, "OK, we are going to create so many jobs we'll take all the scrubbers off the smokestacks, we're not going to worry about pesticides, we don't care if we do pollute, we don't care if there's toxic waste, we've got to provide jobs." And that would be foolish, too. Because once again, we're unbalancing things in one direction or another.

That's what government's all about. And that's what's hard to sell in a candidacy where you're trying to consider these things and not overpromise and not just go before every group and say, "Yeah, I'm for you, I'm for whatever it is you want, I promise you." Because all that winds up with is a presidency where you have overpromised and you can't possibly perform and keep the balances that the president of the United States has to keep—that's in the greatest interest of the greatest number of people. And then when you can't do that, you wind up with a very disenchanted, disgruntled, unhappy bunch of people in this country—just because we were so eager to get into office we promised everything to everybody. And we cannot do that. We have to consider all these different balances.

So would I be happy to have endorsements? I certainly would. I'll accept endorsements. But, am I making that the centerpiece of my campaign? I am not. What I am doing is trying to tailor everything to what is for the greatest good of the greatest number of people so that we truly can perform in office in what is best for the greatest number of people in this country. That to me is just so fundamental. And I think people can make up their own minds.

To bring it back to where you started, though, I'll tell you one thing I do resent about that. And that's the $10-20 million that's going to Democrats to fight Democrats. I think that's tragic. I want to keep our eye on what's important. I want to change the policies of this country, and we can only do that by defeating Ronald Reagan next year. (Loudest and longest applause of the night—fifteen seconds.)

It was, I thought, his best effort to tell people how he would govern and, therefore, what kind of president he would be. It was an effort to tell people he would be a better president than Walter Mondale. In both respects, it was an effort to impose his general election context on a primary electorate. And it had a positive, authentic public service component to it. The applause seemed to me a response both to content and to the conviction with which he spoke. It was not smooth or exciting or complete. But it was heartfelt, and it was a beginning. It was an effort to relate his problem of campaigning from the "middle" to the task of governing the country. It contained a notion of the president as a kind of balance wheel. What it lacked was any intellectual underpinning, any conception—historical, institutional, behavioral—of the American presidency. But it was a beginning.

Flying back to Washington, I recalled this answer in Sioux City. I asked him why he had, only once, addressed this relationship between running and ruling. He said, "I got into that a little bit again last night." (He had spoken to the realtors' convention in Las Vegas.) He continued,

I haven't talked about the middle way and balancing interests because it is just about as exciting as watching mud dry. Can you imagine stacking that up against a Jesse Jackson speech on hunger and poor people and deprivation? I know that's the way you govern. But will it bring people out on a winter's night in Iowa to attend a caucus?

The answer, I thought, begged a much larger question. If simply being himself—and building on his own deeply felt ideas—would not do the trick, what would?

YEAR'S END: THE STATE OF THE CONFRONTATION

Year's end did not mark the end of the Glenn-Mondale confrontation, but it brought the appearance of a new scorekeeper consensus—that John Glenn's summertime momentum had been reversed and that his campaign was not doing as well as expected. It also marked the appearance of evidence to support this theme. And it marked the first time the candidate entertained private doubts about his success. The confrontation had not ended, but it had already delivered its major impulse to the campaign, and it would no longer be the dominant influence on the campaign.

During the year-end pause, a *Washington Post* headline summarized, "Avoiding Mistakes, Mondale Enters '84 With a Widening Lead: Glenn Has Fallen Back Since October." [114] As usual, the conclusion was based on poll results. The Gallup poll, which had showed Glenn trailing Mondale by eleven points in October, found Glenn trailing by twenty-eight points in November and had confirmed this massive shift with a twenty-six-point figure in December. [115] The *Washington Post*-ABC poll showed almost identical figures: Mondale leads of ten points in September, twenty-six points in November, and twenty-one points in December. [116] According to *Time* magazine's poll, Glenn had slipped from the virtual dead heat of a two-point deficit in September to a sixteen-point deficit in December. [117] By these measures, clearly, Mondale's month of endorsements and Glenn's confrontational response had netted out badly for the second-place runner.

That was not all the bad news brought by the horse-race polls. On the Republican side, Ronald Reagan was experiencing a rebirth in approval and, consequently, in his projected pairings against Glenn and Mondale. The president's August approval rate of 43 percent had risen to 53 percent by November. [118] And, whereas all five national polls projected Glenn defeating Reagan as of August and September, all five polls showed Reagan defeating Glenn in October and November. [119] It was small consolation for Glenn to argue, as he had been doing on the campaign trail in November, that "almost every one of the national polls has shown us doing better against Reagan than any other Democrat, and that's been consistent over the past year." If Reagan was going to beat both candidates, Glenn's electability argument no longer gave him much comparative advantage. Those liberal voters who were desperate to defeat Reagan, and who had flirted with John Glenn, could now freely bring their expectations about who would win into line with their real preferences.[120] This switch in Reagan's polls underscored the essential fragility of the electability argument. Once undermined, it would quickly weaken. In the absence of solidly based constituency support, it would disappear.

A measure of this fragility and weakening became available when the *National Journal* returned, in December, to resurvey the state political officials whose strongly pro-Glenn opinions they had collected in July. (See Chapter 2.) The summer interviews had estimated Glenn and Mondale each leading in eleven states; the winter interviews estimated Mondale leading in twenty-three states, Glenn in six. Summing up the wintertime views of these Democratic officials, veteran reporter Dom Bonafede said,

> Glenn, who had been seen by many party activists as their best hope to regain the White House, has faltered in his drive for the nomination after gaining ground last summer.

And he added, significantly, "None of the state party leaders mentioned in December what was frequently emphasized in July: that Glenn offered the best chance for the Democrats to defeat Reagan." [121] As a state chairman put it, "Before he was running as the candidate who could beat Reagan. Now, he's running as the candidate who is ideologically different from Mondale." [122]

From the beginning, exactly what Mondale had hoped to do was to emphasize that difference, to define the context as an intraparty, issued-based contest. John Glenn had helped by allowing himself to be drawn into just such a confrontation. Now, Reagan was helping, too. Indeed, by December Glenn's comparative advantage was gone altogether, as three out of four national opinion polls showed Mondale running a closer race against Reagan than Glenn did. [123] Several important state polls reported the same belief. Iowa Democrats were recorded, in December, as believing, 64-22, that Mondale had the best chance to defeat Reagan.[124] John Glenn would have to give voters another reason for voting for him.

Inside the Glenn campaign, the year's end marked another downturn. The staffers learned that in the fourth quarter of 1983 the campaign had raised less money than Mondale and had failed to meet its fund-raising goal. They had raised $1.6 million to Mondale's $3.3 million and had fallen $200,000 short of their $1.8 million goal. At year's end, the campaign had about a $100,000 cash balance.[125] The shortage of money forced the campaign to cut eighteen people from the seventy-eight-member Washington staff early in January.[126] Following as it did a third quarter in which the campaign had outpaced Mondale, exceeded its goal, and increased the staff, the end-of-year financial report was another indicator of a reversal of campaign fortunes. Money flow is both a measure of and a creator of campaign momentum. Glenn's top money men described their effort as lagging far behind that of Mondale and then attributed the difference to Mondale's two-year lead in fund raising. "We got a late start," said one. "We were behind the eight ball," said another.[127]

Looking back, when it was all over, John Glenn expressed a special sensitivity to this year-end change. "I felt most optimistic when we were having our best success fund raising," he said, "when people cared enough to put their money behind us."

> That's when I felt best—in the summer. I began to have doubts in the late fall and over the holidays. Things weren't coalescing the way I thought they would. I wasn't tasting defeat. But things weren't coming together as I had hoped—organization, fund raising. The money was not coming in the way I had expected.

In sum, public opinion polls, elite interviews, and fund-raising numbers all pointed to a substantial downturn of the Glenn campaign.

Media scorekeepers picked up these indicators, added their first-hand observations, and expressed a year-end consensus on his loss of momentum. They coupled this theme with the idea that Glenn did not have much time left to change the adverse flow. "This was supposed to be the fall when John Glenn showed he had the right stuff to be the Democratic presidential nominee.... It has not worked out that way." [128] "At year's end, Glenn had not yet been able to define his candidacy in terms that capture the imagination of a large body of Democratic voters." [129] "Glenn has had a pretty unproductive year.... The John Glenn camp has [six weeks] to get its act together organizationally and thematically." [130] "Glenn may have fallen too far back to catch up before the caucuses and primaries begin in earnest." [131] "While there is still time to repair the damage, he may have mortally injured his chances." [132] Looking ahead to the early primaries, a reporter wrote, "In Iowa and New Hampshire ... a consensus has emerged that John Glenn, the Democratic candidate with perhaps the most natural appeal, has one of the weakest campaign organizations in the field." [133] Scorekeeping in December and the first week in January was uniformly downbeat. Because media people talk to one another on the campaign trail and because they influence one another (the print media is thought to influence the electronic media), year-end media treatment of the Glenn campaign made its own independent contribution to the loss of momentum.

The relationship of the media to the campaign was even more consequential than that, for, despite their downbeat assessment of the Glenn campaign—as "troubled," "faltering," "stumbling," "lagging," "wilted," "a fizzle," and "alive but barely so"—they resolutely refused to consider the strategic context as anything other than a two-man race. [134] For example, the *National Journal* speculated that Glenn was "mortally injured," but in the next breath stated that "the contest has, for all practical purposes, boiled down to a struggle between Walter Mondale and Ohio Senator John Glenn." [135] Jack Germond and Jules Witcover, after charting Glenn's drop in the polls and describing him as having been "touched up under the pressure of heavy news exposure," concluded, nonetheless, that "as 1984 approaches, the Democratic contest has been reduced to a Mondale-Glenn race." [136] In Iowa, the state's top reporter saw Glenn slipping, but stated, "This is still a Glenn-Mondale fight." [137]

This conclusion may have been their considered judgment, but it is also true that the media needs a contest, that a two-sided contest is easiest for them to portray and sell, that they had invested heavily in this particular two-sided contest, and that they were reluctant to embrace any other scenario. So they continued to lavish virtually all their attention on the Mondale-Glenn contest, content to record Glenn's difficulty (and Mondale's prowess) rather than focus on the changed structure of competition.

This pattern of media behavior had an independent effect on the campaign: media concentration on the Mondale-Glenn race kept John Glenn focused on the same thing. It kept him thinking only about his relationship with Mondale and not with any of the others. In reality, his most pressing strategic problem was not to beat Mondale but to hold second place and to work to inherit the soft or anti-Mondale vote as others dropped out. He should have been concerned with Alan Cranston and Gary Hart. But, as one adviser said when Hart began to surge, "We focused on Mondale. We haven't focused on Hart at all. . . . We just weren't focusing on him." [138] There is not a shred of evidence that John Glenn ever paid the slightest attention to either man—especially, as it turned out, to Hart.

And in a sense the media would not let him. By their institutionalization of the two-man race, they determined that Glenn should fight head-to-head with Walter Mondale until one of them was totally defeated. And they determined that Glenn would not enjoy a moment's respite from these media expectations until such time as he beat Mondale or conceded defeat. By their attention and their expectations, the media severely constricted Glenn's opportunity for strategic maneuver.

Year-end stocktaking for the Glenn campaigners was a time to assess their shortcomings and prepare for the start of the formal nomination process. Public reference to their difficulties centered on the admission that "they had failed to add a political dimension to his image as a war hero and project mercury astronaut." [139] All their polling told them that Democrats preferred a candidate like John Glenn, but that the Democrats did not yet prefer John Glenn. "We found that the opinions of an overwhelming number of Democrats match what John Glenn stands for," said one aide. "What was startling was that most people were not connecting Glenn to the view that they held on the issues." [140] A poll taken at the same time showed a similar lack of definition in terms of Glenn's views. Among Democrats, 58 percent had no impression of him, favorable or unfavorable. [141] And among the general public one-third could not place him on a liberalism-conservatism scale. (See Table 3-1.) The campaigners interpreted Mondale's upsurge in the polls as an indication that "we haven't gotten our message across." [142] They also interpreted that upsurge as evidence of "shakiness in the electorate" and not as evidence of solid support for Mondale. "People's preferences seem to shift month to month," said a spokesman. "We consider this an opportunity for John Glenn." [143] They did not accept the notion that the slide was irreversible, and they remained publicly optimistic about the outcome.

Indeed, the public stance of the Glenn people was that they were moving, on schedule, from one "political season" or one "stage" to another. "We accomplished our major objectives for '83," said campaign manager White. "We showed we can raise money. We are building our organization . . . we think we set the stage for outlining the differences between Walter Mondale and John Glenn in a way that sets a positive theme." [144] In another of his stock-taking comments, White said,

> Nineteen eighty-three was the exhibition season. It was the year when the media and the political insiders had their invisible primary. It was a year when Walter Mondale had all the advantages. This was the year he was supposed to put it away. We held our own. In 1984, the voters have their say. [145]

Communications director Schneiders echoed this year-end theme—that 1983 was preparatory and that "voters are just now beginning to pay attention." [146] From his vantage point, he argued,

> The period we have been in has largely been one of communicating with the heavies in the media who are going to be forming their opinions and making their judgments, so that when we start the direct communication with the voters it will all work together. [147]

These public comments did not convey any sense of urgency.

When asked to comment on Mondale's lead, Glenn answered his "Meet the Press" questioner in a similarly optimistic tone.

> We have good organization now. We're active in—I think we have steering groups in forty-three different states, something like that. We're all set to move into this; so I think these reports of our early demise are greatly overrated.[148]

This set of ideas—White's emphasis on matters that should have been accomplished earlier, Schneiders's notion that they had not yet begun to contact voters, Glenn's insistence on a nationwide organization—suggest a campaign caught in a time warp. Glenn seemed to be falling behind as the campaign-without-voters was coming quickly to its end.

NOTES

1. Joseph Kraft, "Democrats on a Dime," *Rochester Democrat and Chronicle,* May 5, 1983.
2. Dan Balz, "Glenn Tops Mondale, Others in Straw Poll in New Jersey," *Washington Post,* September 14, 1983.
3. David Broder, "Mondale, Glenn Give Democratic Panel Preview of Coming Battle," *Washington Post,* July 15, 1983. On Glenn and straw polls, see *Newsweek,* June 13, 27, 1983.
4. Martin Schram and Dan Balz, "Democrats Begin 1984 Race in Earnest," *Washington Post,* September 6, 1983.
5. George Lardner, Jr., "Democratic Contenders Woo House," *Washington Post,* July 14, 1983; David Rogers, "Mondale Outperforms Glenn," *Boston Globe,* July 14, 1983.
6. Broder, "Mondale, Glenn Give Democratic Panel Preview"; see also Rowland Evans and Robert Novak, "Mondale: Reminders of 1952," *Washington Post,* July 18, 1983.
7. Dan Balz, "Glenn, Mondale on a High Road-Low Road Race to Nomination," *Washington Post,* September 6, 1983.
8. Howell Raines, "Two Democrats in Search of a Southern Strategy," *New York Times,* October 23, 1983.
9. Schram and Balz, "Democrats Begin 1984 Race in Earnest."
10. "Liftoff for Campaign '84," *Newsweek,* October 3, 1983.
11. David Broder, "Democrats: Hey This Is a Pretty Good Fight," *Washington Post,* October 5, 1983.
12. "Liftoff for Campaign '84."
13. Ibid.
14. Raines, "Two Democrats in Search."
15. Dan Balz, "Glenn Shakes Up Campaign After Discord," *Washington Post,* October 27, 1983.
16. Schram and Balz, "Democrats Begin 1984 Race in Earnest."
17. Balz, "Glenn, Mondale on a High Road-Low Road."

18. Jon Margolis, "Mondale and Glenn Take Similar Stands, But Send Out Different Signals to Different Groups of Voters," *Chicago Tribune*, October 30, 1983.

19. Henry Brady and Richard Johnston, "What's the Primary Message: Horse Race or Issue Journalism?" in *Media and Momentum*, ed. Gary Orren and Nelson Polsby (Chatham, N.J.: Chatham House, 1987), 170-175.

20. Dan Balz, "Labor Gets a Warning from Glenn," *Washington Post*, August 30, 1983.

21. Howell Raines, "Mondale and Glenn Vying for Early Lead Head Toward 1984," *New York Times*, September 11, 1983.

22. "Two Big Boosts for Mondale," *Rochester Democrat and Chronicle*, October 2, 1983; Joseph Kraft, "The Mondale Surge," *Washington Post*, October 4, 1983; "Mr. Mondale's Victories," *Washington Post*, October 4, 1983.

23. Michael Barone, "The Mondale-Glenn Dust-Up," *Washington Post*, October 16, 1983.

24. Rowland Evans and Robert Novak, "Glenn's Sand Castles," *Washington Post*, October 3, 1983.

25. Barone, "The Mondale-Glenn Dust-Up"; and Jack Germond and Jules Witcover, *Wake Us When It's Over* (New York: Macmillan, 1985), 101ff.

26. "Two Big Boosts for Mondale."

27. Dan Balz, "Glenn Criticizes Mondale's Tack in Campaign," *Washington Post*, October 5, 1983.

28. Ibid.

29. Ibid.

30. David Broder, "Mondale Wins Cuomo Praise for Citing Differences With Glenn," *Washington Post*, September 29, 1983. See also "Cuomo Tip to Glenn: Just Keep Quiet," *Rochester Democrat and Chronicle*, September 21, 1983.

31. Martin Schram, "A Funny Thing Happened at the Contenders' Forum," *Washington Post*, October 8, 1983.

32. Ibid.

33. Bill Peterson, "Mondale Shifts Strategy, Returns Fire on 'Special Interest' Charge," *Washington Post*, October 10, 1983.

34. Barone, "The Mondale-Glenn Dust-Up."

35. Rowland Evans and Robert Novak, "Mondale Stubs His Toe in New York," *Washington Post*, October 10, 1983.

36. David Broder and Martin Schram, "Mondale Acts to Avert Another '84 Ambush," *Washington Post*, June 15, 1983.

37. Elizabeth Drew, *Campaign Journal* (New York: Macmillan, 1985), 198-205; and Thomas Oliphant, "Mondale Says He'll Confront Hart in New 'Two-Man' Race," *Boston Globe*, March 2, 1984.

38. Peterson, "Mondale Shifts Strategy."

39. Ibid.

40. Ibid.

41. Dan Balz, "Sen. Glenn Defends Tax Vote: Rebukes Mondale for Iowa Attack, Hits Carter Policies," *Washington Post*, October 11, 1983.

42. Martin Schram, "New Critic Glenn Supported Carter Programs in the Senate," *Washington Post*, October 13, 1983.

43. Drew, *Campaign Journal*, 394.

44. Rowland Evans and Robert Novak, "Glenn and the Party," *Washington Post*, October 19, 1983.

45. Dan Balz, "Mondale-Glenn Draw Battle Lines," *Washington Post*, October 12, 1983.
46. Balz, "Sen. Glenn Defends Tax Vote."
47. Barone, "The Mondale-Glenn Dust-Up"; and Germond and Witcover, *Wake Us When It's Over*, 110ff.
48. "Mr. Glenn's Withdrawal," *Washington Post Weekly Edition*, April 2, 1984.
49. Balz, "Mondale-Glenn Draw Battle Lines."
50. Brian Usher, "Glenn Backed Carter Economic Programs, Records Show," *Miami Herald*, October 23, 1983.
51. Broder, "Democrats: Hey This Is a Pretty Good Fight."
52. *Newsweek*, October 24, 1983.
53. Broder, "Democrats: Hey This Is a Pretty Good Fight."
54. Evans and Novak, "Mondale Stubs."
55. Martin Schram, "Candidates' Game Plans Pay Off," *Washington Post*, October 15, 1983.
56. Mary McGrory, "Please!" *Washington Post*, October 13, 1983.
57. Sidney Blumenthal, "Fatecraft as Spacecraft," *New Republic*, November 14, 1983.
58. Howell Raines, "Glenn Accuses Mondale of Being Weak on 'National Defense,'" *New York Times*, November 16, 1983.
59. "Bare Knuckle Time for Glenn, Mondale," *U.S. News and World Report*, December 5, 1983.
60. Martin Schram, "Campaign Takes Turn for the Bitter as Glenn Tests New Strategy," *Washington Post*, November 20, 1983.
61. Ed Yoder, "'Liberated' Candidates Confuse Voters," *Rochester Democrat and Chronicle*, October 18, 1983.
62. "The Candidates Draw Blood," *Newsweek*, October 24, 1983.
63. Evans and Novak, "Glenn and the Party."
64. "The Candidates Draw Blood."
65. Ibid.
66. Dan Balz, "Shakeup in Glenn's Campaign Aimed at Shoring Up Weaknesses," *Washington Post*, November 11, 1983.
67. See Albert Hunt, "John Glenn's Chances for the Democratic Nomination," *Wall Street Journal*, December 28, 1982; Rowland Evans and Robert Novak, "Glenn's Shaky Base," *Washington Post*, April 22, 1983; Martin Schram, "Glenn's Campaign Staff Is Off and Walking," *Washington Post*, April 26, 1983.
68. Meg Greenfield, "Why Mondale Is Falling Short," *Newsweek*, September 17, 1984.
69. Balz, "Shakeup in Glenn's Campaign"; "People," *National Journal*, November 5, 1983; Dan Balz, "Glenn Shakes Up Campaign Staff After Discord," *Washington Post*, October 27, 1983; "Washington Wire," *Columbus Dispatch*, October 30, 1983.
70. Balz, "Shakeup in Glenn's Campaign."
71. Phil Gailey, "Glenn Field Drive Launched in Iowa," *New York Times*, November 7, 1983.
72. *Wall Street Journal*, September 14, 1983.
73. Dan Balz, "Mondale, Glenn Step Up Attacks in War of Words," *Washington Post*, October 19, 1983.
74. David Hess and Brian Usher, "Mondale Is Sorry He Called Glenn 'Anti-Democrat,'" *Philadelphia Inquirer*, October 22, 1983.

75. Dan Balz, "Glenn Hits Democratic 'Litmus Tests,' " *Washington Post*, October 23, 1983; Geoffrey Tomb, "Glenn, Askew Rap Mondale at Conclave," *Miami Herald*, October 23, 1983.

76. *National Journal*, February 11, 1984.

77. *Washington Post Weekly Edition*, December 5, 1983.

78. Schram, "Campaign Takes Turn for the Bitter."

79. Ibid.

80. David Broder, "Glenn Calls Rival Soft on Defense," *Washington Post*, November 1, 1983.

81. Jon Margolis, "Truce Ends for Glenn, Mondale," *Chicago Tribune*, November 17, 1983.

82. Dan Balz, "Glenn Asserts Rival Mondale Can't Deliver," *Washington Post*, November 17, 1983.

83. Howell Raines, "Glenn Steps Up His Attack on Mondale Policies," *New York Times*, November 17, 1983.

84. Dan Balz, "Glenn, Defending His Nerve Gas Vote, Attacks Mondale Anew," *Washington Post*, November 19, 1983.

85. Ibid.; see also Mark Shields, "Glenn's Vote on Nerve Gas," *Washington Post*, October 21, 1983.

86. David Broder, "Mr. Checklist," *Washington Post*, October 13, 1982.

87. Brian Usher, "The Undoing of John Glenn," *Akron Beacon-Journal*, March 25, 1984.

88. Jack Germond and Jules Witcover, "Glenn's Fall Attack on Mondale Could Make or Break his Candidacy," *National Journal*, November 26, 1983.

89. Bill Peterson, "Mondale Leads Rivals in Party by Big Margin," *Washington Post*, December 19, 1983.

90. Ibid.; see also Shields, "Glenn's Vote on Nerve Gas."

91. "The Campaign Goes Underground," *Washington Post*, November 16, 1983.

92. Barry Sussman, *Washington Post*, November 10, 1983.

93. Brian Usher, "Polls," file copy for Knight-Ridder newspapers, November 10, 1983.

94. Ibid.

95. Ibid.

96. Drew, *Campaign Journal*, 282.

97. Ibid., 279.

98. Ibid., 282.

99. On this point, see also Robert Merry, "Why Is John Glenn, So Popular in Past, Running So Poorly?" *Wall Street Journal*, February 1, 1984; Richard Ben Cramer, "The Apple Pie Vision of an American Hero," *Philadelphia Inquirer Magazine*, November 27, 1983; Brian Usher, "A Garbled Message, Poor Delivery, and John Glenn Leaves 'Em Yawning," *Philadelphia Inquirer*, January 9, 1984.

100. Drew, *Campaign Journal*, 279; Howell Raines, "For Glenn, 'The Right Stuff' Seems to be Right," *New York Times*, September 21, 1983.

101. Carl Leubsdorf, "Mondale Seeks Wider Base," *Dallas Morning News*, January 6, 1984; see also Art Harris and Martin Schram, "Six Democratic Hopefuls Strut Their Moderation in New South," *Washington Post*, March 9, 1983.

102. Ken Fuson, "Both Leading Democrats Stump Iowa on Same Day," *Des Moines Register*, November 12, 1983.

103. J. W. Huttig, "Glenn Draws Good Crowd at Stop Here," *Sioux City Journal*, November 12, 1983.

104. Drew, *Campaign Journal*, 285-286.
105. Tom Breen, "Hart, Cranston Seen Posting Iowa Gains," *Washington Times*, February 10, 1984.
106. Ken Fuson and David Yepsen, "The Right Stuff of America," *Des Moines Register*, November 30, 1983.
107. Gailey, "Glenn Field Drive Launched in Iowa."
108. Ibid.
109. Fuson, "Both Leading Democrats."
110. David Yepsen, "National Democrats Forcing a Showdown Over Iowa Caucuses," *Des Moines Register*, November 13, 1983.
111. On this routine, see Brian Usher, "Glenn Campaign Falls Short, But Not For Lack of Humor," *Akron Beacon Journal*, March 21, 1984. Another campaign reporter who writes about this personal side is David Shribman, "Reporter's Notebook: Day of Recalling 'Friendship,' " *New York Times*, February 21, 1984; David Shribman, "With Few Words, Glenn Withdraws," *New York Times*, March 17, 1984.
112. See James Perry, "Democratic Candidates Firmly Dip Their Toes in Presidential Waters:. . . Senator Glenn at a Fish Fry," *Wall Street Journal*, June 15, 1982; James Perry, "On the Trail with Mondale and Glenn: Campaign Is Study in Contrasting Styles," *Wall Street Journal*, January 3, 1984; "Eyes on the White House," *Newsweek*, November 8, 1982; Bill Shipp, "Glenn May Be What the U.S. Needs," *Atlanta Constitution*, October 13, 1982; David Nyhan, "Glenn Much Improved Candidate," *Boston Globe*, June 16, 1983; James Gannon, "A Candidate Tailor Made to Oppose Ronald Reagan," *Des Moines Register*, August 8, 1982.
113. Eugene Kennedy, "John Glenn's Presidential Countdown," *New York Times Magazine*, October 11, 1981. An Ohio editorial board example is Robert Clerc, "Better A 'Dull' Glenn. . . ," *Cincinnati Enquirer*, October 16, 1982.
114. Bill Peterson, "Avoiding Mistakes, Mondale Enters '84 With a Widening Lead: Glenn Has Fallen Back Since October," *Washington Post Weekly Edition*, January 2, 1984.
115. Ibid.; see also "Opinion Outlook," *National Journal*, December 31, 1983.
116. "Opinion Outlook," *National Journal*, December 31, 1983.
117. Evan Thomas, "Highs for Mondale and Reagan," *Time*, December 26, 1983.
118. "Reagan and His Predecessors," *Public Opinion*, February/March 1986.
119. "Trial Heats," *Public Opinion*, October/November 1983.
120. This general sequence is elaborated by Larry Bartels in "Expectations and Preferences in Presidential Nominating Campaigns," *American Political Science Review* (1985). The story of an Iowa voter who followed this path is to be found in "A Peek at Two Political Diaries" by Karen Merrick and Jay Howe, *Des Moines Register*, February 3, 1984.
121. Dom Bonafede, "Democratic State Party Leaders See Mondale Pulling Away from Glenn," *National Journal*, December 17, 1983.
122. Ibid.
123. Gallup, ABC-*Washington Post*, *Los Angeles Times*, and Harris polls still showed Glenn doing better. "Trial Heats," *Public Opinion*, February/March 1986.
124. Bill Peterson and Kathy Sawyer, "Temperature and Glenn Outlook Falling in Iowa," *Washington Post*, January 11, 1984.
125. Thomas Edsall, " '83 New Hampshire Spending May Limit Mondale This Month," *Washington Post*, February 2, 1984; Brooks Jackson, "Mondale Had

Twice the Contributions of Glenn at Year-End," *Wall Street Journal*, February 2, 1984; "Mondale Leads Rivals on Fund Raising," *New York Times*, February 2, 1984; "Mondale Camp Raised $11.4 Million in 1983," *Los Angeles Times*, February 1, 1984.

126. Thomas Edsall, "Fund Raising Problems Force Glenn to Cut Staff," *Washington Post*, January 6, 1984.

127. Bernard Weintraub, "Glenn Narrows Mondale's Lead in Race for Funds," *New York Times*, November 28, 1983; Alan Henry, "Money Helps Make the Candidates," *Chicago Sun-Times*, as printed in *Rochester Democrat and Chronicle*, January 15, 1984.

128. "Mondale's Machine in High Gear: With Glenn Stumbling, Half A Dozen Others Hope for a Chance," *Time*, December 12, 1983.

129. Robert Shogan, "Mondale Could Clinch Nomination Early," *Los Angeles Times*, January 1, 1984.

130. Dan Campbell, " 'Tis the Season for John Glenn To Make His Move," *USA Today*, November 28, 1984.

131. "Glenn: Don't Count Me Out," *Newsweek*, December 26, 1983.

132. Bonafede, "Democratic State Leaders."

133. David Shribman, "Glenn's Backers Worry About Field Organizing," *New York Times*, December 5, 1983.

134. *Newsweek*, December 26, 1983; *Washington Post*, December 26, 1983, January 5, 1984; *Time*, December 7, 1983; *Washington Post*, January 7, 1984; *Dallas Times Herald*, December 9, 1983; *New York Times*, December 27, 1983.

135. Bonafede, "Democratic State Leaders"; Bill Peterson, "Mondale Leads Rivals in Party by Big Margin," *Washington Post*, December 18, 1983.

136. Jack Germond and Jules Witcover, "A Good 1983 for Walter Mondale," *Chicago Tribune*, January 3, 1984.

137. David Yepsen, *Des Moines Register*, November 28, 1983; Keith Love, "Cranston Cites 'Passion Gap' in Mondale Camp," *Los Angeles Times*, December 14, 1983.

138. David Nyhan, "Here's the Lineup—And the Pitches—For N.H.," *Boston Globe*, February 22, 1984.

139. David Shribman, "For Glenn, It's a Problem Putting Image in Focus," *New York Times*, December 18, 1983.

140. Keith Love, "Glenn's Hopes Boosted in California Talks," *Los Angeles Times*, November 24, 1983; Schram, "Campaign Takes Turn for the Bitter"; Dan Balz, "Candidates Reassessing Southern Strategy," *Washington Post*, December 12, 1983; Shribman, "For Glenn, It's a Problem."

141. Hedrick Smith, "Mondale Lead over Nearest Rival in Poll Sets Nonincumbent Record," *New York Times*, February 28, 1984.

142. Shribman, "For Glenn, It's a Problem."

143. Peterson "Avoiding Mistakes, Mondale Enters '84."

144. "Political Notes," *Washington Post*, December 13, 1983.

145. Shribman, "For Glenn, It's a Problem."

146. Steve Berg, "Glenn Practices Tougher Rhetoric in the South," *Minneapolis Tribune*, November 23, 1984; David Shribman, "Glenn as a Campaigner: Elation and Letdown," *New York Times*, January 8, 1984.

147. Bill Hogan, "The Selling of the Candidates," *Washington Journalism Review*, November 1983.

148. Transcript, "Meet the Press," December 11, 1983.

4

A Season of Defeat

THE CAMPAIGN-WITH-VOTERS:
JANUARY-MARCH 1984

As the presidential year began, the campaigner who showed the least public anxiety and the least disposition to alter course was John Glenn. On "Meet the Press" in December he was asked, "You are running behind.... What about campaign plans or events, specific events coming up that might change that?" He answered:

> We're right on target as far as our plans to expand organization in different states, and we move right into this time period now—in late February, where we start out with Iowa and New Hampshire, and then comes that big Super Tuesday on March 13th where we have twelve different states vote on that one day. It will be closer to a national primary day than we have ever had before. And that's what we're gearing toward; we're building right toward that day, and I think we're doing very well.[1]

The answer was not very responsive, but it was in keeping with all his public comments at year's end—that he was moving step-by-step through a preconceived campaign schedule and was now poised to make his final push. He never questioned the wisdom of his original estimate that he needed only fourteen to sixteen months to mount a successful campaign. And he steadfastly maintained that he was moving in strict accordance with the timetables that flowed from that estimate. He still envisioned a fifty-state campaign that would take off on March 13. As he "geared toward" and "built right toward" Super Tuesday, therefore, he contemplated no change of plan.

183

From January to March presidential campaigns grow increasingly public; the sequence of events becomes compressed; and the effects of performance at one point in time speedily transform the context at the next. Survival, we have said, is the ultimate goal of every candidate. As primaries and caucuses have come to dominate the nomination process and as the process has come to be increasingly "frontloaded," the survival rate in the first third of the election year has become minuscule. For most candidates the very earliest hurdles constitute a make-or-break sequence. In 1984 these hurdles were Iowa (February 20), New Hampshire (February 28), and the twelve-state Super Tuesday (March 13). John Glenn failed to survive that three-hurdle sequence.

The seeds of Glenn's nonsurvival were sown well before he approached the threshold in Iowa. The cumulative effects of his campaign—and of his career—simply were recorded as the campaign-with-voters began. In terms of understanding what happened, as it happened, the three voting hurdles constitute a distinct sequence and represent distinct contexts. We shall follow the Glenn campaign through these final reckonings.

For the January-to-March season, the course of the Glenn campaign was one of spiraling decline. The positive momentum of the summer, which had been reversed in the fall, turned into negative momentum in the new year. Poll results worsened, funding dried up, crowds dwindled, organizational plans went unfulfilled, morale dropped, and the campaign manager was replaced. Even fantasy failed, as *The Right Stuff* collapsed at the box office.[2] Indeed, the movie proved to be the only instance in all of 1983 in which "major media attention failed to boost a candidate in the polls."[3]

Media scorekeepers recorded the epidemiology of a classic reverse bandwagon. Between the first of the year and the Iowa caucuses, the campaign was variously described as "floundering," "faltering," "fading," "flagging," "collapsing," "caving in," "wheezing," "plummeting," "plunging," "scrambling," "sagging," "sinking," "skidding," "stumbling," "slipping," and "struggling."[4]

These discouraging descriptions gave the Glenn campaign an additional downward shove. "There's no question that this trend in the media to put the label 'faltering' and 'unraveling' on every story has become a real problem for us," said a top aide. "What we're worried about is that it can quickly become a self-fulfilling prophecy."[5] In an even more subtle way, the media helped make it a self-fulfilling, self-destructive prophecy. The media refused to structure the contest in any form other than a two-person, Mondale-Glenn contest. By so doing the media fixed wholly unattainable expectations for Glenn's performance at the polls, thus magnifying the consequences of his failure to meet them.

The spiraling decline occurred in Iowa, in New Hampshire, and in the southern states separately and almost in the same way. Glenn's negative momentum was a campaignwide phenomenon. But it accelerated rapidly as the voting sequence unfolded. He finished fifth in Iowa with 5 percent of the vote. A week later he finished third in New Hampshire with 12 percent of the vote. Two weeks later, on Super Tuesday, he finished second in Alabama with 21 percent of the vote, fourth in Georgia with 18 percent, and fourth in Florida with 11 percent. Three days after his poor southern showing—and $2.8 million in debt— he withdrew. While his weaknesses were in evidence everywhere, it was his Iowa defeat that, in the sequence of events, knocked him out of the presidential race. This loss compounded every existing problem in every succeeding context. It wiped away all vestiges of the electability assumption. And it destroyed an essential resource—his second-place standing in the competition, his status as the only viable alternative to Walter Mondale. Without it, Glenn could not survive. And he possessed neither the time nor the means to win it back.

THE CAMPAIGN IN IOWA

CONTEXT AND COMMITMENT

The weaknesses of the Glenn campaign in Iowa were the same as those elsewhere—weaknesses of conceptualization, organization, and candidate performance. But in Iowa's context these weaknesses took on candidacy-killing proportions. To begin with, Iowa is the first state to vote. As such, it provides an impulse to everything that follows, and that fact endows it with great importance. Historically, it has given birth to unlikely candidacies such as George McGovern's and Jimmy Carter's and killed likely ones such as Howard Baker's and Bob Dole's. In 1984 the New Hampshire primary followed more closely than ever, predictably magnifying the Iowa impulse. As Iowa has grown in strategic importance, so has media coverage. In 1980 Iowa ranked either first or second (depending upon the study) among all the states in amount of media coverage; 300 reporters and technicians had been in Iowa on caucus night to report the results.[6] The media were certain to be an even louder amplifier in 1984. Strategically located at the front end of a frontloaded sequence, and in the brightest of media glare, Iowa needed to be very well understood.

Further, Iowa is a caucus state. That fact underscored the importance of organization in making certain that political support actually registered itself at the precinct caucuses. Historically, candidates with grass-roots organizing abilities have done particularly well in Iowa—the 1980 organization-based success of George Bush there is an example.[7] Also, the caucus system tends to attract voters who are different from both the general electorate and the party electorate; they are more connected to groups, more activist, more committed to politics. In the Democratic caucuses, these differences have produced a more than normally liberal voting group. Finally, Iowa politics has a certain style, characterized by Samuel Patterson, a veteran student of the state, as "bland," "moderate," and "moralistic." "Above all," says Patterson, "Iowans and their politicians are moralistic about their politics." And he describes their "widely shared 'good government' ethos that downplays conflict and struggle in favor of accommodation, honesty, decency, and standing pat."[8] That, too, had to be taken into account.

Taken separately, these basic matters of context had, by 1976, become well known.[9] Taken together, they demanded that Iowa be approached with very great care and with a commitment disproportionate to all other states except New Hampshire. But the Glenn people seemed never to have incorporated the distinctiveness of Iowa into their thinking. Their campaign never developed a clear and timely strategic sense of what its Iowa component meant—its goals, the amount of effort required, the allocation of resources to that effort, the message they wished to emphasize. They dealt with Iowa more by assumption than with hard thought based on available evidence. For a campaign whose candidate's favorite injunction was to "set goals and go for it," its Iowa component exhibited an unbelievable lack of direction.

The difficulty was built into the campaign from the beginning. Campaign manager Bill White's 191-page strategy memo mentioned Iowa numerous times, but only in bits and pieces, never in more than one sentence in any one place. Vermont drew far more concentrated attention than Iowa. The frontloaded aspect of the process was noted, and "momentum" was mentioned, but little consideration was given to the immensely important Iowa-New Hampshire sequence and its potential impact on future events. Indeed, in a section devoted to the various ways in which the "opposition" might try to deliver the "early knockout" to Glenn's candidacy "in the early states," the memo concludes: "The likelihood of a serious problem here is not great."

There is an assumption here that Iowa would not be a problem—based, it seems, on the general notion that Glenn had a natural constituency there. "Your base is in the Midwest. . . . You are well received in the 'heartland,'" said the memo. That sentiment accords with Glenn's own sense of "at homeness," as he said on the way back from the Arkansas trip. At the same time, White acknowledged Mondale's favorite son status in Iowa. In the only piece of strategic calculation concerning Iowa, he advised Glenn: "Acknowledge your natural appeal in the Midwest, but be complimentary of Mondale's support here as he is also a fellow midwesterner. This strategy is especially important in Iowa. . . ." It is ironic that the one early bit of advice Glenn received was to "be nice to Mondale in Iowa."

Insofar as he did pay attention to Iowa, however, White clearly understood the "retail politics of Iowa." "In caucus states," he generalized, "paid media is generally less important, and a premium is placed on organizational efforts." With respect to Iowa, he declared flatly, "Field organization in Iowa—not media—will determine the outcome." And, accordingly, he urged the early establishment of "a full-time field staff in Iowa" (together with one in New Hampshire and one in Florida).

Early on, it seemed as though Glenn would, indeed, emphasize retail campaigning in the "heartland." The announcement of the hero-senator's candidacy took place against a small-town backdrop in his New Concord, Ohio, birthplace, with a celebration of small-town values.[10] And, during his exploratory period, he expressed his confidence that "small-town Ohio relates to small-town New Hampshire." And he "conceded nothing" in those states.[11] Until their late 1983 polls found them "far behind" Mondale, his campaigners talked of winning in Iowa, of upsetting the front-running Mondale there.[12]

Those who succeeded White never deemed it worthwhile to exploit the small-town connection with a lopsidedly retail campaign there. They thought of Iowa as part of their "unique national campaign" in which there came to be, everywhere, a greater emphasis on media than organization. Iowa was treated as only one among a number of important states, and it took a back seat to the Super Tuesday strategy in planning. The campaigners never considered that Iowa required special attention or special commitment. In sum, they approached Iowa without an Iowa strategy.

One person clearly understood from the beginning of the "presidential thing" exactly how much the campaign's success would revolve around Iowa. He was Bill Connell, Glenn's media adviser in his Ohio campaigns. In a memo to Glenn three weeks before Bill White's memo, Connell advised the candidate to begin organizing seriously in what we might call the momentum states—those states in which closely watched caucuses and primaries provide the arena for a candidate to catch fire. In a section entitled "The Dynamics of March and April," Connell discussed "the importance of the very first tests in Iowa and New Hampshire . . . [because] if there is a clear winner . . . the media will give him a tremendous momentum that will be hard to catch." Conversely, he said, "They are death traps for front-runners who do not win them."

The scenario he envisaged was to "pull off an early win . . . be catapulted into front-runner position . . . and follow up with 'confirming victories' in the South." He concluded, "So a large investment of Glenn's time, staff time, and money in these first tests of strength is a must."

The purpose of the Connell memo was to convince his former client, the senator from Ohio, that "I am, I believe, the best-qualified person to take on this media responsibility for the Glenn campaign." Judging by the "let Glenn be Glenn" advice throughout the memo, it seems that Connell clearly understood the candidate and his strengths. And in another prescient segment of his document, he buttressed his case indirectly by arguing,

> No successful nominee of either party has begun with a nationally experienced staff. Invariably, they brought along with them trusted associates from their early political careers, and those associates had to grow and gain the necessary experience.

Connell was exactly the kind of longtime, astute, personally loyal adviser Glenn needed but never acquired. Connell made his pitch to the candidate and others in December, but he was turned down in favor of a nationally experienced hired gun. From a distance, it appears to have been a large mistake—and a revealing one.

In December Glenn was trailing Mondale by a large margin— twenty-six points, 42-16—in the Iowa poll. His campaigners had become convinced they had no chance of winning there. In recognition of Mondale's long political association with his neighbors, they even conceded that Iowa "may be the toughest state, other than Minnesota, in the country for us." [13] Faced with the possibility of a weak second-place finish, some of Glenn's advisers wanted to get out of Iowa, to skip it entirely.[14] Others argued, "It was [a] Catch Twenty-two. It wasn't Glenn's kind of state, but if we hadn't competed, the press would have said we weren't a national campaign." [15] Glenn worried about it. "Do you think I have to go into Iowa as well as New Hampshire?" he asked an Ohio reporter in April. "I questioned it," he said afterward. "But I was usually a party of one. My advisers told me that we had to run in all the early states if we were to be taken seriously. . . . I didn't push it. I had made the basic decision to run campaigns in all fifty states. We were in it for the long haul."

It is not clear why Glenn became so wedded to the idea of a fifty-state, "long haul" campaign, or why he would boast so optimistically on "Meet the Press" of his forty-three-state organization. Perhaps it was the idea that he could not win the nomination unless he organized everywhere. Perhaps it was the idea that he could only maintain his second-place position by mounting a campaign that was as broadly cast as Mondale's. Perhaps he believed it was the only way to be taken seriously by the media. Whatever the reason, Glenn's devotion to the idea led to the neglect of strategic considerations, such as early starts and momentum, and led to the misallocation of resources. His expressed belief was, "We are in this for the long haul." And, "No candidate is going to win those early elections or freeze anybody out." [16]

The long haul, national campaign idea was not a good reason for staying in the Iowa race, because it did not carry with it the special strategic considerations and the particular commitment of resources that Iowa required. Iowa needs to be thought of as unique, not simply as one interchangeable part of a fifty-part campaign. When it was over, Glenn said he was "ticked off" at those who advised him to compete there.[17]

But he had trapped himself within a set of self-imposed constraints. In mid-January, for example, one journalist noted "the decision this week ... to reduce his campaign schedule in Iowa." [18] Another said, "Glenn has sent out a variety of signals that he would reduce his effort in Iowa." [19] The most important of these was his decision to pass up an all-candidate debate on farm issues at the Iowa Farm Forum, a decision that one close observer called "the biggest mistake he made in the campaign." [20] A similar decision by Ronald Reagan four years earlier was widely thought there to have cost him the state.[21] From inside the campaign, Glenn's scheduling lacked planning. One adviser said, "We decided on a week-to-week basis where he should go. 'We're a few points down in New Hampshire; let's go there for a couple of days. We're slipping in Iowa; let's go to Iowa this week.' That's the way the schedule was made up." From outside the campaign the change was interpreted as a mid-course correction. "Iowa has been written off," said a reporter, "with Glenn just trying to minimize the gap between him and Mondale and avoid a disastrous third-place finish." [22] As Glenn put it, "We don't want to get blasted out of the water in Iowa." [23]

If, in fact, his strategic goal was to stay out of third place—to hold his position as the "alternative"—his competitors in Iowa were Gary Hart and Alan Cranston, not Walter Mondale. As the two candidates pushing a future-oriented message, Glenn and Hart, especially, were natural competitors. They prospected for support among similar voters—those skeptical of Mondale because of his ties to "special interests" or "old ideas." But Glenn campaigned as if the contest was between himself and Mondale, and he paid no attention to anyone else. "Mondale's loss is always Glenn's gain," reasoned one adviser.[24]

Glenn put in a total of thirty-three days in Iowa—only eight of them in 1984—compared to sixty for Hart and fifty-five for Cranston.[25] He did, however, spend more of his money on television than they, and he used up all his allowable funds there.[26] Among all the Democratic candidates, Glenn ranked first in the amount of money spent in Iowa in 1984, but sixth in the number of days there.[27] That allocation of resources ran counter to what anyone who paid special attention to Iowa would have recommended. Through January the official view of the Iowa campaign was, "It would be nice to win the Iowa caucuses; we don't think we've got the time to necessarily win, although we think we can come close."[28] On the eve of the caucuses, however, his campaign manager reflected their unresolved doubts—indeed, their increasing "dread"—concerning the Iowa campaign. "This is not John Glenn's crowd. Walter Mondale runs here almost as a favorite son. So why do you get in a game where you begin 50 yards back?"[29] When it was over, three experienced journalists described the campaign's lack of decisiveness. "Glenn found himself half in and half out of the fight in Iowa."[30] "He and his strategists could never figure out whether to mount a major challenge against virtual native son, Mondale."[31] "An argument raged within the Glenn camp as to whether they should get out of Iowa. They resolved it by getting half in and half out. They cut back John's schedule there, but they spent all the money." Had the Glenn campaigners really understood the strategic significance of Iowa they would either have pleaded *nolo contendere*, gotten out, and lowered expectations or gone all out and improved performance. They did neither. It was a crippling indecision.

ORGANIZATION

Had they more thoroughly understood the historic, sequential, killing power of Iowa, Glenn's strategists might have better appreciated the historic route to success in this organization-intensive state. Early, extensive, face-to-face campaigning and grass-roots organization was the only proven way to secure the degree of commitment that would translate into the amount of work necessary to get people to the caucuses. As one observer put it in early January, "Money and a famous name will not carry a presidential candidate very far in Iowa. Television spots will help little because a favorable image is not enough. A candidate in Iowa needs committed Iowans.... And that takes a gigantic grass-roots effort."[32] Another said, "Iowa may be the only state where a candidate is routinely asked not only how much he is spending on television, but how many precinct captains he has lined up."[33] Campaign manager White understood the imperative of retail politics in Iowa, but the suggestions of his memo were gradually superseded by the media-orientation of the hired guns. The Glenn advisers made a very early decision that they would rely most heavily on the mass media. They would send their candidate in—as in the November trip—to establish a beachhead; but they would not give top priority to the creation of a follow-up, recruiting organization.

From the outset, reports on the state of his organization stressed the inability to capitalize on his personal strengths. Calling his effort "puzzling," one journalist wrote in August, "Despite his gains in the public opinion polls, [Glenn] has been slow to put together an effective campaign organization, according to most Iowa observers." [34] An early December report on the organization concluded,

> In Iowa, Glenn workers have lagged behind in collecting names of possible campaign workers and have failed to follow up enormously successful visits by Mr. Glenn with recruiting efforts that can consolidate political strength and insure that supporters will turn out. [35]

As one Democrat put it at the time, "John Glenn does a tremendous job out here. He does everything right. But when he walks out of the room, the tent collapses." [36] The late November staff shakeup was an acknowledgment of the follow-up problem. When I visited the campaign, there was some visible scurrying to remedy the situation; and I wondered whether it would work. It did not.

In January the new Iowa manager said bravely, "We didn't put a whole lot of resources in this state until December. But this isn't the same campaign it was in December. We're moving." [37] They were not. Within a week, a new campaign manager had taken over in Iowa. When it was all over, a state party official looked back:

> He was very popular. He had the best data base of any candidate, the most people to draw on. More people came through the door to hear him than heard any other candidate. He met more people in Iowa than any other campaign. But they did not contact those people after they met Glenn. They must have thought that once people shook his hand and looked him in the eye, that they would turn out for the caucuses.

It is not clear that they thought very deeply when they made their crucial early decision to contest Iowa but not to make a maximum organizational effort there.

Their Des Moines office had opened in February, four months after Mondale's, with a very inexperienced staff. A state Democratic official who watched them from nearby commented,

> The people who ran the campaign in Iowa from February to November had no political experience and did not know what they were doing. [One of them] had worked part time in the evening for three weeks in a Senate campaign. He walked over

to the Glenn headquarters, and they gave him the top job in Iowa. He had no idea what he was doing, and he didn't know enough to know he didn't know. Just one example: he had one staff member spend three months—when manpower was a scarce resource—looking up the addresses and telephone numbers of all the newspapers, TV, and radio stations in the state. We had all that information here at the state party. Or he could have gotten the newspaper information from the Iowa Press Association and the other information from the Iowa Broadcaster's Association. Just one or two phone calls. He didn't know enough to ask. Someone worked on that for three months!

The Iowa organization drew uniformly unfavorable reviews for its ineffectiveness—until it was finally reorganized in late November. But seven other early caucus and primary states were reorganized at the same time. So even the Iowa shakeup reflected the national campaign emphasis more than any special commitment to Iowa.

By the time they began to reconsider their original decision, there was too little time. "We were late in organizing and we never caught up," said one of Glenn's most prominent Iowa supporters. "Early is everything in Iowa. And we were always late." [38] One of those hired in the November staff shakeup recalled,

When I got to Iowa in December, I got off the plane, and they said to me, "This is our last stand. We've got to pull it out." I said, "Don't tell me that, just give me the numbers." They said, "We're thirty points behind." Thirty points! When we got to the Des Moines headquarters, I looked around and I said, "Where are the volunteers?" They said, "Oh, they're coming in tomorrow." They never came.

In December Glenn had yet to recruit chairs in all of the state's ninety-nine counties; he had no precinct captains at all in the state's most populous county; and his 200-person steering committee had been given nothing to do. [39] These difficulties derived from his earliest strategic decision about getting started.

At the end of January he was still looking for precinct captains. [40] And when he found them, there was no organizational infrastructure to service them. Observers noted that because Glenn decided to stay out of straw poll contests, he had forfeited a chance to test his organization under fire and remedy its deficiencies. A party leader recalled what happened in one of Iowa's six congressional districts.

Our candidate for Congress in the ___th District took over Glenn's headquarters there after Glenn left. When they were cleaning out the office, they found a box which was filled with the caucus manuals for the precinct leaders in the ____th District. Each Glenn precinct captain should have had one on caucus night. Not one of them had been delivered.

He explained this "high level of breakdown."

We found out that Glenn's district coordinator had worked his heart out. He had called the home office time and time again and had never gotten any support or cooperation. He got so frustrated, he said, "I'll get em." And he just didn't deliver the manuals.

The ineffective "home office" had been reorganized for the third time in late January, when state director Jerry Vento replaced Bill White as Glenn's national campaign manager. This move, precipitated by a top-level revolt against White's leadership, once again thrust Glenn's organizational troubles into public view.[41] These late-breaking troubles signaled the complete capture of the candidate by the hired guns. When asked by the press about his new campaign manager—formerly his Iowa manager—Glenn replied, "You probably know him better than I do." [42] It was not a comment that bred confidence in the Glenn organization at any level; and neither did the interview given by the organization's political director and topmost hired gun about that same time. He told a reporter, "This campaign is still in worse shape than any I've ever seen." He also criticized Bill White, described Glenn as "boring," and ended by saying, "I don't take any crap from Glenn, I don't take any crap from anybody." [43] It was further proof of the fatal flaws built into the staff of hired guns.

The Iowa State Democratic chairman provided his post mortem. "Glenn seemed slow to appreciate the value of organization in this state," he said. "There are three basic rules to winning in Iowa: organization, organization, organization. Glenn broke all three." [44] Another Iowa party leader echoed, "Organizationally, it was a disaster. I don't know whether it was the main thing or not. But it probably made it impossible for Glenn to win in Iowa." And a couple of weeks later, a Glenn adviser commented, "We kick ourselves every day.... We got in Iowa late.... We weren't organized." [45] They were self-inflicted wounds.

CONSTITUENCY

Lack of organization was not the only explanation for the lack of troops on caucus day. The campaign staffers never developed a clear idea of who their troops might be. This difficulty, too, resulted from a conceptual flaw in their strategic thinking about nomination politics in general. They conceptualized both Glenn's electability and their support in general election terms, not caucus and primary terms, which left them looking for nominating support among the vaguely defined "constituency of the whole" or "sensible center" or "broad middle" of the Democratic party. In Iowa that description meant, more than anything else, people who do not normally attend caucuses. Among the Iowa electorate, 30 percent to 40 percent are independents, Patterson explained; historically they "do not participate at all" in caucuses.[46]

For Glenn the problem lay in the inapplicability of his appealing Ohio model. His potential constituency was more a figment of that model and its public service underpinnings than the result of a careful analysis of potential caucus-goers. "I keep trying to come back to what's best for all the people in the country, the constituency of the whole if you will."[47] Or, "I don't like back-room politics and the deal making, and I think it's time all the middle ground midstream Democrats get out and get votes and get going."[48] Or,

> I'm getting tired of the radicals of either the left or the right being the ones that control our political system. . . . If we can motivate that great mass of people out there in the middle . . . those are the ones I want involved in the sensible center.[49]

He kept looking for the Iowa equivalent of the rank and file or the across-the-board supporters he had found in Ohio.

During his November trip to Iowa he referred constantly to his Ohio model. At his Sioux City press conference, he was asked about the importance of organizational endorsements. "We've studied very, very carefully the voting patterns of people back in Ohio with regard to that," he answered.

> And you don't find that kind of close correlation between what organizational heads recommend and the voting pattern of their membership. So early on in this campaign, I set out to speak to the people of this country across the board.

What about labor? he was asked.

> Speaking about the rank and file, absolutely, I've done that in Ohio in the past. In Ohio I was not always the choice of organized labor . . . we overcame that by doing just what I was talking about. We went to the rank and file and talked to them. . . . We went in there and said "compare the issues" and laid it out. . . . That's exactly what we did and they responded. So we're doing the same sort of thing nationally.

This was, as we have said, a general election posture—aimed primarily at Ronald Reagan—not a primary election pitch aimed at primary- and caucus-goers. And there seemed no reason to expect it would work in the Iowa caucuses.

Close observers of Iowa politics understood that the "Iowa Democratic party is dominated by liberal activists" and that the caucuses had always been populated by "those who carry the flag of traditional Democratic politics," by "liberal activists," by those "on the liberal side," by "Democratic activists," by people "more liberal" than the Iowa Democrats as a whole.[50] Those were precisely the people Glenn's view tended to exclude. He was looking for the kind of independents whom Patterson identified as historic nonparticipants. Iowa's political writers described his campaign, accordingly, as a general election campaign.[51] In view of caucus voting history, it was the most untutored of gambles to try to reverse that pattern in so short a time in a state of such critical strategic importance.

It was not as if they had any clear idea what their "constituency of the whole" looked like. Glenn's campaigners described their targets variously as "the marine-Elk vote" and as "pickups with shotguns, middle Americans, agribusiness, and blue collar."[52] By a process called geodemographics, they merged poll results and census data in an effort to "pinpoint by ZIP code 65,000 Democratic households in eight clusters." These clusters, in theory, "ought to be teeming with potential Glenn supporters." They described the clusters as "the shotgun and pickup crowd," "new homesteaders," "grain belters," "back country folk," "blue collar and nursery set," "blue chip bluers," "corn town."[53] They planned to contact these people by phone and by mail, hoping to reap 7,000-8,000 caucus votes from their $140,000 effort.[54] They actually managed to reach 20,000-30,000 of these targeted voters. "I'm depending on those people to come out," said Glenn, "I think they will."[55] They did not. John Glenn did not enter the Iowa contest with a committed constituency of any size, and he did not find one while he was there.

The effort to create an Iowa caucus electorate that had never existed before was another manipulative illusion of John Glenn's hired guns. The Democrats who turned out for the Iowa caucuses were, as always, more liberal—by 66 percent to 44 percent—than Iowa Democrats in general.[56] Glenn's intraparty confrontation with Mondale had moved him off of his natural center-left position on issues, away from the middle and toward the conservative end of the spectrum. There were not many caucus voters there.

When it was over, his campaigners acknowledged their total failure with a casual arrogance. "We had identified 20,000-30,000 people who had not gone to caucuses before—and, today, they still haven't."[57] Or,

"We went looking for the sensible center but we found it was the hole in the doughnut." [58] Or, "We made a contribution to text books on Iowa caucuses. Reaching out to nontraditional voters doesn't work. It should save some people a lot of effort in the future." [59] Every Democrat who had ever campaigned in Iowa and every student of Iowa politics could have told them about it. The hired guns might have saved themselves "a lot of effort"—and their candidate a lot of grief—if they had read and listened.[60]

Bill White had sat in on the Hunt Commission deliberations on Democratic party nomination rules and practices, on the impact of rules in the past, and on the anticipated consequences of rules changes. He understood them well. But he did not participate actively in that work and seems not to have thoroughly imbibed the catastrophic potential of the new frontloading rules.[61] And Senator Glenn seems not to have expected him to have done so. "He was an observer there," Glenn said of White. "But we were not key to what that whole arrangement was. That was before I decided to get in. We were interested observers at that time, but that was about it." [62] The Hunt Commission participants made no secret that they had devised a potential life or death sequence in Iowa and New Hampshire.

Perhaps White did understand the sequential significance of Iowa, but followed the strategic advice of the more high-powered hired guns—who had not absorbed much political history either. (Indeed, the top hired gun was already a two-time heavy loser in presidential politics.) Their notion was that the campaign would be largely a media campaign. And they entertained an extravagant faith in what the media could do for their candidate in nomination politics. Knowing little about their candidate, they believed they had signed on with a media star or that they could make him one. Their candidate, with his faith in technology and lack of enthusiasm for the grubbier routines of retail campaigning, was willing to believe them. "I've got my own little theory," he said, "that television has replaced party organization and personal visits as the way you knock on people's doors." [63] It was anything but a theory: it did not even distinguish between organization-intensive Iowa and media-intensive California. And his advisers did not act as if they did either. The lack of state-by-state conceptualization was costly.

In these several matters of campaign conceptualization—strategic priorities, organization, constituency building—the Glenn campaigners suffered from the absence of an intellectual base. The candidate was a pragmatic, can-do person with a great deal of optimism about what technology could accomplish. But he was neither a student of political history nor steeped in the lore of previous presidential campaigns. He did not attach himself to any political tradition. He needed help in thinking seriously about these things, but he did not get it. Instead, he got a campaign that was, at best, extremely risky and highly experimental—a campaign that, in the end, was run by others at his expense.

MEDIA IMAGE AND CONFRONTATION

In the beginning Glenn's media people hoped to piggyback on *The Right Stuff*, and so they began their media campaign in conjunction with it.[64] It was a major miscalculation, but it did not dissuade them from their confidence in their paid media. Even when they gave their organizational component a shot in the arm in December, the aim was "to mount a field organization that will support the communication efforts of the campaign." [65]

Their communication efforts had two aspects. One featured a set of positive ads, some of which emphasized Glenn's military-astronaut heroism and played down his Senate role.[66] Another group of ads stressed his nonastronaut experience and his Senate work on nuclear nonproliferation. All these ads associated him with the idea of excellence and national pride that characterized his astronaut-hero past.[67] Only by inference did they distinguish Glenn from Mondale.

A second set of ads pursued his confrontation with Walter Mondale. The milder of these negative ads used "people on the street" to raise questions directly about Mondale's attachment to special interests. The stronger set of anti-Mondale ads was much more negative and harsh in attacking Mondale for over-promising to special interests, for his attachments to the AFL-CIO, and for the undesirable effects of those relationships. The strongly negative ads were prepared for New Hampshire but never used.[68] In New Hampshire Glenn's campaign ran pro-Glenn ads together with the milder anti-Mondale ads.

In Iowa the campaign ran both groups of positive pro-Glenn ads, but none of the anti-Mondale ads.[69] He began in Iowa with a short burst in October, picked up again in January, and continued off and on until the caucuses. He outspent all the other candidates on television, but there is no evidence that his media campaign changed anything. In the period of greatest concentration from mid-January to mid-February Glenn slipped a couple of points farther behind Mondale in the Iowa poll—from 47 to 16 to 44 to 11 among likely caucus-goers. The day the media campaign began in Iowa, Glenn's media adviser set a goal: "We have to define who John Glenn is and what he stands for." [70] Two weeks later he said, "Clearly, our message, so far, hasn't gotten through." [71] The next day he said, "People now know little about John Glenn." [72] A week later he said, "They know two things about John Glenn: he's an astronaut and he's got a disorganized campaign. They don't even know he's a senator." [73] That same day a reporter commented, "Glenn's television persona is still what it was when he announced his candidacy—indistinct." [74] People even had difficulty with his astronaut image, as one-on-one interviewing unfailingly picked up people who thought he had gone to the moon. In early February a third of those polled nationally said they had not "heard enough" about Glenn to have any opinion about him. The corresponding figures were 5 percent for Mondale and 2 percent for President Reagan. [75] Glenn's media campaign had much to accomplish in less than three weeks—much too much as it turned out.

It was clear from Glenn's Ohio experience that filling in the political blanks in the persona of a marine-astronaut-hero would be difficult and time-consuming. And it was not made easier in his national campaign by the media's insistence on characterizing him as an astronaut rather than as a senator. Not only did the film *The Right Stuff* result in the reinforcement of the astronaut image, but also so did much of the descriptive language with which—as the reader is doubtless now aware—the Glenn campaign was reported. Editorial cartoons had the same effect. The senator was pictured walking around in his astronaut garb—helmet and/or spacesuit; he was shown inside his capsule, waiting for liftoff, lost in space, or crash-landed, as seemed appropriate to the season.

If John Glenn's media campaign had any effect at all in Iowa, it was as a confusing counterpoint to his personal campaign. His media consultants had always believed that his natural advantage and their natural pitch revolved around his strength of character. The astronaut-hero-senator who appeared on television—especially in the Iowa ads—was a person of exceptional character whose accomplishments exemplified unifying values such as peace and excellence. [76] But the campaigning candidate often appeared as something less than—even in conflict with—the portrait of the exemplary individual. The campaign "took a candidate with the image of Dwight Eisenhower," said one commentator, "and turned him into Rocky Graziano." [77]

Whether Glenn weighed the consequences, he continued on the confrontational course he had set in October. Not all of the activity occurred in Iowa, but it reverberated there and had consequences there. Having ended 1983 with a Texas campaign of "escalating criticism" of Mondale, [78] Glenn began 1984 in New Hampshire by accusing the former vice president of having "secret plans" for dealing with the budget deficit and acid rain. [79] And when Mondale struck back by attacking the Ohio senator for "a very poor record on clean air issues," the confrontation was renewed. Glenn countered characteristically by taking it personally. "I came to New Hampshire to do a job on acid rain—Fritz Mondale apparently came here to do a job on me." [80] The comment immediately indicated that the new year would bring no tactical change. Glenn intended to strike hard at Mondale and to insist that the Glenn campaign was positive and hit back only when unfairly attacked.

This stance was Glenn's standard way of reconciling his public service views with his competitiveness. When asked at that time to describe his differences with the front-runner, he told his interviewer, "I've been asked a number of times to give the differences between Mondale and myself. I refuse to do it. I said the important thing is President Reagan. I'll give my view on things." [81] Shades of Syracuse in September. After months of harsh attack and counterattack, Glenn still believed it was important to maintain a posture as the positive campaigner, that it was Mondale, not he, who had started the rough stuff. "When I've come back at him," Glenn continued, "I've raised some questions in return and asked a lot more about his direction than any doubts he cast at me." [82]

His persistence in portraying himself as the injured counterattacker reveals, again, the depth of his attachment to public service politics and its importance to his self-image as a distinctive kind of politician, while at the same time allowing room for the free play of his competitiveness. It is true that in the campaign of a characteristically low-key candidate like Glenn, a little righteous indignation—strategically placed—can be very helpful, as it surely had been in 1974 in Ohio. But indignation is a reaction, and it cannot define a candidate or drive a campaign. Moreover, in early 1984, "who started what" had to be a matter of supreme indifference to the electorate Glenn was trying to reach.

Glenn's refusal to disengage from his confrontation with Mondale indicates a certain strategic inflexibility. While it may be true that his private polls indicated that the strategy had done some damage to Mondale, there was no evidence whatever that it had helped Glenn. But Old Magnet Tail had Mondale in his sights, and he refused to pull off the target. His hired guns encouraged him. "We've got to knock a hole in Mondale's armor," said a top operative.[83] "My instinct is to take out Mondale's knee caps," said another.[84] There was a comforting belief in the Glenn camp that "Mondale has never had to fight for any office he held and will crack as the campaign turns into a punch-counterpunch battle." [85] Privately, they spoke of the Mondale effort as "a glass locomotive" that would shatter at the first obstacle. Glenn also held this view, as his campaign trail comments indicate. So they kept on pressing Mondale and kept waiting for him to stumble.

It was more a fighter pilot's view of the situation than a strategic politician's view. This contest was not just between him and Mondale; it was for the support of a Democratic electorate. Mondale had welcomed that contest in the fall and he welcomed it again—as one in which he held the advantage.

In their early January appearances before New Hampshire's environmentalists, Mondale's advantage with liberal, issue-oriented Democratic constituencies was demonstrated anew. Glenn, struggling—because of the smokestack industries in Ohio—with a steadily changing position on acid rain, delivered a detailed proposal to "a polite, but not enthusiastic," "lukewarm" audience. Mondale, recalling old battles, was "warmly received" by "a cheering audience" as he reminded them symbolically that "on every front, on every issue, we've been together." [86] Talking to Mondale's campaigners, one reporter noted their continuing delight at this kind of confrontation.

> Glenn's thrust evoked a long-planned Mondale parry. At the top levels of the Mondale campaign, his closest advisers believe that any issue-related spat with Glenn helps Mondale because it tends to put the Ohio Senator on the right end of the ideological spectrum, dangerous territory they say in a contest for the Democratic nomination. [87]

It was a New Hampshire example, but an Iowa generalization.

A comparable Iowa example turned out to be Glenn's attack on Mondale for being weak on defense, as it came to be interpreted by an Iowa Democratic party that shows "little support for big military budgets." [88] In general, Glenn's confrontational strategy, as it captured the headlines, tended to drive away the liberals more than it attracted the putative centrists. As this kind of movement occurred, liberals began to paint Glenn as more conservative than he really was. [89] He could not hold the center in any head-to-head confrontation with Mondale. The Mondale campaign knew it; Glenn's did not.

One week after the "secret plans"-acid rain contretemps, Glenn launched his most highly publicized attack—or counterattack—on Mondale. It took place during the first nationally televised all-candidate debate in New Hampshire. As Mondale talked about his plans for cutting the deficit, Glenn jumped to his feet and exclaimed, "That's the same vague gobbledygook we've been hearing. I'm sick and tired of all the vague promises ... without figures attached." He said Mondale's promises would add $170 billion to the deficit. Mondale hit back at Glenn's vote supporting Reaganomics for creating the deficit, while calling Glenn's projections "voodoo numbers" and "baloney figures." Glenn warned of over-promising and big spending. Mondale criticized Glenn votes on the B-1 bomber and "new poison nerve gas" as overspending. Glenn called for sacrifice via his 10 percent surtax on income taxes. Mondale totaled up his budget reduction proposals. This exchange summarized much of their campaign charge and countercharge. It was a heated, face-to-face, shouting, finger-pointing, stand up-sit down argument that dominated the media coverage of the three-hour debate. Scorekeepers recorded that Glenn "lit into," "erupted" at, "exploded" at, "pounced" on, and "blew up" at his opponent.

If there was a consensus view among scorekeepers, it was that there was no clear winner. Glenn won in the sense that he drew attention to himself and, thereby, held his second-place position; Mondale won in the sense that he held his own under attack. There was a good deal of commentary on the contrast between the Glenn of the first two hours—"mute," "lackluster," "laid back," "poised," "relaxed," "calm," "digni-fied," "bland," "tedious," "benign," "even-tempered," "quiet," "con-trolled," "stiff," "wallflower"—and the Glenn of the third-hour con-frontation—"emotional," "indignant," "annoyed," "fiery," "strident," "spirited," "angry," "nasty," and "rousing." [90] The contrast made for enough confusion, apparently, to deprive him of a winning perfor-mance. A quickie *Washington Post* poll (attacked, accurately, by Glenn as "unprofessional and irresponsible") concluded: "John Glenn apparently did himself the least good." It found that the favorability gap between people who watched and people who did not was more damaging to Glenn than to any of the others.[91] A postdebate New Hampshire poll recorded a drop of 5 points—from 17 percent to 12 percent.[92]

The problem for Glenn seemed to be the sense that he was out of character in attacking Mondale, that he came across as excessive and nasty rather than steady and heroic. During the debate, party elder George McGovern deplored "the tendency to clobber the front-runner." He added, "Everyone knows Fritz Mondale is a good, decent Ameri-can. . . ." [93] It was not the sort of rebuke one would expect to see aimed at John Glenn. Indeed, McGovern would continue to rebuild his reputa-tion for high-road wisdom by playing off of Glenn's anti-Mondale posture.[94] The New Hampshire episode exemplified Glenn's mixed message problem. The man in the debate was not the man depicted in the television ads. The dichotomy was a big problem for someone trying to fill out a political persona and gain support. "Whatever Glenn planned for Dartmouth," concluded one scorekeeper later, "it didn't work." [95] Later still, on the eve of the multicandidate Iowa debate, another observer concluded, "His much chronicled 'vague gobbledy-gook' onslaught . . . does not appear to have been a success." [96]

As the Iowa caucuses approached, Glenn applied even more heat—especially on the AFL-CIO-Mondale alliance. On the eve of the televised all-candidate forum in Des Moines, campaign manager White accused Mondale of accepting illegally large amounts of campaign money from organized labor. The Mondale camp retaliated by charging illegalities by Glenn in securing a $2.5 million line of credit from Ohio banks. Both sides threatened to go to the Federal Election Commission.[97] Mondale brushed off the Glenn charge as "trash time in this campaign."[98] Glenn replied to the Mondale charge, "We think Mondale's bottomed out, and now he's trying to prevent us from getting on the air at a crucial time when we see things changing ... they're trying desperately by fair means or foul to stop us from getting the money."[99] He started suggesting more bluntly than ever, "What does Lane Kirkland think he's trying to buy with his $20 million, a president who will never disagree with the AFL-CIO?"[100] It had long been one of Glenn's suppositions, based on his Ohio model, that he could appeal to the rank and file of labor over the heads of their leaders. But he may have vitiated that strategy in Iowa by the vehemence of his attacks. "We didn't have to explain to our members any longer why we endorsed Mondale over Glenn," said one Iowa labor leader.[101]

More than 600,000 Iowans watched or listened to the all-candidate debate one week before the caucuses. To Glenn's campaigners it was "the most important of any so far."[102] Its format made it difficult for Glenn to debate head-to-head with Mondale, and no debate occurred. There were opening and closing statements by each candidate, questions from a panel, and candidate questions to one another, as determined by lot. Glenn did not draw Mondale. Judging by scorekeeper reviews, however, that was the least of Glenn's problems. Only his "strong," "impassioned" opening statement attacking Reagan's foreign policy drew praise.[103] His answers to the questions of others were judged unfavorably as "robot like," "inarticulate," "fumbled," and "all tangled up."[104] So, too, were his questions to fellow candidates—"put his foot in his mouth," "inspired only ridicule."[105] "You're just all confused in that capsule of yours," replied Ernest Hollings to a Glenn question. And he added, "I don't know who is going to pay for the inexperience of John Glenn." Glenn did not respond and was described as "benign and bemused," "flat and frustrated," "sleepy," "feeble," and "listless" in the face of this rebuttal.[106] The man whom his campaigners predicted would be a media star had not yet turned out to be one.

The next morning's headline in the *Des Moines Register* read, "McGovern Fared Well, Glenn Came Off Poorly in Debate, Nagle Says." This assessment by the Democratic state chairman was echoed four days later by Iowa poll results showing that Glenn's performance received the highest unfavorability ratings among all Iowa Democrats and among likely caucus-goers. Both groups ranked him sixth among the candidates in favorability ratings. The pollster concluded, "John Glenn ... did not help himself in the debate."[107] Observers who watched the debate with Iowans reported overwhelmingly negative assessments, such as "just not a really strong candidate," "uncomfortable and inarticulate," "passive and even weak," and noting a "lack of verbal agility."[108] Even his campaigners called it a "disaster."[109] Unlike in New Hampshire, the available evidence indicated that Glenn had lost the debate. At a time when much rested on the candidate's individual effort to pull himself up by his boot straps—to demonstrate political skill, to deliver a message—he failed, conspicuously, to do so.

A few days later Glenn charged that Mondale had made an "untrue" statement during the debate—one regarding Mondale's attitude on consumer issues concerning a national gas pipeline matter. And he began running a harsh radio commercial in New Hampshire challenging Mondale's veracity on the subject. Mondale defended his actions and said, "This has gone too far ... John Glenn has violated the minimum standards of decency.... He should be ashamed of himself."[110] With the fur flying, Charles Manatt, chairman of the Democratic National Committee, sent a warning letter to all candidates. "Personalized attacks or criticisms that could inhibit our ability to win in November should be avoided," he wrote. "Positive presentation of the issues at this stage will be of great value to us all."[111] Three days before the Iowa caucuses, the *Des Moines Register* headlined, "Mondale and Glenn Trade 'Lie' Charges: Manatt Asks for Harmony or Risk Losing to Reagan."[112] On "Face the Nation" two days later, Glenn responded, "I have a five-point program for war and peace. I wish people would concentrate on that. Everyone wants to pick on these little differences between us—the confrontations."[113] But the next day, caucus day, he was calling Mondale the candidate of "the bosses, the power brokers, the kingmakers."[114]

The substance of these confrontations is deservedly lost in obscurity. The point is simply that an essential part of Glenn's strategy called for continuing his confrontations with Mondale right up to the day of the Iowa caucuses. As various scorekeepers saw it: "The message down the stretch [is] overwhelmingly negative."[115] "Mr. Glenn has stepped up his attacks and they reached a crescendo this week";[116] "Glenn has continued to attack Mondale in harsher and harsher terms";[117] exchanges have become "increasingly bitter";[118] they reflect "Glenn's increasingly negative approach";[119] they produce "a torrent of invective [as] Glenn repeatedly slashed at Walter Mondale."[120] When asked why he continued to do it, his Iowa campaign manager commented, "It's his attempt to make a contrast with Mondale, and that's the only way he knows how to do it."[121] It was, of course, Old Magnet Tail's competitive instinct at work, but there is no evidence that this manager or anyone else told him he must stop. To the contrary, they had long since urged him to take that course. Several weeks later, Gary Hart reflected on the "problem John Glenn [faced] when he was constantly attacking Mondale. It's almost Biblical—you destroy your enemy but you destroy yourself. Somebody in . . . [a] campaign has to know how self-destructive those tactics are and how hard it is to repair the damage." [122] But no one did. So the question of February was whether the confrontational element of Glenn's strategy, which had failed to help him in the preceding season, would pay dividends in this one.

It did not. When it was over, there was a solid consensus that the confrontational strategy with its anti-Mondale emphasis had hurt the Glenn campaign. As part of their explanation for Glenn's weak showing, observers cited Glenn's "unsmiling negativism," his "steady stream of attacks on Mondale," "his constant negative attacks on Mondale," "his acerbic attacks on Mondale," "his harsh and negative campaigning against Mondale." [123]

Another part of the explanation was the blurring of Glenn's character. Precisely because it was a deviation from what the media had originally expected from the hero-astronaut, they played up the negative side of the confrontational strategy. "[His] shrill attacks on Mondale clashed with his good guy image." [124] "Outrage doesn't seem to become John Glenn." "He's not that kind of a guy really. It's out of character for him." [125] "When Mr. Glenn tries to act tough, it comes off as mean." [126] "When he attacks, he ends up sounding nasty." [127] "His image has been wholesome, apple pie positive, but he has become an antagonistic, even carping critic." [128] An Ohio reporter believed "the appearance of a split personality" was the "most significant" of all the factors in the Iowa outcome.

> Glenn's strategy was to drag Mondale down by beating Mondale up. It required harsh language. It required suggestions that Mondale was a liar, a shouting match during a debate and negative advertisements depicting Mondale as a wild spendthrift. It failed . . . because Glenn is an unlikely name caller. The mix was like oil and water. . . . [There was] Glenn the hero, the patriot, the nice man. Then there was Glenn the scheming politician engaged in the politics of the negative. . . . Voters became confused by these conflicting political images . . . when voters become confused about a candidate, they don't vote for the candidate. . . . In the Iowa aftermath it became clear the get-tough-on-Mondale strategy had tainted an all-American image.[129]

"The American people just don't believe a hero like John Glenn should

be negative," conceded an adviser—a month later.[130] It was another
tardy admission of a costly strategic error.

The other part of the explanation involved a distinctly Iowa factor.
Patterson emphasizes the high-minded nature of Iowa politics. "Above
all," he says, "Iowans and their politicians are moralistic about their
politics. Iowa politics is blatantly characterized by honesty, fair play,
honorable intentions and good government. . . . Political conflict in Iowa
is remarkably civil and high-minded." [131] The climate was tailor-made
for Glenn, the public service nice guy, but it was particularly inhospitable to Glenn, the rough-and-tumble attacker. And Iowa Democrats seem
to have been particularly put off by the latter. A state party official
generalized,

> When Glenn started attacking Mondale, Iowans didn't like it.
> Iowa Democrats don't like negative campaigning. They were
> victimized by it twice, in the [Dick] Clark and [John] Culver
> [U.S. Senate] campaigns. They don't like people turning the
> machine gun on their own ranks and spraying bullets all
> around. And they don't like the bullets lying all around
> waiting for Republicans to use them against Democrats. That
> hurt Glenn badly.

George McGovern had used the same argument effectively in the two
debates, and it drew a positive response from Iowa Democrats. Glenn's
confrontational strategy was not only inappropriate to him, but also it
was inappropriate to Iowa. And that was a losing combination.

Nearly everything went wrong in the Iowa campaign. There was a
basic lack of understanding of the strategic importance of the state. Or, if
the Glenn people understood it, they did not behave as if they did. From
that perspective, the campaign represented either ignorance or miscalculation, or it was a deliberately perilous experiment run by others at
Glenn's expense. At the end, his primary resources, such as personal
appeal and ideological centrism, had been dissipated; and his secondary
resources, such as organization and political skill, remained undeveloped. His Ohio-generated campaign model and its general election
strategy were inappropriate. His other strategic decisions, from the
delayed start at the outset to the prolonged confrontation at the end,
were faulty. And, now, the media was about to hasten the campaign's
demise with a final downward shove.

EXPECTATIONS AND INTERPRETATIONS

In the weeks preceding the Iowa caucuses, media scorekeepers
created the structure of expectations that would guide their interpreta-

tion of the event. For the most part, the scorekeepers reinforced the structure of competition that had existed since Ted Kennedy's with-drawal—that Walter Mondale was expected to finish first and John Glenn was expected to finish second. That was the way they had played the nomination story for fourteen months. Because they had given more coverage to Mondale and Glenn than to all the other candidates combined, they had a huge investment in their two-man, two-tier version of the story.[132] On the other hand, all the evidence they had amassed and all the descriptive terms they had been applying to that evidence since the end of the year suggested that John Glenn and his campaign were not behaving in accordance with the script, that they had performed so poorly for so long that he was, very probably, no longer in second place.

There was but one piece of evidence in all the accounts of the Glenn candidacy from December 1983 through February 1984 that would have led anyone to think he remained securely in second place. That evidence was the January Iowa poll, which ranked him in second place among likely caucus-goers—twenty-one points behind Mondale and four points ahead of the third-place candidate. The December poll had found him twenty-one points behind Mondale and three points ahead of his nearest competitor.[133] While those polls found him in second place, they also found him much closer to the last place candidate than he was to Walter Mondale. Every other bit of evidence indicated that Glenn was moving in one direction only—back toward the rest of the pack. And it was, after all, only a snapshot poll. Yet the media focused almost exclusively on the simple relationship between Mondale and Glenn rather than on the complex relationship between Glenn and the others. It was in their occupational interest to keep the simple front-runner and challenger story line. As long as they held to it, they were unable to think of John Glenn as anything but the challenger.

There are indications that some of the people keeping score had reservations about this expectation. In early January one noted that Glenn was "slipping so badly in Iowa that he is in danger of finishing third."[134] Two others reported that the temperature was 6° below zero in Iowa and that Glenn's prospects there "have cooled about as much as the weather."[135] A few days later, a third estimate was that "Iowa could become a major embarrassment to Glenn."[136] And at the beginning of February, a *Des Moines Register* story based on interviews with Iowa Democratic politicians headlined, "Leaders: Glenn May Be Red Faced Caucus Night."[137] In mid-February, a reporter wrote, "Glenn's second-place position is probably weakening in the final days here."[138] Another found Glenn "struggling to stay out of third place. And he's doing badly at it."[139] Another said that Glenn, "once a sure second-place finisher, has been losing ground for weeks."[140] And a fourth summed up, "A lot of reporters are raising the question . . . of whether Glenn will finish second here."[141] So there were plenty of doubts about the accuracy of their expectations about Glenn. But they did not alter them.

"Campaign histories," wrote an observer in January, "are replete with instances of reporters and commentators sticking with the early front-runners even as they were being overtaken and eclipsed."[142] Clearly, he had John Glenn in mind. Whatever their doubts, the scorekeepers of 1984 continued to propound the idea that nothing but second would do. "Expectations for Senator John Glenn . . . have fallen through the floor. Glenn's standing has dropped steadily in polls here," began one scorekeeper. "Yet," he concluded, "to meet 'expectations,' Glenn needs to finish second in Iowa."[143] Or, as most other journalists put it, if he could not hold onto a secure second place, he was in trouble. There was unanimity on this score: "the real question . . . is whether Glenn can be denied the solid second-place finish many see as crucial to his campaign";[144] he "would be seriously damaged if edged out of second place";[145] "anything less than second would be disastrous";[146] "anything less than a clear second-place showing could heighten a sense of impending doom";[147] "needs a solid second place . . . to rescue his flagging campaign";[148] "anything less than a second for Glenn means the party's over";[149] "credibility . . . for Glenn means finishing second";[150] "if he comes in third, it could be curtains."[151] It was an expectation he could not meet, not in Iowa. They had every reason to know it, but they held him to it anyway.

When the journalistic community sets its expectations, it is hard for the campaigners to escape from them. In some cases, they do not wish to do so. They may have been co-conspirators in setting the level of expectations. But in a case like Glenn's, where expectations were set far too high, a candidate is constrained to agree because disagreement will appear to concede defeat and may demoralize supporters. So, whether they believed it or were trapped into it, the Glenn campaigners obligingly predicted a second-place finish and 15 percent to 20 percent of the vote.[152]

Bill White said that his candidate needed "a respectable second."[153] Sam Vitali, the new Iowa coordinator, predicted that only Mondale and Glenn would produce "double digits."[154] Gerald Vento said, "If we come in third behind Cranston or Hart, we've got to worry about damage control."[155] Greg Schneiders focused on the longer range. "I'm not willing to say we would drop out if we were third in Iowa or New Hampshire. Being realistic, we'll probably be the alternative to Mondale on Super Tuesday. Being second doesn't rattle him."[156] Robert Keefe avoided the question of Iowa, saying only, "We've got to do well in New

Hampshire. Doing well in the South depends on New Hampshire." [157] John Glenn's comment, made earlier, was even more long range. "I have to win somewhere," he said. "You can't come in second all the time. The worst case for us would be to come in second five times in a row."[158] He was wrong: there was a much worse case than that.

When the Iowa results—a fifth-place finish and 5 percent of the vote—came in and the scorekeepers responded with their predictable interpretation, the total effect on the Glenn campaign could not have been worse. Veteran columnists Jack Germond and Jules Witcover told the essential story.

> Once again, the political expectations game has markedly altered a presidential campaign. Senator John Glenn of Ohio has been effectively eliminated as a serious competitor ... not just because he finished down among the also rans here, but because he did so when the political community and the press fully expected him to finish second, however distantly.[159]

By setting their expectations for him too high and by pressuring his advisers to agree, the media had set John Glenn up for the kill.

The media scorekeepers did not make the Glenn campaign in Iowa fail; it did that all by itself. But they magnified the failure. And they made Glenn's failure *the* story of the Iowa caucuses. Further, by making it *the* story, they effectively took him out of the race. Unwilling to downgrade his standing when they could have done so several weeks earlier, they propped him up so that they could write him off after Iowa. It was almost as if they could not wait for an opportunity to unburden themselves once and for all of their outdated two-man, two-tier story line and get on to a new one. By setting their expectations unrealistically high, they solved a problem for themselves. But they placed a crushing burden on the candidate who needed a very different interpretation— that a big defeat there was to be expected, that Iowa was never his kind of state, and that the real test for him lay ahead.

On the morning after Iowa, the nation's headlines wrote the story: "Glenn Does Poorly," "Glenn Far Back in Pack," "Glenn Is Trampled," "Glenn Falls Well Back," "Mondale's Victory Deals Blow to Glenn," "Glenn Suffers Major Setback," "Big News Is Depth of Glenn's Defeat." [160]

In the accompanying stories, Glenn's performance was described as "a stunning defeat," "a devastating blow," "his last hurrah," "a poor showing," "a crushing and perhaps fatal defeat," "a stunning setback," "an Iowa burnout," "the political choke of the year," "a miserable showing," "a dismal showing," "a misstep," "a debacle," "a public and painful drubbing," "disastrous," "feeble," "embarrassing," "dreary," "a shellacking," "a humiliation," "the beginning of the end," and "the final stages of the most spectacularly bungled presidential campaign in modern American history."

The candidate and the campaign were described as "mortally wounded," "on the ropes," "collapsed in a heap," "hemorrhaging," "reeling," "near collapse," "down in flames," "crashlanded," "the big loser in Iowa," "the loser in the expectations game," "in deep deep trouble," and "wounded and demoralized." The media reached for metaphors: "his back against the wall"; "much of the steam had gone out of [his] campaign"; "the air had gone out of [his] balloon"; "the bottom [had] dropped out"; he was "at the end of his rope"; and "the worst fear [had] come to pass." He was "the only astronaut to splash down before he lifted off." [161] The judgments were merciless and relentless. Iowa was a self-inflicted wound, but the media scorekeepers made it fatal.

The Iowa outcome changed the structure of competition. It took away Glenn's second-place status, left him with no status, and put him in a "political free fall." The negative reverberations were instantaneous. On Tuesday evening the Glenn campaign was conducting a tracking poll in New Hampshire. Just prior to the nightly network news, they found Glenn riding in second place with 19 percent of the vote. Immediately after the Iowa results were reported on the news, Glenn dropped to third place with 9 percent of the vote.[162] When completed, Glenn's New Hampshire poll—which had found Glenn at 25 percent to Mondale's 32 percent shortly before Iowa—found Glenn at 11 percent and Mondale at 34 percent the day after Iowa. Gary Hart was in second place at 25 percent.[163] "We just looked at that stuff," recalled one adviser, "and we said Holy Christ, we're no longer the alternative. We were out of the campaign. There had to be one alternative to Mondale. It was no longer John Glenn." [164] The reverberations were nationwide. A CBS-*New York Times* poll taken four days after Iowa found that Glenn's 7 percent support nationally was half of what it had been a month earlier.[165]

Glenn's New Hampshire campaign manager had noted earlier that "New Hampshire likes an underdog but not a loser." [166] Glenn came out of Iowa a loser, and the loss carried New Hampshire down with it. A New Hampshire pollster attributed Glenn's precipitous fall there largely to people who had originally backed him as the most electable Democrat—a rationale killed in Iowa.[167] After Iowa, all the quantitative indicators of Glenn's media coverage turned negative and scarce.[168] Glenn's expectations momentum was replaced by Gary Hart's expectations momentum. What Iowa did to New Hampshire, New Hampshire subsequently did to the South. "We were wounded meat after New Hampshire," said one top aide when it was all over. "After New

Hampshire, as we moved south, we had a big opening—but we were no longer the alternative." [169]

In the days after Iowa, Glenn spent the lion's share of what would become a $2.8 million campaign debt. His willingness to expend such huge sums in the wake of the Iowa results further indicates how little Glenn's people understood the killing power of the Iowa caucuses. They had not fully understood it before it hit them, and they did not fully understand what it had done to them afterward. As Glenn struggled toward Super Tuesday in the South, an aide said, "We kick ourselves every day. If we hadn't finished fifth in Iowa it might be different now. We got in Iowa late. . . . We weren't organized." [170] When it was all over, the Ohio senator pinpointed Iowa simply as "the place where 'things became unglued.' " [171] One of his top strategists elaborated,

> If you asked me what happened to the Glenn candidacy, I'd answer in one word: Iowa. Pre-Iowa, Glenn's polls showed him within eight or nine points of Mondale in New Hampshire. If he'd come in second in Iowa, he probably would have won New Hampshire. [172]

And if he had won New Hampshire? It was an acknowledgment—finally—of the overwhelming strategic importance of Iowa. It came at least a year and a half too late.

THE CAMPAIGN IN NEW HAMPSHIRE

As the Glenn campaigners approached the New Hampshire primary hurdle, they remained publicly hopeful, but privately mindful, that their survival depended on a second-place finish there. And, for strategic reasons, they predicted one. [173] From the beginning, they had thought of New Hampshire as a more congenial context than Iowa. As a primary state, they felt they would be less dominated by a "liberal establishment," and more susceptible to media appeals. They thought of New Hampshire activists as more conservative and more independent than Iowa activists. [174] John Glenn saw its people "like those in Ohio—very patriotic." [175] And there would be no next-door neighbor running there.

Among observers in the state, there was widespread agreement that Glenn had an excellent opportunity there. The problem was that at the point where he desperately needed to cash in on that opportunity, he had long since squandered his chances. He had no cushion of support awaiting him in New Hampshire, no constituency sufficiently committed to slow the runaway reverse momentum or to give his candidacy some resiliency. The constituency to which he had tailored his appeal—the self-styled "independents" or the self-styled "moderates" did not vote for him. They did give him his best support. But the first group—nearly 40 percent on election day—gave him only 13 percent of its vote; the second group—nearly 50 percent on election day—gave him 16 percent.[176]

New Hampshire was, in fact, much more like Iowa than the Glenn campaigners thought it was. And his difficulties there were similar to those he had in Iowa—except for the multiplicative effect of the Iowa defeat. New Hampshire's nomination politics is less dependent on organized constituencies and more media sensitive than Iowa. Some observers think it is becoming a typically media-intensive state.[177] But conventional political wisdom still has it as a state where nomination politics requires a good deal of personal attention and presence, as a state whose citizens still expect to meet candidates face-to-face and often, and expect to be wooed early, late, and repeatedly by each candidate's campaign. So the political business in New Hampshire gets conducted, as in Iowa, as very much a retail, organization-intensive business. "It's the number of people they make contact with that's important," said its governor.[178] That kind of maximum-contact politics requires a huge commitment of time by the candidate and a large supporting organization to do advance work, organize meetings, recruit volunteers, run voter identification programs, operate phone banks, prepare direct mail, and conduct door-to-door canvassing. As in Iowa, this kind of effort must be undertaken early and gradually.

Walter Mondale's New Hampshire manager set up his campaign there in December 1982. As he described it,

> Putting together a campaign in a state like this one is not like throwing a prefabricated house together. It's brick work. You build an organization by getting people who have been involved in past campaigns to take responsibility in this one. And that is a process that is done one by one over a long period of time.[179]

Ten months later, a reporter looking for Glenn's organizational effort in New Hampshire found none. Like his colleagues in Iowa, he found a "puzzling . . . Glenn gap" between his strength in the public opinion polls and the absence of workers.[180] John Glenn's New Hampshire campaign did not begin in earnest until December 1983. "We've given Mondale a twelve-month headstart here," said Glenn's New Hampshire coordinator when he took over.[181] At the end of October, Gary Hart had spent twenty-eight days in the state, Mondale twenty days, and Glenn eight days.[182] On primary day, Glenn ranked sixth among the Democratic candidates in number of days spent there, just as he had ranked sixth in Iowa.[183] On January 1 Mondale had thirty full-time staff in New Hampshire; Glenn had eight.[184] Hart had nine offices; Glenn had three.[185] At the end of January, Mondale had eleven phone banks going; Glenn had none.[186] Gary Hart had canvassed 40,000 households; Glenn had canvassed none.[187] After the election, a quarter of the voters said they had been contacted by the candidate for whom they voted. Forty percent of this group were Mondale voters, 31 percent were Hart voters, 14 percent were Glenn voters.[188] By all accounts Glenn's organizational lag was as damaging in New Hampshire as it was in Iowa.

The lag resulted from the same strategic decisions that had affected Iowa—John Glenn's long delay in announcing, his attachment to the Ohio model, and the resource priority given to media over organization. In New Hampshire, as in Iowa, Glenn outspent all the Democratic contestants—in a media campaign.[189] And, as in Iowa, it had no detectable impact.

Once again, his campaigners seem not to have understood the imperatives of their early-states campaign. A New Hampshire observer sounded a familiar theme.

> It's the candidate who gets here early ... and really gets to know the people ... who can pull off a surprising upset. It is also important to get here early to line up support with the local leadership across the state.... You have to be organized right down to the grass roots. TV won't do it. Newspaper endorsements won't do it either. You have to work for it.[190]

Other local politicos were more blunt. "This is an organization state as opposed to a media state." [191] "You can't do it with a media campaign. People here expect to be able to meet the candidates." [192] To that suggestion Glenn's media adviser answered, "That's nonsense; people in New Hampshire watch as much television as people in Ohio." [193] A more apt comparison would have been Iowa—where reliance on the media proved equally insufficient. After the primary, a third of New Hampshire's voters claimed to have "met" one or more candidates, and a quarter of the voters claimed to have been "contacted" by the candidates for whom they voted.[194] By the time Glenn faced the New Hampshire voters, the media-fed Hart tidal wave had washed over him. But it is possible to argue that he failed to erect any organizational barriers or any cushion of support to help him weather that storm.

Well before the Iowa-New Hampshire sequence took hold, observers started recording serious weaknesses in New Hampshire. There were headlines: "Glenn Encounters Frost in New Hampshire" (October 1983), "Glenn Team Fighting With Backs to Wall in New Hampshire" (December 1983), "Glenn Campaign Gets Off to Slow Start in New Hampshire as Time Runs Short" (January 1984), "John Glenn's Campaign Remains Stuck on the Launching Pad in New Hampshire" (January 1984), "With Glenn Faltering, Hart Is Seen as No. 2 Finisher in New Hampshire" (January 1984), "Candidates Hope to Overtake Glenn in New Hampshire" (February 1984).

There were also later assessments—all of which had the familiar and frustrating theme of unrealized potential. "This is Senator Glenn's kind of state. These are his kind of Democrats. Yet Mr. Glenn is behind here, when just about every political indicator says he should be ahead.... He failed to organize. He failed to press the flesh New Hampshire style." [195] "The story of Glenn in New Hampshire is a litany of missed opportunities. Voters are far more attuned to his philosophy and policies than Mondale's. But the Glenn camp never located or massaged its potential...." [196] "I still say he probably has the greatest potential, but it hasn't happened. The word 'potential' comes up again and again in conversations about Glenn's chances in New Hampshire." [197] "The natural inclination of New Hampshire is to be more philosophically attuned to John Glenn ... but he didn't do it right. Mondale and Hart did a New Hampshire campaign. Mondale used his name and his organization. Hart utilized his organization and his issue. John Glenn thought he was going to parachute into a motorcade." [198] In mid-January, the Glenn campaigners realized that there was no easy way, no shortcut to hard work in New Hampshire. And they cut back in Iowa to bolster their candidate's New Hampshire trips and their organizational effort there.[199] "We're starting late," admitted his New Hampshire manager in February, "but we've got enough time to do what needs to be done." [200] It was too late. And the Iowa results made it even later than that.

Besides their irreversible impact on his prospects, the Iowa results were interpreted by observers and campaigners as having rendered a verdict on a central element of John Glenn's nomination strategy. The verdict was that the attacks—or, as he would have it, the counterattacks—against Mondale had hurt Glenn. Two days after the caucuses, Mondale's pollster revealed that his polls had showed Glenn's negative rating growing from 9 percent in the summer to 33 percent in February; and he attributed the change to Glenn's "harsh" anti-Mondale campaign. [201] On the same day, Glenn's New Hampshire manager announced that the Mondale-as-tool-of-special-interest ads, which had been running for several weeks there, were being removed and replaced by "entirely positive" ads, merely calling for "Yankee independence." [202] Iowa "told us the people didn't react favorably to the negative approach," explained a top aide.[203]

"The post-Iowa consensus," said one scorekeeper, "holds that Glenn's constant negative attacks on Mondale backfired badly." [204] This "diagnosis that the negative campaigning had hurt Glenn," [205] was supported by the weight of commentary: "attacks on Mondale hurt Glenn particularly in Iowa"; [206] Glenn "was severely punished in Iowa for his combativeness against Mondale"; [207] "Iowans . . . grew clearly less impressed with Glenn's steady stream of attacks on Mondale"; [208] "a strategy of lashing out against Mr. Mondale for his labor ties left Mr. Glenn with no compelling message." [209] The Hart campaigners signaled their agreement by making sure their candidate "talks about himself and not somebody else" in New Hampshire.[210] Said a senior adviser, "People want to hear what we have to say. We don't want to make the same mistake John Glenn made. When the attention turned to him, he was just attacking Mondale." [211] The unequivocal unanimity behind this electoral interpretation finally convinced Old Magnet Tail to pull off a target he had pursued since Melbourne.

No observer denied that Glenn's drumbeat had damaged Walter Mondale, and severely.[212] Mondale "conceded that he had been 'hurt badly' by [Glenn's] TV ads linking him to 'special interests.' " [213] Indeed, Glenn's "special interests" label plagued Mondale for the rest of the election season, first to the benefit of Gary Hart, then Ronald Reagan. But Glenn could not give himself a winning persona by tearing Mondale down. People needed to get a sense of what he would be like as president before they would make him the beneficiary of their doubts about Mondale. Before Iowa Glenn described his "biggest job in New Hampshire" as "dealing with this idea of experience." As he described it,

> I'm head and shoulders above everyone else . . . it's so preposterous that Fritz Mondale leads in experience. Experience doing what? Walking around legislative halls? . . . I just think a president . . . can provide leadership from different background. And I've got it. And I'm the only one who does. . . . If I can get this message across I know what will happen." [214]

He was still working to differentiate himself from Mondale. After his Iowa defeat, he forgot about Mondale and approached his New Hampshire "job" in a more positive way.

The one week between Iowa and New Hampshire voting was not enough time for Glenn to recover. But during that week, observers were given a taste of what a different presentational strategy might have looked like. It was not a fair test of that strategy, but Glenn, along with his ads, abandoned his strong anti-Mondale tone and undertook "to tell people about myself." He finally took the campaign away from the hired guns and "let Glenn be Glenn." He began to talk openly about his astronaut past in an effort to integrate it more thoroughly and more aggressively into his picture of himself. And he was described, in the process, as a more relaxed, more good-humored, more upbeat, more mellow, more natural candidate.[215] "His staff reports," wrote one observer, "that this last week's campaign is more Glenn's personal campaign than in the past, that he has been less apt to pay attention to his aides' advice. 'It's as if he feels more liberated, freer to do what he wants to do.'"[216] He was described as "running the way his supporters hoped he would" and as "going from his gut instincts on this one."[217]

At the heart of the change was a new willingness to confront and talk about his astronaut experience for what it was—a foundation experience in his preparation for the presidency. It was, he said, "something I haven't worn on my sleeve in this campaign," but "I was proud of it then and I'm proud of it now. It was my life on the line. It was not just a political reputation on whether I would get elected or not. It was my life." He was trying to express the idea that he had played in a much bigger league than campaign politics and that it had prepared him for the presidency. "I've had experience under pressure," he said, "and kept my head about me. I'm not a flappable type. I'm not the type who gets up and screams and flaps his arms. . . . I think people are looking for someone who will be calm and make rational decisions."[218]

It seemed a far more relevant comment about his experience than the long vita-like list of his experiences he had been emphasizing during the November trip. Still, he seemed uncomfortable talking about his astronaut past. That, at least, explains his characteristic use of protectionist indignation as the excuse for doing so. "Hollings made that comment [about Glenn being 'up in that capsule'] and Jesse Jackson got a couple of laughs about the 'Right Stuff'—and it hurt for a while," he explained.[219] "I never brought it up first," he said in his now familiar defense. "Two of them brought it up in a very deprecating way, and I'm very proud of those days."[220] He became, as always, the personally abused counterattacker—making what one journalist called "the angry astronaut pitch." "When people deprecate that, they deprecate me, they deprecate my family, they deprecate something that this country thought very important. Those days were very very dear. . . . To have someone cast disparaging remarks at the kind of dedication we had . . . to have someone cast that in a light vein, well, that hurt, yeah, that does hurt."[221]

He had opened the subject in a potentially positive way, and he would go on to talk about the need for "a safe president." "When a person sits in the Oval Office and has to make monumental decisions with regard to pushing that nuclear button or not, I don't want a person to be tested under fire for the first time." [222] It was not yet part of a well-articulated view of the American presidency, but, along with the idea of balancing interests, which he had expressed earlier, it was a beginning. It picked up a quality of leadership—good judgment and steadiness in crisis—that I had observed the day of the Air Florida crash. This quality was closely related to his background and clearly relevant to his future-oriented theme.

Other observers had picked it up, too, after watching and talking with Glenn face-to-face. A member of the *Atlanta Journal*'s editorial board wrote, "There is about Glenn the reassuring manner of a good commander. If one were pinned down by fire, and looking for orders, Glenn's voice would be heard at the same level tenor. . . . His career has been about keeping his head while others about him lost theirs." [223] A *Boston Globe* editorial writer put it,

> If you were in a foxhole, in a big jam and Mondale said go this way, Hart said that way and Glenn pointed in a different direction, you'd go with Glenn. In a tight spot, this marine exudes courage and leadership.[224]

Glenn never built this aspect of his character and his experience into his conception of presidential leadership and, hence, never helped Democratic voters to see and to emphasize it. In post mortems with ordinary New Hampshire voters, Glenn was described as "still an astronaut and always will be." Or, "He has the experience, but people only connect him with space things." [225] He had progressed about as far nationally as he had in Ohio at the end of his 1974 campaign. The transformation from hero to politician continued to be a slow process; apparently he had neither learned how to speed it up nor had he even tried to do so—until it was too late.

Glenn's better integrated discussion of his experience seemed to capture the attention of the scorekeepers, but that attention could be deceptive. They were in a charitable mood toward the also-ran. They were in the process of explaining what a "good guy" this "happy warrior" really was, how "resilient and buoyant," "erect and smiling" he was in the face of adversity.[226] Having helped to kill John Glenn in Iowa, the journalists were engaged in the kind of ritualistic, guilt-reducing rehabilitation they seem to feel necessary as part of a decent burial. Their attention was turning elsewhere. It was turning mostly to Gary Hart, who had replaced Glenn in second place after Iowa. Hart gathered the positive momentum Glenn had lost and defeated Mondale in New Hampshire.

This is not the place to examine the career or the campaign of Sen.

Gary Hart, but his early success is noteworthy for its several contrasts to Glenn's failure. Hart understood nomination politics, and he ran a campaign for the nomination—one directed at caucus and primary constituencies, not general election constituencies. His model, after all, was George McGovern's successful presidential nomination campaign. "I learned a lot in 1972," and "I think I've applied it to this race," he said.[227] "Glenn," he concluded in early December, "is giving up the nomination so that he can win the election." [228] The lessons Hart applied from 1972 were organizational and sequential. "There are three strategies for running a campaign," he said at the outset in Iowa, "endorsements, media, and organization. I've chosen the third. It's the only one I know how to do." [229] And because he understood momentum, he concentrated his scarce organizational resources early and overwhelmingly in the frontloaded states. He ran a grass-roots campaign and kept media expectations low. "All I have to do in the early states is to do better than expected." [230] "If you do well in this state," he said of New Hampshire, "just well enough that the press will say Gary Hart did better than expected, then you get more coverage, your standing in the polls rises and the money flows and then you win." [231]

Hart understood the need to recruit an intensely supportive constituency, and he emphasized the importance of a message in producing commitment. He chose a generational theme of "new ideas" and "new leadership." It was not a message that depended, like Glenn's, on ideological positioning. "To understand the election, you have to get out of the linear left-right spectrum," he argued. "This is not a left-right race. This is a future-past race." [232] Glenn, too, wanted a future-past race. Witness his slogan "Believe in the Future Again" and the hope he had invested in *The Right Stuff* movie, billed as a story of "how the future began." But the movie had flopped, for lack of interest on the part of the most future-oriented voters of all—the young. For them, it was a movie about the past; whatever Glenn did was twenty-two years old. His future was technologically defined, and the young seemed more attracted to a future that was philosophically defined. Hart's "new ideas" promised a break with the past. Articulated by a man without a past, they attracted youthful supporters who remained unaffected by *The Right Stuff.*

Hart's strategy was to hope that the Mondale-Glenn confrontation would expose the weaknesses of both and allow him to emerge as the alternative. By December he had come to believe that "the early line of a two-man race for the nomination is eroding . . . [and] that Glenn is a less and less serious threat to Mondale." [233] "By April 15," he predicted, "this will be a Mondale-Hart race, and then it will be a matter of the new versus the old." [234] In January and February, a scattering of scorekeepers recorded his slow progress.[235] On February 19 Hart predicted more accurately than they: "The big story of the Iowa caucuses is not going to be Mondale, and it's not going to be me. It's going to be the collapse of John Glenn. I mean all the way—right down the tubes." [236] When that happened, Hart became a media sensation. And he became the alternative.

THE CAMPAIGN IN THE SOUTH

After New Hampshire, only pro forma attention was paid to John Glenn.[237] In the two weeks preceding Super Tuesday, for example, "CBS Evening News" devoted twenty-four minutes to Hart, nineteen minutes to Mondale, six minutes to Jesse Jackson, and one minute to Glenn. Although defeated, broke, and deserted by some of his hired guns, Glenn simply could not surrender his plans for the "long haul." "They don't call me Old Magnet Tail for nothing," he said.[238] "The South was supposed to be our territory," he said later. "It was our window of opportunity. And after all we had done, it was very hard to drop out. When you are in it, as I was, for a principle and not just to add a line to a biography, you don't want to quit."

From the outset, the South looked most promising of all to Glenn. Indeed, the clear strategy of the early campaign was to arrive at Super Tuesday as the strong second-place alternative to Mondale, and to catch him there. By the end of 1983 Glenn had spent twice as much time in the South as he had spent in Iowa or in New Hampshire. From the beginning the campaign had attached its hopes to a date beyond Iowa and New Hampshire.[239] "We have to win the South on Super Tuesday, no question about it," said a top adviser in January. "One reason is that people expect us to. The other reason is that if you don't win somewhere you're not going to win in the end." [240] By all informed estimates, the South held great potential for him. But, like New Hampshire, it went unrealized.

His Super Tuesday campaign was accompanied by a familiar story line. "Glenn's potential in the South seems to be everywhere; his organization seems to be nowhere. His strategy is built on a southern base, yet his campaign has no southern coordinator." [241] "This should be Glenn territory, given his military and space background in a region loaded with both, and his comparatively conservative image ... [but he] has failed to capitalize on his assets." [242] "On paper, Glenn seems the dream candidate for this conservative, patriotic part of the nation ... but the paper credentials failed to electrify audiences." [243] "Six months ago, Glenn appeared a perfect candidate here ... a military hero, a space hero and a Senator with a conservative image. . . . But to this day, he has not established a political position in the eyes of the voter." [244]

All these assessments came before the Iowa caucuses. So did downbeat headlines such as: "Glenn's Swing South Shows Gap Between Promise, Performance" (November); "Glenn's Sun Sinks in the South" (December); "Problems Dog Glenn in Southern Swing; Crowds Seem Mainly Impressed with His Former Astronaut Role" (January); "Glenn's Campaign Certainly Isn't Burning Up Atlanta" (February); and "Glenn Launches Last Stand in South" (February). [245]

Like Iowa and New Hampshire, the results in Alabama, Georgia, and Florida were a confirmation of campaign weaknesses that had been accumulating for a long time. The sequential effects of the two earlier contests on these later ones served only to deliver the *coup de grâce*. Glenn's southern problems were the same as elsewhere: weaknesses of organization, political persona, and constituency. The best single barometer for this bundle of problems was Claiborne Darden's poll of nine southern states. In late July, Glenn's season of hope, the poll's results showed him leading Mondale by six points (39-33) in the region. By November he had fallen behind Mondale by fourteen points (29-43), a "dramatic reversal" of twenty points, from which he never recovered. By late January he had slipped further behind, trailing Mondale by twenty-two points (23-45). [246] Super Tuesday produced lower numbers still.

It is not possible to trace the statewide rise and fall of Glenn's southern chances. But there is no doubt that organizational tardiness and weakness were a crippling factor here, too. In early January the southern coordinator was saying, typically, "We are busy doing that which should have been done several months ago. We've got a lot to do in a short time." [247] On the day of the Iowa caucuses, Glenn's southern organization was described as "nearly invisible." [248] Riding into town from the Clarksdale airport on November 10, I had listened to the president of the Mississippi Young Democrats complain. "I've been very disappointed in the Glenn operation in Mississippi," he said.

> They have a group of mickey mouse kids up there in Washington and no organization down here. I met a Mondale guy last week who said he was going to be in Mississippi for five months. That's what we need down here. We have no organization—just a few cats and dogs like Walter and me.

In Oklahoma—like Mississippi, a Super Tuesday caucus state—a similar organizational difference was noted:

> Although Glenn, a former astronaut, has immense popularity in Oklahoma, he has been out organized and out hustled by his

opposition.... By any stretch of the imagination Oklahoma should be in John Glenn's column.... The tide turned on November 1, when Mondale sent ... a team of six outside organizers.... Meanwhile, Glenn's Oklahoma organizers griped for months that its requests for money and manpower were being neglected by the Washington headquarters.[249]

In Alabama, where his hopes were brightest, a party official commented in mid-January that, "The horror story, here as elsewhere, is the lack of organization by the Glenn people."[250] A month later another official there called it "about the worst campaign I've ever seen."[251] In Florida it was a "rag tag effort, hit or miss" until the first full-time organizer arrived the day after Christmas. "I would like to have been here by Labor Day," he said.[252] A month later, a Floridian observer said, "Glenn is doing less and less.... Absolutely nothing is going on down here."[253]

Darden talked about Georgia, emphasizing the campaign's inability to surmount or subsume Glenn's astronaut persona.

Initially, John Glenn had everything in the world going for him in Georgia and Walter Mondale had everything in the world going against him.... [Glenn has had] one of the least effective campaigns we've ever seen. His staff has failed to project him as a candidate. People know he's an astronaut, but they don't know—have no idea—what he stands for as a candidate.... Mondale is going to win in Georgia by default. Glenn let him have it.[254]

At bottom, he said, the problem was the candidate, who failed to convert his natural constituency into a committed one. "There are only three things that count for much in politics," he said, "emotion, emotion, emotion.... John Glenn has not been able to stimulate emotion at all."[255] And, "John Glenn has the lowest hard-core support for a major candidate that we have ever seen."[256]

Glenn continued to prospect for mainstream Democrats without success. Employing another theme that "might have been," he tried, belatedly, to identify small-town Ohio with the small town of the South and its values.[257] He tried reaching "average folks, the kind of people who work from nine to five and then go get a beer or a Coke and go home and watch the Atlanta Braves on television."[258] He tried to sell himself as "the last moderate left in the race." And he ended by pleading with Democrats who liked Reagan to go to the polls and vote for him anyway, as a hedge against a more liberal Democrat.[259] It was ironic that he should have ended in an outright competition for Ronald Reagan's voters—trying, finally, to conduct the primary as if it were a general election!

His appeal revealed one aspect of his constituency problem. The Democrats who most wanted to defeat Reagan were the liberals. But, as Larry Bartels's analysis of post-Super Tuesday voter sentiment shows, John Glenn's favorability ratings dropped among voters with liberal predispositions. They also dropped among the strongest Democratic partisans. In both cases Mondale was strong where Glenn was weak.[260] Glenn's argument that he was the most likely Democrat to defeat Reagan was being directed primarily at more conservative, more independent Democrats, who were relatively content with Reagan. The more Glenn moved away from a liberal constituency, the more he was directing his basic argument at the wrong people. He ended, in the South, by recognizing his dilemma and appealing directly to Reaganite Democrats. But they had no strong incentive to turn out to vote for him.

Glenn ended the race, as he had begun it, without a committed constituency. Some self-styled conservative southern Democrats did come to the polls on Super Tuesday, but they were a minority of the primary electorate—29 percent in Alabama and Georgia, 33 percent in Florida. And while they voted for Glenn in larger numbers than did liberals and moderates, they still gave him only a minority of their votes—33 percent in Alabama, 32 percent in Georgia, 18 percent in Florida.[261] (See Table 4-1.) A minority of a minority is not a winning coalition.

Glenn also ended the race, as he had begun it, without a well-developed political persona. It was a sad indication of that failure that, as Super Tuesday approached, Bill White was still saying that "People need to know what Glenn is all about. . . . People need to be able to equate his five-point program with his leadership. There's a bridge we have to build. . . . "[262] To the end, Glenn retained his basic characterological

TABLE 4-1 Glenn Vote Among Philosophical Groupings in Southern States on Super Tuesday, in percentages

Self-styled philosophy and Glenn vote	Alabama [1] (N=1,349)	Georgia [1] (N=1,293)	Florida [2] (N=1,387)
Conservative voters	29	29	33
Conservative votes for Glenn	33	32	18
Moderate voters	40	42	37[3]
Moderate votes for Glenn	16	16	9
Liberal voters	17	20	30
Liberal votes for Glenn	4	4	6

[1] CBS Exit Poll.
[2] ABC Exit Poll.
[3] Question worded "in between."

strengths; but he had not given them sufficient political content to command primary election support.

As they left the polls, voters were offered a selection of factors to explain candidate choice and asked, for each one, whether it influenced their vote. Table 4-2 describes some of the responses of primary voters in New Hampshire, Alabama, and Florida. It lists the seven factors that drew a positive response from at least 15 percent of the voters in one of the three states. It lists these factors in the order of their average level of importance in the three states combined. That is, an average of 25 percent of the voters in the three states said that the rationale "can be trusted" influenced their vote; and an average of only 13 percent selected "not tied to special interests" as a factor in their choice. The other five factors ranked somewhere between those extremes.

Having identified the group of voters for whom each factor was important, we next recorded the percentage of that group who voted for John Glenn. Thus, of the 26 percent of New Hampshire voters who said "can be trusted" influenced their vote, 19 percent of them voted for Glenn. As a corollary, larger percentages will have voted for other candidates on that basis—in this case, 37 percent for Hart, 22 percent for Mondale, 22 percent for others.

Finally, we looked only at those who voted for Glenn and recorded the factors they identified as influencing their vote. Viewed in this way, for example, 40 percent of the Glenn voters in New Hampshire said that "can be trusted" influenced their choice of Glenn. And, if we look at the percentage of Glenn's New Hampshire voters who were influenced by the six other factors, we can see that more of them were influenced by "can be trusted" than by any other factor—followed by "not tied to special interests" and "can beat Reagan."

Taken as a whole, Table 4-2 indicates that Glenn was not strongly identified with any of the seven factors by these primary electorates. On average, he was most strongly associated with those voters (30 percent of them) for whom "not tied to special interests" was influential. But Gary Hart attracted more voters on this ground—in each state separately, and with a three-state average of 39 percent. Glenn's attacks had done damage to Mondale and created an issue, but the chief beneficiary was Gary Hart. Glenn's next strongest attraction came from among those voters for whom "can be trusted" was an important factor. On average, 27 percent of those voters influenced by "can be trusted" voted for Glenn; but he trailed Mondale in both New Hampshire and Alabama on this score. And his three-state average was slightly lower than Mondale's. The same lack of strong identification holds also with regard to Glenn's third highest score—on the "strong leader" factor. Among voters who took leadership into account, Glenn was outranked by

Mondale and Hart in both New Hampshire and Georgia and by Mondale and Glenn and Jackson in Alabama.

In the matter of experience, about which Glenn had worried so much, he did indeed lose heavily to Mondale in all three states—11-51 in New Hampshire, 11-76 in Alabama, 14-74 in Georgia. It was a very influential, high-profile factor for Mondale; and it was not a factor that Glenn voters cited as important. But it was not a matter of overwhelming concern to voters generally. Two factors that outranked it in influence were "cares about people" and "has new ideas." The first was very strongly associated with Mondale; the second was very strongly associated with Hart. On both these factors, the association with Glenn was minuscule across the board.

A final factor—"can beat Reagan"—was of considerable importance to voters and is of special interest to us because of its prominence as a theme of Glenn's campaign. Among voters for whom electability mattered, far more had come to think positively of Mondale in this regard than Glenn by the time of New Hampshire (48 percent-15 percent). And by Super Tuesday Hart had joined Mondale in this respect. Among Glenn voters, electability lingered as a rationale for their vote in New Hampshire and all but vanished afterward.

Overall, John Glenn was not strongly identified with any particular factor in any particular state. If the three primary electorates and the seven influential factors are considered separately, Glenn outscored his rivals in only two of the twenty-one instances—among the 42 percent of Alabama's voters influenced by "not tied to special interests" and among the 33 percent of Georgia's voters influenced by "can be trusted." As these two instances indicate, his assets lay, as he had always believed, in his strength of character. Among all primary voters and among his own voters, Glenn's relative strengths lay in his trustworthiness and in his independence.[263] Yet even in these areas of his greatest appeal, other candidates had a greater appeal. He did not, in the end, establish for himself a high positive profile on any dimension.

So John Glenn could not survive. In the end he could not give people a positive, sustainable reason for making him their president. Nonsurvivors, it is said, "don't lose, they just run out of money." Perhaps more to the point, John Glenn just ran out of time. There is evidence that voters did not stabilize their images of him till after he was driven from the race.[264] We know that in Ohio his development of a statewide political persona—image, message, skills, issues—took a great deal of time. One can assume it would take a great deal of time to make him into a national politician, too. So many things went wrong, it is probably not possible to say that if he had given himself more time and if he had understood Iowa better he could have won. But if he had done

TABLE 4-2   Factors Influencing Voter Choice: Glenn Vote
in Three Primary Electorates

Factor influencing vote choice	New Hampshire (N=1,278)	Alabama (N=1,349)	Georgia (N=1,293)	Three-state average
"Can be trusted"				
All voters influenced by factor	26%	27%	23%	25%
Influenced by factor who voted for Glenn	19	29	33	27
Glenn voters influenced by factor	40	41	43	41
"Cares about people"				
All voters influenced by factor	21	22	19	21
Influenced by factor who voted for Glenn	6	8	6	7
Glenn voters influenced by factor	10	9	6	8
"Has new ideas"				
All voters influenced by factor	23	16	18	19
Influenced by factor who voted for Glenn	8	9	4	7
Glenn voters influenced by factor	14	8	4	9
"Can beat Reagan"				
All voters influenced by factor	22	16	18	19
Influenced by factor who voted for Glenn	15	6	8	10
Glenn voters influenced by factor	27	5	8	3
"Experience"				
All voters influenced by factor	17	18	16	17
Influenced by factor who voted for Glenn	11	11	14	12
Glenn voters influenced by factor	15	11	13	13

Factor influencing vote choice	New Hampshire (N = 1,278)	Alabama (N = 1,349)	Georgia (N = 1,293)	Three-state average
"Strong leader"				
All voters influenced by factor	13%	17%	16%	15%
Influenced by factor who voted for Glenn	19	24	24	22
Glenn voters influenced by factor	20	22	21	21
"Not tied to special interests"				
All voters influenced by factor	21 [1]	9	10	13
Influenced by factor	17	42	30	30
Glenn voters influenced by factor	30	19	16	22

Source: CBS News-*New York Times* Exit Poll.
[1] New Hampshire wording = "Is his own man."

those things, he might well have survived longer. To what end, however, we cannot say.

Three days after Super Tuesday, Glenn formally acknowledged his inability to survive. "I'd like nothing better than to stay in the race," he said. But he had had no success; he had no prospects for success; and he was $2.8 million in debt. "When I began this campaign last April," he remarked, "I said that I wasn't running for president just to add another line to my resumé. It turned out I'm glad that wasn't the purpose." "Although my campaign for the presidency will end," he concluded, "my campaign for a better America will continue." [265] The presidential campaign moved on, and John Glenn went back to work in the Senate.

NOTES

1. Transcript, "Meet the Press," December 11, 1983.
2. Brian Usher, "The Film Is Not the Stuff Glenn Had Hoped For," *Philadelphia Inquirer*, December 9, 1983; Jeff Greenfield, "Shattering the Campaign's Political Myths," *Boston Globe*, February 26, 1984; Louis Peck, " 'Right Stuff' Doesn't Launch Glenn," *USA Today*, December 14, 1984.
3. William Adams, "Media Coverage of Campaign '84, A Preliminary Report," *Public Opinion*, April/May 1984.
4. See *Washington Post*, January 6, 23, 25, 26, February 3, 14; *New York Times*,

January 9, 27; *Cleveland Plain Dealer*, January 5, 11, 23, February 14, 20; *Chicago Tribune*, January 9, 23, February 15; *Los Angeles Times*, January 31, February 15; *Boston Globe*, January 17, February 3, 14; *Washington Times*, January 23, February 16; *Wall Street Journal*, February 1; *Philadelphia Inquirer*, January 28; *Manchester Union Leader*, February 1; *Miami Herald*, February 1, *Hartford Courant*, February 2; *St. Petersburg Times*, February 18; *Akron Beacon Journal*, January 13. All dates are 1984.

5. Dan Balz and Martin Schram, "Taking A Southern Route, Glenn Lightens His Load of Adversity," *Washington Post*, January 23, 1984.

6. William C. Adams, "As New Hampshire Goes. . .," and Emmett Beull, " 'Locals' and 'Cosmopolitans': National, Regional, and State Newspaper Coverage of the New Hampshire Primary," in *Media and Momentum*, ed. Gary Orren and Nelson Polsby (Chatham, N.J.: Chatham House, 1987), 49, 61; Kevin Klose, "Up From Obscurity," *Washington Post*, February 20, 1984.

7. See James Flansburg, "Reagan Seen Losing Steam in Iowa Race," *Des Moines Register*, December 16, 1979; Daniel Pedersen, "Bush Tops in Reaching GOP Voters, Poll Finds," *Des Moines Register*, December 18, 1979; Daniel Pedersen and Arnold Garson, "Race Close: 'I've Won,' Bush Says," *Des Moines Register*, January 22, 1980; JoAnne Davis, "Nation Takes Notice as Bush Polishes Style in GOP Race," *St. Louis Globe Democrat*, November 23, 1979; Dave Goldberg, "Politicking at the Grass Roots," *Rochester Democrat and Chronicle*, December 23, 1979.

8. Samuel Patterson, "Iowa," in *The Political Life of the American States* by Alan Rosenthal and Maureen Moakley (New York: Praeger, 1984), 87, 89, 97.

9. See Pevrill Squire, "Iowa and the Nomination Process" (Paper prepared for University of Iowa Shambaugh Conference, "First in the Nation: Iowa and the Presidential Nomination Process," Iowa City, February 7-8, 1988). But see also the post-1988 analysis by David Broder, "Oh, Well, So Much for the Importance of Iowa," *Washington Post Weekly Edition*, March 14-20, 1988.

10. See Bill Peterson, "Glenn With Hero's Send-Off Launches Bid for Presidency," *Washington Post*, April 27, 1983; "Glenn: Another Liftoff," *Newsweek*, May 2, 1983; Albert Hunt, "Glenn Officially Enters Democratic Race for President," *Wall Street Journal*, April 22, 1983.

11. David Broder, "Mr. Checklist," *Washington Post*, October 13, 1982.

12. "Glenn Challenges Mondale in Iowa," *Cleveland Plain Dealer*, December 17, 1983; Bill Peterson and George Lardner, Jr., "Temperatures and Glenn Outlook Falling in Iowa," *Washington Post*, January 11, 1984.

13. Peterson and Lardner, "Temperatures and Glenn Outlook"; see also Jonathan Moore, ed., *Campaign for President: The Managers Look at '84* (Dover, Mass.: Auburn Press, 1986), 50. On Mondale's long cultivation of Iowa, see Wayne Svoboda, "Politics Here There Everywhere in Iowa," *Des Moines Register*, January 14, 1980; Bill Peterson, "In Iowa, Mondale Is Far Ahead," *Washington Post*, August 16, 1983.

14. Brian Usher, "The Undoing of John Glenn," *Akron Beacon Journal*, March 25, 1984.

15. Ben Bradlee, Jr., and Walter Robinson, "Glenn Abandons Quest for Presidency," *Boston Globe*, March 17, 1984.

16. Richard Dunham, "Glenn Focuses on National Issues in Texas," *Dallas Times Herald*, January 24, 1984; Chris Black and Thomas Oliphant, "Stalled Glenn Camp Ponders Ad Assault," *Boston Globe*, January 26, 1984.

17. Bradlee and Robinson, "Glenn Abandons Quest for Presidency."

18. Larry Eichel, "Competitors Face Tough Choices on Use of Resources to Beat Mondale," *Philadelphia Inquirer*, January 19, 1984.

19. Dan Balz, "Senator Glenn Changes Chief of Campaign in Shakeup," *Washington Post*, January 27, 1984.

20. David Broder and Dan Balz, "Mondale Says Nomination May Be Clinched Soon," *Washington Post*, February 22, 1984. See also *New York Times*, January 23, 27, 1984; *Washington Post*, January 20, 1984; *Philadelphia Inquirer*, January 20, 1984.

21. Arnold Garson, "Reagan Sags, Carter Soars in Iowa Poll," *Des Moines Register*, January 11, 1980; Flansburg, "Reagan Seen Losing Steam in Iowa Race"; Pedersen and Garson, "Race Close; 'I've Won,' Says Bush."

22. Joseph Rice, "Glenn Team Sizes Up Competition in Early Primaries," *Cleveland Plain Dealer*, January 23, 1984.

23. Jack Germond and Jules Witcover, "A Bit of Strategic Enthusiasm," *Baltimore Sun*, January 12, 1984.

24. Sidney Blumenthal, "Over and Out," *New Republic*, February 13, 1984.

25. Hugh Winebrenner, *The Iowa Precinct Caucuses* (Ames: Iowa University Press, 1987), 141; John Dillin, "Iowa Caucuses Reshuffle Field of Democrats," *Christian Science Monitor*, February 22, 1984.

26. Ed Bark, "Democrats Go On Sale in Iowa's Prime Time," *Dallas Morning News*, February 13, 1984.

27. Winebrenner, *The Iowa Precinct Caucuses*, 141.

28. Ken Fuson and James Healy, "Glenn Replaces National Campaign Director," *Des Moines Register*, January 27, 1984.

29. Bill Peterson, "Mondale Keeps Lead in Iowa; Glenn Slips," *Washington Post*, February 20, 1984.

30. Dan Balz, "Grounded By His Debts, Glenn Drops '84 Hopes," *Washington Post*, March 17, 1984.

31. Carl Leubsdorf, "What Happened to Glenn? First, Start With the Candidate," *Dallas Morning News*, February 24, 1984.

32. Julia Malone, "Cranston's Maximum Effort in Iowa," *Christian Science Monitor*, January 17, 1984. Some pre-1988 analyses expressing this wisdom are: Paul Taylor, "What Do You Call the Front Runners in Iowa? Nervous," *Washington Post Weekly Edition*, December 22, 1986; John Milne, "Keeping in Touch Remains Key in Iowa," *Boston Globe*, September 28, 1987; David Rogers, "Organizational Skills Could Play a Pivotal Role in the Outcome of Iowa Presidential Campaigns," *Wall Street Journal*, January 11, 1988; David Yepsen, "Gephardt, Dole Lead Final Poll," *Des Moines Sunday Register*, February 7, 1988.

33. Larry Eichel, "The Race in Iowa Is For Second," *Philadelphia Inquirer*, February 13, 1984.

34. Bill Peterson, "In Iowa Mondale Is Far Ahead," *Washington Post*, August 1, 1983.

35. David Shribman, "Glenn Backers Worry About Field Organizing," *New York Times*, December 5, 1983.

36. Ibid.; Kurt Anderson, "Crashing Back to Earth? " *Time*, January 23, 1984. On the "name of the game" importance of collecting names in Iowa, see Bruce Mohl, "Top Hart Aide in Iowa Seen Joining Dukakis," *Boston Globe*, June 7, 1987.

37. Brent Larkin, "Mondale Is Winning With the Right Staff," *Cleveland Plain Dealer*, January 23, 1984.

38. Peterson and Sawyer, "Mondale Says Nomination May Be Clinched Soon."

39. Shribman, "Glenn's Backers Worry."

40. "How Iowa Plays Politics," *Newsweek*, January 30, 1984.

41. For example, these headlines of January 27, 1984: "Glenn Replaces Campaign Chief in Abrupt Shift," *Washington Post*; "Glenn Ousts Campaign Aide Amid Campaign Discord," *Wall Street Journal*; "Glenn Reorganizes Campaign Again as Standing in Poll Declines," *New York Times*.

42. Martin Schram, "Glenn Says He's in Sensible Center Between Reagan, Mondale," *Washington Post*, January 28, 1984.

43. Jack Germond and Jules Witcover, *Wake Us When It's Over* (New York: Macmillan, 1985), 136-137.

44. Bill Peterson and Kathy Sawyer, "Mondale Triumphant in Iowa," *Washington Post*, February 21, 1984.

45. John Dillin, "Glenn's Hopes Rest With Moderates," *Christian Science Monitor*, March 8, 1984.

46. Patterson, "Iowa," 93.

47. Ken Fuson and David Yepsen, "The Right Stuff for America?" *Des Moines Register*, November 25, 1983.

48. Fred Barnes, "Glenn Stresses the Future in His Candidacy," *Baltimore Sun*, November 30, 1983.

49. David Espo, "Revitalized, Glenn Accentuates Positive," *Nashua (N.H.) Telegraph*, January 30, 1984.

50. The following all in the *Des Moines Register*: David Yepsen, November 11, 1983; Fuson and Yepsen, "The Right Stuff for America?"; David Yepsen and Ken Fuson, "Leaders: Glenn May Be Red Faced Caucus Night," February 6, 1984; James Gannon, "Glenn Talks Like a President, Making For a Dull Campaign," January 16, 1984. See also James Flansburg, editorial page editor of the *Register*, in Robert Merry, "Iowa: Barren Ground for Glenn," *Wall Street Journal*, February 17, 1984. For a 1987 update, see Thomas Edsall, "It's Hard To Be in Two Places at Once," *Washington Post Weekly Edition*, September 7, 1987; E. J Dionne, Jr., "Poll of Voters in Iowa Finds Liberal Views," *New York Times*, November 1, 1987. Scholarly confirmation is provided in an excellent later paper by Walter Stone, "How Representative Are the Iowa Caucuses?" (Paper prepared for presentation at Conference on Iowa Caucuses, Iowa City, February 6-8, 1988).

51. Fuson and Yepsen, "The Right Stuff for America?"

52. Germond and Witcover, "A Bit of Strategic Enthusiasm"; Jane Mayer, "In Iowa Campaign, Vote Getting Begins With Getting on TV," *Wall Street Journal*, February 6, 1984.

53. Bill Peterson, "Hopefuls Vie to Go With the Gain," *Washington Post*, February 18, 1984.

54. Ibid.; Larry Eichel, "In Iowa, They Ask: Who's 2nd?" *Philadelphia Inquirer*, February 13, 1984.

55. Steve Bera, "Glenn Launches Last Stand in the South," *Minneapolis Tribune*, February 19, 1984.

56. David Elbert, "Poll: Caucuses Not Representative," *Des Moines Register*, February 18, 1984.

57. Martin Schram, "Glenn's Spirit of Excellence Gets Lost in Rough and Tumble," *Washington Post*, February 23, 1984.

58. Deborah Orin, "Glenn Aides Ready 'I Quit' Speech," *New York Post*, March 15, 1984.

59. David Shribman, "Glenn Says His Enthusiasm Is Undampened," *New York Times*, February 22, 1984.
60. To George McGovern for one. See "Glenn's Liftoff Fizzles Out," *Newsweek*, March 5, 1984. See also Howell Raines, "Politics Seems Predictable Until...," *New York Times*, January 9, 1984.
61. Dan Balz, "How the Campaign Is a Sprint to Super Tuesday," *Washington Post Weekly Edition*, January 16, 1984.
62. Transcript, "Meet The Press," December 11, 1983.
63. Mayer, "In Iowa Campaign."
64. Blumenthal, "Over and Out"; also Sidney Blumenthal, "Statecraft as Spacecraft," *New Republic*, November 14, 1983.
65. Dan Balz, "Glenn Hoping To Make Up Lost Time, Reorganizes at the Top," *Washington Post*, December 15, 1984.
66. Bill Peterson, "Glenn's Image Makers Play Up the Hero, Play Down the Senator," *Washington Post*, October 16, 1983.
67. Jack Germond and Jules Witcover, "In Iowa, Glenn Is Trying To Surmount His Reputation as an Astronaut Hero," *National Journal*, January 14, 1984; Fred Barnes, "Glenn Airs TV Commercials Stressing Aim To Seek Peace," *Baltimore Sun*, January 10, 1984; Martin Schram, "Early Leaders of the Presidential Pack Lure the News Hounds," *Washington Post*, January 18, 1984.
68. Martin Schram, "Glenn Switches to 'Mild Stuff' in Ad Campaign Against Mondale," *Washington Post*, January 26, 1984; Rowland Evans and Robert Novak, "Spots Against Mondale," *Washington Post*, January 25, 1984.
69. John Dillin, "In Iowa, Mondale's Almost Hometown Boy," *Christian Science Monitor*, February 14, 1984; Ed Bark, "Democrats Go On Sale In Iowa's Prime Time," *Dallas Morning News*, February 14, 1984; Robert Shogan, "Glenn Trims Schedule, Pulls Negative Ads," *Los Angeles Times*, January 31, 1984.
70. Martin Schram, "4 Democrats Launch Media Blitz in New Hampshire and Iowa," *Washington Post*, January 13, 1984.
71. Schram, "Glenn Switches to 'Mild Stuff.'"
72. Shribman, "Glenn Reorganizes Campaign Again."
73. Dudley Glendenen, "Candidates Map TV Barrage in 2 Key States," *New York Times*, February 1, 1984.
74. John Corry, "Critics Notebook: Candidates," *New York Times*, February 1, 1984.
75. William Flanigan and Nancy Zingale, "Changing Perceptions of Presidential Candidates During the 1984 Primary Season" (Paper prepared for Western Political Science Association Meeting, Las Vegas, March 28-30, 1985).
76. Bill Peterson, "Glenn's Image Makers Play Up the Hero."
77. Schram, "Glenn's Spirit of Excellence Gets Lost."
78. See *Dallas Times Herald, Dallas Morning News, Austin American-Statesman* for December 19, 1983.
79. David Shribman, "Glenn Stepping Up His Attack," *New York Times*, February 7, 1984; Larry Eichel, "Glenn Says Mondale Offers A Platform of 'Secret Plan,'" *Philadelphia Inquirer*, February 7, 1984.
80. Deborah Orin, "It's War as Dem Hopefuls Clash Over Acid Rain," *New York Post*, February 9, 1984; Cass Peterson, "Mondale Tilts With Glenn on Clean Air," *Washington Post*, February 9, 1984.

81. "Inquiry," *USA Today*, January 6, 1984.
82. Ibid.
83. Dan Balz, "Ready To Make Quick Decisions, Vento Maps Glenn's Race Anew," *Washington Post*, January 29, 1984.
84. Blumenthal, "Over and Out"; see also Jon Margolis, "Glenn on Offensive, Pressures Mondale," *Chicago Tribune*, January 10, 1984.
85. Orin, "It's War."
86. Cass Peterson, "Mondale Tilts With Glenn." Cass Peterson, "3 Democrats Outline Plans On Acid Rain," *Washington Post*, January 9, 1984; Sarah Fritz, "Mondale Puts Anti-Clean Air Label On Glenn," *Los Angeles Times*, January 10, 1984.
87. Thomas Oliphant and Jerry Ackerman, "Acid Rain: An Issue Hard to Ignore in N.H.," *Boston Globe*, January 11, 1984.
88. Yepsen, *Des Moines Register*, November 11, 1983.
89. Brian Usher, "A Garbled Message, Poor Delivery and John Glenn Leaves 'Em Yawning," *Philadelphia Inquirer*, January 9, 1984; "Glenn's Drive to Centerfield Not Getting Him to First Base," *Washington Times*, January 23, 1984.
90. The following stories all dated January 16, 1984: David Broder, "Democrats Exchange Brickbats," *Washington Post*; Martin Schram, "Each Candidate Scored Points, Though Some Strayed From Plans," *Washington Post*; Howell Raines, "Debate Among Democrats Draws Sharpest Exchange of Campaign," *New York Times*; Robert Merry, "Democratic Candidates Debate Marked By Clashes Between Two Front Runners," *Wall Street Journal*; Ernest Furgurson, "Sharp Retorts Are Climax of 3-Hour Debate," *Baltimore Sun*; Robert Shogan, "Rivals Zero In On Mondale in Debate," *Los Angeles Times*; Myron Waldman, "Democrats Do Shouting at Debate," *Newsday*; Thomas Oliphant and Curtis Wilkie, "Angry Clash Highlights Democratic Debate," *Boston Globe*: Thomas Brazaitis, "Glenn, Mondale Spar in Debate," *Cleveland Plain Dealer*; and David Nyhan, "Ex-Vice President's Problem with Television," *Boston Globe*. The following stories all dated January 17, 1984: Howell Raines, "The Democratic Debate: Reagan May Be the Chief Beneficiary," *New York Times*; Fred Barnes, "Democratic Debate May Aid Reagan," *Baltimore Sun*; Don Campbell, "Debate Defies a Boring Label," *USA Today*; Larry Eichel, "Debate's Free Wheeling Format Served All of the Democratic Candidates Well," *Philadelphia Inquirer*; David Broder, "The Real Winner," *Washington Post*; and Joseph Kraft, "On to Round One," *Washington Post*. Larry Eichel, "With New Pecking Order, Democrats to Debate Anew," *Philadelphia Inquirer*, February 23, 1984.
91. Barry Sussman, "Poll Sees Debate Aiding Mondale, Jackson Most," *Washington Post*, January 17, 1984; Dan Balz, "Glenn Labels Post-ABC Debate Poll Unprofessional," *Washington Post*, January 18, 1984.
92. Joel Blumenthal, "Poll Says Reagan, Undecided Voters Beat Democrats," *Manchester Union Leader*, January 28, 1984.
93. Broder, "Democrats Exchange Brickbats."
94. David Broder, "The Democratic Debate: McGovern Earns Respect," *Des Moines Register*, February 15, 1984; Paul West, "McGovern Charming Democrats Again," *Dallas Times Herald*, February 17, 1984; Steve Ned, "McGovern Raising His Profile," *Chicago Tribune*, February 18, 1984; Fred Barnes, "Iowans Show McGovern 'Tremendous Goodwill,'" *Baltimore Sun*, February 18, 1984.

95. Morton Kondracke, "The Candidates Cross-Examined," *New Republic*, January 24, 1984.

96. Larry Eichel, "Mondale's Position Is Still Secure After 31 Outings At Candidate Debates," *Philadelphia Inquirer*, February 10, 1984.

97. James Healey and Tom Witosky, "Glenn Worker Says Mondale Campaign Takes Too Much Labor Help," *Des Moines Register*, February 11, 1984; Bill Peterson and David Broder, "Glenn-Mondale Campaigns Trade Allegations of Financial Irregularities," *Washington Post*, February 11, 1984; Walter Robinson, "Mondale Aides Question Bank Loans Made To Glenn," *Boston Globe*, February 14, 1984; Walter Robinson, "Glenn Aide Disputes Claims on Bank Loans," *Boston Globe*, February 15, 1986.

98. Thomas Oliphant, "Glenn Secures Line of Credit for Campaign," *Boston Globe*, February 15, 1984.

99. Thomas Oliphant, "Glenn Criticizes Globe Story on Campaign Loan," *Boston Globe*, February 14, 1984.

100. Thomas Oliphant, "Glenn Says Mondale Is Trying to 'Buy' the Nomination," *Boston Globe*, February 14, 1984.

101. Peterson and Sawyer, "Mondale Says Nomination May Be Clinched Soon."

102. David Yepsen and James Healey, "Democratic Rivals to Debate Today at D.M. Civic Center," *Des Moines Register*, February 11, 1984.

103. David Yepsen, "McGovern Fared Well, Glenn Came Off Poorly in Debate, Nagle Says," *Des Moines Register*, February 13, 1984; John Hyde and Ken Fuson, "Mondale Reacts to Foes' Charges," *Des Moines Register*, February 13, 1984; Robert Healy, "Winners and Losers in Iowa Debate," *Boston Globe*, February 13, 1984.

104. Note 103, *supra*; Jack Germond and Jules Witcover, "Three Scored Well in Iowa Debate," *Des Moines Register*, February 13, 1984; Paul West, "Glenn Can't Get Off Launch Pad in Iowa," *Dallas Times Herald*, February 16, 1984.

105. Healy, "Winners and Losers in Iowa Debate"; Ed Bark, "Glenn Never Leaves the Pad at Iowa Debate," *Dallas Morning News*, February 13, 1984.

106. Notes 100-102, *supra*; Deborah Orin, "Front Running Jitters Put Mondale Road Team on the Fritz," *New York Post*, February 15, 1984; Tom Breen, "Glenn Lets Chance Slip to Score on Mondale," *Washington Times*, February 13, 1984; Sandy Greeley, "It May Be First in the Nation, But Politics Rates a Big Yawn in Iowa," *Des Moines Register*, February 17, 1984.

107. David Elbert, "Poll Finds McGovern 'Won' Debate," *Des Moines Register*, February 17, 1984.

108. Martin Schram, "TV Debate Seemed Night of Long Shots," *Washington Post*, February 13, 1984; Steven Roberts, "From One Living Room in Iowa, Opinions on the 8," *New York Times*, February 13, 1984; Robert Merry, "Mondale Becomes Punching Bag as Rivals Hit Him With Complaints at Iowa Debate," *Wall Street Journal*, February 13, 1984.

109. Curtis Wilkie, " 'Uncommitted' Vying for 2nd in Iowa," *Boston Globe*, February 19, 1984.

110. Thomas Oliphant, "Glenn Raps Mondale on Gas Pipeline Role," *Boston Globe*, February 16, 1984.

111. James Healey, "Mondale and Glenn Trade 'Lie' Charges," *Des Moines Register*, February 17, 1986.

112. Ibid.

113. Martin Schram and Kathy Sawyer, "Close Contestants for Second Place in Iowa Defend Attacks on Mondale," *Washington Post*, February 20, 1984.

114. Ken Fuson, James Healey, and David Yepsen, "Iowa Caucuses Today; Reagan to Visit State," *Des Moines Register*, February 20, 1984.
115. Thomas Oliphant, "Glenn Alters His Campaign Strategy," *Boston Globe*, February 17, 1984.
116. David Shribman, "Glenn Steps Up Attacks on 2 Rivals," *New York Times*, February 15, 1984.
117. Curtis Wilkie, "Problems Beset Glenn in Iowa," *Boston Globe*, February 16, 1984.
118. "Glenn Aide Rebuts Mondale Camp Loan Charges," *Chicago Tribune*, February 16, 1984.
119. Dan Balz and Kevin Klose, "Glenn, Mondale Trade Charges Over Debate Statement," *Washington Post*, February 17, 1984.
120. "Mondale: Testing Time," *Newsweek*, February 20, 1984.
121. Wilkie, "Problems Beset Glenn in Iowa."
122. David Broder, "Self-Destructing Candidates," *Washington Post Weekly Edition*, April 23, 1984.
123. "The Glenn Gap and the Fritz Blitz," *New York Times*, February 22, 1984; Martin Schram, "Democratic Runners See Campaign Hurdles Stamped 'Mondale,'" *Washington Post*, February 22, 1984; Brent Larkin, "Mondale Win Signals 'Beginning of the End,'" *Cleveland Plain Dealer*, February 22, 1984; Thomas Brazaitis and Brent Larkin, "Glenn Defends 'Right Stuff,'" *Cleveland Plain Dealer*, February 24, 1984; Paul Magnuson, "Organized Labor Leaves Its Mark on Mondale's Victory in Iowa," *Hartford Courant*, February 22, 1984.
124. Larry Eichel, "Hart Getting a 2d Look as N.H. Voters Go To Polls Today," *Philadelphia Inquirer*, February 28, 1984.
125. Steve Berg, "Glenn Launches Last Stand in South," *Minneapolis Tribune*, February 19, 1984.
126. "A Matter of Style in Iowa," *Hartford Courant*, February 22, 1984.
127. "Notes from Iowa," *Dallas Morning News*, February 22, 1984.
128. Robert Turner, "New Opportunities in the Realigned Democratic Race," *Boston Globe*, February 23, 1984.
129. Brent Larkin, "The Old Glenn's Back—Is It Too Late?" *Cleveland Plain Dealer*, February 27, 1984.
130. Orin, "Glenn Aides Ready 'I Quit' Speech."
131. Patterson, "Iowa," 87, 89, 97.
132. Schram, "Early Leaders."
133. Peterson and Lardner, "Temperatures and Glenn Outlook."
134. Jon Margolis, "Politics as Abstract Philosophy," *Chicago Tribune*, January 9, 1984.
135. Peterson and Lardner, "Temperatures and Glenn Outlook."
136. Malone, "Cranston's Maximum Effort in Iowa."
137. February 6, 1984.
138. John Dillin, "Mondale Way Ahead in Iowa, but Watch Out for Hart," *Christian Science Monitor*, February 16, 1984.
139. Bill Peterson, "Iowa's No. 1 Question Is 'Who's in Third,'" *Washington Post*, February 15, 1984.
140. Wilkie, "Uncommitted Vying for 2nd Place In Iowa."
141. Orin, "Front Running Jitters."
142. Schram, "Early Leaders."
143. Bill Peterson and Kathy Sawyer, "'Expectations' the Big Foe," *Washington*

Post, February 21, 1984.

144. Phil Gailey, "Iowa Caucuses: A Possible Surprise?" *New York Times*, February 6, 1984.

145. Howell Raines, "In Iowa Caucuses, the Vote Isn't Secret and That Puts a Spin on the Ball," *New York Times*, February 10, 1984.

146. Breen, "Glenn Lets Chance Slip to Score on Mondale."

147. Carl Leubsdorf, "Winners and Losers in Iowa May Not Be What They Appear," *Dallas Morning News*, February 1, 1984.

148. David Colton and Don Campbell, "Nothing Like Monday's Free-For-All," *USA Today*, February 17, 1984; see also Don Campbell, "Presidential Hopefuls Hurting for Votes," *USA Today*, February 20, 1984.

149. Brent Larkin, "In Iowa, Conflicting Signs for Glenn," *Cleveland Plain Dealer*, February 20, 1984.

150. Jack Germond and Jules Witcover, "Can Debaters Bring Mondale to His Knees," *Des Moines Register*, February 10, 1984. See also Jack Germond and Jules Witcover, "Candidates Play Expectations Game," *Des Moines Register*, February 4, 1984.

151. Joseph Kraft, "On To Round One," *Washington Post*, January 17, 1984.

152. David Yepsen, "Caucus Story May Not Be Finished," *Des Moines Register*, February 19, 1984; Donald Rothberg, "Big News Is Depth of Glenn Defeat," *Jackson (Miss.) Daily News*, February 21, 1984.

153. Thomas Brazaitis, "Glenn Endures Tough Sledding In the North," *Cleveland Plain Dealer*, February 14, 1984.

154. Wilkie, "Problems Beset Glenn in Iowa."

155. Larry Eichel, "The Question In Iowa Is Who Will Finish Second," *Philadelphia Inquirer*, February 20, 1984.

156. Rebecca Powers, "John Glenn Grasps For the 'Sensible Center,'" *Detroit News*, February 15, 1984.

157. Ibid.

158. James Perry, " 'Farm Kid' Mondale Wooing the South, Where the Nomination May Be Decided," *Wall Street Journal*, January 17, 1984.

159. Jack Germond and Jules Witcover, "Going Down: Glenn; Moving Up: Hart," *Baltimore Sun*, February 22, 1984.

160. These January 21 headlines are from: *Wall Street Journal; Washington Post; Washington Times; Boston Globe; Dallas Times Herald; Jackson (Miss.) Daily News; Dallas Morning News.*

161. Descriptions are from stories accompanying headlines in note 160, *supra*, as well as stories in: *New York Times; Baltimore Sun; New York Daily News; USA Today; Christian Science Monitor; Columbus Journal; Columbus Dispatch; Cleveland Plain Dealer; Philadelphia Inquirer; Los Angeles Times; Chicago Tribune; New York Post.*

162. Moore, *Campaign for President*, 54; Dudley Clendenin, "Residents Under Siege of Candidates Barrage," *New York Times*, February 27, 1984.

163. Germond and Witcover, *Wake Us When It's Over*, 160-161.

164. Ibid.

165. Hedrick Smith, "Mondale Lead Over Nearest Rival in Poll Sets Nonincumbent Record," *New York Times*, February 28, 1984.

166. *New York Daily News*, February 15, 1984. See also "Countdown to Super Tuesday," *Newsweek*, March 5, 1984.

167. David Lightman, "Few Surprises Expected in New Hampshire," *Hartford Courant*, February 26, 1984.

168. Emmett Buell, " 'Locals' and 'Cosmopolitans': National, Regional and State Newspaper Coverage of the New Hampshire Primary," and Henry Brady and Richard Johnston, "What's the Primary Message: Horse Race or Issue Journalism?" in Orren and Polsby, *Media and Momentum*, 92-93, 155-160.

169. Interview with William Hamilton and Robert Teeter, "Politics: 1986 and Beyond," *Public Opinion*, October/November 1985.

170. Dillin, "Glenn's Hopes Rest With Moderates."

171. Thomas Brazaitis, "Glenn Wonders Why Hurrahs Didn't Last," *Cleveland Plain Dealer*, March 23, 1984.

172. Bradlee and Robinson, "Glenn Abandons Quest for Presidency."

173. Fox Butterfield, "Hart After Iowa Sees 2-Man Race," *New York Times*, February 22, 1984.

174. Transcript of interview with John Glenn, "Meet the Press," February 26, 1984; *Boston Globe*, February 22, 1984.

175. Ernest Furgurson, "The Day After: Mondale Basks, Hart Attacks," *Baltimore Sun*, February 22, 1984.

176. CBS-*New York Times* exit poll.

177. David Broder, "That Quadrennial Phenomenon Known as the Iowa Bump," *Washington Post Weekly Edition*, February 8-14, 1988; John A. Farrell, "Biden's Campaign in N.H. Appears to be Stumbling," *Boston Globe*, August 10, 1987; Orren and Polsby, *Media and Momentum*.

178. Ernest Furgurson, "Rural or Urbane, Democrat or Republican, N.H. Voter Is Nothing If Not Important," *Baltimore Sun*, February 28, 1984; see also Chris Black, "1984 Presidential Hopefuls Woo N.H.," *Boston Globe*, August 25, 1983. A 1987 update of this wisdom will be found in "New Hampshire Focus Is on Activists A Year Before Election" by David Shribman, *Wall Street Journal*, February 24, 1987; William Mayer, "The New Hampshire Primary: A Historical Overview," in Orren and Polsby, *Media and Momentum*, 33.

179. David Broder, "A Mondale Champion," *Boston Globe*, February 2, 1984.

180. David Broder, "Can the Glenn Campaign Shape Up," *Washington Post Weekly Edition*, November 14, 1983.

181. Hedrick Smith, "Glenn Team Fighting With Backs To Wall in N.H.," *New York Times*, December 20, 1983.

182. David Broder, "Glenn Encounters Frost in New Hampshire," *Washington Post*, October 31, 1983.

183. David Broder, "Hart Defeats Mondale in New Hampshire Upset," *Washington Post*, February 29, 1984.

184. John Dillin, "Glenn Campaign—Undergoing Repairs," *Christian Science Monitor*, January 31, 1984; Larry Eichel, "Hart and Askew Winning Surprising Backing in N.H.," *Philadelphia Inquirer*, January 14, 1984.

185. Note 184, *supra*; *Boston Globe*, February 17, 1984.

186. David Nyhan, "Mondale Tops In Phone Battle," *Boston Globe*, January 30, 1984.

187. Eichel, "Hart and Askew."

188. CBS-*New York Times* exit poll.

189. *Public Opinion*, August/September 1984, 49.

190. Dillin, "Glenn Campaign—Undergoing Repairs."

191. Carl Leubsdorf, "Organization Called the Key to Crucial New Hampshire Primary," *Dallas Morning News*, February 28, 1984.

192. Mike Littwin, "It's Polite To Shake Hands All Around," *Los Angeles Times*,

January 31, 1984.

193. Brazaitis, "Glenn Endures Tough Sledding."
194. CBS-*New York Times* exit poll.
195. Dillin, "Glenn Campaign—Undergoing Repairs."
196. David Nyhan, "Mondale Finds Going Smooth in N.H.," *Boston Globe*, February 6, 1984.
197. Brazaitis, "Glenn Endures Tough Sledding."
198. Leubsdorf, "Organization Called the Key." Also, Aram Bakshian, "Is It Now Bedtime For Glennzo?" *Washington Times*, February 24, 1984.
199. Larry Eichel, "Competitors Facing Tough Choices on Use of Resources to Beat Mondale," *Philadelphia Inquirer*, January 19, 1984; Robert Shogan, "Glenn Trims Schedule, Pulls Negative Ads," *Los Angeles Times*, February 1, 1984.
200. Howell Raines, "Iowa Race May Answer New Hampshire Riddle," *New York Times*, February 17, 1984.
201. Curtis Wilkie, "Candidates Assessing Strength For N.H.," *Boston Globe*, February 22, 1984.
202. Broder and Balz, "Mondale Says Nomination May Be Clinched Soon"; Howell Raines, "8 Democrats Gird for Key Primary in New Hampshire," *New York Times*, February 26, 1984; Howard Fineman, "The Video Battle for Votes," *Newsweek*, February 6, 1984; David Nyhan, "Peace Emerges as the Big Issue in N.H.," *Boston Globe*, January 15, 1984.
203. Ernest Furgurson, "Glenn Folds Maine Campaign, Shifts From Anti-Mondale Strategy," *Baltimore Sun*, February 23, 1984.
204. Brent Larkin, "Mondale Win Signals Beginning of the End," *Cleveland Plain Dealer*, February 22, 1984.
205. Elizabeth Drew, *Campaign Journal* (New York: Macmillan, 1985), 252.
206. Usher, "The Undoing of Glenn."
207. Mary McGrory, "Reality Catches Up With Democratic Candidates in the N.H. Debate," *Boston Globe*, February 2, 1984.
208. Schram, "Democratic Runners See Campaign Hurdles."
209. Howell Raines, "Mondale Works To Bolster Lead as Others Adjust to New Lineup," *New York Times*, February 22, 1984; see also Curtis Wilkie, "Mondale Rolls in Iowa; Glenn Falls Well Back," *Boston Globe*, February 21, 1984; Larry Eichel, "Hart Getting a 2nd Look as N.H. Voters Go to Polls Today," *Philadelphia Inquirer*, February 28, 1984.
210. *Boston Globe*, February 23, 1984.
211. Sara Fritz, "Hart Finds His 'Ideas' Pitch Less Than Ideal," *Los Angeles Times*, February 26, 1984.
212. Jack Germond and Jules Witcover, "Super Tuesday Primaries May Be Mondale's Last Chance to Save His Campaign," *National Journal*, March 10, 1984. See also *Los Angeles Times*, February 27, 1984; *Boston Globe*, February 17, August 23, 1984; *Washington Post*, February 22, 1984.
213. *Los Angeles Times*, March 6, 1984; Dan Balz and David Broder, "Rivals Issue Challenges," *Washington Post*, March 1, 1984; Thomas Oliphant, " 'Special Interest' Question Arises as Mondale Seeks VP," *Boston Globe*, July 4, 1984; Reagan Raps Mondale on Tax Increase Issue: Glenn Accuses Reagan of 'Political Charade,' " *Boston Globe*, August 21, 1984.
214. Martin Schram, "Mondale's Song Is a New Hampshire Hit," *Washington Post*, January 31, 1984.
215. Raines, "8 Democrats Gird for Key Primary"; Dan Balz, "Astronaut Glenn

Returns, Running as Backers Hoped," *Washington Post*, February 28, 1984; Eichel, "Hart Getting a 2d Look"; Myra MacPherson, "New Hampshire, the Primary Prize," *Washington Post*, February 28, 1984; Deborah Orin, "Mondale Plays It Cool at Head of Pack," *New York Post*, February 27, 1984.

216. Brent Larkin, "Glenn Looks for Surprises in N.H. Race," *Cleveland Plain Dealer*, February 28, 1984.

217. Balz, "Astronaut Glenn Returns"; Fred Barnes, "Glenn Now Comfortable About Touting Experience He Gained as Astronaut," *Baltimore Sun*, February 27, 1984.

218. Barnes, "Glenn Now Comfortable."

219. Bernard Weinraub, "Glenn Maintains Upbeat Mood in the Wake of Disappointment," *New York Times*, February 26, 1984.

220. Larkin, "Glenn Looks for Surprises in N.H. Race."

221. Weinraub, "Glenn Maintains Upbeat Mood."

222. *New York Times*, March 5, 1984.

223. Dick Williams, "John Glenn Decides to Campaign—Finally," *Atlanta Journal*, February 15, 1984.

224. David Nyhan, "The Big Choice," *Boston Globe*, March 8, 1984.

225. Steve Sakson, "Nashuans Assess Results," *Nashua (N.H.) Telegraph*, February 29, 1984.

226. Mary McGrory, "Reality Catches Up With Democratic Candidates in the N.H. Debate," *Boston Globe*, February 26, 1984; Balz, "Astronaut Glenn Returns"; Myra MacPherson, "The Great Contenders," *Washington Post*, February 28, 1984; Martin Schram, "New Hampshire Debate Changed a Few Voters' Minds," *Washington Post*, February 25, 1984.

227. Wesley Pruden, "Most of the Drama Is Hype," *Washington Times*, February 28, 1984. See also Marjorie Hershey, *Running for Office* (Chatham, N.J.: Chatham House, 1984), 66.

228. *Time*, December 7, 1983.

229. Bill Prochnau, "Shades of '76," *Washington Post*, February 8, 1984.

230. David Broder, "Hart Seen Moving Up in New Hampshire," *Washington Post*, February 6, 1984.

231. Larry Eichel, "Hart and Askew Winning Surprise Backing in N.H.," *Philadelphia Inquirer*, January 14, 1984.

232. *New York Times*, March 7, 1984.

233. Thomas Oliphant, "Hart Announces He'll Compete in Vermont Test," *Boston Globe*, December 7, 1983.

234. Dennis McDonald, "Hart Says His Campaign Still Alive," *Des Moines Register*, December 16, 1983.

235. Among the best of the pre-Iowa articles on Hart are Frank Lynn, "An Interview with Gary Hart," *New York Times*, January 2, 1984; George Lardner, "New Ideas Democrat Has Had His Eyes on the Presidency," *Washington Post*, January 17, 1984; Robert Merry, "Gary Hart's Drive For the White House Is Fueled By Old-Fashioned Staff Work," *Wall Street Journal*, January 26, 1984; David Yepsen, "Hart Turns On the Heat, Revives His Campaign in Iowa," *Des Moines Register*, January 31, 1984; Sara Fritz, "With Glenn Faltering, Hart Is Seen as No. 2 Finisher in New Hampshire," *Los Angeles Times*, January 31, 1984; Larry Eichel, "Media Coverage Is Moving Hart to Center Stage," *Philadelphia Inquirer*, February 7, 1984; Fred Barnes, "Hart Effort Begins To Attract Attention," *Baltimore Sun*, February 7, 1984; Dillin, "Mondale Way Ahead in Iowa."

236. Schram, "Democratic Runners See Campaign Hurdles."
237. CBS memo; also Adams, "Media Coverage of Campaign '84: A Preliminary Report."
238. MacPherson, "The Great Contenders."
239. "Showdown in the South," *Newsweek*, December 19, 1983.
240. David Shribman, "Glenn Shifts Focus on South in Strategy To Show Strength," *New York Times*, January 23, 1984.
241. Martin Schram, "Mondale Covering Crucial Bases in South," *Washington Post*, March 15, 1983.
242. *USA Today*, January 20, 1984.
243. Ronald Ostrow, "Problems Dog Glenn on Southern Swing: Crowds Seem Mainly Impressed With His Former Astronaut Role," *Los Angeles Times*, January 25, 1984.
244. Steve Berg, "Glenn Launches Last Stand in South," *Minneapolis Tribune*, February, 20 1984; see also Richard Dunham, "Glenn Trails in Texas Despite Fund Raising Lead," *Dallas Times Herald*, December 14, 1983.
245. These headlines appeared in the following: *Washington Post*, November 21, 1983; *New York Post*, December 7, 1983; *Los Angeles Times*, January 25, 1984; *St. Petersburg Times*, February 18, 1984; *Minneapolis Tribune*, February 20, 1984.
246. Rowland Evans and Robert Novak, "Has Glenn Lost the South? *Washington Post*, December 7, 1983; Berg, "Glenn Launches Last Stand in South."
247. Carl Leubsdorf, "Mondale Digging In in the South," *Dallas Morning News*, January 10, 1984; see also Rudy Abramson, "Mondale, Glenn Focus on South," *Los Angeles Times*, December 4, 1983.
248. Berg, "Glenn Launches Last Stand In South."
249. Richard Dunham, "Glenn Campaign Grounded Despite Oklahoma Popularity," *Dallas Times Herald*, February 11, 1984.
250. *USA Today*, January 20, 1984.
251. Bill Cornwell, "Glenn's Campaign Certainly Isn't Burning Up Atlanta," *St. Petersburg Times*, February 18, 1984.
252. Howell Raines, "Two Democrats In Search of Southern Strategy," *New York Times*, October 23, 1983; *Los Angeles Times*, December 4, 1983; *Boston Globe*, January 7, 1984.
253. Don Campbell, " '84 Nomination May Ride On Dixie's Political Winds," *USA Today*, January 20, 1984.
254. Cornwell, "Glenn's Campaign"; Brent Larkin, ". . . While the Fight Heats Up in the South," *Cleveland Plain Dealer*, February 12, 1984; Jack Germond and Jules Witcover, "Georgia, Alabama May Be Glenn's Last Chance to Derail Mondale's Express," *National Journal*, February 14, 1984.
255. Dillin, "Glenn's Hopes Rest With Moderates."
256. Hedrick Smith, "Experts Say the South Looks Bleak for Glenn," *New York Times*, February 27, 1984.
257. Bill Kling, "Glenn's Tack In Dixie: Fiscal Responsibility," *Washington Times*, January 19, 1984.
258. Cornwell, "Glenn's Campaign."
259. "Glenn Calls On Voters in South To Go to Polls," *Los Angeles Times*, March 7, 1984.
260. Larry Bartels, *Presidential Primaries and the Dynamics of Public Choice* (Princeton, N.J.: Princeton University Press, 1988), Appendix, Table A-15.
261. The figures follow those of the CBS-*New York Times* exit polls.

262. *Los Angeles Times,* March 1, 1984.
263. A study of the national electorate found that, in comparison with the other major candidates, Glenn outranked Reagan, Mondale, Hart, and Jackson in terms of integrity, but ranked second in terms of empathy, second in terms of competence, and third in terms of leadership. In sum, his ratings on "personal traits" were described as "very high." Brady and Johnston, "What's the Primary Message," 168-169.
264. See Henry Brady, "Is Iowa News" (Paper presented at Conference, "First in the Nation: Iowa and the Presidential Nomination Process," University of Iowa, Iowa City, February 7-9, 1988); and Brady and Johnston, "What's the Primary Message."
265. Balz, "Grounded by His Debts, Glenn Drops '84 Hopes"; David Shribman, "With Few Words, Glenn Withdraws," *New York Times,* March 17, 1984; Bradlee and Robinson, "Glenn Abandons Quest for Presidency."

Seasons of Recovery and Renewal

THE SEASON OF RECOVERY:
MARCH 1984-SEPTEMBER 1985

The presidency was the dominant goal of John Glenn's second term in the Senate, and his presidential campaign was its dominant event. When he withdrew from the race, his term still had two years to run. Given our interest in the full six-year cycle, we need to consider two questions: How did the senator interpret his electoral experience? What effect did that interpretation have on his subsequent political activity? A senator's electoral interpretation always has an important impact on his or her subsequent behavior—in Washington and at home. Indeed, it was Glenn's interpretation of his 1980 reelection victory in Ohio that triggered his quest for the presidency. That victory became the crucial connection between two sets of activities. Moreover, we would expect the interpretation of his nomination campaign to provide an enlightening link between that career detour and his subsequent activity in Washington and at home.

INTERPRETING THE ELECTION

Because the Glenn presidential campaign drew a good deal of attention, a number of postelection interpretations were immediately available. It may be helpful to look at them briefly as a prelude and backdrop to the candidate's reflections. All of them, by scorekeepers and participants alike, were incomplete. Scorekeepers offered up their interpretations on the run. Few, if any—other than those from Ohio— stayed to talk with the candidate after he withdrew. The nomination process flowed swiftly on, and the reporters went with the flow. They wrote their wrap-up obituaries by weaving their earlier observations into an interpretive form and then moved on to cover the live candidates. Participants, too, had little incentive to dwell on a campaign that soon became a minor—and disappointing—episode in a longer, more consequential drama. When, for example, two dozen "managers" of the various campaigns met in December, along with several media scorekeepers, to recreate the 1984 presidential campaign, the manager from the Glenn campaign contributed only 3 pages of commentary to a 253-page story. When invited to present the perspective of the Glenn campaign, he replied—to the amusement of his colleagues—"Do I have to use the whole minute? (laughter)" [1] The quip was a reminder that failure is an orphan, and it was a clear signal that a full-blown electoral interpretation would not be forthcoming. None came from any other source either. Nor will one be presented here.

However, the thrust of our analysis provides a context that easily accommodates partial interpretations. Given the magnitude of Glenn's failure, it is hardly possible to argue that he ever had much chance of survival. On the other hand, because nearly every observer (and participant) felt there was an enormous gap between potential and performance, it is equally impossible to argue that his candidacy received its fairest test. Our view is that it did not. While he probably could not have won, he certainly could have done better. In that case, the questions become: What went wrong? How could the campaign have done better? What helpful changes could have been made? Implicitly, at least, these questions have been the subject of our analysis. Here and there, we have suggested changes that, if implemented, would have given the Glenn campaign a fairer test: an earlier start; a stronger reliance on retail-oriented organization; a surer understanding of the candidate's predispositions, strengths, and weaknesses; a more informed conceptualization of nominating constituencies; a more positive integration of the marine-astronaut and the politician in the presentation of his persona; a heightened appreciation of the strategic importance of Iowa; less reliance on hired-gun campaigners; a more fully developed conception of the American presidency.

Each of these suggestions represents a part of the explanation of the gap between potential and performance—partial interpretations of what happened. They tend to focus attention on the shortcomings of the campaigners, the candidate, or both, as did the electoral interpretations of scorekeepers and participants. Journalistic interpretations tended to place heaviest blame on the campaigners; the campaigners, on the other hand, tended to put the heaviest blame on the candidate. Our own set of remedies suggests both interpretations are valid.

There was, of course, a broad interpretation that might subsume all others. It was that the time was not right for a candidacy like Glenn's, one that emphasized a theme of national unity as expressed by a hero of exemplary character. Perhaps Glenn was doomed from the start, no matter what campaign and candidate problems developed. In his previous toughest fight, in 1974, he had been aided by a context in which a nonpolitical hero was much advantaged. Perhaps, in 1984, the context was a disadvantage. As one of Glenn's advisers put it early on, "It's like two surfers on two very different waves. Form and style and ability help. But what's most important is who's on the right wave." [2]

At the Democratic mini-convention, Walter Mondale issued a call-to-arms, the rest-of-us-against-the-rich, us-against-them, little-guys-versus-big-guys polarizing rhetoric; Glenn offered bromidic rhetoric as he promised a unified effort in meeting the challenges of the future. Perhaps the Democrats wanted ideological warfare. Perhaps—as we suggested in connection with *The Right Stuff*—it was the ideological future rather than the technological future they wished to embrace. A number of observers thought that interpretation was the case. [3] Had that been the voter preference, it would be obvious that John Glenn did not have a chance to win the Democratic nomination. That interpretation would render most of the post mortems irrelevant, which is a possibility. But we shall leave this large assessment to future analysts and pursue our astigmatic, over-the-shoulder look at the electoral aftermath.

As they reflected on the potential-performance puzzle, scorekeepers stressed, as they had from the beginnings of their vigil, the shortcomings of the organization—first the amateurishness of Senate staffer Bill White, later the aggrandizement of the hired guns. We are, by now, thoroughly acquainted with those indictments. So their emergence in post mortem interpretation is no surprise. In the most extensive post mortem, the reporter who followed the campaign longer and knew it better than any other observer pointed to the instability and the internecine warfare inside the organization as a major cause of campaign failure. Under the headline "The Undoing of Glenn: Amateurs, Strife Wreck A Campaign," he wrote, "Infighting raged for months inside the Glenn campaign among the factions known to each other as 'the Ohio gang' and 'the gurus,' 'the hired guns,' and 'the Capitol Hill boys.'" [4] The Ohioans, led by Bill White, he said, "made tons of organizing and administrative mistakes"; but "as the hired guns, led by ... Robert Keefe, took control" of the campaign, "even stranger things began to happen to John Glenn." [5] Given the deficiencies of the campaigners, he argued, the candidate never had a chance.

Another prominent journalist rendered his similar postelection judgment that Glenn was "the worst managed candidate of 1984," because "[his] hired hands somehow managed to make a national hero who is also a decent, attractive human being into a politically unmarketable product." [6] A veteran Ohio reporter asked: "So what happened to the wholesome political figure who offered himself for the presidency? For $12 million, they converted an attractive political package into the ugly duckling of the 1984 campaign." [7] Focusing on the hired guns, a national reporter who traveled often in the Glenn entourage said afterward,

> He was not well served by the mercenaries. They had no commitment to John Glenn. They were all looking out for their own careers. As soon as things began to fall apart, they deserted him like rats on a sinking ship. Everyone covered his own ass. Everyone blamed everyone else. They didn't give a damn about John Glenn.

Others concurred in this harsh judgment. But one of the most knowledgeable among them put the verdict in a more charitable form. "Some of these people," he said, "were good at their crafts. But they did not know John Glenn. And they had no idea how to run a John Glenn campaign."

The gap between potential and performance was acutely felt by the hired guns. They had signed on expecting to make a president out of the hero-candidate, and they had failed completely. Not surprisingly, their interpretations tended to emphasize the candidate's shortcomings. Most of these notions have already been discussed. A different post mortem view was held by the person closest to Glenn on the campaign trail—it was that Glenn had started his campaign *too early*. Glenn, he said, would have done much better had he announced just before the formal campaign season, in the fashion of Dwight Eisenhower. That strategy, he reasoned, would have maximized the impact of Glenn's heroism while minimizing his liabilities as a practical politician. Glenn, he argued afterward, performed poorly because he was "devastated" by "competing day after day in the nitty gritty of politics for nine months." [8] The campaign-without-voters, he said, involved "a lot of political battles, in-fighting, straw polls, endorsements, fund raising, all the things John Glenn is least suited to do." [9] He portrayed his candidate as "fumbling around terribly in a political environment he was never comfortable in." [10] It was, altogether, an exceedingly negative judgment on Glenn's capabilities as a retail campaigner.

Another important adviser dwelled more on Glenn's difficulties as a media campaigner because of his inability to cope with the marine-astronaut image. "Early on," recalled this adviser,

> we found that people had an image of him as an astronaut hero, and that it was hard for them to remove him from the past,

regardless of what we did in the media. It was difficult to put together a new coalition with someone 62 years old, semi-bald, with basic traditional values. He was undone by his past.[11]

As might be expected, this adviser played up the "disastrous" effect of the movie in reinforcing rather than overcoming the astronaut image.[12]

A third top campaigner spoke afterward of the candidate's communication difficulties generally. "When his announcement came," he said, "expectations were extremely high. He soared and people expected he would present the vision of the future and articulate it. That never happened."[13] Altogether, these judgments betray the disappointment of the hired guns that John Glenn was not the candidate they thought he was and could not be made into the candidate they wanted. They came to believe that the task they had undertaken was impossible.

Between the two interpretive nodes, one blaming the campaigners and one blaming the candidate, Glenn's view was that there was blame enough to go around. "It was my campaign," he told a reporter shortly after his withdrawal, "but I'm not doing a mea culpa, taking it all on my broad shoulders. There were lots of people who did things that were not right. I'm not going out and praise everybody. But it was absolutely my campaign, and I'm not going to blast anybody."[14] When he talked about what happened, however, he tended to focus on neither the campaigners nor himself, but rather on the least tractable features of the nominating campaign. In the manner of the losing politicians studied by John Kingdon, he rationalized his failure by attributing it primarily to factors over which no one in his camp had much control.[15] The formally prescribed campaign sequence, the occupational incentives of the media scorekeepers, the issue context of 1983-1984, the ambitions and talents of his rivals—these were the "uncontrollables" that bulked largest in Glenn's mind.

When I went to Washington to talk with him in mid-May, I asked the senator whether he had done any post mortems and whether he felt like doing any. The atmosphere in which we spoke was a sufficient answer to the second part of the question. He was gracious but subdued, in striking contrast to the irrepressibly upbeat mood of our preceding conversation in the same office ten months earlier. From the outset, it was obvious that he certainly did not "feel like" reliving the campaign. But he persevered—in bits and pieces.

In response to the first part of my question, he said,

> No, we haven't done any post mortems. Naturally there are some things we would do differently if we had it to do over again. We didn't win. But it was my campaign. I'm not blaming anybody. As far as sitting down and post morteming the whole

thing, figuring out just what we would do differently, no, we haven't done that. We've got a $3 million debt. That's what keeps me awake nights.

He was, understandably, preoccupied with his debt. It clouded his future and reminded him of his past.

The debt was the only aspect of his failure that produced any second guessing or self-criticism during our talk.

> I think I would have trusted my own judgment more. It was my campaign. I made all the decisions. But I didn't inject myself into the process as much as I should have. Three or four times during the campaign I said, "All right, I'm going to take myself off the road for ten days, come back to Washington and check out the whole organization." Each time, my advisers would say, "You can't do that. We've got six house parties in New Hampshire and four fund raisers in Iowa. They are going to raise so much money. They've worked so hard to put them together. You can't tell them you aren't coming." So I went. I never did come back and take charge of fund raising the way I should have.

Fund raising had been for Glenn the barometer of his falling hopes at the end of 1983, and it remained the most visible and most durable measure of his defeat. If he harbored any other items of self-doubt, they were either crowded out by his financial situation or too painful to confront at all.

I asked him if he had stumbled into the debt or had taken it on deliberately. He said, "We knew what we were doing," and added, "if I had it to do over, I would do it again." He reviewed the February context in which he secured his $2.5 million bank loan. And in so doing he offered some partial explanations for his defeat. "When we came up to Iowa, I was in second place," he said.

> Our polls showed that I was doing pretty well and that Mondale's vote was soft. I had been attacking Mondale, and it was having an effect. Mondale's polls, they told us later, showed the same thing. I was not attacking on a personal basis. I was being responsible about it—or, I thought I was. . . . (So he took out the loan for $2.5 million.) Then Gary [Hart] came in second. The media expectations were that I should finish second. And when I didn't meet their expectations, they blew it all out of proportion to what it really meant. They set the expectations and when you don't meet their expectations, that's their story. They make you fit their story. The difference was only about 6,000 votes between Gary in second place and me in

forty-fifth place or wherever it was I finished. Tell me, why should 6,000 votes out of 100 million make so much difference? And why should there be this serial effect—especially in small states—where one result has such an overwhelming effect on the next one?

He took out the loan when he thought he had a chance.[16] And he continued to draw down that loan through Super Tuesday because he believed he still had a chance. And, as his account went, if it were not for the prescribed sequence of contests and the media's role in interpreting the results, he would have done better than he did.

The difficulty was that the early sequence of contests and the media's role in producing "serial effects" were well-known facts of life in the nominating process. Glenn did not admit that his campaign had failed to digest those facts beforehand. Nor did he seem to fully appreciate them afterward. "I made the decision to run campaigns in all fifty states," he said.

We had more districts covered in Illinois than Mondale. We had every district, except a few, covered in Pennsylvania. We were in this for the long haul. Gary took all his resources and put them into Iowa and New Hampshire. He paid no attention to the other states. He could shoot crap, throw in his entire bundle. And if everything went his way, he would win big. It worked for him. And I give him credit. But we had strength in all the states. We raised a lot more money than he did, so that we could stay in it till the end. But the serial effects of those little states made it impossible.

There was no sense that his was the wrong strategy, or that Hart's was a rational alternative strategy, or that he would do it differently another time. It was as if he had only recently discovered the potency of these serial effects and remained uncertain as to how he might have coped with them.

He expressed the general sense that the electoral context had been inhospitable, but he did not interpret the outcome as proof that his general election strategy or his constituency-of-the-whole idea had been faulty. When I asked about the problems of a centrist candidate, he replied,

The sensible center, the moderates don't come out to vote. If you arranged the voters across the spectrum, you'd have a bell-shaped curve, with most people lumped in the center as moderates. But it's the extremes who come out to vote. . . . The caucuses are the worst, because people have to come out and sit for four hours. The extremes get excited enough to do that. Then you've got labor. The leaders stand there with their clipboards checking to see who has gone to vote—you go, you go, you go. I don't know whether it's legal to outlaw caucuses, but I'd like to do it. That's one of the problems this year—too many caucuses. That and the serial effect of one state on another are two problems I think we have to deal with. . . . We need regional primaries or even a national primary. I would be in favor of a national primary. Let's just vote. Is there any other country that has serial primaries the way we do? Let's discuss the issues and vote.[17]

He did not convey the notion that he would or could accommodate to the existing system.

Glenn's words lead one to wonder whether he ever had contemplated an accommodative strategy. As he did not discuss or second guess any of his strategy decisions, the question remains unanswered. Implicit in his postcampaign desire to change the system is the idea that the electorate in a national primary would be different from the electorate in a statewide caucus or primary. But he did not, nor had I ever heard him, from Ohio in 1980 to Iowa in 1983, articulate any distinction between primary electorates and general election electorates. Nor did he express a clear recognition that he had always been a stronger candidate in a general election than in a primary.

When I asked him who his "strongest supporters" in the campaign were, he replied, "They were people who believed as I did on the issues—moderates. They were people who would say, 'We compared your position to Mondale's on such and such an issue and we agree with you.'" On the evidence, he did not have many supporters of this sort. There may have been a large number of moderates under the bell curve, but they did not become strong supporters. In his term, they apparently were not "excited" enough or sufficiently encouraged by others (like labor leaders) to vote for him. Why not? One reason Glenn mentioned was the issue context of the election. "If it was a matter of shall we go to war or not go to war," he said, "the moderates will come out to vote. But if it's a matter of economy, then it's marginal whether they'll come out to vote. Certainly they won't brave a snowstorm, as in New Hampshire." But the nature of the issues was not the major problem, in Glenn's view. The main problem was simply that the elections in which he was defeated were not fought out "on the issues" at all. If they had been, the moderates would have been stirred, they would have agreed with him, and he would have done better.

I asked him if he understood the problems he was getting into in Iowa. "We knew what we were getting into," he said.

But we thought we could get our issues across. As it turned out, the media ran the race. And they never focused on the issues. It was always some joke someone told, or who wore what color suit to distinguish himself from the others or who looked tired or who sat erect or who slouched or who wore what shoes that the media focused on. Is that any way to elect a president and the leader of the free world, for goodness sakes? What about issues? You never read about the issues. For the media, everything has to be visual. They want table-pounding and handwaving. Issues aren't visual enough.

It was his longest and most vigorous reflection. And it was the one he had emphasized in his earliest post mortem interviews. "I do not think the race was decided on the issues," he had told an Ohio reporter. "That's what makes me feel sad about the whole thing." He added,

In the debates, there wasn't much attention paid to our differences. We had some substantive differences. Somehow we were supposed to spell them out in sixty seconds. "What is your foreign policy? You've got sixty seconds to answer." All people can do is get a general impression: Are you calm, are you agitated.... It focused more on that than it did on substance.[18]

A major problem for him, he believed, was that he had been "too specific" on the issues and that the candidates who were "far less specific" fared better in the debates than he.[19] "I would doubt," he had said to another reporter, "that out of these forums and debates, my views were any better known."[20]

Electoral politics and candidate support should be based on issues, Glenn believed. But the occupational incentives of the media pulled his campaign in the opposite direction. "Now I'll defend the media, too," Glenn continued.

There were eight of us in the race, so it was hard for them to sort out our views. With three people in the race, they can do it much easier. The other day, the [*Washington*] *Post* ran a full page comparing the three men on the issues. You could go right down the page, compare the three on each issue and decide on the one you agreed with the most.

This view expresses the public service notion of an election campaign. It is akin to his preference for the national primary—"Let's discuss the issues and vote." Voting on the issues is the electoral equivalent of making legislative decisions on the merits.

In another postcampaign interview he acknowledged his difficulties in coping with his identification as an astronaut. Again, he felt that media treatment had hurt him. "Almost every write-up that went out about me," he said,

> was "Glenn on the launching pad" and "will the rocket fizzle?" and all the connotations that kept that in the foreground. The movie came out in the middle of all this, which once again refocused attention in that area and, I think in some respects, prevented us from maybe filling in the gaps of information that we should have been able to fill in.[21]

There seems to be an acceptance here that his problem was the one his advisers had identified for the media—"filling in the blanks"—and not the top-to-bottom integration of his prepolitical and political experiences.

When Glenn deliberately sought to harness the media in the service of his issues, the result, he said, was that the visual aspects were reported and the issue content was ignored. In our conversation, he discussed his experience with national defense issues.

> When I was down in Pine Bluff, Arkansas, at the end of the campaign talking about defense, and about my military experience compared to Hart's lack of military experience . . . there was a man who had an old P-17 fighter—in great shape. I took it up to fly it, and the media started grinding away. There I was on the evening news flying the plane, but nothing about my views on defense. The next day, same thing. I made a speech criticizing Hart's ideas on defense. I said he would wreck our national defense with those kooky ideas of his. And I stood in front of a line of tanks to make the issue visual. Then I drove one of the tanks. There I was in pictures all over the country driving the tank, peeking out from under the helmet, and not one word about my views on defense. The media only wanted the visual stuff. I don't like it—but I suppose it will ever be thus.

His complaint reflects his continued discomfort with political routines that diverge from his public service ideal. He could not bring himself to believe that he drove the tank primarily to get his picture on the news. He believes that publicity-seeking on behalf of the issues is legitimate, whereas pure publicity-seeking is not. We have suggested that there may be a bit of self-deception here, but it represents an unchanging feature of his political outlook.

In summary, John Glenn interpreted his campaign as having been conducted on the issues. Such strong support as he had was based on the issues. There was a great deal of potential issue-based support available to him, but it could not be mobilized because the caucus system in Iowa militated against moderates and because the serial effects of Iowa and New Hampshire made it impossible to recoup. Above all, he believed, it was the media's lack of interest in the issues that kept him from communicating with his potential supporters in Iowa; and it was the media's attention to horse-race momentum that lay behind the serial effects that followed. His issue-based campaign was thwarted, in the final analysis, by factors over which he had little control.

In all of this interpretive discussion he had focused very little on himself. Probing around the edges of his candidacy, I asked whether—as the scorekeepers had so unanimously agreed and as their descriptions had convinced me—he had altered substance and/or style after Iowa. He said he had not.

> That was the media's view. But it was wrong. They thought that after Iowa I would be down in the dumps and when I wasn't— when I showed that Iowa wasn't the end of the world—they interpreted it as a change. Again, they set an expectation and they wrote the story to fit their expectation. I suppose they thought that if they had been in my shoes, they would have been downhearted and when they saw me come in and take charge they decided it must be the new John Glenn. But I was just the same John Glenn I'd always been.

He was at pains to point out that he had not changed. But it was a view at odds with the people who watched him.

In another gentle probe, I asked whether he had learned anything from the campaign that would make him a better senator or change his behavior in the Senate. Again, he did not mention any major lessons or changes. "I don't think it would have as much effect on me," he began,

> as it would on some of the other candidates—because of my background. There's hardly any place in the country I hadn't been. There are places, of course, but I've lived in all sections of the country and I've traveled around a great deal. Some of the others have traveled from home to Washington and given a few speeches here and there. But I think I had a lot less to learn about the country than most of the others. But if you mean did I learn more about the views of particular people, as a result of meeting the political people in various areas, the answer is yes.

When I had first observed Glenn's presidential campaign in 1981, I felt he was learning as he went about the country. Now, at the end, it seemed as if his education had stopped fairly early on. His campaign had collapsed in the very section of the country where he felt most at home, but he did not mention it.

He went out of his way to buttress the idea that he did not have a great deal to learn about the essentials of his campaign. "On the matter of issues, too, my background gave me an advantage over the others," he continued.

> Ohio, as I've said before, contains just about every interest there is in our country. So I was pretty much up to speed on all the issues when I started. For a congressman from Nebraska, a steel mill or coal mine would be quite a shock. But I'd been exposed to all the diversity our country has to offer. Ohio has everything but a sea port like Seattle and palm trees. The Ohio resources commissioner heard me say that so much, he says he's going to plant palm trees in southern Ohio.

When I asked him if being a senator helped or hurt him in the campaign, he returned to the idea that he was "up" on the issues. "I think it's a help. You are involved," he said of being a senator.

> You have a staff here and sources of information that keep you up to speed on the issues. And if you don't have what you need you can hire it real quick around here. You are more likely to read *CQ* and *National Journal*. If you read them regularly, you don't miss much. On the other hand, when you are off campaigning and you have to miss votes back here, that bothers you. I never missed a vote where I was the key vote. And I flew back for several that I thought were important.

His idea was that the issues he studied in the Senate prepared him for his issue-oriented presidential campaign; in other words, that the experience of Sen. John Glenn was ample preparation for candidate John Glenn.

His remarkable constancy came out most forcefully when I asked him whether he felt he should have started his campaign earlier. He answered by recapitulating his fundamental public service view of politics. "I didn't decide to run right after Reagan's inauguration the way Walter Mondale did," he began.

> I waited to see how Reagan's policies worked out. If they had worked out for the good of the country I would not have run. But as things went along, I thought his policies were not what the country needed—cutting programs that helped the needy, butchering research. . . . I decided to run. But it took nearly two years to make that judgment. I don't see how you can judge

policies in much less than that. I know it sounds self-serving, but I didn't get in it for the glamour and the glory. I got in it because I believed that my policies are in the best interest of the country and Ronald Reagan's are not. Mondale didn't wait to see whether Reagan's policies would work. He started with all the blocs lined up and the list of names from his White House days. . . . He got started earlier than anyone except Carter. If you have to start that early, it means the best people will not run for the presidency. . . . I thought we would put together a campaign in fourteen to fifteen months, and I still think we could have done it. But we didn't; so that's that.

These were comments I had heard and read many times before. Long ago I had come to believe they were fundamental to John Glenn's view of himself as a politician.

This belief was fortified one more time when, closing out the meeting, we walked to the door of his office. He wanted to explain himself once more—in much sharper tones.

I didn't get in the race for the glory. I got in it because I believed in principles I felt were for the greatest good of the country. Mondale got in it so early that it seems to me crass or cynical or all of the above. He got in it for reasons of personal advancement. He didn't wait to see what would happen to the country. He said, "I'm going to run no matter what." I know this sounds self-serving, but I wanted what was best for the country. I got in it for principle and that's why I didn't want to get out. Getting out has been a trauma. And the $3 million debt is an even bigger trauma.

The interview ended on the same note with which it had begun—the debt.

Glenn also had returned to another familiar theme—one much more firmly associated with him—the motivational distinction between ego politics and public service politics. Glenn's presidential campaign did not change his political attitudes or predispositions very much: all elements of this post mortem point to that conclusion. John Glenn, the nonsurviving presidential candidate was essentially the same person as the marine-astronaut who ran for public office in 1964, 1970, and 1974. He wanted to do one more thing for his country; he was signing up for one more hitch in the marines. He believed, as always, that his motives were preferable to those of most other politicians because his early dosage of fame had given him a broader, less self-interested perspective on politics. He believed that the best man was the man with the best political motives, that the best man deserved to win, that he was the best man, and that voters would recognize his qualities and support him. These were his core beliefs, and they reflected what he saw as his essential political strength.

Other people who watched his campaign at close range captured aspects of Glenn's attitude. An attentive journalist commented,

> John Glenn was gulled by the polls into thinking he was a strong presidential candidate. But it was only name recognition. I think the polls told him what he was powerfully disposed to hear—that he could do it. Let's not forget he had heard presidential talk from the beginning of his career in public life.

A campaign adviser said,

> His view was that he had "made" president. He'd earned the rank ... [that] what we need in the presidency is just a good man, a guy who is just the best all-around man for the office. ... [And] he says, "Look I'm the guy, and why can't they see it?" [22]

"John Glenn is not a traditional politician," said an Ohio reporter. "He doesn't reach out to other people and ask them for help. ... He seems to feel that 'I'm John Glenn. My record speaks for itself. I don't have to be a shill and sell myself like a traditional politician.'" One of his top Senate staffers spoke more sharply, "He's an amateur—not because of ability but because of arrogance. I've seen him in political situations where he does what has to be done. He thought that all he had to do was enter the race—John Glenn, the big hero—and everyone else would be blown away." None of these observations quite captures the permanence or the patterning of Glenn's public service politics as we have traced it throughout his career. But each of them is consistent with it.

Despite his assertion that it was the obstacles placed in the way of his issue-oriented campaign that "saddened" him the most and despite his interpretive focus on those obstacles, the fact is that the voters failed to credit his public service motivations and failed to recognize him as the best man. And that must have saddened him. We have repeatedly observed how fiercely he protects his personal reputation. Indeed, despite his devotion to issues of policy, the only "issue" that invariably engages his passions and his competitive spirit is an attack—or a perceived attack—on those personal qualities that mark him as a public service politician. He fought strenuously to protect his character, his integrity, his devotion to public service when he felt they were under attack by Howard Metzenbaum or Mario Cuomo or Walter Mondale or Jesse Jackson or Ernest Hollings. Indeed, his political campaigns almost invariably centered more on his personal qualifications than on his issues. To have had several nominating electorates ignore or reject those distinctive qualities about which he cared most deeply must surely have contributed to his personal trauma.

These comments are speculative. Glenn did not acknowledge that aspect of his disappointment. Instead he concentrated on external factors and shielded himself from electoral interpretations involving the specific shortcomings of Glenn the candidate. In the earliest postelection period, at least, Glenn was not prepared to address that kind of interpretation in any but the vaguest "it was my campaign" sense. "There have been some very fair articles in the [Ohio] papers," said one aide in May, "but the senator has gotten livid when he sees them. It's as if he doesn't want to see any criticism of himself." Another aide said that Glenn had just vetoed a post mortem op-ed article by one of the campaigners because it could be interpreted as putting the blame on him. Candidate-centered interpretations, it seemed to me, would have to come from elsewhere.

Earlier we suggested that Glenn's basic distinction between ego politics and public service politics may mask his ambition—even from himself. Perhaps the same distinction may mask his failures—even from himself. Perhaps it blinds him to the inherent difficulty of pursuing a political ambition while preserving a nonpolitical reputation. Whatever the case, there is nothing of artifice or demagoguery about John Glenn. No one in America more deeply and more genuinely wants to serve his country than he does. His belief in the distinction between public service politics and ego politics is profound and irreversible. It is the product of his long pre-Senate experience. It is his core political conceptualization. And it has guided his political life from its beginning. As a framework for political action it has helped him to achieve success, but it may also have contributed to his failure. Whatever the case, it survived the presidential campaign intact. John Glenn remained essentially unchanged by the campaign and by the interpretation he placed upon it. It was unlikely, therefore, that his electoral interpretation would have much effect on his subsequent reelection campaign.

SURVIVING THE DEFEAT

When a presidential campaign detour ends, each nonsurvivor must return to the life he or she was leading before the "presidential thing" began. Nonsurviving senators return to the sequential rhythms of governing and campaigning. It cannot be easy. But it can be done. The "Senate's Club of Failed Ambitions" has had a distinguished membership—Robert Taft, Hubert Humphrey, Edmund Muskie, Henry Jackson, Howard Baker, and Robert Dole. These senators and others took up where they left off and enjoyed productive careers following a losing presidential campaign.[23] There *are* difficulties. More than anything else in the world, ambitious politicians hate to lose. Furthermore, "This society really punishes losers—even honorable losers," said one who knows, George McGovern.[24] And Walter Mondale said the same thing, "This country doesn't like losers." [25] The difficulties are both short term and long term. For the short term there is a period of decompression. "There's no question it's a letdown," said McGovern. "You're out of the limelight; you're out of the main arena." [26] But more serious and longer lasting is the reentry problem at home. McGovern, Frank Church, and Birch Bayh all lost their subsequent reelection bids because, it is believed, the pursuit of their presidential ambition put them out of sync and out of touch with their constituents. [27] For the nonsurvivors, therefore, there is yet another round of survival problems to face. John Glenn faced all of them in the spring and summer of 1984.

He addressed the main problem immediately by devoting much of his withdrawal news conference to politics in Ohio. He served notice on potential pretenders that he would seek reelection to the Senate in 1986. And he emphasized that the "presidential thing" had brought no sense of separation from his electoral roots. His staff had continued to work on Ohio problems, he said, and he had not missed any votes of importance to Ohio. "We've represented Ohio very well during this whole time period." And he thanked Ohioans profusely for their support. "When we started out,"

> I was concerned there might be that kind of criticism, that people would feel I was deserting my Ohio duties to run. But I found, everywhere I went back home across Ohio, people were very proud and supportive. They saw it as an opportunity for Ohio and Ohioans to have more impact on the whole federal government.[28]

To punctuate his future intentions, he left for a round of home state visits immediately after his news conference.

In succeeding weeks he moved to shore up his party and labor bases, with appearances at statewide functions of each.[29] And he stayed at it during the fall. "In 1984, after the presidential campaign," he said later,

> We were worried about the reaction, about a possible fall off. So I spent a lot of time in Ohio over the next four or five months. That impressed people. And in the fall campaign I crisscrossed Ohio doing nothing but campaigning for state senators and

state representatives. That impressed the party people particularly. The result was that there was no fall off.

Glenn even effected a reconciliation with Howard Metzenbaum, his Ohio Senate colleague, with whom he had had the most bitter and longest lasting political differences, by rushing to his support against an unfair media attack.[30]

When the media recorded Glenn's withdrawal, they were anything but unfair. Their reports retained the same glow they had taken on after Iowa—highlighting the defeated senator's strength of character. Partly, we have suggested, this reaction is a guilt-ridden, ritualistic rehabilitation of someone they have helped to defeat. But partly it reflects their informed estimate of the defeated candidate's real strengths. In Glenn's case, scorekeepers said of his withdrawal that he "went out saluting—upbeat and with the sure sense of himself that has marked his political career . . . [and] with his good humor and cheerful disposition intact." [31] He exhibited, they said "personal grace," "dignity and pride," "grace and style." [32] One wrote,

> There was nobody smarter in technical terms, none more honest, none more admirable in terms of personal courage and ability to focus the discipline of a lifetime . . . in the [presidential] field. He just wasn't a very good pol. . . . [He was] an eminently qualified U.S. Senator, as determined and dedicated and as decent a public servant as you can get in this country. But not a good pol.[33]

John Glenn was returning to the Senate with journalistic admiration for him as a person solidly intact.

In December 1983, when Glenn was in the process of falling twenty-five points behind Mondale in the presidential sweepstakes, George Gallup had asked Americans which men they most admired in the world. John Glenn ranked eighth; Walter Mondale ranked tenth. There is evidence here (sampling problems aside) that the wider public—while they did not want him for their president—still wanted him for their hero.[34] In sum, John Glenn's return to Senate politics was floated on a base of undiminished regard for the personal qualities so crucial to his previous success. It was the most favorable possible augury for his future.

OBSERVATIONS AND REFLECTIONS: SAN FRANCISCO, JULY 1984

When we talked in May, he was already in a time of transition back to antebellum politics. I did not observe the transition inside the Senate, but I did see some of its natural strains when I dropped in on the senator and his staff during the Democratic National Convention in mid-July. It was, in the words of family, staff, and friends, "a hard time for him." It was a sustained, emotional, one-week reminder of all that he had gone through, of what might have been, and of what was not to be.

We had talked in May about the convention. He clearly was not looking forward to it. "I'm a delegate," he said,

> I'll go and support the Democratic ticket. There are things I disagree with Mondale about and there are things I disagree with Hart about. . . . So it's not a happy prospect. Especially with all the hoopla and posturing that goes on at the convention. . . . If I hadn't been involved the way I was, didn't have a $3 million debt, and wasn't running for reelection, I wouldn't want to be a delegate and I wouldn't go. . . . If the convention is cut and dried, I'll go, do my duty, and go home early. If it's not settled, then I'll stay.

At another point in our talk, he suggested that the nomination might not be settled quickly. And he revealed a tiny residual reluctance to close the books on 1984. "It may turn out to be a brokered convention," he speculated.

> I've been watching the "other-than-Mondale" numbers—Hart plus Jackson plus uncommitted. If they got close to Mondale, they wouldn't turn to candidates like me who have dropped out. It would be Mondale or Hart. I don't know what they would do for the second spot. I'm not looking for the second spot.

Surprisingly, considering the magnitude of voter rejection, the idea of the vice presidency was alive in his mind. But, considering his self-confidence and the huge investment he had made in the politics of 1984, the idea was not surprising. From his public comments, it was clear he would have accepted if asked.[35] He never thought it a real possibility, but the fact that he thought about it at all indicates how difficult and time-consuming the readjustment to nonpresidential politics can be.

The senator from Ohio came to the convention because he had to. He had to maintain his ties to Ohio politics. ("I'll be with the Ohio delegation and be voting with them and be active in the convention with the Ohio delegation.") And he had to start raising money. ("Anytime you have a debt that's steeper than the San Francisco hills out there, I can guarantee you it's a problem. We're trying every fund-raising operation in the world.") Most probably, he also expected to be invited to play some sort of public, party-unifying role. He scheduled a half-dozen media interviews for the day of his arrival. But when he reached San Francisco, he was already upset by evidence that he would not be given any special opportunity. He had, instead, been notified by letter that he had been assigned, along with many others, to read a section of the platform. The letter, with the instructions, had the impersonal salutation "Dear Podium Participant." It was a disdainful and insensitive relegation of a proud ex-candidate to the party ranks from which he had—over the last two years—emerged.[36]

Glenn was upset. And he reacted in a manner that further reduced his chances of any public role. He refused to accept the first invitation and then refused a second one. Waving a second, hand-delivered letter, he exclaimed,

> This shows you how dumb they are. After I withdrew, they called me to say how difficult it must have been. Since then I have not had one word from them. Then I got a letter last week addressed to "Dear Podium Participant," telling me when and where to appear for my makeup so I could deliver part of the platform. I told them, no, that I wasn't going to do that. They didn't ask me to speak. Then just now I got another message. It's not addressed to Podium Participant but something just about like that. I told my staff to shut that down. I'm not going to do it.

It was a sour note on which to start his "hard time." And it rankled throughout the week. When, for example, Walter Mondale removed Chairman Charles Manatt and then rehired him, Glenn was more critical than any other leader of the Ohio delegation of Mondale's "flip flop, flop flip," which he called "disunifying," "divisive," "wrong," "damaging," and "a mistake" even after it had been put to rest.[37] "He should put a positive face on everything," said an aide. "He should support Mondale and not feel happy when Mondale screws up. But he's down and he's negative right now."

Nearly all of Glenn's press interviews that week took place the Sunday he arrived, the day before the convention began. Typically he was asked how he felt under the circumstances, what was he going to be doing at the convention, whom was he going to support, what were his opinions on convention events (like the Manatt affair), and what were his plans. On the matter of how he felt, he described it variously as "disappointment," "a hangover," "a tinge of regret," "nostalgia," "bittersweet." But at the same time, he invoked his familiar public service rationale. "I'd be lying if I didn't say it was a disappointment. My reason for running was not a self-serving reason, but for what I thought was best for the country," he was quoted in the *San Francisco Chronicle*. On Columbus television he said, "You have a tinge of regret that you're not here under different circumstances. I didn't get in this to advance my political career, but because I felt very strongly about the future of this country." And in the *Youngstown Vindicator*, "My hopes for two years were that I'd be here in another capacity. I didn't want to be here for my own advancement but because I thought the President was leading the country in ways we shouldn't be going." He took special pains to differentiate himself from other politicians. But it was instructive to note that what he seemed to care about so deeply was of no interest to the people with whom he was speaking. The distinctiveness of his motives had ceased to be of any help to him with others. It was an argument that probably had had a short half-life in his campaign, too.

On the matter of support, he remained uncommitted—there were only 4 in a delegation of 175. On the matter of his plans, he told the Ohio scorekeepers he was going to campaign hard for Democrats in Ohio. He said he was already hard at work in the Senate, and he pointed to his accomplishments there. "I'm not going to turn off or sit in the corner," he said.

> You don't accomplish anything by doing that. You have to get in and do what you can. We can influence the platform committee. I went back to the Senate and got our soldiers' education bill through. . . . It's disappointing that I can't work for change at the level I wanted. But the Senate is not a bad level.

It was an upbeat, future-oriented look that belied his downbeat feelings.

On the specifics of his campaign, he talked only about his problems with the issues. "If there's one thing I did," he told a reporter, "almost to my detriment in my campaign, it was that I was too specific. When you are too specific, you give people things to shoot at. . . . I believe I was more specific than any other candidate." And, in another interview, "I thought my moderate views and my specific views were needed. I'm sorry I was so specific that it hurt me." Another Ohio scorekeeper who talked with Glenn in private said afterward,

> He still thinks he lost because he didn't get his issues across. He talked about his five-point program and he complained that he had to buy TV time to present it. He still thinks politics is about issues. Do you think the people who voted for Mondale know his positions on five issues? Of course not. Politics is about something else. People vote for a person. John doesn't see it that way. He still won't say it hurts him to lose. He still doesn't admit it was his fault. He's a marine. He stands at attention, sticks his chin out and says "I can take it." The idea that it's the issues is an optimistic view. It keeps him from recognizing that it's really his fault.

On the available evidence, the ex-candidate had changed neither his views nor his stance on the campaign. And we should not have expected him to.

One of the downside features of the transition period is the long lonely fall from public attention. For Glenn, it had begun after Iowa, but evidence of just how far he had fallen could be found everywhere at the convention. At a couple of points he deliberately chose not to inject himself into the picture, for example, the refusal to be a "podium participant" and an earlier decision not to try to be named chairman of the Ohio delegation. "He could have had the delegation chairmanship," said a staffer, "but he kept saying he didn't want it." So he helped to make himself a nonstory at the convention. Christopher Madison of the *National Journal* chose the Ohio delegation as the subject of his feature column in the *Journal*'s thirty-page "Convention Daily," published and distributed each day of the convention to delegates and spectators. None of Madison's five columns was about the ex-candidate. "I thought about doing something with Glenn," he said, "but frankly there just wasn't a story there."

An Ohio reporter was more emphatic. "John Glenn is a nonentity in the Ohio delegation," he said.

> We've been asking ourselves, "What is he going to be doing at the convention?" The answer is, "Nothing." His press people say he's a leader, a unifier. Hell, John Glenn is a genial folk hero. [Gov.] Dick Celeste is the one on the move. When my editor was handing out assignments, I said, "We forgot John Glenn." He said, "Oh, yes, he's going to be here, isn't he. Oh, yeah."

"He held a press availability yesterday [Monday]," said another Ohio reporter, "and he didn't have anything to say. Nobody could figure out why he did it." Calling Glenn "the forgotten man," still another Ohio reporter wrote that of 150 Ohio delegates surveyed before the vice-presidential selection, only 4 suggested Glenn for the position.[38]

In one lengthy blow-by-blow chronicle of the convention, Glenn rated one sentence: "John Glenn is here, almost unnoticed, trying to raise money to pay off his still substantial debt."[39] One of the national reporters who had traveled with him during the campaign devoted a full-length article to Glenn's activities at the convention. It was head-lined "Glenn Becomes Another Also-Ran: Face in the Crowd." Its lead sentence read, "He was the forgotten man." And the article described the Ohio senator as "but a face in the crowd," "an afterthought," "all but unnoticed," and "faded as a public figure."[40] For the man who exactly one year before had believed he could be president, these were hard knocks. He was especially sensitive to the thrust of the nationally syndicated article just mentioned.

But there were compensations. On Tuesday morning Glenn came to the meeting of the Ohio delegation (he had not come on Monday) to hear the speeches of two men who had survived longer than he. From their warm words, he received further indication that his personal reputation had survived his political disappointment. Gary Hart began his speech by calling Glenn "one of the finest people I've ever met in politics."

> More than anyone I know, he is a decent human being. I know he's sick of hearing this, but he is an authentic American hero, a gentleman, a decent, decent human being. . . . Of the original eight candidates, no one represented such a barrier to my candidacy. Yet I retained his friendship . . . through many ups and downs. I may have said some harsh words, but he was always warm and candid with me. Thank you very much, John.

These words drew a great deal of applause, as if they accurately described John Glenn as the delegates knew him or thought they knew him. After Hart, came Jesse Jackson, and he, too, began with public sentiments about Glenn nurtured in private relationships. "During my campaign, one man stands out. No one was more mindful of me. He reached out to me in a tender moment of the campaign. My special thanks to Senator Glenn." Those remarks also drew applause.

The next morning, the senator performed his one semipublic function. He gave a short pep talk, a party unity speech, to the delegation. The state party chair introduced the senator, saying, "One of the nice parts of this job is the opportunity to introduce people you respect."

> One person I've worked with and been proud to work with is a person dedicated to public service, who works hard at it, who doesn't choose the glamour, who's a work horse and not a show horse. This has been hard for him. As a citizen of Ohio I couldn't be prouder of our senior senator, John Glenn.

This introduction was followed by a standing ovation. It had none of the enthusiastic, foot-stamping "Run Jesse Run" or "Gary-Gary" that the Ohio delegation heaped on the surviving candidates. But it had warmth produced, it seemed, by genuine respect.

So, too, did their singing of "Happy Birthday" to him after his speech, at the suggestion of the governor. Glenn then went to the microphone and said, "Now you've loused up my day. I was trying to forget it." It was a touch of the unspoiled hero that had for so long underwritten his national appeal. His speech to the delegation was statesmanlike. But he read it. Nowhere in it did he give anything of himself—no personal reminiscences, no mention of his campaign. As usual, he made no effort to forge an emotional bond. It reminded me again of his communication difficulties in politically structured settings—a problem I had often noted since 1980. But the warm burst of applause when he ended conveyed the sense that these people from Ohio had come to expect this kind of performance and were not asking for anything else; they had decided they liked him anyway. Whatever he was, they had become, over time, comfortable with him, and that, too, augured well for his eventual recovery—both emotionally and politically.

SENATORIAL CHANGES

It was two years before I had another opportunity to observe John Glenn in action. It was 1986, and he was campaigning for reelection in Ohio. With the major exception of his debt, the transitional difficulties he had experienced were behind him. We cannot trace the decompression and reentry process, but there is good evidence to support the view that he had immersed himself again fairly quickly in the governing-campaigning sequence of his senatorial life. We know that at the moment of his withdrawal, he was already preoccupied with reelection. And we know that soon after his withdrawal he made two changes that helped position him for that contest. As such, they signaled an effort to close the book—except for the debt—on the "presidential thing."

The first change was to give increased attention to the public relations aspects of his job. It was, we have often noted, a much neglected activity in Glenn's Senate operation. "I have never tooted my horn around here" was a trademark Glenn comment. His effort to redress the situation was the result of more political learning as well as an interpretation of his reelection effort. The change was a dramatic upgrading of the job of press secretary within his Senate staff. During my earliest contact with the Glenn office, the chief press person was called the press assistant and drew a salary that ranked fourteenth among his staff members. During the heart of his presidential run (October 1983-March 1984), the renamed director of communications drew the sixth highest salary on the staff. But this person also became, in the course of the presidential campaign, the closest adviser to the senator, his shadow on the campaign trail. He became Glenn's interlocutor in the running dialogue with the nation's scorekeepers. It was said by his Senate aides that Glenn gained a totally new appreciation of what an active press secretary could do for him in an electoral situation. The indispensability of a press intermediary was, indeed, something Glenn had learned from the presidential race. If the media were as powerful a force in his defeat as his interpretation of it indicated, then he would have to cope with it more aggressively than he had before.

With his reelection uppermost in mind, he quickly appointed his top campaign speechwriter as his press secretary in the spring of 1984. And he gave him, for that year, the second highest salary in the office. By 1985 the press secretary was the highest paid person on Glenn's personal staff, representing an importance to Glenn and to the rest of the staff that would have been unthinkable earlier. In the Ohio press, the new appointee was given credit for improving Glenn's speaking style and his persona.[41]

The most tangible and visible of the press secretary's innovations was undertaken in anticipation of the 1986 campaign. He engineered the production of a newsletter mailed statewide to all of Glenn's constituents—listing some forty of his accomplishments. It was the *first* newsletter of John Glenn's ten-year Senate career. During his 1980 campaign, as we have seen, Glenn professed to be ready to take such a step, but it apparently took the presidential campaign to convince him. It is another example of the very slow, very gradual way in which the marine-astronaut absorbed the ways of most working-level politicians. His new-found appreciation of the press-related parts of his job positioned him favorably for his reelection campaign.

In January 1985, when the new Congress convened, Glenn made his second important change. He left the Foreign Relations Committee to become a member of the Armed Services Committee. It was an unusual move. He sacrificed ten years of seniority on what was traditionally the Senate's most prestigious committee. The move was a surprise. "He'll never leave Foreign Relations," a top staffer had told me six months before. "That's his real interest." But he did. He first petitioned the party leadership to make an exception to the rules and allow him membership on both committees. When they declined, he chose Armed Services.

The choice represented a coming to terms with the prospect of a lifetime career as a senator from Ohio. His presidential failure brought on a period of self-examination about how he wanted to spend that career. Although Foreign Relations may have been his real interest, Armed Services represented his real love—technology. Whereas Foreign Relations had long been a favorite launching pad for presidential ambitions, Armed Services had more obvious rewards for the reelection-oriented. In discussing his intentions publicly, he stressed the increasing dominance of the defense budget over national policy, the need for efficiency and competence in handling that budget, the relevance of his background and experience to that need, and the opportunity to ensure that Ohio received its fair share of defense expenditures.[42]

On the campaign trail in Ohio, I asked him why he did it. "Two reasons," he answered,

> I had become disenchanted with Foreign Relations. It didn't do much. Aside from confirmations, our influence was nil. In foreign affairs, things are so changeable, tipping first one way, then the other. It's not like dealing with hardware. For a long time I had wanted to get on the Armed Services Committee. Its work is less ethereal and more concrete. You know how much of this and that you have and how much the Russians have. . . . I'm more comfortable dealing with armed services questions than foreign relations questions. They are better suited to my particular talents and expertise. And I think you can have just as much influence on foreign policy from Armed Services. In fact, I don't know how you can separate the two fields.

He continued,

> I'm the most junior man on the [Armed Services] committee, and so I sit way down at the end of the table. I don't particularly like that. I was third ranking on Foreign Relations. But if we control the Senate, Claiborne Pell will be chairman and Joe Biden is next. So I would have had no chance of being chairman. On Armed Services I get more questions than most others because of my background, so that my expertise more than makes up for my lack of seniority.

"I don't want to brag," he continued,

> but when it comes to airplanes or SDI, I know more than anyone else on the committee. And the other members look to me more than to anyone else on the committee. I've made that my special responsibility. For ten days each of the last two summers, I've toured laboratories involved in SDI to familiarize myself with their operations and their problems. That's how I learned what I described at the press conference [at Battelle] this morning. And that was only one system. I have to understand many many more.

He sounded as if he had found a comfortable long-term home where his technological and military know-how would count for far more and where his policy-making influence would be undiminished.

He had another reason for shifting committees: he wanted to be reelected. "I regard this as a great victory not only for me, but for the people of Ohio. As a member of the committee, I intend to do all I can to insure that Ohio gets its fair share of defense dollars. That will mean more jobs and that can't do anything but help Ohio." [43] People at home understood what the move meant to them. "This turn of events could be especially beneficial in Greater Dayton," said one editorial there, "because the Defense Department is our area's number one employer—with a $1.7 billion payroll at Wright Patterson Air Force Base and at the Defense Electronics Supply Center." [44] Two months after this editorial, $12.8 million for Wright Patterson's Institute of Technology was cut from the budget. [45] Glenn fought successfully to have the funds restored. He won lavish praise at home for his "uphill effort" when "all the signals were negative" and for this "tribute to standing with his colleagues." "Glenn remarked," closed one editorial, "that the reprieve was confirmation that it made great sense to Ohio to shift [committees]. ... That it was." [46] The benefits of the shift—for a senator mindful that Ohioans might think him out of touch, not certain how they would react to his recent failure, and soon running for reelection—were obvious from the outset and were made quickly manifest. And they soon bulked unusually large in his campaign for reelection.

THE SEASON OF RENEWAL:
OCTOBER 1985-NOVEMBER 1986

The Second Reelection Campaign

From our perspective, the central question of John Glenn's second reelection campaign is: What effect, if any, did his presidential campaign have on his Senate campaign and, therefore, on his constituency career? We know that as soon as the national campaign failed, he started thinking about the statewide one. And we have described two concrete steps he took as a reaction to the failed campaign to position himself favorably for the next one. So we know there was some impact on Glenn. The more important question has to do with the impact on his constituents in Ohio. Did the failure of his 1983-1984 presidential campaign effect the 1986 election outcome? After all, Glenn's presidential adventure had been a widely recognized flop. He had run, in his own words, "in the worst possible way." The magnitude of the defeat might have an adverse effect on the senator's reputation with the voters, which in turn might have an adverse effect on his reelection.

Some people certainly thought it might. "John Glenn's abortive presidential bid has some Ohioans wondering about the Senator's political strength," began the February 1985 analysis of a conservative

Republican newsletter.[47] In August an Ohio scorekeeper echoed, "Some political observers in Washington . . . say Glenn's dismal showing in the 1984 presidential race shows he's fallible." [48] The next February, Republicans in Ohio were reported as believing that "Glenn's disastrous 1984 presidential campaign has made Glenn vulnerable for the first time." [49] In the words of one GOP county chairman, "Glenn showed he could be beat. He flat out died in that [presidential] race. That really made an impression on a lot of people in Ohio." [50] "One might think," said an Ohio scorekeeper, "that after a bruising and somewhat humiliating loss, Glenn would be vulnerable to a challenge at home. After all, rejection is often the most fatal disease in politics." [51] None of the commentators regarded Glenn's defeat as likely. But they all regarded it as an open question.

So did the conservative six-term Republican member of Congress, Tom Kindness, who announced his candidacy for Glenn's seat in September 1985. "Kindness is hoping," wrote one Ohio reporter,

> that Glenn's unbeatable image as the All American hero and ultimate Mr. Nice Guy has been tarnished by his dismal showing in the presidential race. . . . The Kindness camp believes this perceived tiny crack in Glenn's public facade will allow it to paint Glenn as too liberal and out of touch with most Ohioans. Kindness supporters also believe Glenn's problems in paying off his $2.8 million presidential debt and his poor attendance record during the primary campaign will hurt him in 1986.[52]

The "too liberal" and "out of touch" themes were those used by Glenn's challenger, without success, in 1980.[53] The hope was that in 1986, because of the "tiny crack" of the presidential race, old themes would gain new credibility. The further hope was that Glenn's current difficulty with his presidential campaign debt would allow the challenger to widen the crack. "We believe," said one Republican adviser, "that John Glenn is going to hang himself in his presidential debt problem." [54]

From the beginning, the Kindness campaign was viewed as "an uphill fight." But the race was regarded by the Ohio operative of the National Republican Senatorial Committee as "a sleeper campaign . . . one that I think is doable." The committee pledged Kindness its maximum allowable $715,000 as seed money. And the committee's Ohio poll was thought to contain hope. It showed the electorate split down the middle on party preference in Senate voting. It showed voter disagreement with Glenn on some spending and social issues. And it found pluralities that agreed with descriptions of Glenn as "a great astronaut but not a good legislator," "wishy washy," not "in touch with the needs of the people of Ohio," "too involved with D.C.," and "not effective in getting things done." Such, at least, was Kindness's interpretation of the committee poll.[55] One of his top consultants commented,

> Glenn's people would have you believe Glenn is not vulnerable, that he is too popular and has a broad base of support. . . . [But] no one is prepared to run through a wall for John Glenn in Ohio. No one feels he is indispensable. . . . When you ask Ohioans about Glenn they say he was an astronaut. That was a fairly monumental achievement, but that was a quarter of a century ago.[56]

"The most important thing about Glenn's profile," echoed Kindness, "is that he has broad support, but it's soft . . . he's still recognized as a national hero; no one has really analyzed him as a politician. That will change as we get into the campaign."[57]

On those optimistic notes, the challenger launched a slam-bang attack on the incumbent as a "sideline senator," "an inactive, ineffective senator." In his September announcement, he acknowledged Glenn's status as a "national hero" but charged that

> [his] hero status has not been translated into leadership or effectiveness for Ohio . . . in the Senate he has not been effective. He has not been a frontline senator, but a sideline senator.[58]

For contrast, Kindness adopted the campaign slogan, "On the Front Line—for Ohio." "It's a classic case," he said, "of a person who's gone to Washington and forgotten the people who sent him there."[59]

Soon the challenger embroidered his "frontline-sideline" theme with specific indictments—that Glenn employed only three staffers in his Ohio offices, that he had made only four trips to Ohio that year, and that during his second term Glenn "proposed only two laws that have actually been enacted."[60] The first two charges were demonstrably wrong. The third charge was, at best, ambiguous. All three vanished amid an inconclusive semantic wrangle over Glenn's own nine-page list of his "actual legislative accomplishments." Glenn's list, fired off to the Ohio media in rebuttal to his opponent's accusation, was the brainchild of his new, campaign-tested press secretary. It was a major, tangible payoff from one of his "postpresidential" changes. The rebuttal letter called into question the credibility of the challenger at a time when he had almost no name recognition and badly needed some bona fides to get his campaign off the ground.

That early skirmish was not the only, or the most severe, jolt to the challenger's budding campaign. On January 27, as part of his effort to separate the hero from the politician, Kindness told a Youngstown audience that Ohio had "sent an astronaut to do a Senator's job." [61] On January 28 the space shuttle *Challenger* exploded. The accident sent the nation into shock and grief, and Americans turned to the astronaut-senator for explanation, consolation, and perspective. John Glenn's Senate office logged 600 media requests of one sort or another.[62] The vice president of the United States asked the senator to accompany him to Cape Canaveral to console the families of the astronauts. His picture and his comments appeared on the television networks, in the papers, on radio talk shows, and at memorial ceremonies—nationally and in Ohio. It was one of John Glenn's finest weeks of national service, and it was wholly dependent on his experience as an astronaut. It also reminded people of the blend of heroism and strength of character that had always been the source of his appeal as a public figure. It vastly compounded the problem of an opponent who was trying to make the case that he was an astronaut in a senator's job.

Even more interesting was the light the episode cast on the matter of Glenn's political persona. For a while, the astronaut-senator became known in the way he had wanted so much to be known during his presidential campaign. Ohio headlines read: "The Calmest Man," "Glenn Had Right Stuff After Tragedy," "Glenn Reassured Stunned Nation," "Glenn Strives to Comfort the Grieving," "Glenn Back in the Public Eye," "Tragedy May Boost Glenn Effort," and "Rough Days for Kindness." [63] In the articles beneath the headlines, the scorekeepers demonstrated what candidate John Glenn had needed to demonstrate but could not—that astronaut and senator could be integrated into an appealing public persona, that coolness and compassion in crisis situations were essential qualities of leadership, and that John Glenn's experience could help certify such qualities. It was a case of life surpassing art. Events had revealed the relevance of the "right stuff" as no movie could.

Ohio's scorekeepers wrote:

The calmest man in town was John Glenn . . . he had the best perspective I heard on the 11:40 shocker . . . freckled and hard jawed [he] still showed The Right Stuff . . . tough and fatalistic and American.[64]

Since the shuttle accident Glenn has reemerged as the space hero he once was, this time serving to comfort the families of the *Challenger* crew, as well as his Senate colleagues and the public.[65]

Glenn found himself facing more cameras, microphones

and people than he did during most of his 1984 campaign. . . . Reporters agreed that Glenn handled himself well. The senator . . . is at his best when dealing with human concerns that genuinely move him.[66]

Glenn's words always were reassuring. . . . Reaction to Glenn's role was positive. One of John Glenn's finest moments, remarked one person. Glenn, without asking, had assumed a national leadership role, one that eluded him during months [of campaigning].[67]

Glenn is never better, perhaps, than in a crisis situation in which he offers more than ordinary expertise. . . . The senator has seldom come across more effectively . . . than in the wake of the *Challenger* disaster. Most Ohioans, whatever their political leanings, surely felt a sense of pride in how Glenn handled himself.[68]

Glenn was the calm reassuring voice of authority and reason on national television . . . [he] offered a warmth and strength that came through on national television.[69]

As retrospectives, these comments hinted, if they did not demonstrate, that the failure of the candidate and his hired guns to develop a persona and a conception of the presidency that integrated Glenn's two sets of life experiences lay not in the absence of raw material but in the absence of understanding. The presidential candidate had not understood the strength that could be drawn from open and searching discussions of his marine-astronaut experience. It was his natural strength. The hired guns had not understood that the only way to run a campaign or conceptualize leadership was in terms of Glenn's natural strength. They had not understood, either, that the person himself, rather than a variety of artistic renditions, would be the best instrument for conveying it.

Glenn formally announced for reelection in February, one day before the twenty-fourth anniversary of his space flight. In his speech he talked openly about it. One newspaper headlined its account of his announcement "Glenn Campaigns on Astronaut Origins." And its story began:

Senator John Glenn formally opened his reelection campaign today by reminding Ohioans of his accomplishments as an astronaut and emphasizing his reputation for independence.[70]

As he toured the state, however, other reporters drew different leads from his all-purpose remarks. Some echoed the presidential campaign: "Sen. John Glenn . . . called himself a 'Senator who thinks for himself' and said his political philosophy is rooted in 'the sensible center' between extreme liberals and conservatives."[71] Others highlighted his

claims to have helped Ohio: "Sen. John Glenn announced his candidacy
... boasting that he has saved thousands of jobs in Ohio and helped
bring millions of dollars into the state."[72] Other reporters gave top
billing to his comments on foreign policy.[73]

The announcement was floated on a base of favorable voter
opinion—one that showed no signs of erosion. Indeed, in the near term,
Glenn's statewide job performance ratings had been getting stronger. In
answer to the question "How would you rate the job John Glenn is
doing as one of Ohio's Senators?" Glenn's "excellent" and "good"
ratings had each risen steadily from 1984 to 1986. In combination, they
showed favorable voter ratings of 54 percent in October 1984, 59 percent
in May 1985, and 65 percent in March 1986.[74] These data tended to
support a body of opinion in Ohio holding that, as one journalist put it,
"Politically, there is no evidence [that] the damage done to Glenn's
national reputation as a legitimate presidential prospect has significantly
wounded his home state standing."[75] "The guy is an institution," said a
prominent Republican. "He's what the people of Ohio want. His
presidential race left a lot to be desired, but it didn't weaken him at all in
Ohio. In fact, he may be stronger."[76] The March 1986 survey indicated
that Glenn retained the "across the board" support that had been
traditional for him in Ohio. His favorability rating stood at 68 percent
among Democrats and 60 percent among Republicans. It stood at 65
percent in three of the four regions of Ohio and at 57 percent in the
fourth. And 83 percent of the respondents felt they knew enough about
John Glenn to rate his job performance.

These figures disclosed none of the vulnerability Kindness had
hoped for. Equally discouraging for him, the March survey found that
only 7 percent of the Ohio voters knew the challenger well enough to
rate his job performance. In a head-to-head contest among voters with
an opinion, the March figures showed the incumbent at 78 percent and
the challenger at 23 percent. Glenn's own poll, taken in December,
showed the contest at 62 percent to 17 percent, with 21 percent having
no opinion.[77] The challenger faced both a threshold problem of name
recognition and the larger problem of Glenn's continued appeal to Ohio
voters.

In May Kindness launched a four-week statewide "name recognition media blitz" designed to introduce himself and, in the process, to
contrast "the fighting frontline senator Ohio needs" with the "sideline"
incumbent Ohio had.[78] In July he began to exploit Glenn's troubles with
his presidential campaign debt—especially the $1.9 million of it owed to
four Ohio banks.[79] In January Glenn had asked the banks for a one-year
moratorium on all payments.[80] As part of his May offensive, the
challenger seized the opening and went on the radio with ads calling

this request for "special treatment" "wrong," "not fair," and "probably illegal." And he linked Glenn's request for a "special bank deal" to an ongoing savings institution scandal in Ohio.[81] It was the opening shot of an attack that continued till election day, and it resulted directly from the presidential campaign.

As matters developed, Glenn's debt became the challenger's central issue, his major effort to widen that "tiny crack" of vulnerability some people believed was the residue of the presidential failure. So it would not be for want of trying if the exploitation of Glenn's presidential flop were to fail. Indeed, Kindness did not have to work hard to keep the issue alive in the spring and summer. "Glenn Trapped With Debt as Issue," headlined one analysis in February.[82] The banks gave Glenn an extension he could not meet; Glenn informed the banks that he would be unable to make any payments until after the Senate campaign; Kindness asked the Federal Election Commission (FEC) to investigate the legality of the debt; the FEC announced that Glenn's debt arrangements had violated the law; Glenn sued to nullify the FEC finding. From May to July, the issue dominated Ohio headlines:

> May 16, *Cincinnati Enquirer,* "Glenn to Bank, Hold On: Senator Vows to Pay Campaign Debt, Someday"
> May 17, *Dayton Journal Herald,* "Kindness Asks Glenn to Tell All About Loans"
> May 18, *Cleveland Plain Dealer,* "Glenn's Debt Remains His Millstone"
> June 17, *Cincinnati Enquirer,* "Kindness Asks FEC to Probe Glenn Debt"
> June 21, *Youngstown Vindicator,* "FEC Finds Glenn's Bank Loans In Violation"
> June 22, *Akron Beacon Journal,* "Glenn Says He Didn't Violate Public Trust"
> June 24, *Cleveland Plain Dealer,* "Kindness Attacks Glenn Loans"
> July 12, *Dayton Daily News,* "Sen. Glenn, 4 Banks Beat FEC to Court on Loan Issues"
> July 16, *Cincinnati Enquirer,* "Glenn's Campaign Debts Become Issue"
> August 3, *Cincinnati Enquirer,* "Glenn's Presidency Dream Turns to Debt Nightmare"

In mid-July the challenger launched a new series of radio spots blasting Glenn on the debt. He took out half-page ads in Ohio newspapers detailing "The Legal Case Against John Glenn." [83] In an

August 11 fund-raising letter to PACs, the challenger's campaigners began,

> John Glenn is in trouble. Because of his debt problems, his lack of leadership and his liberal voting records, we are in a position to win in November. Over 60 percent of Ohioans recognize Glenn's debt problems. By a margin of 7 to 1, they feel he should not get special treatment.

By midsummer the matter of Glenn's debt was clearly the campaign's dominant issue. The challenger was getting every chance to widen the "tiny crack."

For his part, Glenn was running a "frugal," low-key campaign, sitting on what he assumed was a comfortable lead. "Taking all the polls together, we're running in the low to mid-sixties," he said in late October. "I'd be satisfied with that." But he also stressed that the presidential campaign experience had given him greater confidence. "There's a different air about this campaign [than 1980]," he said.

> It's postpresidential. . . . The presidential campaign is so intense that every little thing you do is watched carefully and magnified and interpreted—interpreted negatively, too, if at all possible. . . . But after you've campaigned in the big time—and that's about as big time as you can get—you gain confidence in your ability to handle things. So I'm much more relaxed than I ever was before.

It was a comment about growth in self-confidence not unlike his comments about his early Senate experience. The marine-astronaut learned about politics gradually and not always easily. One thing he had learned, apparently, from his 1984 experience was to campaign as if it never happened. In two days of travel with him in October, he did not mention it once without being asked—except for his single stump joke. His one main five-minute TV campaign spot contained not a hint that he had ever run for president. Nor did any of his three thirty-second spots. Nor did any of his campaign literature. It affected him. He learned from it, but he did not speak of it.

He addressed the debt issue whenever he had to, but no more than he had to. "I have always viewed the loans as a personal moral obligation," he said when asked.[84] And he would add, "It's not a matter of 'if,' it's a matter of 'when,' " regarding repayment.[85] When the legality of the loan was challenged, he responded, "I have always tended to my legal affairs with the utmost care, and I view this matter as a point of personal honor." [86] He rested his case heavily on his reputation for personal probity, and he asked for public trust on that basis. His campaign slogan was "Strength and Integrity—An Ohio Tradition." He was asserting his core political strength, his storehouse of personal voter trust resting upon character, and putting it to the test. Whatever the legalities of the matter were—and they soon vanished inside the courts—the essence of the matter was John Glenn's trustworthiness. And it came to be interpreted as such on both sides.

The more central the issue became to his campaign, the more the challenger's rhetoric centered on the character of the incumbent. For example, Kindness said that Glenn should have "a very heavy conscience" because of his "terrible breach of public trust." [87] Or, "Right now, I'm wondering what John Glenn's word is worth." [88] Or, "It's ironic that John Glenn has the courage to be the first man in space, but doesn't have the courage to open his files." [89] Or, "He's campaigning on the basis of integrity and strength. I question the integrity of anyone who would deceive the public for two years on the financing of his campaign." [90] Or, "I believe the people of Ohio have yet to know what this integrity thing is all about." [91] It was a frontal attack on the essence of John Glenn's political strength, and it provoked the same response that earlier personal attacks had: his anger, his competitiveness became fully engaged in the defense of his character and his reputation.

Predictably, then, his 1986 response followed the counterattacking pattern of his 1974 and 1984 campaigns. But, because he did not feel he was fighting for his life, his reaction was relatively mild. In the beginning, he was content to say of his opponent's campaign, "It's all about the debt. He's not addressed how to provide for the future of Ohio or this nation." [92] But as the attack escalated so did the familiar Glenn indignation. He came to characterize his opponent's campaign as "all a personal attack thing—cut and shoot politics." [93] He called it "a negative, smear-type campaign," designed "to talk down my character or question my integrity." As for himself, "I've never engaged in one [a smear campaign] and won't now. But he has." [94] As always, Glenn turned aside reporters' suggestions that he, too, was being negative, insisting that he was only pointing out "differences of voting records" not "false, personal-attack types of things." [95] When asked to treat the challenger's remarks as standard political rhetoric, he answered, "No, sir. At one news conference, he questioned my integrity. I resent that." [96] Once again, the public service politician was in action.

This time, however, he defended himself more with sorrow than anger. "The people of Ohio know I have lived my entire life honestly and above board," he said, "and I'm sorry my opponent is now questioning my integrity for political purposes." [97] Or, "I know he's unhappy with the way things have gone for him. . . . Still, I've never been up against an opponent who has been so negative. I think it's going to rebound against him." [98] And, "If we are to resort to just tearing each other down, we demean our whole system of government." [99] As always, his defense against personal attacks was based on his view of public service politics.

Privately, Glenn evinced a higher level of wrath. "This is the first time I ever had an opponent whose principal effort has been to tear me down. Oh, I've had little things here and there, but nothing like this. He's attacking my integrity—with absolute untruths." He was anxious to be able to interpret the results of the election as a repudiation of negative campaigning. When I asked him whether 1986 was not a replay of 1980, he shook his head vigorously. "It's completely different," he said.

> I never had an opponent who was so negative. He is conducting a completely negative campaign. My other opponents differed from me, but on the issues. This guy is saying things that are outrageous. He says I've only had two staff members in the state. I've always had somewhere between nine and twelve—averaging about ten. I don't know where he got that number. He made a statement that I had only been in Ohio four times last year. Why, I've been here four times in one week. He says I never got a single piece of legislation passed last session. I have nine pages of things I got done last session. I'd love to get a vote of 75-80 percent so that I could say Ohioans have rejected negative campaigning, that we won't have that sort of thing ever again in this state.

His final sentiment derives, too, from his devotion to public service politics.

Ohio voters reelected Glenn by a margin of 62 percent to 38 percent, with a plurality of 770,000 votes. It was less than his 69 percent, 1.6 million-vote victory of six years earlier, but voter turnout was 800,000 less than in 1980. And the challenger conceded that those votes would have gone overwhelmingly to Glenn. [100] The newspapers called it an "easy victory" and a "landslide." From ABC exit polls it appeared he had won another "across the board" general election victory, attracting "virtually every group in the state." He received at least two-thirds of the vote in every age, ethnic, and educational category. He received more than 90 percent among Democrats, and the same among Mondale voters. He won two-thirds of the vote among independents, half of the Reagan voters, and one-third of the Republicans. [101] It was a convincing renewal of his mandate to help govern the country with, as he put it, "the independence and independent judgment I've sought to exercise for the past twelve years." [102]

Glenn also placed a broader public service interpretation on his victory—as he had hoped he could. He said he was "genuinely upset and disappointed" by the negative campaigning of his opposition. He said he hoped his reelection

> signals that the voters are fed up with campaigns that rely on the kind of personal attacks and innuendo that only demean our democracy, that cheapen our politics and insult our intelligence.[103]

He added that he hoped "the revulsion [among Ohio voters] spreads to every state in this great land until it is finally and forever wiped from the face of our political system." [104] That we should find him returning over and over again to this theme, which I first heard in Ohio in 1980, is indicative not just of Glenn's passion for public service politics but of the continuing conflict between the values embodied in that view of politics and the realities of everyday political life.

As for the question of whether the presidential campaign failure would lead to a senatorial campaign failure, the answer is it did *not*. Whatever survival problems he encountered in the country, he had none at home. There is not a bit of evidence that Glenn was damaged in Ohio by his performance nationally. And it was not for lack of any reminder. His opponent had delivered some hard shots, aimed directly at his character.

From inside the Glenn campaign, the view was that the challenger never made the slightest headway. When I arrived the third week in October, a top aide greeted me, "The campaign is over." He explained,

> Kindness raised $1.2 million . . . $700,000 from the Republican committee, $500,000-$600,000 himself. Their strategy was to attack John Glenn's character, on the theory that if they could destroy that, there would be nothing left. . . . They tried to make the issue into a corruption issue, that Glenn was tied in illegally with the banks through the loan. So they went on TV in the summer with this message. In December we took our benchmark poll and we were ahead 62-17. In July, after they had been on TV steadily for a month or so, we took another poll to see what had happened. Nothing. Our lead was 62-21. And they had shot their wad.

From outside the campaign, the view was similar. "Kindness is trying to puncture Glenn's All-American image," wrote one scorekeeper that same week.

> About all it has produced so far are newspaper editorials deriding Kindness as a "Johnny One-Note." . . . More to the point, the public doesn't appear to be particularly interested.[105]

An inspection of eleven newspaper endorsements shows that among the ten that endorsed Glenn, five mentioned the debt difficulty and five did not. Those that mentioned it dismissed it as "not a valid reason for" a vote or as having "little substance" or by saying, "nobody really thinks John Glenn's senatorial votes are for sale." [106] Of those that mentioned it, three went out of their way to praise his "honesty" and "integrity." [107] The major theme was Glenn's record of achievement in the Senate, his growth in stature and promise, and his specific accomplishments for Ohio.[108] To whatever degree the Senate contest could be interpreted as a referendum on his presidential campaign, to that degree the voters had said that it did not matter to them. The senator had proved to be as invulnerable an ex-presidential aspirant as could be imagined. His career in the constituency continued to prosper and solidify. Ohio voters seem prepared to underwrite whatever course his subsequent Washington career might take.

How do we account for this result? In part we would have to recognize what Glenn had done since the spring of 1984 to shore up his reputation at home. He had worked visibly for the Ohio party. He had worked visibly for the Ohio economy. And he campaigned that way, too. He devoted both days of my visit to helping state senators running for reelection. And he traded everywhere on the new connection between his Armed Services membership and increased defense spending in Ohio. When asked, at the very outset of an interview at Ohio State University, to "go over some of the highlights" of his Senate record, he began,

> Well, okay, I'm very proud of my record in the Senate over the past twelve years. We've been very active in a number of areas, one bringing jobs home to Ohio here. Very proud of that. I've held a number of defense seminars, contracting seminars across Ohio—five of them in the last two years. Since I've been on the Armed Services Committee, we've brought in about $3 billion worth of additional contracting back into Ohio here.

And he went on to cite an impressive list of specifics. He highlighted this accomplishment, too, in each of his press conferences during my visit.

His main five-minute TV spot opened with a description of the Chernobyl nuclear plant accident, followed by a reference to the recent leak of radioactivity in southern Ohio and Glenn's instant intervention in that local problem, followed by a recitation of the other tangible benefits he had brought to the state.[109] Several editorial endorsements praised his recent upsurge in Ohio-oriented work.[110] Altogether, these various activities were an effective barrier against any charge that, in his pursuit of personal ambition nationally, he had neglected Ohio.

However important his constituency services may have been, they provided, at bottom, preventive maintenance. They did not reach to the core of Glenn's reputation and support. That core rested—as his own polling affirmed—on the "strength," "integrity," and "tradition" embodied in his campaign slogan. The voter's sense of Glenn's personal trustworthiness had been most directly tested in the campaign, and it was found to be unshakable. Constituent trust takes a long time to develop. In his twelve years in public life, Glenn had gradually achieved and solidified that trust. As he campaigned in 1986, he talked about it in precisely that way. I asked why he was (seemingly) having such an easy time. He answered,

> Well, it took a long time. I've been in Ohio politics for twenty years. Don't forget I took my lumps in the beginning. I lost a primary. I battled the governor and Metzenbaum. If anyone in Ohio ever earned his political spurs it was me.... So— considering all that—do I have good rapport with the people of Ohio now? I sure do.

Over time, the people of Ohio had gotten used to him and had come to trust him. It was not what he changed that accounted most for his 1986 triumph, but what he did not change.

OBSERVATIONS AND REFLECTIONS: OHIO, OCTOBER 1986

To travel with John Glenn in October 1986 was to hear the echoes of earlier travels. Consider, for example, the constancy of his policy interests. During a tour of Battelle Institute, a high-tech research company in Columbus, his enthusiasm for "scientific breakthroughs" and his technical knowledge shone as he alternately probed and lectured and extolled the company officials guiding him. The next day, at each of five county seat rallies, he keynoted his remarks with his concern for education and research. To a gathering in a Zanesville shopping mall, he put it,

> If I had to pick two things that made this country what it is, made Ohio what it is, more than anything else it would be, one, that we set out to have an education second to none, to educate all our people ... and then along with that, we put forth the basic fundamental breakthrough research that let us learn the new things first.

It was the same policy passion around which he had centered his campaign three years (and six years) before.

Equally familiar were the patriotic, concern-for-country attitudes that underlay his belief in public service politics. At every one of his five stops he blasted negative campaigning as "a disgrace to our political system" and "demeaning to the entire body politic." At Newark's American Legion Hall, he called the right to vote "a sacred trust."

> I've been through a couple of wars with some of you here, too. We've seen people die so that we can have the right to decide our future.... I can't break faith with people like that. I'd get out and vote just in memory of those people that I knew that are no longer with us, if nothing else, because what they stood for was this country of ours.

In front of the county courthouse in Logan, he delivered his interpretive version of the Pledge of Allegiance.

> We say that we're going to be *one nation*. We never again are going to be north and south or east or west or black or white. We're going to be one nation; we're going to stand before the rest of this world as a nation, a land of opportunity, of freedom and hope that will set the path for the future that other nations can follow. *One nation under God.* How many nations around this world can put that in the preamble or a pledge or say that they're going to take their direction from on high? And we say that in this country, whether you're Jewish or Gentile or Catholic or Protestant or Buddhist or Moslem or American Indian believing in the Great Spirit, that we say we realize as a nation there is a higher power. If we would call on that higher power, that somehow the word will come through to us as to what our relationship with our fellow people will be and with other nations around this world. Then we say we're going to be *indivisible*, not going to be divided, not going to be rich against poor, male against female, labor against management. And then comes six magic words, if there ever were, that should lead all of our political activity, whether it's in the state house or the national Capitol. We say *with liberty and justice for all*—the liberty of opportunity and the justice of equality. And that to me goes just—it goes beyond being a Democrat, Republican, independent, or whatever. It just should—something that we should just have as our guiding light at whatever level of government we operate.

His version of the pledge had been another of the staple ingredients of his presidential campaign.

In a couple of isolated instances, an observer could trace lessons learned from the earlier campaign, lessons that extended the education of the senator in the workaday political arts. Early in the exploration stage of the "presidential thing," during a meeting with reporters,

Glenn had stumbled witlessly into expressions of interest in a voluntary Social Security program. And he had paid a heavy price for this naiveté (for a Democrat) within the political community. In October, in a formal speech at the Fitzimmons Senior Citizens Center in Dayton, he went out of his way to excoriate this idea. "I pledge to each and every one of you here today that we will fight—and we will defeat—any attempt to kill Social Security by making it a voluntary program." [111] He had learned.

In his earlier campaign, as Glenn struggled with the articulation of a vision, he expressed it privately as the "We're Number One" vision. "He'd say," said one adviser, " 'I don't see why America can't be like those styrofoam fingers at the football game—We're Number One! We're Number One! We're Number One!' Sometimes he'd go on like that five or six times." But, said the adviser, that vision was only "a shibboleth ... just an empty styrofoam finger.[112] Campaigning in Newark in 1986, as he talked about the value of the space program for America's future, he went out of his way to attack the emptiness of the "We're Number One" formula.

> The purpose of this program is not just to see if we can send people up and down and keep them alive as a stunt. It's to do the very basic fundamental research that's necessary to keep us in a leadership position. And leadership not just to wave our fingers in the air like we do after a ballgame and say, "We're Number One, We're Number One, We're Number One." But leadership here means we're not copying some other nation. We have control of our own destiny.

Again, he had learned. He was still learning, in bits and pieces, the various tools of the working politician's trade.

These few instances aside, the overwhelming impression from my brief visit was how little John Glenn had changed in interests, themes, and attitudes from the person who had pursued the presidency. If the voters of Ohio had not been much affected by Glenn's presidential campaign, neither had Glenn. My feeling in October 1986, therefore, dovetailed with the feeling I had in May 1984 that he had not been changed much by his campaign experience. These later impressions fit with my earliest conclusion that his six-year stint in the Senate had not changed Glenn's attitudes and behavior a great deal either. The shaping of the senator and of the presidential candidate had occurred during his lengthy, intense, successful, and altogether extraordinary prepolitical career. The politician was still only a thin cloak for the marine-astronaut.

Although John Glenn might not have changed much since his presidential campaign, the atmosphere of his Senate campaign was totally different. He was at home, in familiar, friendly territory. He was reinforcing old ties, not reaching to create new ones. He was in the protectionist, not the expansionist, time of his constituency career. And he was comfortable in that stage. Doubtless, as he said, his "big time" presidential campaign had increased his confidence as a campaigner. But it was not any change in skills or style that was different in Ohio. It was the changes in context that mattered.

Flying home from Arkansas in 1981, Glenn had expressed his strong identification with "Ohio and the small towns of the Midwest ... [where] people are proud of their country ... love their country ... [and] put the flag out on Flag Day," and his corresponding difficulty understanding "the cynicism of the two coasts." At the time that I had traveled with Glenn in 1983, the eastern media scorekeepers had demonstrated that cynicism toward what they had dubbed "the annotated Pledge" [of Allegiance]. One of them wrote that it was "unadulterated hokum" and ridiculed its usage as exemplifying the "utter rigidity" of Glenn's performance on the stump.[113] But it was the authentic John Glenn. And in Ohio, as he knew it would be, it was accepted at face value. He no longer campaigned in a setting where his questioners assumed he was not what he said he was. His use of the pledge in 1986 drew applause at the courthouse in Logan and at the senior citizens center in Dayton. The day before, during the pledge at Steubenville High School, said a staffer, some people had cried.

At a press conference after his tour of Battelle, a question about Glenn's position on the strategic defense initiative triggered an impenetrable fifteen-minute disquisition on state of the art technology. It was a familiar replay of communication difficulties that had brought on harsh judgments about his "boring" persona in the national media. But at Battelle the reporters smiled, put down their pencils, turned off their cameras, and waited patiently for him to finish. They were extremely indulgent. He apologized, saying, "I didn't mean to give a whole campaign speech." Then he pointed to the reporter who had asked the question and joked, "I didn't do it. You did. You made me." "I went on too long," he admitted afterward. But he laughed when a staffer kidded him about his propensity to induce "MEGO," which stands for "my eyes glaze over." "I have a hard time stopping. One thing runs into another. . . . Sometimes I have two or three separate endings. One time I had four. The staff takes bets on it when I speak." A difficulty thought to be crippling in the 1983 context now took the form of an established inside joke, shared by reporters, candidate, and staff. All of them— apparently the voters, too—seemed comfortable living with the presumed political shortcomings of the senator from Ohio.

Indeed, most of the problems that had plagued him during the national campaign—the problems I had observed and written about in

1983—were absent from the Ohio campaign. Most noteworthy, perhaps, was the absence of two former problems, an undeveloped political persona and a supportive constituency.

The problem of experience, which bedeviled him during my 1983 trip, was nowhere to be found in 1986. Observers outside of Ohio had wanted to know how his experience would relate to his performance as president; observers in Ohio seemed not to worry about his performance in the Senate. They had some sense of the kind of senator he had been, and they were satisfied. Editorial writers called him "diligent and principled," "a man of international reputation," "a leader in such matters as nuclear proliferation," "a diligent and productive protector of Ohio's best interests," "a source of pride and reassurance," "independent and pragmatic [in] his approach to issues," and "close enough to the political center to have the ear of members of both parties." [114] Their endorsements expressed comfortableness and familiarity. His record is "in keeping with Ohio's mainstream image. Much of [his] appeal comes from his avoidance of extremist positions," said one writer.[115] "It is hard to imagine the Senate without him—which is one of the reasons he deserves reelection," said another.[116] They did not, as presidential campaign observers had, ask him to take new leads. They asked only that he provide more of the same. There were no worries about future performance. The Armed Services Committee, said one endorsement, "is where he belongs, given his interests and background. Now he seems well perched to begin his most productive time in the Senate." [117] In Ohio, experience was his major asset, not his major problem.

During the presidential run, the largest part of his experience problem had been the astronaut background, which, as he put it in Iowa, "overwhelmed other things." [118] It was the oldest obstacle to the creation of his political persona. It had plagued him from the beginning in Ohio, and his opponent had raised it again in 1986. But gradually, as we have chronicled, he had blunted its impact in Ohio. The voters apparently had come to recognize and to value him both as an astronaut and as a senator. The passage of *time* had eased the difficulty. But time was a luxury he did not have in the short span of a presidential campaign. Unable to integrate astronaut and senator into a viable conception of presidential leadership, he could not cope with the problem nationally.

In Ohio he exhibited an ease with his prepolitical past that I had not seen before—not in 1980 nor in any of my subsequent trips with him. The most illuminating example came at the end of his five-stop swing through central Ohio, in Newark. After his talk, he was presented with a scale model of the rocket booster used on the suborbital flight preceding his, and asked to autograph it for the local seventh grade science class. He started reflecting extemporaneously on his experience with the space program. It was a ten-minute reminiscence of the sort I had never heard, nor heard of, during the presidential campaign. And it might not have worked in that context anyway, as it assumed he was among people who valued his prepolitical experience.

Now, among friends, he talked about his service as back-up to Alan Shepard, about his preflight discussions with his family, about his reaction to the *Challenger* tragedy, about his trip to Cape Canaveral with George Bush to talk to the families of the crew, and about the importance of space research and exploration to America's continued leadership among nations. It was personal and statesmanlike. It gave something of himself and something of his wisdom. He showed none of the uncertainty he had displayed during his presidential quest about the relevance of his prepolitical experience to his activity as a politician. It conveyed a natural, comfortable sense of his political persona.

A second problem of the presidential campaign, Glenn's inability to locate a strongly supportive primary constituency, was totally absent in 1986. Here he had no need to locate such a constituency. He was running in a general election and seeking a general election constituency, the kind of across the board, rank and file constituency he had always found in Ohio. And it was the kind of constituency he was most comfortable being with, talking to, and reaching for. It was the kind of constituency contemplated by his politics of public service—a constituency of the people, of the whole. It was a hero's constituency. It was the kind he contemplated when he expressed his commitment to the largest political community—the country or the greatest good for the greatest number. Many had commented in 1983 and 1984 that Glenn lacked passion. But that judgment focused on his attitudes toward cause-oriented elements within the party, toward elements of a primary constituency. Glenn's natural constituency and his passion lay elsewhere. As he put it, "I felt passionately about my country when I was sitting on top of that booster." [119] His broad focus hurt him in the presidential race, but it helped him in the Senate race.

Glenn's problem—when it was a problem—stemmed not from a lack of concern for the intense, partial, segmented interests within the community. Rather, his problem was that he typically failed to distinguish between general election and primary constituencies for the purposes of seeking support. He paid special attention, in 1986, to senior citizen groups (via one TV spot and five appearances) and women's groups (via one special mailing and three appearances). He did so, however, because he felt they "didn't have a good feel for what I've done—in those areas," and not because he thought of them as primary constituents.[120] He did not think about politics in terms of his strong supporters or in terms of cultivating a primary constituency. Nor did he present his candidacy in that way. Nor, not surprisingly, did people see him that way.

I had first wondered, in 1980, who in Ohio would fight, bleed, and die for John Glenn, and I had found no answer there. I returned with the same question in 1986. And, again, I found no answer. I found no cadre of enthusiasts, no group of dedicated volunteers to articulate what they were fighting for. Glenn, as far as I can tell, never distinguished between his primary and general election constituencies. I have concluded that Glenn simply does not think in terms of people who kill themselves to get him elected, and he does not organize or campaign that way. So long as the context allows him to embrace a large undifferentiated constituency, so long as the context makes possible a general election campaign, John Glenn will be comfortable—and invincible. Those are the conditions that prevailed in Ohio in 1986.

The same conditions had prevailed in 1980. In that year, Glenn's spectacular general election success and his microcosmic view of his supporting constituency may have led him to overestimate the ease with which he could achieve similar success elsewhere. During my first visit to Ohio in 1980, he had expressed the view that his state was a microcosm of the United States. He repeated this view whenever we talked, almost as an article of faith. He did so again on the trail in 1986. "I used to say it was [a microcosm], but after campaigning all over the country I became more convinced than ever that it was true." To the degree that he internalized that view, he would think about 1983-1984 in terms of a syllogism: Ohio is a microcosm of the United States; I succeeded in Ohio; therefore, I will succeed in the United States. But such a syllogism would be faulty. Because it was based on general election success, it did not contemplate support problems in nominating elections. Because it assumed Ohio was a microcosm, it would keep him from conceptualizing a different political setting.

Ohio was *not* a microcosm in the way that he most needed it to be, as training ground for a presidential run. It may have been that Glenn's presidential race did not reflect, as his Ohio challenger suggested, a lack of interest in Ohio but rather too exclusive an interest in Ohio. His attachment to the general election model, which had produced such spectacular success in Ohio, may have helped undermine his success elsewhere. Running for the presidency, we conclude, is different from running for the Senate. Senators who wish to try it will need to do a good deal of reconceptualization if they are to succeed.

During the years that John Glenn pursued his goal of higher office, his party did not control the Senate. So, while he yielded some of his governing influence in those years, he did not sacrifice the degree of influence that flows from a formal position inside the Senate. Two years after his withdrawal, however, his party took back control of the Senate, and he succeeded to a formal institutional position—chairman of the Governmental Affairs Committee. With official position came the opportunity to become, for the first time in his career, a person of national political importance. We have chronicled the political growth of a "mature amateur" who has been characteristically slow to warm to the political process and to assume political leadership. Each step in that direction has been gradual and time-consuming. And his development as a political figure, when he became chairman, remained incomplete. The greatest lesson of the failure of his presidential campaign was, after all, that he had yet to be perceived and accepted as a national leader. Through 1986 he still gave evidence of a protectionist's style of campaigning and a loner's style of governing. Yet our chronicle tells us that, over time, he has learned to become enough of a working politician to achieve success in both arenas—broadly and spectacularly in Ohio, narrowly and modestly in the Senate. As of January 1987, therefore, time, talent, hope, and room remained for the achievement of still another goal—to be a Senate leader in the making of public policy.

Should he move in that direction, a question naturally arises: What could John Glenn learn to aid him in taking this next step? The answer may be that political leadership in the Senate may require some attitudes and actions that may not fit easily with those ideas about politics that have superintended his career so far. Through 1986 Glenn pursued his political ambitions within the set of constraining notions we have labeled public service politics. These ideas embody a view of politics that has guided and shaped his political activity. They triumphed—eventually—in Ohio, but not nationally. So some suspicion seems warranted that they might have to be modified still further to underwrite successful leadership in the Senate. Just as defeat was a teacher in Ohio, so too can defeat be a teacher nationally, as long as ambition remains. With a somewhat more open ambition and a somewhat warmer embrace of the political process, John Glenn's greatest public achievements could lie ahead. Then his presidential odyssey would seem more like another well-learned political lesson than a personal disappointment.

NOTES

1. Jonathan Moore, ed., *Campaign for President* (Dover, Mass.: Auburn House, 1986), 17.
2. Martin Schram, "Mondale and Glenn Bet on Divergent Paths to the

Presidency," *Washington Post*, October 3, 1983.

3. David Broder, "Election '84: A Class Struggle," *Washington Post Weekly Edition*, January 16, 1984; Richard Reeves, "The Ideological Election," *New York Times Magazine*, February 19, 1984; Peter Hart and Richard Wirthlin, "Moving Right Along? Campaign '84's Lessons for 1988," *Public Opinion*, December/January 1985.

4. Brian Usher, "The Undoing of Glenn," *Akron Beacon Journal*, March 25, 1984.

5. Ibid.

6. David Broder, "The Envelopes, Please...," *Washington Post Weekly Edition*, November 19, 1984.

7. Brent Larkin, "Glenn's Mistake Was Listening Too Much," *Cleveland Plain Dealer*, March 21, 1984.

8. Johanna Neuman, "Glenn's Campaign: A Textbook Case of Botched Chances," *Cleveland Plain Dealer*, March 21, 1984.

9. Moore, *Campaign for President*, 18.

10. Jack Germond and Jules Witcover, *Wake Us When It's Over* (New York: Macmillan, 1985), 135.

11. Dom Bonafede, "Campaign Pollsters—Candidates Won't Leave Home Without Them," *National Journal*, May 26, 1984.

12. Ibid.

13. David Shribman, "With Few Words, Glenn Withdraws," *New York Times*, March 17, 1984.

14. Usher, "The Undoing of Glenn."

15. John Kingdon, *Candidates for Office: Beliefs and Strategies* (New York: Random House, 1968).

16. See also Chris Burnett and Cliff Treyens, "Glenn's Presidency Dream Turns to Debt Nightmare," *Columbus Dispatch*, August 3, 1986.

17. See also Tom Diemer, "Glenn Wants All Primaries To Be Held on the Same Day," *Cleveland Plain Dealer*, June 19, 1985; Tom Price, "Glenn Seeks Election Reforms," *Dayton Journal Herald*, June 19, 1985.

18. Tom Brazaitis, "Glenn Wonders Why Hurrahs Didn't Last," *Cleveland Plain Dealer*, March 23, 1984.

19. Ibid.

20. AP, "Glenn Feels 'Scalded' By Political System," *Ashtabula Star-Beacon*, April 18, 1984.

21. Germond and Witcover, *Wake Us When It's Over*, 116; AP, "For Glenn, Returning to Senate Bit Like 'Good News-Bad News,'" *St. Mary's Evening Leader*, March 24, 1984.

22. Germond and Witcover, *Wake Us When It's Over*, 117.

23. Helen Dewar, "Senate's Club of Failed Ambitions," *Washington Post*, March 10, 1980.

24. Kathy Sawyer, "Since Saturday Debate, McGovern Finds Self in a Friendlier State," *Washington Post*, February 17, 1984.

25. Paul Taylor, "To Run or Not to Run—What Is the Answer?" *Washington Post Weekly Edition*, March 30, 1987.

26. Dewar, "Senate's Club."

27. Eve Lubalin, "Presidential Ambition and Senatorial Behavior" (Ph.D. diss., Johns Hopkins University, 1981), chap. 13; Stephen Salmore and Barbara Salmore, *Candidates, Parties and Campaigns* (Washington, D.C.: CQ Press, 1985), chap. 4.

28. Bill Sternberg, "Sen. Glenn Reassuring Ohioans He Hasn't Been Neglecting State," *Canton Repository*, March 21, 1984. See also Jerry Cando, "A Deeply Stung John Glenn Plans to Rebuild Home Base," *Columbus Citizen Journal*, March 31, 1984; Dan Balz, "Grounded by His Debts, Glenn Drops '84 Hopes," *Washington Post*, March 17, 1984.

29. Keith White, "Glenn Jokes About Himself," *Cincinnati Enquirer*, May 4, 1984; Bob Westen, "Glenn Courts Labor, Urges Party Voting," *Cincinnati Enquirer*, June 20, 1984.

30. Tom Price, "Glenn, Metzenbaum Seem to Have Buried the Hatchet," *Dayton Daily News*, September 10, 1984. When Metzenbaum came under attack in his 1988 Senate campaign, Glenn again came to his aid with a supportive TV ad. Mary Beth Lane, "The Best and Worst Campaigns of 1988," *Campaigns and Elections*, January/February 1989.

31. Balz, "Grounded By His Debts."

32. Deborah Orin, "Glenn to Abort Failed Mission," *New York Post*, March 16, 1984; Jody Powell, "John Glenn: Defeated but Not Demeaned," *Los Angeles Times*, March 19, 1984; Shribman, "With Few Words."

33. David Nyhan, "Why Glenn Didn't Have a Chance," *Boston Globe*, March 18, 1984.

34. "The Ten Men and Women Admired Most in 1983," *Washington Post Weekly Edition*, January 30, 1984.

35. Sternberg, "Sen. Glenn Reassuring Ohioans."

36. William Hershey and Brian Usher, "No Hoopla as Glenn, Celeste Arrive," *Akron Beacon Journal*, July 15, 1984; Brent Larkin and Tom Brazaitis, "Miffed Glenn Rejects Offer to Speak to Dems," *Cleveland Plain Dealer*, July 15, 1984.

37. Lee Leonard, "Young Preaches Unity to Ohio Delegation," *Columbus Citizen Journal*, July 17, 1984; Gene Jordan, "Ohioans Agree Move Was Error," *Columbus Dispatch*, July 16, 1984; Jerry Condo and T. C. Brown, "Ohio Delegates Glad to See End to Manatt Flap," *Columbus Citizen Journal*, July 16, 1984; Chris Madison, "View From Ohio's Delegation: Quiet Please," *National Journal Convention Daily*, July 16, 1984.

38. Tom Diemer, "Most Ohio Dem Delegates Support a Woman VP," *Cleveland Plain Dealer*, July 15, 1984.

39. Elizabeth Drew, *Campaign Journal* (New York: Macmillan, 1985), 539.

40. David Shribman, "Glenn Becomes Another Also-Ran," *Wall Street Journal*, July 23, 1984.

41. Tom Diemer, "Glenn Chipping Away At Bland Image," *Cleveland Plain Dealer*, August 17, 1986; Randy Wynn, "Congress Plays to the Camera," *Youngstown Vindicator*, September 9, 1986; George Embrey, "Glenn Back in the Public Eye," *Columbus Dispatch*, May 25, 1986.

42. Tom Price, "Glenn Seeks Assignments on 2 Senate Committees," *Dayton Journal Herald*, January 10, 1985; William Hershey, "Former Astronaut Glenn Still Keeps an Eye on Controls," *Akron Beacon Journal*, March 11, 1985; "Glenn Likely For New Panel," *Cleveland Plain Dealer*, February 9, 1985.

43. "Glenn Set to Join Armed Services Panel," *Columbus Dispatch*, February 9, 1985.

44. "Glenn Would Help this Area with Armed Services Post," *Dayton Journal Herald*, February 19, 1985. See also Laurence S. Newman, Jr., "Glenn Is in Another Uphill Run," *Dayton Journal Herald*, January 11, 1985.

45. Tom Price and Mary Beth Lane, "Wright-Pat Institute Project Is Cut,"

Dayton Journal Herald, April 11, 1985.

46. "Glenn's Recovery for AFIT Is a Most Welcome Reprieve," *Dayton Journal Herald,* May 17, 1985. See also "Glenn Earns AFIT Credit, Cap, Too," *Dayton Daily News,* May 19, 1985.

47. Stuart Rothenberg, ed., "Ohio Senate: Does Glenn Have Right Stuff? " *The Political Report,* February 22, 1985.

48. R. Chris Burnett, "Kindness: Is He Up to Challenging Glenn? " *Columbus Dispatch,* July 28, 1985.

49. William Hershey, "Kindness Facing a Foe Who Wins Big," *Akron Beacon Journal,* February 9, 1986.

50. Adam Condo, "GOP Hopes for a Kindness Upset Fading Fast," *Cincinnati Post,* October 10, 1986.

51. Keith White, "Glenn Contest May Not Be Much," *Gannett News Services,* October 4, 1985.

52. Susan Smith, "A 1984 Loser on the Road, Glenn Faces Test At Home," *Akron Beacon Journal,* August 29, 1985. See also Tom Price, "Kindness to Challenge Glenn for Senate Seat," *Dayton Journal Herald,* September 5, 1983; Bertram de Souza, "Rep. Kindness to Challenge Glenn for Senator in '86," *Youngstown Vindicator,* July 28, 1985.

53. Robert E. Miller, "Glenn Runs Scared," *Alliance Review,* September 15, 1980; Steve Wilson, "John Glenn Running Scared Despite Polls," *Cincinnati Enquirer,* October 26, 1980; Steve Wilson, "Few Got Excited About Betts' Challenge to Glenn," *Chillicothe Gazette,* November 1, 1980.

54. AP, "Glenn, Kindness Race to be Duel with Dollars," *Cleveland Plain Dealer,* January 7, 1986.

55. Letter to PAC directors, Kindness for Senate Committee, December 28, 1985.

56. Adam Condo, "Kindness Campaign Depicts Glenn as Ineffective Senator," *Columbus Citizen Journal,* December 10, 1985.

57. Ron Cordray, "Representative Kindness Lacks Kind Words for Glenn," *Washington Times,* October 2, 1985.

58. Press release, Kindness for Senate Committee, September 23, 1985.

59. Interview with Tom Kindness, *Columbus Dispatch,* August 8, 1986.

60. Randy Wynn, "Budget Bid Is Ravaged," *Youngstown Vindicator,* October 28, 1985; Jim Newton, "Glenn, Kindness Square Off in Senate Race," *Hamilton, Fairfield Journal News,* March 31, 1986; Adam Condo, "Kindness, Glenn: Underdog vs. Hero," *Cincinnati Post,* July 14, 1986; Kindness letter to Glenn, Kindness for Senate Committee, January 15, 1986; Howard Wilkinson, "Opponent Criticizes Sen. Glenn," *Cincinnati Enquirer,* January 17, 1986.

61. Neil Durbin, "Kindness Raps Glenn Performance," *Youngstown Vindicator,* January 28, 1986.

62. Tom Price, "Showdown for the Senate," *Dayton Daily News,* October 5, 1986.

63. From, in order, *Dover-New Philadelphia Times-Reporter, Dayton News Journal, Columbus Dispatch, Cleveland Plain Dealer, Cincinnati Enquirer.*

64. Sandy Grady, "The Calmest Man," *Dover-New Philadelphia Times-Reporter,* January 30, 1986.

65. Joe Rice, "Tragedy May Boost Glenn Effort," *Cleveland Plain Dealer,* February 2, 1986.

66. Randy Wynn, "Glenn Had 'Right Stuff' After Tragedy," *Dayton Daily News,* February 2, 1986.

67. R. Chris Burnett, "Glenn Reassured Stunned Nation," *Columbus Dispatch,*

February 2, 1986.
68. Robert Webb, "Rough Days for Kindness," *Cincinnati Enquirer*, February 6, 1986.
69. Embrey, "Glenn Back in the Public Eye."
70. Tom Price, "Glenn Reminds Ohioans of his Accomplishments," *Dayton Daily News*, February 19, 1986.
71. "Sen. Glenn's Campaign Seeks 'Sensible Center,' " *Dayton Journal Herald*, February 21, 1986.
72. UPI, "Glenn Pushes Ohio Jobs in Bid for Third Term," *Ravenna-Kent Courier Journal*, February 20, 1986; Bertram de Souza, "Glenn Brings Campaign to Youngstown," *Youngstown Vindicator*, February 20, 1986.
73. Brent Larkin, "Glenn Seeks Reelection, Attacks Marcos," *Cleveland Plain Dealer*, February 20, 1986.
74. Mary Grace Poidomani, "Poll Shows Glenn Has 3-1 Edge," *Akron Beacon Journal*, March 31, 1986; Tim Miller, "Glenn Is Far in Front of Kindness in Poll," *Dayton Journal Herald*, March 31, 1986.
75. Brent Larkin, "GOP Views Glenn As 'An Institution,' " *Cleveland Plain Dealer*, February 13, 1985.
76. Ibid.
77. See note 74, *supra*. Later poll results are found in Michael Curtin, "Celebrezze, Glenn Lead Challengers," *Columbus Dispatch*, September 11, 1986; Robert White, "Celebrezze, Glenn Lead Races, Poll Finds," *Cincinnati Post*, September 23, 1986.
78. AP, "Kindness to Blitz Ohioans," *Akron Beacon Journal*, March 14, 1986; Jackie Jadronk, "Senator Glenn Faces Big Guns," *Cincinnati Enquirer*, May 9, 1986; Stuart Rothenberg, ed., "Ohio Senate, Not Handled With Kindness," *The Political Report*, August 15, 1986.
79. Condo, "Kindness, Glenn: Underdog vs. Hero."
80. William Hershey, "Glenn Asks Help on Loans," *Akron Beacon Journal*, January 31, 1986; R. Chris Burrett, "Glenn Asks Four Banks for Extension on Debt," *Columbus Dispatch*, January 31, 1986.
81. Cliff Treyens, "Campaign '86," *Columbus Dispatch*, May 1, 1986; "60 Radio Ad," Kindness for Senate Committee; "The Ohio Thrift Panic," *Newsweek*, April 1, 1985; John Berry, "A Shortage of Confidence, Not Funds, Caused the Ohio Crisis," *Washington Post Weekly Edition*, April 1, 1985.
82. *Akron Beacon Journal*, February 28, 1986.
83. See *Columbus Dispatch*, June 21, 1986.
84. Lewis Beck, "Glenn Disputes Panel over Campaign Loan Debt," *Cincinnati Enquirer*, June 22, 1986.
85. William Hershey, "Double-Barreled Money Problems," *Akron Beacon Journal*, May 16, 1986.
86. "FEC: Glenn Loans Violate Election Law," *Canton Repository*, June 22, 1986.
87. Randy Wynn, "FEC Finds Glenn's Bank Loans in Violation," *Youngstown Vindicator*, June 21, 1986.
88. William Hershey, "Glenn Says He Didn't Violate Public Trust," *Akron Beacon Journal*, June 22, 1986.
89. Jim Underwood, "Kindness Targets Glenn Assets, Warner Tie," *Dover-New Philadelphia Times-Reporter*, June 24, 1986.
90. Louis Peck, "Kindness Takes the Offensive," *Cincinnati Enquirer*, September 12, 1986.
91. "Glenn's Campaign Debt Doesn't Faze Voters," *Cleveland Plain Dealer*,

October 21, 1986.

92. Scipio Thomas, "Glenn: Loan Commotion Overshadows Real Issues," *Dayton Daily News*, May 16, 1986.

93. William Hershey, "It's a Sweet Race for Glenn," *Akron Beacon Journal*, October 27, 1986.

94. Lee Leonard, "Glenn: Kindness Nothing Like Name," *Martin's Ferry Times Leader*, September 28, 1986.

95. Tom Price, "Glenn Attacks Kindness," *Dayton Daily News*, October 25, 1986.

96. AP, "Kindness Hoping for 'Surprise' in Race With Glenn," *Youngstown Vindicator*, November 3, 1986.

97. Peck, "Kindness Takes the Offensive."

98. Adam Condo, "Kindness Fights an Uphill Battle," *Cincinnati Post*, November 3, 1986.

99. Price, "Glenn Attacks Kindness."

100. Rich Exner, "Kindness Long Shot Against Ohio Astronaut Glenn," *Ravenna-Kent Record Courier*, October 27, 1986.

101. "Glenn Support Built on Variety of Sources in State," *Dayton Daily News*, November 5, 1986.

102. AP, "Glenn Jubilant at Winning 63% Over Kindness," *Mansfield News Journal*, November 5, 1986.

103. Tom Price, "Glenn Defeats Kindness, Takes Another Senate Term," *Dayton Daily News*, November 11, 1986.

104. "Glenn Jubilant at Winning." In 1987 Glenn returned to this view of his election contest in his second Senate floor defense of Sen. Howard Metzenbaum against an attack on him, *Congressional Record*, July 29, 1987, S10812-16.

105. Louis Peck, "Glenn's Debt Is Campaign's Hottest Topic," *Cincinnati Enquirer*, October 26, 1986.

106. *Toledo Blade*, October 29, 1986; *Akron Beacon Journal*, October 23, 1986; *Dayton Daily News*, October 14, 1986.

107. Note 106, *supra*.

108. Ibid.; *Youngstown Vindicator*, October 24, 1986; *Cleveland Plain Dealer*, October 10, 1986; *The Cincinnati Post*, October 27, 1986; *The Lorain Journal*, October 14, 1986; *Mansfield News Journal*, October 14, 1986; *Cincinnati Enquirer*, October 27, 1986; *Ohio AFL-CIO Focus*, October 1986. Only one major paper, *Columbus Dispatch*, October 12, 1986, did not endorse Glenn.

109. William Hershey, "Glenn Asks Radiation Probe," *Akron Beacon Journal*, October 11, 1986; Tom Price, "Glenn Wants Probe of Fernald Incident," *Dayton Daily News*, October 11, 1986; Anne Brataas, "Senate Group to Meet on Fernald," October 12, 1986; Randy Ludlow, "Glenn Proposes Nuclear Cleanup," *Cincinnati Post*, October 21, 1986.

110. *Toledo Blade*, *Cincinnati Post*, *Lorain Journal*.

111. John Glenn, "Keeping Faith With Older Americans" (Speech delivered at Fitzimmons Senior Center, Dayton, Ohio, October 24, 1986). Also delivered to senior citizens groups in Youngstown, Cincinnati, Toledo, and Cleveland.

112. Germond and Witcover, *Wake Us When It's Over*, 117.

113. Joe Klein, "The Right Stuff," *Rolling Stone*, November 24, 1983.

114. See notes 106, 108, *supra*.

115. *Youngstown Vindicator*.

116. *Cincinnati Enquirer*.

117. *Dayton Daily News.*
118. Phil Gailey, "Democrats' Iowa Campaign Ends With Sharp Attacks on Mondale," *New York Times,* February 20, 1984.
119. From the *New York Daily News,* as reported in *Warren Chronicle Tribune,* August 21, 1983.
120. Tom Price, "Glenn Means to Stay Ahead," *Dayton Daily News,* October 27, 1986.

Epilogue

Four years after John Glenn's presidential campaign ended, the memory of it resurfaced, and the revival, like the original event, had real consequences for his political career. The full story is known only to Michael Dukakis, the 1988 Democratic presidential nominee, but published accounts from May to July 1988 give the strongest indication that the Ohio senator very nearly became the Democratic nominee for vice president. The most frequently stated reason why he did not was the perception of his 1984 campaign.

The earliest journalistic speculations pronounced Glenn a leader among potential Dukakis running mates. In May, well before Dukakis turned his attention to the matter, Glenn was labeled a "natural choice" to balance a ticket headed by an eastern governor without experience in foreign policy or national defense matters.[1] By the end of the month, Glenn was called "the current favorite in the Dukakis veepstakes."[2]

The recitation of Glenn's credentials echoed scorekeeper evaluations during his presidential season of exploration. "He brings you *Reader's Digest* values and some pretty good defense credentials."[3] "Maybe only five members of the U.S. Senate are asked for their autograph. He's No. 1."[4] "A former astronaut, fighter pilot and war hero, and a moderate voice on foreign policy questions, [he] might provide some help on national security."[5] He is a "national hero with no controversial baggage ... [and] solid foreign policy credentials."[6] One southern leader described him as "a plus in the South,"[7] and another added, "Glenn has that something that is national in scope."[8] The clincher was that Glenn's massive home state popularity would almost certainly deliver Ohio's twenty-three electoral votes to the Democrats. He was, as before, widely recognized as a person with sterling personal qualities and proven vote-getting prowess in his state.

As a counterweight to these assets, however, the early handicappers invariably mentioned the events of Glenn's 1984 campaign. They described him as "still a bit tarnished by his disappointing bid for the top spot in 1984."[9] They said he might be "even duller than Dukakis in public speeches; he had trouble igniting popular passion in his 1984 presidential bid."[10] And they added, "One serious problem: Glenn still owes $2.4 million, mostly to Ohio banks, from his 1984 presidential campaign."[11] The Ohio senator came to the new situation burdened with other people's recollections of his presidential candidacy.

When Mike Dukakis addressed the matter in June, and when "sources" close to his campaign began to be quoted, the pattern of conflicting considerations remained. In late June one source talked about Glenn to the reporters from Dukakis's hometown *Boston Globe:*

> He is very steady and has foreign policy credentials and national stature, and there is little doubt that he could bring Ohio with its 23 electoral votes to the ticket. There would be no downside risk with Glenn. However, the problem, as 1984 showed, is that he does not communicate his strengths well as a campaigner. The result is that people see him as a former astronaut and he can't move them beyond that image.[12]

A day later, Dukakis "aides" were described as worried about Glenn's "track record as a political candidate," about how he "bombed badly in the Iowa caucuses," about how he absorbed "a stinging series of defeats" that left him "saddled with an embarrassing debt of $2.4 million, which he still owes." "Glenn is hampered," the *Globe* reporter concluded, "by his lackluster performances when he ventured into national politics in the past, and skeptics are questioning his creativity, his abilities as a campaigner and his managerial skills."[13] Nonetheless, the article cataloguing all these reservations was headlined, "Glenn Emerges As a Leading Choice in Democratic Running-Mate Derby." And the next day the *Globe's* Dukakis-watchers wrote, "For several days, journalists and politicians have speculated that Glenn—with a household name, a patriotic, astronaut-hero's image and moderate political views—is a virtual shoo-in for the ticket."[14]

When Mike Dukakis journeyed to Ohio in early July to campaign with Glenn, the senator was still being described by the press as "the heroic former astronaut who remains the most frequently touted choice to be the governor's running mate."[15] Sharing the platform with him in Dayton, Dukakis showered Glenn with positive, albeit inconclusive, signals. "I don't know why John Glenn can't chair Howard's [Senator Metzenbaum] campaign and run for the vice presidency," he told the crowd. Then, as the *Boston Globe* reported it,

> The governor plunged on: "I've been taking a poll all over America about running mates. What do you think about John Glenn?" As the crowd cheered, Dukakis walked over to Glenn and they shook hands. Both men beamed and the governor put his arm around Glenn's shoulder affectionately. After the

crowd quieted down, Dukakis turned to Glenn and said, "Sounds unanimous to me, John."

"John and I had a good conversation," he said afterward. But he added, "I've had good conversations with other people." [16] Media scorekeepers described Dukakis's performance as "teasing" the senator.[17]

Only John Glenn knows how interested he was in the vice-presidential office. Our analysis throughout this book tells us he would have wanted the job. For the dutiful fighter pilot-astronaut, it was one more hitch in the marines; for the public service politician, it was one more chance to serve his country. It was, moreover, a job he had wanted and failed to get once before, in 1976. "He seems quietly willing," said an early May report.[18] Glenn responded humorously by suggesting Neil Armstrong and by mocking his 1984 campaign. "I humiliated my family, gained 16 pounds and went over $2.5 million in debt. Other than that, it was a great experience." [19] As the preconvention season progressed, other frequently mentioned candidates took themselves out of the running. But Glenn did not. In June he filled out all questionnaires and forwarded the personal and financial records Dukakis asked of him. "The mere fact of his availability," said one *Globe* reporter, "has pushed his name up among the candidates." [20] During his Ohio appearance with Dukakis in early July, Glenn, wrote another, "did little to disguise his availability." [21] The *Globe* described him as "available, even anxious, to be asked." [22] No one doubted he would accept if asked.

Most of the handicappers believed to the end that he would be asked. *Newsweek's* "Conventional Wisdom Watch" made Glenn their top pick almost every week from May 9 to announcement day.[23] An early California poll, a late Minnesota poll, and an eleventh-hour survey of prominent Democrats by *Newsweek* showed Glenn bringing strength to the ticket.[24] In early July the *Wall Street Journal* said, "Glenn leads the VP sweepstakes.... Politicians from both the South and industrial states push the Ohioan; most pollsters and Republicans agree he'd be the strongest running mate." [25] The Bush campaigners believed, to the end, that Glenn would be the choice.[26] Among the journalists covering the Dukakis campaign, thirteen of twenty predicted the same thing.[27] Two days before the selection, a *New York Times* reporter called him the "morning favorite of Washington insiders." [28] The day of the announcement, the same reporter called him a "compelling choice." [29]

He was not compelling enough. As the convention drew close, sources spoke of the Dukakis campaign's efforts "to develop a vice-presidential option other than Sen. John Glenn." "Since mid-June," continued this report, "the early favorite among politicians has been

Glenn.... [But some Dukakis people] have raised questions about Glenn's campaigning skills." [30] "The governor seemed close to picking Mr. Glenn," said another report, "then backed off as questions were raised about the failure of the Ohio Democrat's 1984 presidential campaign." [31]

Among the post mortems there is general agreement that Dukakis's final choice came down to two men and that Glenn was the last man out. There is also agreement on his special point of vulnerability. Calling Glenn "the final alternative to [Sen. Lloyd] Bentsen," one summary said that the Dukakis inquiries had "turned up many warnings that Glenn might wear no better as a national campaigner than he did when he was unsuccessfully seeking the presidential nomination in 1984." [32] A second account said, "Dukakis' choice ... came down to two seasoned, moderate-to-conservative politicians." And it quoted one of the campaigners: "It was almost like a replay of Glenn's 1984 presidential race. He looked great on paper, but there was doubt about how he would look in the flesh." [33] John Glenn was not to be given a chance to prove them wrong.

Realistically, the events of 1988 put an end to John Glenn's chances for higher office and, perhaps, to his desire for it as well. In that sense, this epilogue is a definitive conclusion to a story that began with one person's senatorial ambition. As it turned out, Glenn's unsuccessful presidential campaign mattered more to the development of his political career than we could have known in 1986. Although it had no effect in Ohio in that year, its fullest effects were not registered nationally until 1988. There is a durability to political events and to the interpretation of those events by politicians that confirms our assumption that experience at one point in a career affects experiences at a later point and, therefore, that careers must be studied sequentially, over time. Circumstances may intervene at points in the sequence to create an opportunity, should ambition exist, for a major career change. John Glenn had the ambition and two—maybe three—such opportunities. None worked out.

Doubtless, Glenn was disappointed ("relieved," he said) at the turn of events in 1988.[34] Doubtless, he did not relish the rehashing of his 1984 troubles.[35] Doubtless, too, he would have wished for the chance to show how he had profited in terms of political learning—as he always had—from his experiences since 1984.[36] Instead, the earlier experience, as it remained in the memory banks of America's politicians, could not be erased, reinterpreted, or overcome. The original failure to achieve his ambition appears to have contributed to a subsequent failure as well.

So his expansionist goals continued to go unmet. On the other hand, his protectionist goals had been met in full; he retained all the personal strengths of heroism-plus-character with which he began. The epilogue ends, then, where the book had already ended. In the fall of 1988 John Glenn remained a United States senator, with his exemplary personal reputation fully intact, with the official resources to accomplish much where he was, and with a senatorial career that was far from finished.

NOTES

1. Paul Taylor, "Must the Democrats Look South to Find 270 Electoral Votes?" *Washington Post Weekly Edition*, May 9-15, 1988.
2. "Washington Wire," *Wall Street Journal*, May 20, 1988.
3. Taylor, "Must the Democrats Look South?"
4. "Washington Wire," *Wall Street Journal*, July 2, 1988.
5. David Shribman, "Leading Democrats Begin to Focus on Selection of Dukakis's Running Mate as Primaries Near End," *Wall Street Journal*, May 10, 1988.
6. Margaret Carlson, "Is Nunn Really the One? " *Time*, May 9, 1988.
7. Sam Nunn, quoted in "Washington Wire," *Wall Street Journal*, May 20, 1988.
8. Bert Lance, quoted by Dennis Farney, "Lance, Taking Time Out from Smelling the Roses, Advises Jackson, Looks to Possible Convention Role," *Wall Street Journal*, June 13, 1988.
9. Taylor, "Must the Democrats Look South."
10. Carlson, "Is Nunn Really the One? "
11. "Washington Wire," *Wall Street Journal*, May 20, 1988.
12. Thomas Oliphant and Ben Bradlee, Jr., "Dukakis To Meet With Key Senators," *Boston Globe*, June 28, 1988.
13. Curtis Wilkie, "Glenn Emerges as a Leading Choice in Democratic Running-Mate Derby," *Boston Globe*, June 29, 1988.
14. Thomas Oliphant and Curtis Wilkie, "Three Senators on Dukakis' Short List," *Boston Globe*, June 30, 1988.
15. Ben Bradlee, Jr., "Dukakis Plays the Tease in Meeting with Glenn," *Boston Globe*, July 2, 1988.
16. Ibid.
17. Ibid.; Richard Berke, "Dukakis Courts Prospect for Ticket," *New York Times*, July 9, 1988; Elizabeth Drew, "Letter from Washington," *New Yorker*, August 15, 1988; "Washington Wire," *Wall Street Journal*, July 8, 1988; "The Politics Page," *National Journal*, July 16, 1988.
18. Carlson, "Is Nunn Really the One? "
19. "Campaign '88," *Boston Globe*, June 10, 1988.
20. Wilkie, "Glenn Emerges."
21. Bradlee, "Dukakis Plays the Tease."
22. Thomas Oliphant, "A Five-Week Process Ended at Kitchen Table," *Boston Globe*, July 13, 1988.
23. See "Conventional-Wisdom Watch," *Newsweek*, May 9, 23, 30; June 13, 27; July 18, 1988. A summary appears in Jonathan Alter and Mickey Kaus, *Newsweek*, October 31, 1988.
24. For the California poll, see "Campaign '88," *Boston Globe*, June 10, 1988; for

the Minnesota poll, see Chris Black, "Poll Watch," *Boston Globe*, July 7, 1988; for the *Newsweek* poll, see "Convention Crunch: The VIP Poll," *Newsweek*, July 18, 1988.

25. "Washington Wire," *Wall Street Journal*, July 2, 1988.
26. Thomas Oliphant, "Risks in Choosing Texas Senator for Ticket," *Boston Globe*, July 14, 1988.
27. "Overheard," *Newsweek*, July 25, 1988.
28. Michael Oreskes, "Striving to Formulate a Ticket That Sells," *New York Times*, July 12, 1988.
29. Michael Oreskes, "Dukakis Nears Choice on Running Mate," *New York Times*, July 12, 1988.
30. Thomas Oliphant and Michael Frisby, "Dukakis Gets Together With Former Foes Gephardt and Gore," *Boston Globe*, July 6, 1988.
31. E. J. Dionne, Jr., "Jackson Distances Himself From Remarks About Gore," *New York Times*, July 9, 1988.
32. David Broder and Paul Taylor, "Dukakis' Recipe For a Running Mate," *Washington Post Weekly Edition*, July 18-24, 1988.
33. Oliphant, "A Five-Week Process."
34. Chris Burnett, " 'No' From Dukakis Isn't Glenn's First," *Columbus Dispatch*, July 13, 1988.
35. "Glenn Reported Miffed At Pick," *Boston Globe*, July 19, 1988; "Hero's Due? " *Newsweek*, July 25, 1988.
36. Evidence that he *had* learned is to be found in the favorable reviews of his nominating speech for Lloyd Bensten. See Curtis Wilkie, "Countdown '88," *Boston Globe*, July 24, 1988; "Conventional Wisdom-Watch," *Newsweek*, August 1, 1988.

Index